EYEWITNESS TRAVEL GUIDES

BERLIN

EYEWITNESS TRAVEL GUIDES

BERLIN

Main Contributor: MAŁGORZATA OMILANOWSKA

LONDON, NEW YORK,
MELBOURNE, MUNICH AND DELHI
www.dk.com

Produced by Wydawnictwo Wiedza i Życie, Warsaw

MANAGING EDITOR Ewa Szwagrzyk
SERIES EDITOR Joanna Egert
DTP DESIGNER Pawel Pasternak
CONSULTANT Nils Meyer
ILLUSTRATIONS Andrzej Wielgosz,
Lena Maminajszwili, Dorota Jarymowicz
PHOTOGRAPHY Dorota and Mariusz Jarymowicz
CORRECTION Bożena Leszkowicz
PRODUCTION Anna Kożurno-Królikowska, Ewa Roguska

Dorling Kindersley Limited
EDITORS Nancy Jones, Esther Labi, Hugh Thompson
SENIOR EDITOR Helen Townsend

CONTRIBUTORS Małgorzata Omilanowska,
Jürgen Scheunemann, Christian Tempel
MAPS Maria Wojciechowska, Dariusz Osuch (D. Osuch i spółka)

Reproduced by Colourscan, Singapore
Printed and bound by South China Co. Ltd., China

First published in Great Britain in 2000
by Dorling Kindersley Limited
80 Strand, London WC2R 0RL
Reprinted with revisions 2002, 2003, 2004, 2005, 2006

Copyright 2000, 2006 © Dorling Kindersley Limited, London
A Penguin Company

A CIP catalogue record is available from the British Library.

ISBN 1 4053 1092 8

Floors are referred to throughout in accordance with British
usage, ie the "first floor" is the floor above ground level.

**The information in this
Dorling Kindersley Travel Guide is checked annually.**
Every effort has been made to ensure that this book is as
up-to-date as possible at the time of going to press. Some
details, however, such as telephone numbers, opening hours, prices,
gallery hanging arrangements and travel information are liable to
change. As a result of the return of the German government to
Berlin, and the large amount of construction
work under way, whole areas of the city are in a constant state
of change. The publishers cannot accept responsibility for any
consequences arising from the use of this book, nor for any material
on third party websites, and cannot guarantee that
any website address in this book will be a suitable source of
travel information. We value the views and suggestions of
our readers very highly. Please write to: Publisher, DK
Eyewitness Travel Guides, Dorling Kindersley, 80 Strand,
London WC2R 0RL, Great Britain.

CONTENTS

A child's drawing of Fernsehturm,
Siegessäule and Funkturm

INTRODUCING
BERLIN

Bomb-damaged Kaiser-Wilhelm-
Gedächtnis-Kirche (see pp152–3)

The Spree river passing by the Nikolaiviertel *(see pp88–9)*

One of Germany's many hearty
dishes *(see pp232–233)*

Modern architecture by the former
Checkpoint Charlie *(see p141)*

Berliner Dom
(see pp76–7)

HOW TO USE THIS GUIDE

This Dorling Kindersley travel guide helps you to get the most from your visit to Berlin. It provides detailed practical information and expert recommendations. *Introducing Berlin* maps the city and the region, and sets it in its historical and cultural context, and describes events through the entire year. *Berlin at a Glance* is an overview of the city's main attractions. *Berlin Area by Area* starts on page 52. This is the main sightseeing section, which covers all of the important sights, with photographs, maps and illustrations. *Greater Berlin* covers the nearby historic city of Potsdam, as well as three walking tours. Information about hotels, restaurants, shops and markets, entertainment and sports is found in *Travellers' Needs*. The *Survival Guide* has advice on everything from using Berlin's medical services, telephones and post offices to the public transport system.

FINDING YOUR WAY AROUND THE SIGHTSEEING SECTION

Each of eight sightseeing areas in Berlin is colour-coded for easy reference. Every chapter opens with an introduction to the area of the city it covers, describing its history and character, and has a *Street-by-Street* map illustrating typical parts of that area. Finding your way around the chapter is made simple by the numbering system used throughout. The most important sights are covered in detail in two or more full pages.

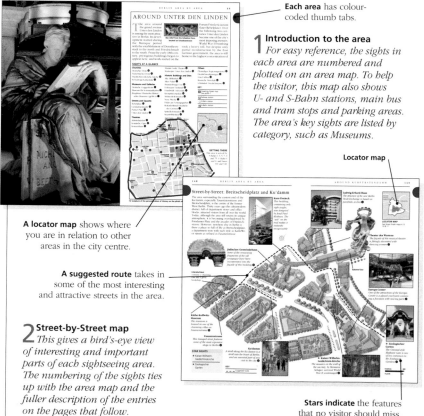

Each area has colour-coded thumb tabs.

1 Introduction to the area
For easy reference, the sights in each area are numbered and plotted on an area map. To help the visitor, this map also shows U- and S-Bahn stations, main bus and tram stops and parking areas. The area's key sights are listed by category, such as Museums.

Locator map

A **locator map** shows where you are in relation to other areas in the city centre.

A **suggested route** takes in some of the most interesting and attractive streets in the area.

2 Street-by-Street map
This gives a bird's-eye view of interesting and important parts of each sightseeing area. The numbering of the sights ties up with the area map and the fuller description of the entries on the pages that follow.

Stars indicate the features that no visitor should miss.

BERLIN AREA MAP

The coloured areas shown on this map *(see inside front cover)* are the eight main sightseeing areas used in this guide. Each is covered in a full chapter in *Berlin Area by Area (see pp52–205)*. They are highlighted on other maps throughout the book. In *Berlin at a Glance*, for example, they help you locate the top sights. They are also used to help you find the position of three walks *(see pp198–205)*.

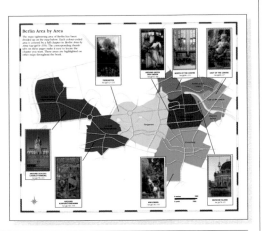

Numbers refer to each sight's position on the area map and its place in the chapter.

Practical information provides everything you need to know to visit each sight. Map references pinpoint the sight's location on the *Street Finder* map *(see pp300–323)*.

3 Detailed information

All the important sights in Berlin are described individually. They are listed in order following the numbering on the area map at the start of the section. Practical information includes a map reference, opening hours and telephone numbers. The key to the symbols is on the back flap.

The visitors' checklist gives all the practical information needed to plan your visit.

Story boxes provide information about historical or cultural topics relating to the sights.

4 Berlin's major sights

Historic buildings are dissected to reveal their interiors; museums and galleries have colour-coded floorplans to help you find the most important exhibits.

The list of star sights recommends the places that no visitor should miss.

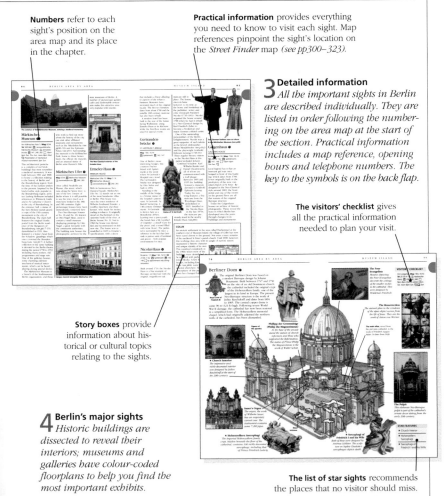

INTRODUCING BERLIN

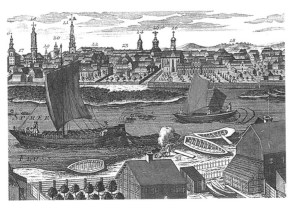

FOUR GREAT DAYS IN BERLIN

As Berlin is laid out on an epic scale, these four days are organized so that you can take in as much of the city as possible. They guide you to all the interesting monuments, museums and art collections Berlin has to offer, as well as giving you ideas for family

Sanssouci statue

fun and where to go shopping. There's a lot of things to do each day, but nothing is rigid and as all the places mentioned are cross-referenced, you can look up the details and tailor the day to suit your stamina. The price guides include cost of travel, food and admission fees.

HISTORY AND CULTURE

- See Brandenburger Tor
- Walk along Wilhelmstrasse
- Lunch at a brasserie
- Zeughaus/Museum Island
- Checkpoint Charlie

TWO ADULTS allow at least €84

Morning
Start on the Unter den Linden at the city's most famous landmark, **Brandenburger Tor** *(see p67)*, one of the few remaining historic city gates. Continue east on Unter den Linden and turn left into Wilhelm-strasse, where the **Reich's Chancellery** and **Hitler's office** *(see p66)* are to your left at No. 77 Voss Strasse. Another grim reminder of Germany's Nazi past is just

The Rotunda gallery of the Altes Museum, Museum Island

round the corner. **The Topographie des Terrors** *(see p140)*, at the site of the former Gestapo and SS HQ, details crimes at the excavated torture cells. An original section of the Berlin Wall that used to run just behind Neo-Renaissance **Martin-Gropius-Bau** building is nearby *(see p140)*. From here, walk back along Wilhelmstrasse to 39 Unter den Linden for lunch at the brasserie **Dressler** *(see p236)*.

Afternoon
Tour the German history section at the **Zeughaus (Deutsches Historisches Museum)** *(see pp58–9)*. Then head north along the canal to **Museum Island** *(see pp71–85)*, a world-class museum complex, and explore the Altes Museum or the Pergamonmuseum with its famous Pergamon Altar. Detour to Kreuzberg by walking south on Friedrich-strasse to **Checkpoint Charlie**, the border crossing, and visit the nearby museum **Haus am Checkpoint Charlie** *(see p141)*.

Children and animals at the Zoologischer Garten, Berlin

A FAMILY DAY

- Visit the zoo
- A quick self-service lunch
- Hands-on technology fun
- Studio tour at the Filmpark

FAMILY OF FOUR allow at least €158

Morning
Start at the **Zoologischer Garten** *(see p150)*, one of Germany's oldest and biggest zoos. Leave the zoo via the Hardenbergplatz exit and walk east towards the Kaiser-Wilhelm-Gedächtniskirche on bustling Breitscheidplatz. Enjoy the jugglers and street artists on the square, then pop in to see the heavenly blue light in the church's modern section. Lunch at the Marché Mövenpick, set up like a street market on the elegant **Kurfürstendamm** *(see pp147–155)*.

Afternoon
Catch a bus on Kurfürstendamm to the **Deutsches Technikmuseum**

(*see p144*), with its planes, vintage cars, trains, boats and hands-on experiments to try. Bus back to Zoologischer Garten and then take the S-Bahn to Potsdam-Babelsberg to its **Filmpark Babelsberg** for a tour of Germany's biggest studio complex (*see p205*). You can get a simple dinner in Kreuzberg or Neukölln.

A SHOPPING DAY

• Shop at KaDeWe
• Stroll to Savignyplatz
• Snack on the go
• Friedrichstadtpassagen chic

TWO ADULTS allow at least €45 (cost of lunch and travel only)

Morning
Begin at **Kaufhaus des Westens**, called KaDeWe by Berliners, Europe's second biggest department store (*see p155*). Then explore the Tauentzienstrasse, a popular, affordable shopping avenue, and continue on Kurfürsten-damm – the further west you go, the more elegant the shops and boutiques. Take detours into even more chic side streets such as **Fasanen-, Meineke-, Uhland-, Bleibtreu-** and **Schlüterstrasse** as you head to **Savignyplatz** (*see p154*) with its many boutiques and eateries.

Afternoon
Take the S-Bahn from Savignyplatz towards the east and exit at Friedrichstrasse. Walk north; once over Unter den Linden, you'll find

The impressive French department store, Galeries Lafayette

the huge complexes of the **Friedrichstadtpassagen** including the French **Galeries Lafayette** and the über-luxurious **Quartier 206**, alongside top designers Gucci, Versace and Donna Karan. If not yet shopped out, walk back north on Friedrich-strasse and then east on Oranienburger Strasse to **Hackescher Markt**. This is a hip area of mostly alternative-style, young fashion, as well as clubs, bars and pubs.

BERLIN OUTDOORS

• A walk to Grunewald forest
• Boat trip to Pfaueninsel
• The Tiergarten
• Schloss Bellevue

TWO ADULTS allow at least €43

Morning
From the S-Bahn station Grunewald walk south (about 60 minutes) to **Jagdschloss Grunewald** (*see pp212–13*), a lovely hunting palace with an art gallery,

past fine historic villas. Continue through the forest to **Wannsee lake** (*see p181*) or walk back to the S-Bahn and get off at Wannsee station. Take a bus ride to the ferry for a walk on **Pfaueninsel**, a nature reserve (*see pp208–209*). Head back to the S-Bahn to Potsdam-Hauptbahnhof to enjoy the lovely **Park Sanssouci** with its beautiful palace – a gem of Prussian Rococo architecture (*see pp192–6*).

Afternoon
From Potsdam, take the S-Bahn to the green lung of Berlin, the vast **Tiergarten** (*see pp113–35*). Follow the Strasse des 17. Juni east and climb the **Siegessäule** (*see pp132–33*), the victory column with a great view of the city. Follow Spreeweg to **Schloss Bellevue** (*see p133*), official Presidential seat. To finish, walk southwest to **Neuer See**, a pretty lake in the park. Rent a boat at the Café am Neuen See and return there for supper.

Gardens of Sanssouci palace, in Park Sanssouci

Putting Berlin on the Map

Berlin, the capital of the Federal Republic of
Germany, has a population of approximately 3.5
million and covers 889 sq km (343 sq miles). Situated
in the eastern part of the country, in the middle of the
Brandenburg region, Berlin occupies the flatlands on
the banks of the Havel and Spree rivers, which merge
in the Spandau district. The whole city is
criss-crossed with numerous canals.

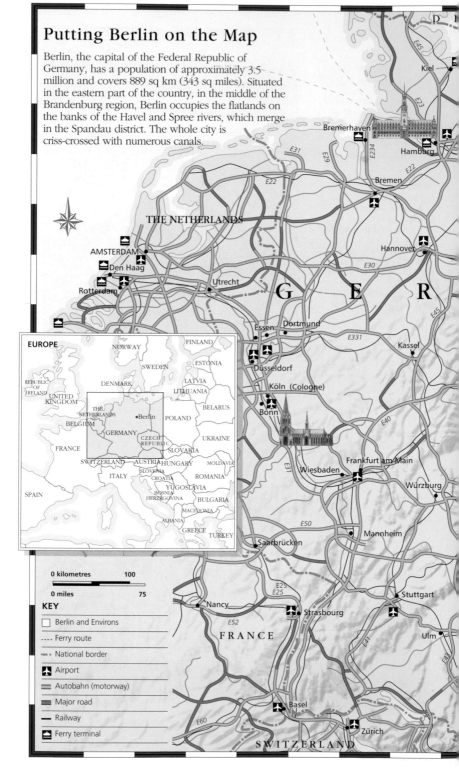

EUROPE

KEY

☐	Berlin and Environs
----	Ferry route
–·–	National border
✈	Airport
===	Autobahn (motorway)
▬	Major road
—	Railway
⛴	Ferry terminal

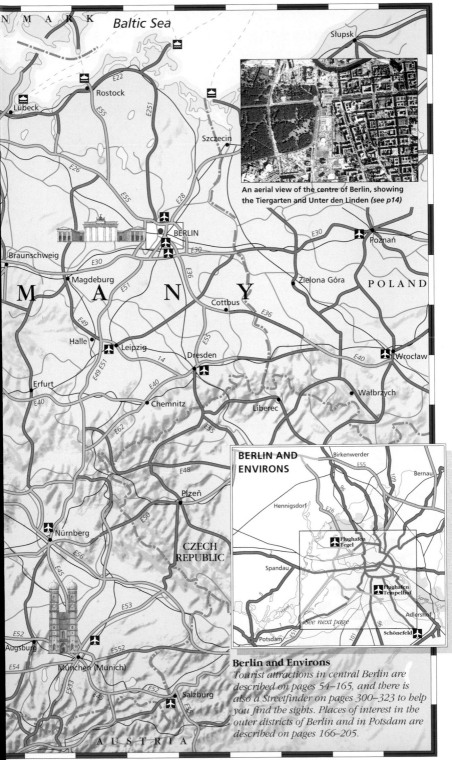

An aerial view of the centre of Berlin, showing the Tiergarten and Unter den Linden *(see p14)*

Berlin and Environs

Tourist attractions in central Berlin are described on pages 54–165, and there is also a Streetfinder on pages 300–323 to help you find the sights. Places of interest in the outer districts of Berlin and in Potsdam are described on pages 166–205.

Greater Berlin

Berlin in its present form was created in 1920, through an amalgamation of several towns and villages surrounding the historic centre. It now consists of 12 administrative districts, some of which were formerly separate municipalities, such as Spandau. The city is surrounded by recreational areas, including lakes and woodlands. To the southwest lies the city of Potsdam with its splendid palaces, which can be reached easily by public transport.

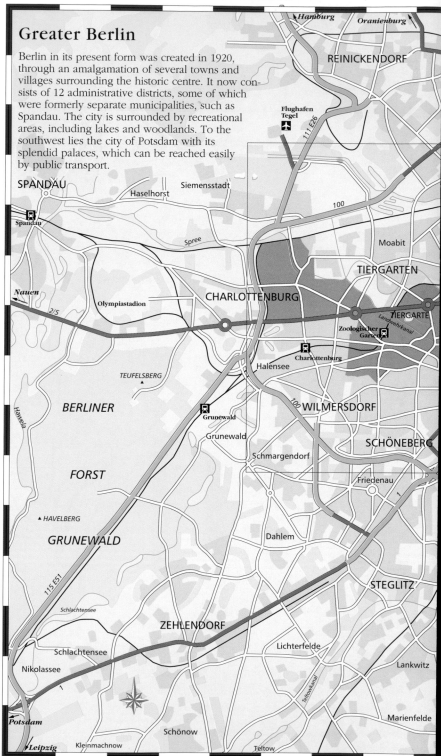

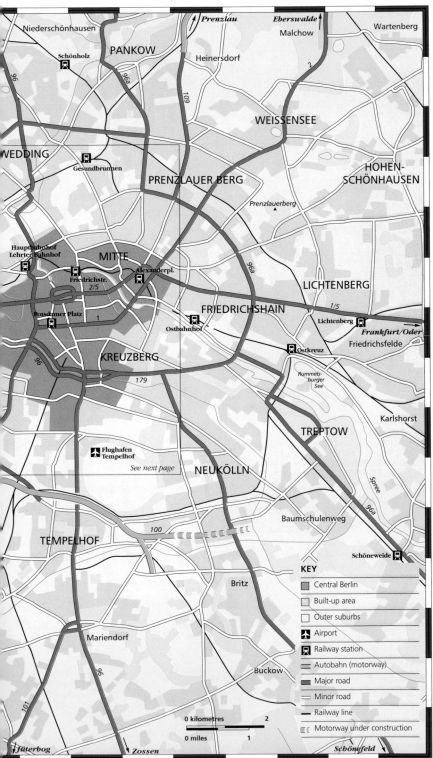

Niederschönhausen

PANKOW

Schönholz

↑ *Prenzlau*   *Eberswalde*↑
Malchow   Wartenberg

Heinersdorf

WEISSENSEE

WEDDING

Gesundbrunnen

PRENZLAUER BERG

HOHEN-
SCHÖNHAUSEN

Prenzlauerberg ▲

Hauptbahnhof
Lehrter Bahnhof

MITTE

Friedrichstr.
2/5

Alexanderpl.

LICHTENBERG

963

FRIEDRICHSHAIN   1/5

Ostbahnhof

Lichtenberg

Potsdamer Platz   1

Frankfurt/Oder→
Friedrichsfelde

Ostkreuz

KREUZBERG

179

Rummels-
burger
See

Karlshorst

TREPTOW

Flughafen
Tempelhof

See next page

NEUKÖLLN

Spree
96a

Baumschulenweg

100

TEMPELHOF

Schöneweide

KEY

Britz

	Central Berlin
	Built-up area
	Outer suburbs
✈	Airport
🚊	Railway station
	Autobahn (motorway)
	Major road
	Minor road
	Railway line
	Motorway under construction

Mariendorf

Buckow

0 kilometres   2

0 miles   1

↑*Jüterbog*   ←*Zossen*   *Schönefeld*↘

Central Berlin

Central Berlin is divided into eight colour-coded sightseeing areas. The historic core is located along the eastern and northern banks of the Spree river, around the grand boulevard Unter den Linden and on Museum Island. West of the centre is the sprawling green Tiergarten. To the south is Kreuzberg, an area renowned for its alternative lifestyle. Further west is Kurfürstendamm, the centre of former West Berlin. Finally, at the edge of the city centre is the summer residence of the Prussian kings, the Schloss Charlottenburg.

Around Schloss Charlottenburg
The Baroque Charlottenburg Palace, named after Sophie Charlotte (wife of Friedrich III), is one of Berlin's greatest tourist attractions. Its magnificent rooms contain many beautiful objects (see pp156–65).

Kulturforum, Tiergarten
The Kulturforum is a cluster of interesting museums and libraries. It is also the home of the Berlin Philharmonic (see pp112–35).

KEY

▣	Major sight
🚉	Railway station
Ⓤ	U-Bahn
Ⓢ	S-Bahn
Ⓟ	Parking
✚	Church
✡	Synagogue

Around Kurfürstendamm
The Kurfürstendamm, or Ku'damm as it is often called, is the main thoroughfare of western Berlin. This area contains numerous shops, restaurants, bars and cinemas (see pp146–55).

Rotes Rathaus, East of the Centre
This monumental town hall, which replaces the former medieval Rathaus, dates from the 1860s. It is decorated with terracotta bas-reliefs, (see pp86–97).

Berliner Dom, Museum Island
On this island are Berlin's Protestant cathedral, with its Neo-Baroque interior and massive dome, and a museum complex (see pp70–85).

Hamburger Bahnhof

HERBSTR.

CHAUSSEESTR.

INVALIDENSTR.

HANNOVERSCHESTR.

HEIDESTR.

TORSTR.

TORSTR.

ROSENTHALER STR.

ALTE SCHÖNHAUSER STR.

MOLLSTR.

MITTE

LUISENSTR.

FRIEDRICHSTR.

ORANIENBURGER STR.

Alter Jüdischer Friedhof

KARL-LIEBKNECHT-STR.

OTTO-BRAUN-STR.

KARL-MARX-ALLEE

Bahnhof Friedrichstrasse

Pergamon-museum

Fernsehturm

ALEXANDERSTR.

SCHILLINGSTR.

Berliner Dom

J.-F.-DULLES-ALLEE

ENTLASTUNGSSTR.

SCHEIDEMANNSTR.

DOROTHEENSTR.

Zeughaus

Altes Museum

Marienkirche

GRUNERSTR.

STRALAUER STR.

Spree

STRASSE DES 17. JUNI

Tiergarten

GARTEN

UNTER DEN LINDEN

BEHRENSTR.

BEBEL-PLATZ

WERDERSTR.

BRETE STR.

MÜHLENDAMM

NEUE ROSSTR.

STRALAUER STR.

BRÜCKENSTR.

LENNÉ STR.

WILHELMSTR.

FRANZÖSISCHE STR.

MARKGRAFENSTR.

NEUE JAKOBSTR.

TIERGARTENSTR.

Kunstgewerbe-museum

LEIPZIGER

STRASSE

WALLSTR.

Gemälde-galerie

SIGISMUNDSTR.

HEYDT STR.

STAUFFENBERGSTR.

GENTHINER STR.

LÜTZOWSTR.

POTSDAMER STR.

KURFÜRSTENSTR.

KOCHSTR.

ORANIENSTR.

STRESEMANNSTRASSE

ANHALTER STR.

FRIEDRICHSTR.

LINDENSTRASSE

SCHÖNEBERGER STR.

GITSCHINER STR.

KREUZBERG

BLÜCHERSTR.

URBANSTR.

PRINZENSTR.

HORNSTR.

GROSSBEERENSTR.

ZOSSENER STR.

BAERWALDSTR.

YORCKSTR.

YORCKSTR.

GNEISENAUSTR.

KREUZBERGSTR.

Viktoriapark

KATZBACHSTR.

DUDENSTR.

MEHRINGDAMM

Galeries Lafayette, Friedrichstrasse
This department store combines history with ultra-modern architecture (see pp54–69).

Viktoriapark, Kreuzberg
This park is situated on a hill in the Kreuzberg district, whose inhabitants include many Turks and eccentric artists (see pp136–45).

0 metres	500
0 yards	500

THE HISTORY OF BERLIN

Berlin is one of the younger European capitals. The first written reference to the small fishing settlement of Cölln appeared in the year 1237. Together with the equally insignificant settlement of Berlin on the opposite bank of the Spree river, it was to become first a successful trading city under the control of the Margraves of Brandenburg, then capital of Prussia, and finally, the capital of Germany. Following World War II and the 1949 armistice, Berlin became a central arena for the Cold War. In 1991, after the fall of the Berlin Wall, the city became the capital of the newly-united Federal Republic of Germany.

EARLY SETTLEMENTS

During the first centuries AD the banks of the Spree and Havel rivers were inhabited by various tribes, most notably the Germanic Semnones. By the end of the 6th century the Semnones were competing for land with Slavic tribes, who built forts at what are now the Berlin suburbs of Köpenick *(see p175)* and Spandau *(see p185)*. Five hundred years later the Slavic tribes were finally defeated following the arrival of the warlike Saxon, Albrecht the Bear of the House of the Ascanians, who became the first *Markgraf* (Margrave, or Count) of Brandenburg. The banks of the Spree river were now resettled with immigrants from areas to the west including the Harz mountains, the Rhine valley and Franconia.

Statue of Albrecht the Bear

BEGINNINGS OF THE MODERN CITY

Berlin's written history began in the early 13th century, when the twin settlements of Berlin and Cölln grew up on opposite banks of the Spree river, around what is now the Nikolaiviertel *(see p90)*. Trading in fish, rye and timber, the towns formed an alliance in 1307, becoming Berlin-Cölln, a deal celebrated by the construction of a joint town hall.

Following the death of the last Ascanian ruler in 1319, Brandenburg became the object of a long and bloody feud between the houses of Luxemburg and Wittelsbach, with devastating effects for the area's inhabitants. In 1411 the desperate townspeople appealed to the Holy Roman Emperor for help, receiving in response Friedrich von Hohenzollern as the town's special protector. Then in 1415 Rome duly rewarded Friedrich by naming him Elector of Brandenburg, a fateful appointment that marked the beginning of the 500-year rule of the House of Hohenzollern.

TIMELINE

1134 Investiture of Albrecht the Bear	**1197** First mention of Spandau	**1237** First written reference to Cölln	**1307** Signing of the treaty between Cölln and Berlin	**1359** Berlin and Cölln join Hanseatic League		**1415** Friedrich von Hohenzollern appointed Elector of Brandenburg
1100	**1150**	**1200**	**1250**	**1300**	**1350**	**1400**
1157 Albrecht the Bear defeats Slavic tribes and is crowned Margrave of Brandenburg	**1209** First documented mention of Köpenick		**c.1260** Berlin is enlarged			
			1244 First written reference to the settlement of Berlin	*Silver denarius of 1369*		

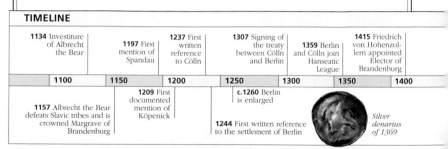

◁ **Adolf von Menzel's symbolic painting *Borussia*, or *Prussia* (1868), at the Ephraim-Palais**

Deposition from the Cross (c.1520), a pane of a
Gothic polyptych from the time of the Reformation

THE EARLY HOHENZOLLERNS

In 1432 Berlin and Cölln were formally unified. By 1443 Elector Friedrich II, son of Friedrich I, had begun construction of the town's first castle, the future Stadtschloss *(see p71)*. This was part of his plan to make Berlin-Cölln the capital of Brandenburg and to reduce the powers and privileges of its citizens. Despite fierce opposition from the local population, the castle was built. By 1448 all opposition had been violently crushed, and in 1451 the castle became the Elector's official residence. To symbolize the consolidation of Hohenzollern power, he added an iron chain and padlock around the neck of the city's heraldic bear.

By the time Friedrich's nephew Johann Cicero became

Elector in 1486, Berlin-Cölln was formally established as the capital of the March of Brandenburg.

REFORMATION AND THE THIRTY YEARS' WAR

During the first half of the 16th century, the radical religious ideas of Martin Luther (1483–1546) spread quickly throughout the whole of Brandenburg. In 1539 the new Protestantism was adopted by the Elector, Joachim II Hector, and most of the town's aldermen.

For a time the city grew fast, boosted by the arrival of religious refugees from the Netherlands, as well as Italian artists invited by the subsequent elector, Joachim Georg. However, successive epidemics of the bubonic plague occurred in 1576, 1598 and 1600, checking the town's growth. The effect was compounded by the advent of the Thirty Years' War which raged from 1618 to 1648, turning the whole of the Holy Roman Empire into a bloody battlefield. In 1627 the Elector of Brandenburg had fled, relocating his court to the less exposed town of Königsberg. By 1648 the population of Berlin-Cölln had fallen to just 6,000, its population being decimated by famine and disease.

BERLIN UNDER THE GREAT ELECTOR

The fortunes of Berlin were turned by the arrival of Friedrich Wilhelm von Hohenzollern, who ascended the Brandenburg throne in 1640. Under the rule of this man, later known as the Great Elector, Berlin experienced a period of an unprecedented growth. The city's population

A falconer on a
16th-century tile

TIMELINE

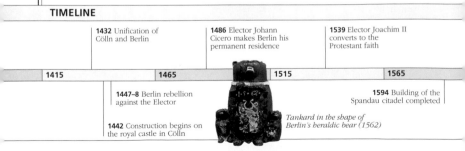

1432 Unification of
Cölln and Berlin

1486 Elector Johann
Cicero makes Berlin his
permanent residence

1539 Elector Joachim II
converts to the
Protestant faith

| 1415 | 1465 | 1515 | 1565 |

1447–8 Berlin rebellion
against the Elector

1594 Building of the
Spandau citadel completed

1442 Construction begins on
the royal castle in Cölln

*Tankard in the shape of
Berlin's heraldic bear (1562)*

The former Stadtschloss (Berlin Castle), with Lange Brücke in the foreground, c.1685

THE CAPITAL OF PRUSSIA

The successor to the Great Elector, Friedrich III inherited the title in 1688. Thirteen years later he raised Brandenburg's status to that of a kingdom, and was crowned King Friedrich I of Prussia. Ambitious and with a taste for luxury, Friedrich became a powerful patron of the arts. Under his rule Berlin acquired its Academies of Fine Arts and Science. Artists transformed the castle into a Baroque palace. The Zeughaus *(see pp58–9)* and the summer palace or Schloss in Lietzenburg, later renamed Charlottenburg *(see pp160–61)*, were built at this time.

rose to 20,000 by 1688 at the end of Friedrich Wilhelm's long reign.

In 1648 work started on the modern fortification of the city. The Lustgarten *(see p74)* was established opposite the Stadtschloss and the road later to become known as Unter den Linden *(see p60)* was planted with lime trees. The city's economic power increased following the building of the canal linking the Spree and Oder rivers, which turned Berlin into the hub of all Brandenburg trade.

Berlin began to expand in all directions with the creation of new satellite towns – first Friedrichswerder, then Dorotheenstadt and Friedrichstadt, all between 1650 and 1690. They would all be absorbed into a unified city of Berlin in 1709.

In 1671 several wealthy Jewish families expelled from Vienna settled in Berlin, while following the 1685 Edict of Potsdam, large numbers of French Huguenots flocked to Brandenburg, forced out of their homeland after Louis XIV repealed the Edict of Nantes. Both these events came to play a major role in the future development of the city.

Friedrich II (1740–86)

The next ruler of Prussia, Friedrich Wilhelm I (1713–40), was unlike his father and soon became known as the "Soldier-King". His initiatives were practical: Berlin was further expanded and encircled with a new wall, not for defence but as a measure against the desertion of conscripted citizens. Pariser Platz *(see p67)*, Leipziger Platz *(see p126)* and Mehringplatz *(see p144)* were all built at that time, and the population reached 90,000.

The next king was Friedrich II (1740–1786), otherwise known as Frederick the Great or "Alter Fritz" (Old Fritz). An educated man who appreciated art, he oversaw the city's transformation into a sophisticated cultural centre. He was also an aggressive empire builder, sparking the Seven Years' War of 1756–63 with his invasion of Silesia, during which Berlin was briefly occupied by Austrian and Russian troops. The city's development continued, however, and at the time of Friedrich II's death in 1786, its population numbered 150,000.

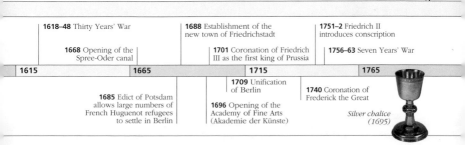

1618–48 Thirty Years' War	1688 Establishment of the new town of Friedrichstadt	1751–2 Friedrich II introduces conscription
1668 Opening of the Spree-Oder canal	1701 Coronation of Friedrich III as the first king of Prussia	1756–63 Seven Years' War
1615	**1665**	**1715**	**1765**

1685 Edict of Potsdam allows large numbers of French Huguenot refugees to settle in Berlin

1696 Opening of the Academy of Fine Arts (Akademie der Künste)

1709 Unification of Berlin

1740 Coronation of Frederick the Great

Silver chalice (1695)

The Baroque Period

Berlin's Baroque Period lasted from the second half of the 17th century to the end of the 18th, and saw the expansion of Berlin-Cölln from a small town, devastated by successive epidemics of bubonic plague and the ravages of the Thirty Years' War, into a rich and cosmopolitan metropolis. Population growth was rapid, aided by the official amalgamation of Berlin-Cölln with the previously independent communities of Dorotheenstadt, Friedrichstadt and Friedrichs-werder. New city walls were built, as were many substantial buildings, including the Akademie der Künste, the Charité and Schloss Charlottenburg.

EXTENT OF THE CITY

■ 1734   □ Today

Flute Concert
This painting by Adolf von Menzel shows the arts-loving King Friedrich II (1740–86) giving a flute recital for his guests in the music room of the Schloss Sanssouci.

Nikolaikirche

Frederick the Great
The famous French-born portrait painter, Antoine Pesne, created this portrait of Friedrich II of Prussia, heir to the Prussian throne, in 1739.

Rococo Tureen
This elaborate silver tureen, decorated with a gilded lemon, was made in the Berlin workshop of Georg Wilhelm Marggraf und Müller in 1765.

Stadtschloss
(Royal Palace)

Love in the Italian Theatre (1714)
French painter Jean-Antoine Watteau (1684–1721) was a favourite with King Friedrich II, and as a result many of his works can still be seen in Berlin.

Rondell (now Mehringplatz)

Oktogon (now Leipziger Platz)

Zeughaus (Former Arsenal)
The splendid Baroque Zeughaus was completed in 1730. Used to store weapons until 1875, it will house the Deutsches Historisches Museum. This view of it was painted in 1786 by Carl Traugott Fechhelm.

King Friedrich I
This medallion bears the likeness of the first King of Prussia (1688–1713). The work of sculptor and architect Andreas Schlüter (1660–1714), it adorns the king's tomb.

Quarré (now Pariser Platz)

BERLIN IN 1740

This map shows the layout of the city's 18th-century fortifications, with various landmark buildings. Contrary to today's convention, this map was drawn with the north pointing down, rather than up.

Unter den Linden

BAROQUE ARCHITECTURE IN BERLIN

Many of Berlin's Baroque buildings have been destroyed, but in the city centre some fine examples still exist. Don't miss the Zeughaus *(see pp58–9)*, two fine churches in Gendarmenmarkt – the Deutscher Dom and the Französischer Dom *(see pp64–5)* – the Parochialkirche *(see p97)* and Sophienkirche *(see p104)*. Another Baroque highlight, even though it is largely a reconstruction, is Schloss Charlottenburg *(see pp158–9)* with its delightful park.

Schloss Charlottenburg

Antique scroll depicting the grand boulevard of Unter den Linden, 1821

BEGINNINGS OF THE MODERN ERA

By the time Friedrich Wilhelm II (1786–97) ascended the throne of Prussia, the country's era of absolute rulers was nearing an end. New trends associated with Romanticism were gaining popularity, and there was an explosion of ideas from outstanding personalities such as writers Gotthold Ephraim Lessing (1729–81) and Friedrich and August-Wilhelm von Schlegel.

Throughout Europe, French Emperor Napoleon Bonaparte (1769–1821) was waging war, defeating the Prussians in 1806 at the battles of Jena and Austerlitz. As French troops moved in to occupy Berlin, Friedrich Wilhelm took his court to Königsberg, while Berlin's pride, the horse-drawn chariot *(Quadriga)* crowning the Brandenburg Gate, was dismantled and taken to Paris.

By the end of 1809 the royal court had returned to Berlin, and, having received huge reparations, Napoleon and his troops finally left the city. In 1814 the *Quadriga* was returned to Berlin, and a year later Napoleon was defeated at Waterloo. Granted the mineral-rich lands of the Rhineland and Westphalia at the subsequent Congress of Vienna, Prussia enjoyed rapid industrialization during the next 30 years, particularly in Berlin. By 1837 August

Borsig had opened his locomotive factory in the city, and in 1838 the first train ran on the Berlin–Potsdam railway.

Many outstanding buildings were designed at this time by Karl Friedrich Schinkel *(see p187)*, including the Neue Wache *(see p60)* and the Schauspielhaus, renamed the Konzerthaus *(see p64)*. Berlin University (now Humboldt Universität) was established in 1810 and became a major seat of learning, attracting famous lecturers such as philosophers Georg Hegel (1770–1831) and Arthur Schopenhauer (1788–1860).

In 1844, however, recession hit Europe, leaving a quarter of all Prussians in poverty. Hunger riots rocked the city in April 1847 and by 1848 Berlin saw a people's uprising in which over 250 demonstrators were shot dead by the Prussian army.

BUILDING AN EMPIRE

In 1861 Friedrich Wilhelm IV (1840–1861) was forced by madness to cede the throne to his brother, Wilhelm (1861–1888). Otto von Bismarck was soon appointed Chancellor, with a foreign policy to install Prussia in Austria's place at the head of all German-speaking states. In 1864 Prussia declared war on Denmark, and successfully acquired Schleswig-Holstein.

Portrait of Friedrich Wilhelm IV

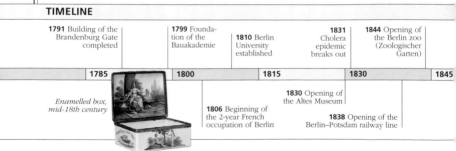

1791 Building of the Brandenburg Gate completed

1799 Foundation of the Bauakademie

1810 Berlin University established

1831 Cholera epidemic breaks out

1844 Opening of the Berlin zoo (Zoologischer Garten)

| 1785 | 1800 | 1815 | 1830 | 1845 |

Enamelled box, mid-18th century

1830 Opening of the Altes Museum

1806 Beginning of the 2-year French occupation of Berlin

1838 Opening of the Berlin–Potsdam railway line

In 1866, following war with Austria, Prussia established dominance over the North German Confederation, an association of 22 states and free towns. In 1870 Prussia went to war with France, annexing the provinces of Alsace and Lorraine. Bismarck's next move was the proclamation of a German Empire on 18 January 1871, with Berlin as its capital and King Wilhelm I as Kaiser (Emperor). Thanks to the colossal reparations paid by France, and the abolition of trade barriers, Berlin now entered another period of rapid industrial growth, accompanied by a population explosion. By 1877 Berlin's population had grown to one million; by 1905 it was two million.

Poster advertising the Berlin Secession Exhibition of 1900, by Wilhelm Schulz

TRIUMPH AND DISASTER

The late 19th century saw an explosion of scientific and cultural achievement in the city, including the completion of a new sewage system in 1876, dramatically improving public health. By 1879 electric lamps lit the streets

Berlin's original Reichstag (parliament) building, constructed in 1894

and in 1881 the first telephones were installed. A year later the first urban train line, the S-Bahn, was opened. Berlin's cultural and scientific life flourished, headed by such outstanding personalities as writer Theodor Fontane, painter Adolf von Menzel and bacteriologist Robert Koch. In 1898 Max Liebermann *(see p67)* founded the hugely influential Berlin Secessionist movement, with members including Käthe Kollwitz and Max Slevogt.

As the city prospered, political developments in Germany and throughout Europe were moving towards the stalemate of 1914. Initially, the outbreak of World War I had little effect on the life of Berlin, but the subsequent famine, strikes and total German defeat led to the November Revolution in 1918, and the abdication of Kaiser Wilhelm II.

The Berlin Congress of 1878 by Anton von Werner

1871 Berlin becomes the capital of the German Empire	**1878** Berlin Congress takes place	**1888** Year of three Kaisers	**1902** Operation of the first underground train (U-Bahn)	**1914** Outbreak of World War I
1860	1875	1890	1905	1920
1879 Technische Universität established	**1882** Opening of the S-Bahn, the first urban train line	*Mosaic by Martin-Gropius-Bau*	**1907** Completion of the Kaufhaus des Westens (KaDeWe)	**1918** Abdication of Kaiser Wilhelm II

Capital of the German Empire

On 18 January 1871, Berlin became the capital of
the newly-established German Empire, fulfilling the
expansionist ambitions of the Prussian Chancellor
Otto von Bismarck. Bringing together many previously independent German-speaking regions, the new
Empire stretched beyond the borders of present-day
Germany, into what are now France, Poland, Russia
and Denmark. Massive reparations paid by France
after her defeat in the Franco-German war of 1870
stimulated the rapid growth of a fast-industrializing
Berlin, accompanied by an explosion of scientific and
artistic invention. Standing at just 300,000 in 1850, by
1900 the city's population had reached 1.9 million.

EXTENT OF THE CITY

| ■ 1800 | □ Today |

**House of
Hohenzollern**
*Mosaics depicting the
Hohenzollern rulers
decorate the bombed
remains of the Kaiser-
Wilhelm-Gedächtnis-
kirche (see pp152–3),
completed in 1895.*

The Stadtschloss
*The Stadtschloss was the royal
residence at the declaration of
the Prussian Empire in 1871.
Decorating the Rathausbrücke,
in the foreground, was the magnificent statue of the Great Elector,
now in the courtyard of Schloss
Charlottenburg (see pp160–61).*

Prussian
nobles

Members of
Parliament

Riehmers Hofgarten
*In the late 19th century a
huge number of buildings
were erected, from tene-
ment blocks to grand
buildings like this one.*

Neptunbrunnen
*This exuberant fountain
(see p92) created by sculptor
Reinhold Begas in 1891 was
a present to Wilhelm II from
the Berlin town council.*

Hackescher Markt Station
Formerly called Bahnhof Börse, this is one of Berlin's first S-Bahn stations, built to a design by Johannes Vollmer and opened in 1902.

Vase with Portrait of Wilhelm II
Designed by Alexander Kips and bearing a portrait of Kaiser Wilhelm II, this vase was mass-produced at the Berlin Königliche-Porzellan-Manufaktur. Pieces were often presented to visiting heads of state.

Empress Augusta Victoria

Heir to the throne, Wilhelm

Black mourning clothes for women and black armbands for men were obligatory after the deaths of the two Kaisers, Wilhelm I and Friedrich III, in 1888.

Diplomatic corps

Prussian Chancellor Otto von Bismarck

Kaiser Wilhelm II

OPENING OF THE REICHSTAG

This enormous canvas, painted by Anton von Werner in 1893, portrays Kaiser Wilhelm II giving a speech to the Members of Parliament, nobles and other dignitaries at the official opening of the Reichstag. This important event took place only 11 days after the coronation of the new Kaiser.

Charlotte Berend
The arts flourished in the years before World War I. This 1902 portrait of an actress is by Berlin artist Lovis Corinth.

The burning of one of the thousands of buildings belonging to Jews on *Kristallnacht*, November 1938

Brecht, while from the UFA film studio came such classics as *The Cabinet of Dr Cagliari* and *Metropolis*. Jazz was popular, and the Berlin Philharmonic gained worldwide fame. Architecture flourished with Walter Gropius and Bruno Taut, while Berlin scientists Albert Einstein, Carl Bosch and Werner Heisenberg were all awarded the Nobel Prize.

THE WEIMAR REPUBLIC

On 9 November 1918 two politicians simultaneously proclaimed the birth of two German Republics. Social democrat Philipp Scheidemann announced the founding of a Democratic Republic, while hours later Karl Liebknecht, founder of the German communist movement, declared the Free Socialist Republic of Germany. Rivalries between the two groups erupted in January 1919 in a week of rioting, crushed by the Freikorps army who also brutally murdered communist leaders Karl Liebknecht and Rosa Luxemburg.

In February 1919 the National Assembly elected Social Democrat Friedrich Ebert President of the German Republic. In 1920 urban reform dramatically increased the size of Berlin, causing the population to swell to 3.8 million. Berlin, like the rest of the country, fell on hard times, with rising unemployment and rampant hyper-inflation.

At the same time, the city became the centre of a lively cultural life. Leading figures in theatre included Max Reinhardt and Bertolt

Ein Volk, ein Reich, ein Führer!

Nazi propoganda poster of Hitler, printed in 1938

THE THIRD REICH

The world stock-market crash of October 1929 and the ensuing Depression put the fragile German democracy under great pressure, paving the way for extremist politicians. On 30 January 1933 Adolf Hitler was appointed Chancellor. The Reichstag fire in February was used as a pretext to arrest communist and liberal opponents, and by March 1933 Hitler's Nazi (National Socialist German Workers) Party was in control of the Reichstag. Books by "un-German" authors were burned in front of the Alte Bibliothek, and works of art deemed to be "degenerate" were removed from museums.

Inferno (1946), Fritz Koelle

The 1936 Olympic Games in Berlin were meant as a showcase for Aryan supremacy. Although Germany won 33 gold medals, the real hero was the black US athlete Jesse Owens, with four gold medals.

The effects of the Nazi regime were felt particularly by Jews and intellectuals, many of whom were

TIMELINE

1919 Proclamation of the Weimar Republic

1926 The Funkturm (radio tower) is opened

1930 Opening of the Pergamonmuseum

1938 Kristallnacht on the night of 9–10 November

1945 Germany surrenders on 8 May

24 June 1948–12 May 1949 Soviet blockade of Berlin

1920	1930	1940	1950	196

1928 Premiere of *The Threepenny Opera* by Bertolt Brecht

1920 Urban reform creates Greater Berlin

1933 Hitler accedes to power

1939 Outbreak of World War II on 1 September

1942 Wannsee Conference

Poster depicting the German race

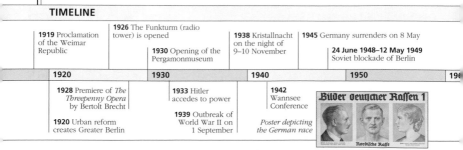

forced to emigrate. On the night of 9–10 November 1938, known as *Kristallnacht* (Night of the Broken Glass), thousands of synagogues, cemeteries, Jewish homes and shops throughout Germany were looted and burned.

WORLD WAR II

Hitler's invasion of Poland on 1 September 1939 signalled the start of World War II. For the citizens of Berlin, food shortages were followed in August 1940 by British air raids. By 1941 the goverment policy of the mass deportation of Jews to concentration camps had begun. Other groups targeted included homosexuals, priests and Romany gypsies. In January 1942, at a conference held in a villa in Wannsee *(see p181)* it was decided to embark on a systematic extermination of all European Jews. The unsuccessful attempt to assassinate Hitler in 1944 ended up with Nazis murdering many members of the German resistance.

After nearly four years of bitter warfare, the tide began to turn against the Germans. In April 1945 more than 1.5 million Soviet soldiers invaded Berlin. On 30 April Hitler committed suicide, and Germany conceded defeat.

BERLIN DIVIDED

The Potsdam Conference of 1945 *(see p199)* divided Berlin into four sectors, occupied respectively by Soviet, US, British and French troops. This put the devastated city at the centre of the Communist-Capitalist Cold War. On 24 June 1948 the Soviet authorities, in their attempt to annex the whole city, introduced a blockade of its Western sectors. The Allies responded with the Berlin Airlift, which thwarted the Soviet plans. On 12 May 1949 the blockade was lifted.

Historic buildings at the Gendarmenmarkt destroyed by British and American bombs, 1945–6

The same year saw the birth of the Federal Republic of Germany, with its capital in Bonn, and the German Democratic Republic (GDR), with the capital in East Berlin. West Berlin remained as a separate enclave. On 17 June 1953 workers' strikes in the GDR and East Berlin turned into an uprising which was bloodily crushed by the authorities. In their attempt to staunch the ever-rising flood of refugees, the GDR authorities decided in 1961 to surround West Berlin with a wall, and shoot at anyone attempting to cross it.

The political changes which occurred all over Eastern Europe in 1989 led to the fall of the Berlin Wall and the opening of the frontiers between the two republics. On 3 October 1990, Germany was officially reunified and Berlin once again became the capital. The government moved here in 1991.

Celebrations as the Berlin Wall falls, 9 November 1989

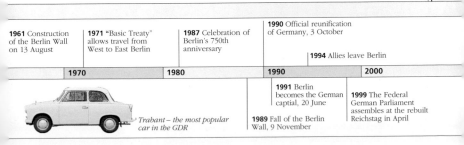

1961 Construction of the Berlin Wall on 13 August

1971 "Basic Treaty" allows travel from West to East Berlin

1987 Celebration of Berlin's 750th anniversary

1990 Official reunification of Germany, 3 October

1994 Allies leave Berlin

1970   1980   1990   2000

Trabant – the most popular car in the GDR

1991 Berlin becomes the German captial, 20 June

1989 Fall of the Berlin Wall, 9 November

1999 The Federal German Parliament assembles at the rebuilt Reichstag in April

BERLIN AT A GLANCE

More than 150 places of interest are described in the *Area by Area* section of this book. These include a range of sights from historic monuments, such as the Nikolaikirche *(see p90)*, to modern landmarks like the ambitious showcase architecture of the new Potsdamer Platz district *(see p126)*; from the peace of the Botanical Garden *(see p177)* to the noisier charms of Berlin's long-established zoo *(see p150)*. To help you make the most of your stay, the following 16 pages provide a time-saving guide to the very best that Berlin has to offer. Museums and galleries, historic buildings, parks and gardens, modern architecture, the legacy of the divided city and famous Berliners all feature in this section. Below is a top ten selection of attractions that no visitor should miss.

BERLIN'S TOP TEN ATTRACTIONS

Pergamonmuseum
See pp80–83.

Schloss Charlottenburg
See pp160–61.

**Kungstgewerbe-
museum**
See pp118–21.

Gemäldegalerie
See pp122–5.

Nikolaiviertel
See pp88–9.

Zoologischer Garten
See p150.

Brandenburger Tor
See p67.

Fernsehturm
See p93.

Reichstag
See p134.

**Kaiser-Wilhelm-Gedächt-
nis-Kirche** *See pp152–3.*

◁ Interior of the Reichstag *(see p134)*, with its new dome designed by Sir Norman Foster

Berlin's Best: Museums and Galleries

Ancient Greek vase

Berlin boasts some of the finest museum collections in the world. Since 1990 many of the collections previously split between East and West Berlin have been brought together in new venues. One example is the Gemäldegalerie collection, a magnificent collection of Old Master paintings. Berlin's major museum complexes are located on Museum Island, around Schloss Charlottenburg, at the Kulturforum and at Dahlem.

Kunstgewerbemuseum
The arts and crafts collection at the Kunstgewerbemuseum (see pp118–21) is among the most interesting in Europe. One of its many treasures is this 17th-century gold elephant-shaped vessel.

Around Schloss Charlottenburg

Tiergarten

Around Kurfürstendamm

Gemäldegalerie
This world-famous collection illustrates the history of European painting from the 13th to the 18th centuries. Originally part of a triptych, The Adoration of the Magi *(1470) was painted by Hugo van der Goes (see pp122–5).*

Museumszentrum Dahlem
This huge complex houses several museums devoted to ethnography and non-European art (see p178).

0 metres	750
0 yards	750

Hamburger Bahnhof

Featuring artists such as Joseph Beuys and Andy Warhol, as well as the renowned Flick Collection, this museum of modern art is housed in the former Hamburger railway station (see pp110–11).

Deutches Historisches Museum

Once building works are finished, the Baroque Zeughaus will contain the Museum of German History. Everyday objects as well as works of art will be used to illustrate historical events (see pp58–9).

North of the Centre

East of the Centre

Pergamonmuseum

This museum owes its name to the reconstructed Pergamon Zeus altar, which stands in its main hall (see pp80–83).

Around Unter den Linden

Museum Island

Altes Museum

The ground floor of Karl Friedrich Schinkel's Neo-Classical building has been used since 1998 to exhibit a collection of Greek and Roman antiquities (see p75).

Kreuzberg

Deutsches Technikmuseum

The development of a range of industrial technologies, from locomotive-building to brewing, is illustrated in this entertaining museum (see pp144–5).

Jüdisches Museum

Berlin's Jewish museum was designed by Daniel Libeskind, an American architect of Jewish descent. The form of the building is based on the Star of David (see p141).

Exploring Berlin's Museums

Majolica plate, Kunstgewerbemuseum

Despite being damaged during World War II, Berlin's numerous museums are still among the finest, and the most heavily subsidized, in the world. Many collections were split up when the city was partitioned in 1946, and although the process of bringing them together again is under way, some collections are still scattered around different sites, and many of the older museums are undergoing refurbishment.

Picasso's *Head of the Faun* (1937) in the Sammlung Berggruen

ANCIENT ART

The art of ancient Egypt is shown at the **Ägyptisches Museum** (Egyptian Museum). The jewel of this museum is the bust of Queen Nefertiti. Works of art from Ancient Greece and Rome are kept in the 19th-century **Altes Museum** (Old Museum). Another large collection of antiquities can be found in the **Pergamonmuseum**, where visitors can see several reconstructed architectural wonders, including the Pergamon Zeus altar and the Market Gate from Miletus. The museum also holds an impressive collection of Middle Eastern art, including a reconstruction of the Babylonian Ishtar Gate.

Bust of Nefertiti, Ägyptisches Museum

German and Italian sculpture is housed in the **Bodemuseum**, while the **Alte Nationalgalerie** (Old National Gallery) displays 18th- and 19th-century art, including paintings by the German Romantics, amongst which are famous landscapes by Caspar David Friedrich.

A collection of sculpture from the late-16th to the mid-19th centuries can be seen in the **Schinkel-Museum**. The **Neue Nationalgalerie** (New National Gallery) is filled with late 19th- and early 20th-century paintings and sculpture. Art Nouveau and Art Deco works are featured at the **Bröhan-Museum**, while works by modern greats, such as Pablo Picasso, Paul Klee

and Georges Braque, are on show at the **Sammlung Berggruen** (Berggruen Collection).

The **Brücke-Museum** displays the works of German Expressionists, and contemporary art is exhibited in the **Hamburger Bahnhof**.

Arts and crafts, from the Middle Ages to the present, are displayed at the **Kunstgewerbemuseum** (Museum of Applied Arts). The **Bauhaus-Archiv** displays applied arts from the influential inter-war Bauhaus movement.

Two recent additions are the **Newton-Sammlung**, which contains the life's work of 20th-century photographer Helmut Newton, while the reopened **Berlinische Galerie** shows the city's collection of modern art and architecture.

FINE ART AND DESIGN

Berlin's largest collection of 13th- to 18th-century European painting is displayed in the **Gemäldegalerie** (Picture Gallery). Here are works by old masters including Dürer, Rembrandt, Titian, Botticelli and Caravaggio. In the same museum complex is the **Kupferstichkabinett**, with drawings and prints from the Middle Ages to the present.

Old masters can also be seen in the **Jagdschloss Grunewald**, a Renaissance palace home to German and Dutch paintings from the 14th to 19th centuries. A large collection of predominantly 17th-century paintings is housed in the **Bildergalerie** (Gallery of Paintings) in Potsdam.

Étienne Chevalier with St Stephen by Jean Fouquet, Gemäldegalerie

NON-EUROPEAN ART

Those interested in Asian art should visit the **Museums-zentrum Dahlem**. This complex houses three large collections: the Museum für Ostasiatische Kunst (Museum of East Asian Art), the Museum für Indische Kunst (Museum of Indian Art) and the Ethnologisches Museum (Museum of Ethnography), which explores the heritage of non-European nations.

The **Museum für Islamische Kunst** (Museum of Islamic Art) is located in the same building as the Pergamonmuseum.

Totem pole, Ethnologisches Museum

HISTORY

The collection of the **Deutsches Historisches Museum** (Museum of German History) traces German history from the Middle Ages to the present. The **Hugenotten-museum** (Huguenot Museum), located in the tower of the Französischer Dom, charts the history of the city's Huguenots.

The **Centrum Judaicum** (Jewish Centre) in the Neue Synagogue (New Synagogue), and the **Jüdisches Museum** (Jewish Museum), in a new building by Daniel Libeskind, are devoted to Jewish history and cultural heritage.

Berlin has several museums associated with World War II. The **Topographie des Terrors** (Topography of Terror) exhibition is displayed at the site of the former Gestapo and SS headquarters. A deeply shocking collection of documents concerning the Holocaust is kept at the **Haus der Wannsee-Konferenz**. The tools of terror used on the citizens of the German Democratic Republic can be seen at the **Stasi-Museum**, while the **Haus am Check-point Charlie** (House at Checkpoint Charlie) museum tells the stories of those who crossed the Berlin Wall. The **Alliiertenmuseum** focuses on life during the Cold War.

TECHNOLOGY AND NATURAL HISTORY

The **Museum für Natur-kunde** (Museum of Natural History) contains the world's biggest dinosaur skeleton. Also popular with visitors is the **Deutsches Technik-museum** (German Technology Museum), in a large site around a former railway station. German movie history (including original costumes worn by divas such as Marlene Dietrich) is presented at the **Filmmuseum Berlin**. Those interested in technology should also visit the **Museum für Post und Kommunikation** (Museum of Post and Communications).

SPECIALIST SUBJECTS

Berlin is not short of specialist museums. There are museums devoted to laundry, sugar and even hemp. Lovers of theatre and literature can visit the one-time home of Bertolt Brecht (1898–1956), now the **Brecht-Weigel Gedenkstätte** (Brecht-Weigel Memorial). Worth a visit to see the magnificent Wurlitzer organ alone is the **Musikinstrumenten-Museum** (Musical Instruments Museum). The outdoor **Domäne Dahlem** (Dahlem Farm Museum) shows 300 years of local farm life and exhibits old-fashioned tools.

FINDING THE MUSEUMS

A wide array of exhibits in the Musikinstrumenten-Museum

Berlin's Best: Historic Architecture

Berlin is a relatively new city. It expanded slowly until the first half of the 19th century, and then grew with increasing rapidity from around 1850 onwards. Although many of the city's finest architectural treasures were destroyed by World War II bombing, it is still possible to discover many interesting historic buildings (for more information, *see pp38–9*). In nearby Potsdam *(see pp190–205)* you can visit the splendid Schloss Sanssouci. Set in magnificent parkland, the palace was built for Friedrich II (1740–1786) and extended by subsequent rulers.

Schloss Charlottenburg
The construction of this Baroque royal palace at Charlottenburg was begun in 1695. Subsequent extension works took place throughout the 18th century (see pp160–61).

Around Schloss Charlottenburg

Tiergarten

Around Kurfürstendamm

Schloss Bellevue
This Rococo palace by Philipp Daniel Boumann is now the official residence of the President of the Federal Republic of Germany.

The Reichstag
This massive Neo-Renaissance building was designed in 1884 by Paul Wallot. Its elegant new dome is the work of British architect Norman Foster (see p134).

Schloss Sanssouci
This small palace was the favourite residence of Friedrich II.

Neues Palais
The Neues Palais combines elements of Baroque and Neo-Classical style.

POTSDAM PALACES

The summer palace of Schloss Sanssouci gives its name to Potsdam's Park Sanssouci, a royal complex with highlights including the grand 18th-century Neues Palais and the small but charming Schloss Charlottenhof.

0 metres	750
0 yards	750

Brandenburger Tor
*This Neo-Classical gate stands at
the end of Unter den Linden.
Crowned by a Quadriga (chariot)
driven by the Goddess of Victory, it
is the symbol of Berlin (see p67).*

Zeughaus
*Upon completion of re-
building, this Baroque
arsenal will house the
Deutsches Historisches
Museum (see pp58–9).
Its courtyard will contain
masks of dying warriors
by sculptor Andreas
Schlüter (1660–1714).*

Marienkirche
*This Gothic church,
founded in the 13th
century, contains a
striking 15th-century
mural. It is one of the
city's oldest buildings
(see pp94–5).*

North of the Centre

East of the
Centre

Around Unter
den Linden

Museum
Island

Kreuzberg

Rotes Rathaus
*Berlin's main Town Hall is named
"red" after the colour of its brick
exterior, not the political
persuasion of the Mayor (see p90).*

Berliner Dom
*This enormous cathedral, built
between 1894 and 1905, is an
example of the Neo-Renaissance
style in Berlin (see pp76–7).*

Konzerthaus
*Built in 1820 to replace a theatre
destroyed by fire, this beautiful building
on the Gendarmenmarkt was designed by
Karl Friedrich Schinkel (see pp64–5).*

Exploring Berlin's Historic Architecture

Until the industrial revolution of the late 19th century, Berlin was little more than a small town surrounded by villages. As a result, the city's oldest buildings are concentrated in the central core around Unter den Linden and along the Spree river, an area which suffered heavy damage during World War II. Older country residences, however, as well as some important newer buildings, can be seen in former villages such as Wedding and Charlottenburg, which now form part of Greater Berlin.

14th-century Gothic doorway of the Nikolaikirche in the Nikolaiviertel

MIDDLE AGES AND RENAISSANCE

The **Nikolaikirche** is the oldest building in central Berlin. The base of its massive front tower is Romanesque and dates back to about 1230, although the church itself is Gothic and was built between 1380 and 1450. The second Gothic church in the city centre is the **Marienkirche**. Nearby are the ruins of a **Franciscan friary**, and the **Heiliggeistkapelle**. Many medieval churches outside the city centre have survived the war. Among the most beautiful is the late-Gothic **Nikolaikirche** in Spandau, dating

from the early 15th century. A further ten village churches, most dating from the 13th century, can be found hidden among high-rise apartment buildings. **St Annen-Kirche** in Dahlem, however, still enjoys an almost rural setting.

The few surviving secular structures include fragments of the **city walls** in the city centre, and the **Julius-turm** in Spandau, a huge, early 13th-century tower which stands in the grounds of the Spandau Citadel. Berlin's only surviving Renaissance buildings are the **Ribbeckhaus** with its four picturesque gables, the **Jagdschloss-Grunewald**, a modest hunting lodge designed by Casper Theyss in 1542, and the **Spandau Citadel** (or fortress), a well-preserved example of Italian-style military defence architecture. Finished in 1592, the construction of the Citadel was begun in 1560 by Christoph Römer using plans by Italian architect Francesco Chiaramella da Gandino. It was brought to completion by Rochus Guerrini Graf zu Lynar (the Count of Lynar).

BAROQUE EXPANSION

The Thirty Years' War (1618–48) put a temporary stop to the town's development, and it was not until the Peace of 1648 that new building work in the Baroque style began. One of the first of the city's Baroque buildings is the late 17th-century **Schloss Köpenick**. More buildings followed, many of which survive today. They include the **Parochialkirche**, the **Deutscher Dom** and the **Französischer Dom**, as well as the magnificent **Zeughaus**, built between 1695 and 1730. During this period Andreas Schlüter (1664–1714) designed the now-demolished Stadt-schloss (Royal Palace), while Johann Arnold Nering (1659–95) designed **Schloss Charlotten-burg**. Other surviving Baroque palaces include **Palais Podewils** and **Schloss Nieder-schönhausen**. One of the few buildings dating from the reign of Friedrich Wilhelm I (1713–40) is the **Kollegienhaus** at Linden-strasse No. 14 , designed by Philipp Gerlach and built in 1733. During the reign of Friedrich II (1740–86), many buildings were erected in the late Baroque and Rococo styles. These include **Schloss Sanssouci** in Potsdam and the **Alte Bibliothek** building on Unter den Linden, which completed the Forum Fridericianum project, now better known as Bebelplatz (*see pp56–7*).

Detail of the Zeughaus

NEO-CLASSICISM AND ROMANTICISM

The Neo-Classical architecture of the late-18th and early-19th centuries has given Berlin much of its basic form. One dominant figure of this period was Carl Gotthard Langhans (1732–1808), creator of the **Brandenburg Gate** and of **Schloss Bellevue**. Even more influential, however, was Karl

Renaissance-style defence, the Citadel building at Spandau

Friedrich Schinkel *(see p187)*. His work includes some of Berlin's most important public buildings, including the **Neue Wache**, the **Altes Museum** and the **Konzerthaus**. Many of Schinkel's residential commissions are also still standing, with some such as **Schloss Klein Glienicke** and **Schloss Tegel** open to the public. Schinkel's Neo-Gothic work includes **Schloss Babelsberg** and the **Friedrichswerdersche Kirche**.

Elegant Neo-Classicism at Karl Friedrich Schinkel's Schloss Klein Glienicke

INDUSTRIALIZATION AND THE MODERN AGE

The second half of the 19th century was a time of rapid development for Berlin. After Schinkel's death, his work was continued by his students, Ludwig Persius (1803–45) and Friedrich August Stüler (1800–65). Stüler designed the Neo-Classical **Alte Nationalgalerie** between 1866 and 1876. Some splendid Neo-Romanesque and Neo-Gothic churches and several notable public buildings in various styles were also produced at this time. The spirit of the Italian Neo-Renaissance is seen in the **Rotes Rathaus** designed by Hermann Friedrich Waesemann, and in the **Martin-Gropius-Bau**, by Martin Gropius in 1877. Late Neo-Renaissance features are used in Paul Wallot's **Reichstag** building and in Ernst von

Decorative frieze on the Martin-Gropius-Bau

Ihne's **Statsbibliothek** building. Julius Raschdorff's **Berliner Dom** shows Neo-Baroque influences. Much of the religious architecture of the period continued in the Neo-Gothic style, while Franz Schwechten designed the **Kaiser-Wilhelm-Gedächtnis-Kirche** in the Neo-Romanesque style. Many structures of this period are built in the modernist style inspired by the industrial revolution, the textbook example being the huge power station, **AEG-Turbinenhalle**, designed by Peter Behrens in the 1890s.

BETWEEN THE TWO WORLD WARS

The greatest architectural achievements of this period include a number of splendid housing estates, such as the **Hufeisensiedlung** designed by Bruno Taut and Martin Wagner in 1924, and **Onkel-Toms-Hütte** in Zehlendorf. An interesting example of the Expressionist style is Erich Mendelsohn's **Einsteinturm** in Potsdam. Art Deco is represented by Hans Poelzig's **Haus des Rundfunks**, the country's first Broadcasting House. Hitler's rise to power in the 1930s marked a return to the classical forms which dominated German architecture of the Fascist period. Representatives of this period include the **Tempelhof Airport** Terminal building and the **Olympia-Stadion**, built for the 1936 Olympic Games.

20th-century Neo-Renaissance detail of the massive Berliner Dom

HISTORIC BUILDINGS

Reminders of the Divided City

In 1945, as part of the post-war peace, Berlin was divided into four zones of occupation: Soviet, American, British and French. Hostilities erupted in June 1948, when the Soviets blockaded West Berlin in an attempt to bring the area under their control. The ensuing year-long standoff marked the start of the Cold War. By the 1950s, economic problems in the East had led to bloodily-suppressed riots and a mass exodus to the West. In 1961 the East German government constructed the infamous Berlin Wall *(die Mauer)* to contain its citizens. Between this time and reunification at the end of 1989, more than 180 people were shot trying to cross the Wall.

Berlin Wall
Protected to the east by land mines, the Wall, known by the East German authorities as the "Anti-Fascist Protection Wall", surrounded West Berlin and was 155 km (95 miles) long (see p168).

Memorial to Soviet Soldiers
Part of West Berlin, the area around this monument to Red Army troops killed in the 1945 Battle of Berlin was closed for many years due to attacks on its Soviet guards (see p135).

Around Schloss Charlottenburg

Tiergarten

0 km 1
0 miles 0.5

KEY

■ Berlin Wall

Around Kurfürstendamm

BERLIN BEFORE REUNIFICATION

The Wall cut the city in half, severing its main transport arteries, the S-Bahn and U-Bahn lines. West Berliners were excluded from the centre of the city. Running along the Wall was a no-man's-land, now Berlin's biggest building site.

KEY

■ Berlin Wall

■ Sector boundaries

✈ Airport

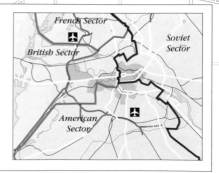

French Sector
British Sector
Soviet Sector
American Sector

Tränenpalast (Palace of Tears)
Until 1989 the Tränenpalast, next to the final S-Bahn station in East Berlin, was a border checkpoint for S-Bahn passengers heading west.

Checkpoint Charlie
This border crossing between the American and Soviet sectors was used by foreign citizens and diplomats. It was the location of many dramatic events during the years of the Cold War.

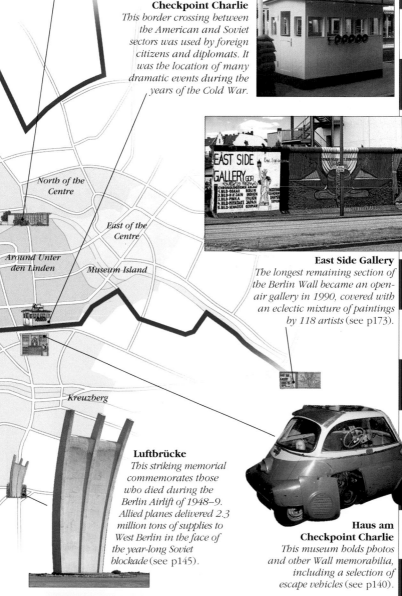

North of the Centre

East of the Centre

Around Unter den Linden

Museum Island

Kreuzberg

East Side Gallery
The longest remaining section of the Berlin Wall became an open-air gallery in 1990, covered with an eclectic mixture of paintings by 118 artists (see p173).

Luftbrücke
This striking memorial commemorates those who died during the Berlin Airlift of 1948–9. Allied planes delivered 2.3 million tons of supplies to West Berlin in the face of the year-long Soviet blockade (see p145).

Haus am Checkpoint Charlie
This museum holds photos and other Wall memorabilia, including a selection of escape vehicles (see p140).

Berlin's Best: Modern Architecture

Following Berlin's devastation in World War II, intense post-war reconstruction turned the city into a giant building site. With the help of architects from several countries the city acquired many modern structures and estates, ranked among the best in the world. The city's reunification in 1990 and the reinstatement of Berlin as the main seat of government gave rise to a second wave of building activity, carried out on a scale unprecedented in Europe. The architectural elite are participating in the design of the new Berlin, and the sites in the city centre that stood empty until 1990 are being filled with new buildings at an incredible rate.

Bauhaus-Archiv
This cubist structure was completed in 1978 to house the Bauhaus museum. It was designed much earlier by Walter Gropius (1883–1969), director of the Bauhaus art school from 1919 to 1928.

Around Schloss Charlottenburg

Tiergarten

Around Kurfürstendamm

Kant-Dreieck
This building, with its pure forms and the eccentric sail-like structure mounted on the roof, is the work of Josef Paul Kleihues.

Nordische Botschaften
Built between 1997 and 1999, the five interconnected embassies of the Scandinavian countries are an example of daring architectural design. The building's green shutters adjust to the intensity and direction of available sunlight.

Kammermusiksaal

Both the Berliner Philharmonie building (1961) and the adjacent Kammermusiksaal, or chamber music hall (1987), were designed by Hans Scharoun. The latter was built posthumously by Edgar Wisniewski, Scharoun's pupil.

Galeries Lafayette

This elegant department store in Friedrichstrasse, designed by Jean Nouvel, brings Parisian chic to the heart of Berlin.

Quartier Schützenstrasse

This part of the city features the work of Italian architect Aldo Rossi. With high-rise blocks and bold colour schemes, the area shows modernity and classical forms standing side by side.

North of
the Centre

East of the Centre

Around Unter
den Linden

Museum
Island

Kreuzberg

0 metres 750

0 yards 750

Gemäldegalerie

The new Gemäldegalerie, designed by the Hilmer and Sattler Partnership, was opened in June 1998. The main hall is particularly elegant.

Sony Center

This ultra-modern steel-and-glass building was designed by German-American architect Helmut Jahn. It houses offices, entertainment venues, the Kaisersaal and Sony's European headquarters.

Exploring Berlin's Modern Architecture

Around the world architects are forever designing buildings with innovative and interesting structures, but in Berlin this creative process is happening on an unprecedented scale. The city is a vast melting pot of trends and styles, where the world's greatest architects scramble for new commissions and where the buildings compete with each other in the originality of their form and in their use of the latest technology.

Haus der Kulturen der Welt in the Tiergarten

FROM 1945 TO 1970

World War II exacted a heavy price from Berlin. The centre was reduced to rubble and the partitioning of the city made it impossible to carry out any co-ordinated reconstruction. In 1952, East Berlin decided to develop **Karl-Marx-Allee** in the Socialist-Realist style. In reply, West Berlin employed the world's greatest architects to create the **Hansaviertel** estate. Le Corbusier built one of his *unités d'habitation*, while the American architect, Hugh A Stubbins, built the Kongresshalle (now the **Haus der Kulturen der Welt**). The West's response to the cultural venues inherited by the East Berliners, including the opera, the library and the museums, was the **Kulturforum** complex. The complex included such magnificent buildings as the **Philharmonie**, designed by Hans Scharoun, and the **Neue Nationalgalerie**, designed by Mies van der Rohe. While West Berlin acquired its huge "trade temple"– the **Europa-Center**, constructed in 1965, East Berlin boasted its **Fernsehturm** (television tower), built in 1969.

FROM 1970 TO 1990

The continuing rivalry, as each part of the city tried to outdo the other, resulted in the construction of East Berlin's **Palast der Republic** in 1976. The West replied with the ultramodern **Internationales Congress Centrum** in 1979. The Kulturforum complex was further extended with designs by Scharoun, including the **Kammermusiksaal** and the **Staatsbibliothek** (library). The impressive **Bauhaus-Archiv** was developed from a design by Walter Gropius. In 1987 Berlin celebrated its 750th anniversary, which in the East saw the completion of the huge **Nikolaiviertel** development, with its pre-war allusions. In the West, the IBA's 1987 scheme gave the town its enormous new post-modernist housing estates in Kreuzberg and also in the **Tegel** area.

POST-REUNIFICATION ARCHITECTURE

The government district is under construction within the bend of the Spree river. Its designers include Charlotte Frank and Axel Schultes. The **Reichstag** building has been famously remodelled by Norman Foster. **Pariser Platz** has been filled with new designs by Günther Behnisch, Frank O Gehry, Josef Paul Kleihues and others. The magnificent **Friedrichstadtpassagen** complex became the scene of rivalry between Jean Nouvel and Oswald M Ungers. Many interesting office buildings have sprung up around town, including **Ludwig-Erhard-Haus** by Nicholas Grimshaw and the nearby **Kant-Dreieck** by Josef Paul Kleihues. Housing has also been transformed, with perhaps the most original example being Aldo Rossi's **Quartier Schützenstrasse**. The city has also acquired some fine museums, including the new **Gemälde-galerie** designed by the Hilmer and Sattler Partnership, and the Deconstructivist style **Jüdisches Museum**, designed by Daniel Libeskind.

Neue Nationalgalerie at Kulturforum designed by Mies van der Rohe

Potsdamer Platz

In the short space of a few years a new financial and business district has sprung up on the vast empty wasteland surrounding the Potsdamer Platz. It boasts splendid constructions designed by Renzo Piano, Arata Isozaki and Helmut Jahn. As well as office blocks, the area has many public buildings, including cinemas and a theatre, as well as a huge shopping centre – the Arkaden, plus luxury hotels, restaurants and several bars.

The Beisheim Center is a mix of exclusive apartments and international hotels.

The Sony Center

POTSDAMER PLATZ

POTSDAMER STRASSE

ENTLASTUNGSSTRASSE

LANDWEHRKANAL

The Sony Tower, *designed by Helmut Jahn, is the most modern building in Potsdamer Platz and is curved on one side and flat on the other.*

This office building, which is the tallest in Potsdamer Platz, was designed by the architects Kollhoff & Timmermann Partnership.

Arkaden, opened in autumn 1998, immediately became one of the city's favourite shopping centres.

| 0 metres | 100 |
| 0 yards | 100 |

The Debis House, *designed by Italian architect Renzo Piano.*

Berlin's Best: Parks and Gardens

Berlin is undoubtedly one of Europe's greenest capital cities, with the sprawling Tiergarten at its centre. However, most of Berlin's districts have their own smaller parks and gardens, too, some of them with children's play areas and nature trails. To the west of the city is the vast Grunewald, a beautiful area of forest which contains mountain bike trails and scenic paths for walkers and cyclists. In summer, numerous lakes, rivers and canals provide excellent facilities for water sports.

Zoologischer Garten
Popular with children, Berlin's zoo has some 14,000 animals, representing 1,400 different species. It is the oldest zoo in Germany (see p150).

Schloss Charlottenburg
The well-maintained grounds of this royal palace were designed in the French Baroque style (see pp160–61).

Around Schloss Charlottenburg

Around Kurfürstendamm

Botanischer Garten
Established from 1899 to 1910 in Dahlem, this botanical garden is one of the biggest in the world (see p177).

Park Babelsberg
This vast landscaped park was designed by Peter Joseph Lenné, and now lies within the Potsdam city limits. It surrounds the picturesque Schloss Babelsberg (see pp210–11).

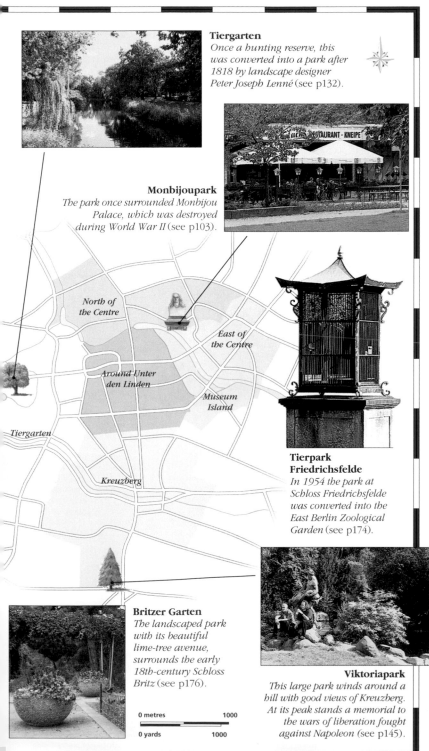

Tiergarten
Once a hunting reserve, this was converted into a park after 1818 by landscape designer Peter Joseph Lenné (see p132).

Monbijoupark
The park once surrounded Monbijou Palace, which was destroyed during World War II (see p103).

North of the Centre

East of the Centre

Around Unter den Linden

Museum Island

Tiergarten

Kreuzberg

Tierpark Friedrichsfelde
In 1954 the park at Schloss Friedrichsfelde was converted into the East Berlin Zoological Garden (see p174).

Britzer Garten
The landscaped park with its beautiful lime-tree avenue, surrounds the early 18th-century Schloss Britz (see p176).

Viktoriapark
This large park winds around a hill with good views of Kreuzberg. At its peak stands a memorial to the wars of liberation fought against Napoleon (see p145).

| 0 metres | 1000 |
| 0 yards | 1000 |

BERLIN THROUGH THE YEAR

Like all major European capitals, Berlin offers a wide range of activities throughout the year. The best seasons for cultural and sporting events are spring and autumn, when the city hosts many spectacular fairs and exhibitions. During summer the city's population shrinks, as many locals head for their holiday destinations. But the weather is often pleasant, and rarely

Karneval der Kulturen

very hot, so this is a good time for serious sightseeing. In winter, although it can get quite cold, it is possible to spend time visiting museums or simply walking around the city. The streets teem with shoppers during the run up to Christmas. A more detailed programme of events can be obtained from tourist information offices *(see p278)* or on the internet at www.berlinonline.de/kultur.

The Karneval der Kulturen in the streets of Kreuzberg

SPRING

In springtime, Berlin holds many interesting fairs and cultural events in its squares, parks and gardens, allowing the visitor to appreciate fully the beauty of the city as the trees and flowers burst into life. With the arrival of the warmer weather, another natural resource springs to life as cruise and rowing boats start operating on the Spree river and the city's canals.

MARCH

ITB-Internationale Tourismus-Börse *(mid Mar)*. The biggest European fair devoted to tourism where representatives from all parts of the world try to attract visitors to their countries.
Music-Biennale Berlin *(2nd week in Mar)* is a busy festival of experimental, electronic and contemporary music held on odd-number years.

Rassehunde-Zuchtschau *(weekend mid-Mar)* is a huge show for pedigree dogs and pedigree dog lovers.
Berliner Motorradtage *(end Mar)*. Motorcyclists from all over Germany converge on Berlin for this specialist event.

APRIL

Festtage *(Apr)*. A series of popular concerts and operas performed by world-class musicians in the Philharmonie and at the Staatsoper.
Easter *(exact date varies)*. Huge markets open around the Kaiser-Wilhelm-Gedächtnis-kirche, Alexanderplatz and other central locations as the city prepares for the feast.
Britzer Baumblüte *(all of Apr)* is a month-long spring festival organized in Britz, a suburb in the south of the city famous for its windmills.
Neuköllner Frühlingsfest *(all of Apr)* Hasenheide. Traditional springtime festival celebrating the new season.

MAY

German Women's Tennis Open *(early May)*. Each year this tournament attracts the world's top women players. The current strength of German tennis ensures huge crowds turn up eager to cheer on the home players.
Luft- und Raumfahrtaus-stellung Berlin-Brandenburg *(early May)*. This festival and air show of civil, military and space craft fills the skies above Schönefeld airport.
Theatertreffen Berlin *(May)*. This important Berlin theatre festival has been running since 1963, and provides a platform for theatre productions from German-speaking regions worldwide.
Karneval der Kulturen *(late May)*. For three days, the streets of Kreuzberg district are brought to life by singing and dancing in this colourful display celebrating multicultural Berlin.

Street recitation of poetry during the Theatertreffen Berlin in May

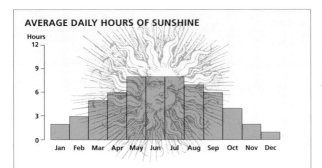

AVERAGE DAILY HOURS OF SUNSHINE

Hours

Sunshine Chart
In Berlin, the highest number of sunny days occurs in May, but June, July and August also enjoy good weather. The cloudiest month is December, followed by January and November.

SUMMER

Summertime in Berlin is marked by many open-air events. There are concerts of classical music and opera performances, as well as open-air concerts and festivals for the young, including the famous Love Parade. It is also possible to take advantage of the good weather by taking a walk or bicycle ride in the Grunewald, or even swimming in the nearby lakes of Wannsee or Müggelsee.

An outdoor artist at work in the Potsdamer Platz

JUNE

Deutsch-Französisches Volksfest *(early Jun–mid-Jul).* This German-French folk festival takes place near Kurt-Schumacher-Damm.
Jazz Across the Border *(throughout Jun).* This jazz festival is organized by the Haus der Kulturen der Welt.
Konzertsommer im Englischen Garten *(mid-Jun–end Jul)* is a schedule of open-air concerts.
Christopher Street Day *(end Jun)* features a gay and lesbian parade with revellers in extravagant outfits, held around Ku'damm. At night,

the party continues in the city's many gay clubs and kniepen.
Berliner Theatermarkt an der Deutschen Oper *(end Jun)* is a programme of open days at the opera.
Open-Air-Classic *(end Jun–early Jul).* Series of operas in Waldbühne with a gala finale in Gendarmenmarkt.

JULY

Bach Tage Berlin *(1st week in Jul)* features concerts of Johann Sebastian Bach's music, performed in concert halls throughout the city. The festival lasts nine days during which around 30 concerts are held.
Heimatklänge *(mid-Jul–end Aug).* A spectacular array of groups give open-air concerts in this world music festival; every Wednesday to Sunday.

AUGUST

Deutsch-Amerikanisches Volksfest *(30 Jul–22 Aug).* A programme of entertainment

Ku'damm full of revellers on Christopher Street Day

with an American theme that always draws the crowds.
Berliner Gauklerfest *(late Jul–early Aug).* Stalls on Unter den Linden selling speciality foods, while crowds are entertained by acrobats and musicians.
Kreuzberger Festliche Tage *(end Aug–early Sep).* This is a large multi-event festival of traditional classical music held in Kreuzberg.

Prokofiev's *The Love of Three Oranges* performed in the Komische Oper

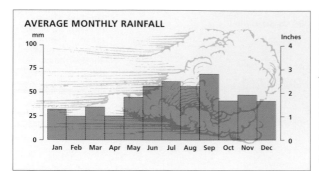

AVERAGE MONTHLY RAINFALL

Jan Feb Mar Apr May Jun Jul Aug Sep Oct Nov Dec

Rainfall Chart
The lowest amount of rainfall occurs in February and again in April, as the temperature begins to rise. The amount of rain in September can dampen the enthusiasm of the unprepared visitor. Unexpectedly heavy cloudbursts can also occur during the summer months.

AUTUMN

Autumn in Berlin is marked by major cultural events. In September the city's hotels fill with visitors arriving for the Berliner Festwochen, to hear concerts given by some of the world's top artists and to make the most of the wide range of culture on offer. Autumn is also a time for major sports events, including the Berlin Marathon, the third biggest in the world after New York and London.

SEPTEMBER

Internationales Stadionfest (ISTAF) *(first week Sep)*. International track and field event in the Olympiastadion.
Internationale Funkausstellung *(early Sep, every two years)*. High-tech media and computer fair at the Internationales Congress Centrum *(see p182)*.

Internationales Literaturfestival *(mid Sep)*. Readings, lectures and special events featuring old and new writing from around the world.
Berliner Festwochen *(throughout Sep)*. A major festival with concerts, theatre, exhibitions and meetings.
Berlin-Marathon *(3rd Sun in Sep)*. This international running event attracts thousands of runners and brings the city's traffic to a halt for several hours.
Art Forum in Berlin *(end Sep)*. Artists and art collectors from all over Europe gather for this five-day modern art fair.
Popkomm *(end Sep)*. This is Europe's biggest pop music fair, which also has a very lively club and dance programme/festival.

Participants in the September Berlin-Marathon

OCTOBER

Tag der Deutschen Einheit *(3 Oct)*. Berlin celebrates the reunification of Germany by staging an annual grand parade through the streets.

NOVEMBER

Jazz Fest Berlin *(early Nov)*. Held annually since 1964, this respected jazz festival kicks off in the Haus der Kulturen der Welt *(see p134)*.
Treffen Junge Musik-Szene *(early Nov)*. Music for the younger generation.
Jüdische Kulturtage *(throughout Nov)*. A festival devoted to Jewish arts and culture with films, plays, concerts and lectures.
Internationales Reitturnier *(3rd week in Nov)*. International horse-jumping.
KinderMusik Theater Wochen *(Nov)*. This is a great feast of theatre and music for the very young, and the young at heart.

Marching through the Brandenburg Gate during Deutschland Fest

AVERAGE MONTHLY TEMPERATURE

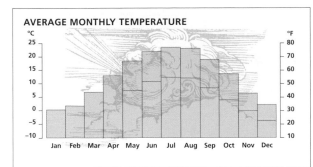

Temperature Chart
Average maximum and minimum temperatures are shown here. The warmest months are June, July and August when the temperature exceeds 20°C. Winters are cold and temperatures can drop below –5°C in January, with the chance of heavy snowfalls or extreme frost.

WINTER

Berlin's winters are usually cold and the temperature can sometimes drop to below zero, with a carpet of snow lining the streets. During December, the city prepares for Christmas with many traditional markets. January brings numerous Carnival balls, while the major event in February is the great cinema gala – the Berlin Film Festival.

Berlinale – the grand festival of world cinema

DECEMBER

Weihnachtsmärkte
(throughout Dec). In the month before Christmas the city is dotted with picturesque fairs and festive stalls selling Christmas gifts and regional culinary specialities.
Christmas (Weihnachten)
(25–26 Dec). As in many other European cities, Berlin's traditional celebrations include Christmas trees, present-giving, family gatherings and communal feasts.
New Year's Eve (Silvester)
(31 Dec) is celebrated in hotels, restaurants, discos, clubs and in private homes; another traditional activity is the popping of champagne corks at the Brandenburg Gate.

JANUARY

Berliner Neujahrslauf
(1 Jan). For those unaffected by the previous night's revelry, this 4-km (2.4-mile) run along the city streets starts off at the Brandenburg Gate.
Sechs-Tage-Rennen *(late Jan).* This meeting in the Velodrome features a six-day bicycle-race and other events.

Berliner Team-Marathon
(22 Jan). Race organized by Sport Klub Charlottenburg.
Lange Nacht der Museen
(end of Jan) A series of events organized by Berlin's museums which stay open until midnight or later.
Internationale Grüne Woche
(last week of Jan). This giant fair is devoted to agriculture and food; it provides an ideal opportunity to sample delicacies from all over the world.

Christmas shopping in the KaDeWe department store

FEBRUARY

Berlinale – Internationale Filmfestspiele *(2nd and 3rd week in Feb).* This gala of cinematography attracts big movie stars and features the best films of the season. It is held in tandem with the **Internationales Forum des Jungen Films** which features low-budget movies during the Filmfestspiele *(see p97).*
Berliner Rosenmontagskonzerte is a series of classical music concerts.

PUBLIC HOLIDAYS

Neujahr New Year (1 Jan)
Karfreitag Good Friday
Ostermontag Easter Mon
Tag der Arbeit Labour Day (1 May)
Christi Himmelfahrt Ascension Day
Pfingsten Whitsun
Tag der Deutschen Einheit (3 Oct)
Weihnachten Christmas (25–26 Dec)

BERLIN AREA
BY AREA

AROUND UNTER DEN LINDEN

The area around the grand avenue Unter den Linden is among the most attractive in Berlin. Its development started during the Baroque period with the establishment of Dorotheen-stadt to the north and Friedrichstadt to the south. From the early 18th century, prestigious buildings began to appear here, and work started on the

Bas-relief from the Schadow-Haus, located on Schadowstrasse

Forum Friedericianum (later Bebelplatz). Over the following two centuries Unter den Linden became one of the city's most imposing avenues. World War II bombing took a heavy toll, but despite only partial reconstruction by the East German government, the area is still home to the highest concentration of historic buildings in Berlin.

SIGHTS AT A GLANCE

Churches
Deutscher Dom **18**
Französischer Dom **16**
Friedrichswerdersche Kirche **14**
St-Hedwigs-Kathedrale **11**

Museums and Galleries
Deutsche Guggenheim **7**
Museum für Kommunikation **22**
Zeughaus (Deutsches Historisches Museum) (pp58–9) **1**

Streets and Squares
Bebelplatz **10**
Gendarmenmarkt **15**
Pariser Platz **24**
Unter den Linden **2**

Theatres
Admiralspalast **31**
Komische Oper **29**
Konzerthaus **17**

Maxim Gorki Theater **32**
Staatsoper Unter den Linden **12**

Historic Buildings and Sites
Alte Bibliothek **9**
Altes Palais **8**
Brandenburger Tor **25**
Holocaust Denkmal **26**
Humboldt Universität **4**
Kronprinzenpalais **13**
Mohrenkolonnaden **20**
Neue Wache **3**
Palais am Festungsgraben **33**
Reiterdenkmal Friedrichs des Grossen **5**
Spittelkolonnaden **21**
Staatsbibliothek **6**

Others
Ehemaliges Regierungsviertel **23**
Friedrichstadtpassagen **19**
Hotel Adlon **27**
Russische Botschaft **28**
S-Bahnhof Friedrichstrasse **30**

KEY
Street-by-Street map *See pp56–7*

🚆 Railway station

Ⓢ S-Bahn station

Ⓤ U-Bahn station

GETTING THERE
This area is served by S-Bahn 1, 3, 5, 7, 9 and 75; U-Bahn 6 and 9; and buses 100 and 348.

0 metres   400
0 yards   400

◁ **Sculpture of the personification of History on the plinth of Schiller's monument, Gendarmenmarkt**

Street-by-Street: Around Bebelplatz

The section of Unter Den Linden between Schlossbrücke
and Friedrichstrasse is one of the most attractive places
in central Berlin. There are some magnificent Baroque
and Neo-Classical buildings, many of them designed by
famous architects. There are also some restored palaces
that are now used as public buildings. Of particular
interest is the beautiful Baroque building of the
Zeughaus (the former Arsenal), which now houses the
German History Museum.

Humboldt Universität
*The entrance to the courtyard
is framed by two guardroom
pavilions and is crowned
with the allegorical
figures of Dawn
and Dusk* ❹

Staatsbibliothek
*This Neo-Baroque
building, designed
by Ernst von Ihne,
was built between
1903 and 1914. It
houses a collection
that dates from the
17th century* ❻

**Equestrian Statue
of Frederick
the Great**
*The impressive
statue dates
from 1851 and
is the work of
Christian Daniel
Rauch* ❺

Deutsche Guggenheim
*The building, which was
rebuilt after World War II,
provides exhibition space for
the fifth branch of the famous
Guggenheim museum* ❼

KEY

– – – Suggested route

Altes Palais
*This Neo-Classical
palace was built between
1834 and 1837 for the
future Kaiser Wilhelm I. It
was reconstructed after
World War II* ❽

Alte Bibliothek
*The west side of Bebelplatz features a
Baroque building with an unusual
concave façade. Locals have nick-
named it the "chest of drawers"* ❾

★ Neue Wache

Since 1993, this monument has served as a memorial to all victims of war and dictatorship **3**

★ Zeughaus (Deutsches Historisches Museum)

A new wing designed by I M Pei has been added to this beautiful Baroque building. The Zeughaus pediment shows the Roman goddess of wisdom **1**

LOCATOR MAP
See Street Finder, maps 6, 7, 15 & 16

| 0 metres | 100 |
| 0 yards | 100 |

Unter den Linden

This magnificent avenue was replanted with four rows of lime trees in 1946 **2**

UNTER DEN LINDEN

Kronprinzenpalais

The rear elevation of the palace pavilion features a magnificent portal from the dismantled Bauakademie building **13**

HINTER DER KATH. KIRCHE

BEBELPLATZ

Staatsoper Unter den Linden

Unter den Linden's opera house is Germany's oldest theatre building not attached to a palace residence **12**

★ Friedrichswerdersche Kirche

In this Neo-Gothic church, designed by Karl Friedrich Schinkel, is a museum devoted to this great architect **14**

St-Hedwigs-Kathedrale

Bas-reliefs (1837) by Theodore Wilhelm Achtermann adorn the cathedral's supports **11**

Bebelplatz

Designed in the 18th century as the Forum Friedericianum, this square was renamed in 1947 in honour of social activist, August Bebel. The Nazis burned books here in 1933 **10**

STAR SIGHTS

* ★ Zeughaus (Deutsches Historisches Museum)

---

* ★ Neue Wache

---

* ★ Friedrichswerdersche Kirche

Zeughaus (Deutsches Historisches Museum) **①**

This former arsenal was built in the Baroque style in 1706 under the guidance of Johann Arnold Nering, Martin Grünberg, Andreas Schlüter and Jean de Bodt. It is a magnificent structure; its wings surrounding an inner courtyard, its exterior decorated with Schlüter's sculptures, including masks of dying warriors in the courtyard. Since 1952 it has housed the German History Museum. The museum recently reopened following a major refurbishment by the Japanese-American architect I M Pei, which included the construction of a glass canopy for the central courtyard and an entire new wing to house temporary exhibitions.

Warrior's mask, courtyard arcade

Soldiers Plundering a House
This painting by Sebastian Vrancx dates from around 1600 and depicts a scene from the religious wars which ravaged the Netherlands during the 16th century.

Prisoner's Jacket
This jacket, which once belonged to a concentration camp prisoner, will be used to illustrate the horrors of the Nazi regime.

GALLERY GUIDE
The ground floor houses exhibits from 1918 to the present day. The first floor contains collections dating from early history to the beginning of the 20th century. A subterranean pathway links the Zeughaus to the Pei Wing which houses temporary exhibitions.

KEY

☐	Early Civilizations and the Middle Ages
☐	1500–1648
☐	1648–1789
☐	1789–1871
☐	1871–1918
☐	1918–1945
☐	1945–1949
☐	1949 to present day
☐	Non-exhibition rooms

Steam Engine
The history of the Industrial Revolution will be illustrated with exhibits such as this 1847 steam-powered engine.

★ Martin Luther
This portrait, painted by Lucas Cranach the Elder in 1529, will be the focal point of an exhibition devoted to the Reformation.

First floor

VISITORS' CHECKLIST

Unter den Linden 2. **Map** 7 A3, 16 E2. **Tel** 20 30 40. Ⓤ & Ⓢ Friedrichstrasse. 🚌 100, 157, 200, 348. ⬜ 10am–6pm daily. **www**.dhm.de

Europa
A group of Meissen porcelain figurines, depicting the continents, possibly designed by Johann Joachim Kändler.

Unter den Linden
Carl Traugott Fechhelm's painting shows Berlin's grandest avenue, Unter den Linden, at the end of the 18th century.

Saddle
This valuable mid-15th-century saddle is decorated with graphic carved plaques made of ivory.

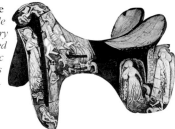

Museum Cinema

Ground floor

★ Gloria Victis
The death of a friend in the final days of the Franco-Prussian War (1870–71) inspired French artist Antonin Mercié to create this moving allegory.

STAR EXHIBITS

★ Martin Luther

★ Gloria Victis

Unter den Linden as depicted in Franz Krüger's *Opernplatz Parade* (1824–30)

Unter den Linden ❷

Map 6 E3, 6 F3, 15 A3, 16 D3.
Ⓢ *Unter den Linden.* 🚌 *100, 200, 348.*

One of the most famous streets in Berlin, Unter den Linden starts at Schlossplatz and runs down to Pariser Platz and the Brandenburg Gate. It was once the route to the royal hunting grounds that were later transformed into the Tiergarten. In the 17th century the street was planted with lime trees, to which it owes its name. Although removed around 1658, they were replanted in four rows in 1820.

During the 18th century, Unter den Linden became the main street of the westward-growing city. It was gradually filled with prestigious buildings that were restored after World War II. Following the reunification of Germany, Unter den Linden has acquired several cafés and restaurants, as well as many smart new shops. This street is also the venue for many interesting outdoor events; it is usually crowded with tourists and students browsing the bookstalls around the Humboldt Universität and the Staatsbibliothek.

Neue Wache ❸

Unter den Linden 4. **Map** 7 A3, 16 E2. Ⓢ *Hackescher Markt.* 🚌 *100, 200, 348.* 🕐 *10am–6pm daily.*

This war memorial, designed by Karl Friedrich Schinkel and built between 1816 and 1818, is considered to be one of the finest examples of Neo-Classical architecture in Berlin. The front of the monument is dominated by a huge Doric portico with a frieze made up of bas-reliefs depicting goddesses of victory. The triangular tympanum above the pediment shows allegorical representations of Battle, Victory, Flight and Defeat.

The building was originally used as a royal guardhouse, but during 1930 and 1931 it was turned it into a monument to the soldiers killed in World War I. In 1960, following its restoration, Neue Wache became the Memorial to the Victims of Fascism and Militarism. Then, in 1993 it was rededicated once again, this time to the memory of all victims of war and dictatorship.

Inside the building is an eternal flame and a granite slab over the ashes of an unknown soldier, a resistance fighter and a concentration camp prisoner. Under the circular opening in the roof is a copy of the 20th century sculpture *Mother with her Dead Son*, by Berlin artist Käthe Kollwitz, who lost her own son in World War I.

Humboldt Universität ❹

HUMBOLDT UNIVERSITY

Unter den Linden 6. **Map** 7 A3, **Tel** 20930. 16 D2. Ⓢ & Ⓤ *Friedrichstrasse.* 🚌 *100, 200, 348.*

The university building was constructed in 1753, for Prince Heinrich of Prussia, the brother of Frederick the Great. The university was founded in 1810 on the initiative of Wilhelm von Humboldt. It became the Berlin University but was renamed in von Humboldt's honour in 1949.

The overall design of the palace, with its main block and the courtyard enclosed within a pair of wings, has been extended many times. Two marble statues (1883) by Paul Otto stand at the entrance gate and represent Wilhelm von Humboldt (holding a book) and his brother Alexander (sitting on a globe), who was a famous explorer. The entrance gate leads to the courtyard, which was designed by Reinhold Begas.

Many famous scholars have worked at the University, including philosophers Fichte and Hegel, physicians Rudolf Virchow and Robert Koch and physicists Max Planck and Albert Einstein. Among its graduates are Heinrich Heine, Karl Marx and Friedrich Engels.

After World War II, the University was in the Russian sector of the divided city and the difficulties encountered by the students of the western zone led to the establishment of a new university in 1948 – the Freie Universität *(see p179)*.

Humboldt University courtyard with statue of Hermann Helmholtz

Reiterdenkmal Friedrichs des Grossen ❺

EQUESTRIAN STATUE OF FREDERICK THE GREAT

Unter den Linden. **Map** 7 A3. Ⓢ & Ⓤ *Friedrichstrasse.* 🚌 *100, 200, 348.*

This is one of the most famous monuments in Berlin, featuring a massive bronze statue 5.6 m (18.5 ft) in height and standing on the centre lane of Unter den Linden. It was designed by Christian Daniel Rauch and created between 1839 and 1851. It depicts Frederick the Great on horseback, wearing a uniform and a royal cloak. The base of the high plinth is surrounded

by statues of famous military leaders, politicians, scientists and artists. The top tier of the plinth is decorated with bas-reliefs depicting scenes from the life of Frederick the Great. Out of line with GDR ideology, the monument was removed to Potsdam, where until 1980 it stood by the Hippodrome in Park Sanssouci.

Staatsbibliothek ❻

STATE LIBRARY

Unter den Linden 8. **Map** 7 A3, 16 D2. **Tel** *266 23 03.* Ⓢ & Ⓤ *Friedrichstrasse.* 🚌 *100, 200, 348.* 🕐 *9am–6pm Mon–Fri , 9am–1pm Sat.*

The nucleus of the State Library collection was the library belonging to the Great Elector – Friedrich Wilhelm – founded in 1661 and situated in the Stadtschloss. At the end of the 18th century it was moved to the Alte Bibliothek building. Its current home was designed by Ernst von Ihne and constructed between 1903 and 1914 on the site of the Academy of Science and the Academy of Fine Arts. This impressive building was

severely damaged during World War II and underwent extensive restoration. The collection, numbering 3 million books and periodicals, was scattered during the war, including a collection of priceless music manuscripts, which ended up in the Jagiellonian Library in Cracow, Poland.

After the war only part of the collection was returned to the building in Unter den Linden, and the rest was held in West Berlin. Since reunification, both collections are once again under the same administration.

Deutsche Guggenheim ❼

Unter den Linden 13–15. **Map** 7 A3, 16 D3. **Tel** *202 09 30.* 🕐 *11am–8pm daily (to 10pm Thu).* Ⓢ & Ⓤ *Friedrichstrasse.* 🚌 *100, 200, 348.* 📷

The Deutsche Guggenheim building is home to the German branch of the New York-based Guggenheim Foundation. The museum does not have its own permanent collection, but is regularly used to display a variety of temporary exhibitions.

The ivy-clad Staatsbibliothek building on Unter den Linden

A window with a heraldic shield on the Altes Palais

Altes Palais ❽

THE OLD PALACE

Unter den Linden 9. **Map** 7 A3,
16 D3. Ⓢ & Ⓤ *Friedrichstrasse.*
🚌 *100, 200, 348.* ⬤ *to the public.*

This Neo-Classical palace,
near the former Opernplatz
(Bebelplatz), was built for the
heir to the throne – Prince
Wilhelm (later Kaiser Wilhelm
I). The Kaiser lived here all his
life. He was able to watch the
changing of the guards every
day from the ground-floor
window on the far left.

The palace, built from 1834
to 1837, was designed by Carl
Ferdinand Langhans but its
splendid furnishings were
destroyed during World War II.
The palace was subsequently
restored, and is now used by
Humboldt Universität.

Alte Bibliothek ❾

THE OLD LIBRARY

Bebelplatz. **Map** 7 A3, 16 D3.
Tel 20 930. Ⓢ & Ⓤ *Friedrichstrasse.*
🚌 *100, 200, 348.*

The Old Library, known by
locals as the *Kommode* or
"chest of drawers" after its
curved façade, is actually one
of the city's most beautiful
Baroque buildings. It was
designed by Georg Christian
Unger and built around 1775
to house the royal library
collection. In fact, Unger based
his design on an unrealized
plan for an extension to the
Hofburg complex in Vienna
by Josef Emanuel Fischer von
Erlach some 50 years earlier.
The concave façade of the
building is accentuated by the
insertion of three breaks,
surrounded at the top by a

row of massive Corinthian
pilasters. The building now
houses the law faculty of
Humboldt University.

Bebelplatz ❿

Map 7 A3, 16 D3. Ⓢ & Ⓤ *Friedrichstrasse.* 🚌 *100, 200, 348.*

Once named Opernplatz
(Opera Square), Bebelplatz was
to be the focal point of the
intended Forum Friederic-
ianum, an area designed by
Georg Wenzeslaus von
Knobelsdorff to mirror the
grandeur of ancient Rome.
Although the initial plans were
only partly implemented, many
important buildings rose
around the square with the
passage of time.

On 10 May 1933 Opernplatz
was the scene of the infamous
book burning act organized by
the Nazi propaganda machine.
Some 25,000 books written by
authors considered to be
enemies of the Third Reich

were burned. These included
works by Thomas and Hein-
rich Mann, Robert Musil and
Lion Feuchtwanger.

Today, a monument at the
centre of the square, designed
by Micha Ullman in 1995,
commemorates this dramatic
event. A translucent panel
inserted into the road surface
provides a glimpse of a room
filled with empty bookshelves.
Next to it is a plaque bearing
the tragically prophetic words
of the poet Heinrich Heine,
written in 1820: "Where books
are burned, in the end people
will burn."

St-Hedwigs-Kathedrale ⓫

ST HEDWIG'S CATHEDRAL

Bebelplatz. **Map** 7 A4, 16 D3, E3.
Tel 203 48 10. Ⓢ & Ⓤ *Hausvogtei-
platz.* 🚌 *100, 200, 348.* ⬤ *10am–5pm
Mon–Sat (to 4:30pm Sat), 1–5pm Sun.*

This huge church, set back
from the road and crowned
with a dome, is the Catholic
Cathedral of the Roman Arch-
diocese of Berlin. It was built
to serve the Catholics of Silesia
(part of present-day Poland),
which became part of the
Kingdom of Prussia in 1742
following defeat in the
Silesian Wars of 1740–63.

The initial design, by Georg
Wenzeslaus von Knobelsdorff,
was similar to the Roman Pantheon. Construction began in
1747 and the cathedral was
consecrated in 1773, although

The façade of St-Hedwigs-Kathedrale featuring beautiful bas-relief sculptures

work continued on and off until 1778. Its design was modified repeatedly. Later, additional work was carried out from 1886 to 1887. The cathedral was damaged during World War II, and rebuilt between 1952 and 1963.

The crypt holds the tombs of many bishops of Berlin, a 16th-century Madonna and a Pietà dating from 1420. It is also the resting place of Bernhard Lichtenberg, a priest killed in a concentration camp and beatified as a martyr by Pope John Paul II.

Bas-relief of Apollo and Mars on the façade of the Staatsoper

Staatsoper Unter den Linden ⑫

STATE OPERA HOUSE

Unter den Linden 7. **Map** 7 A3, 16 D3. *Tel* 20 35 45 55. Ⓢ & Ⓤ *Friedrichstrasse.* 🚌 100, 200, 348.

The early Neo-Classical façade of the State Opera House is one of the most beautiful sights along Unter den Linden. It was built by Georg Wenzeslaus von Knobelsdorff in 1741–3 as the first building of the intended Forum Fridericianum. Following a fire, the opera house was restored from 1843 to 1844 under the direction of Carl Ferdinand Langhans, who altered only its interior.

Following wartime destruction, the opera house was rebuilt from 1952 to 1955, almost from the ground up. It has played host to famous singers, musicians and artists; one of its directors and conductors was Richard Strauss, and its stage designers included Karl Friedrich Schinkel.

The imposing façade of the Kronprinzenpalais

Kronprinzenpalais ⑬

CROWN PRINCE'S PALACE

Unter den Linden 3. **Map** 7 A3, B3, 16 E3. Ⓢ & Ⓤ *Friedrichstrasse.* 🚌 100, 200, 348. ⏰ 10am–6pm Thu–Sat, Mon, Tue (to 10pm Thu).

This striking late-Neo-Classical palace takes its name from its original inhabitants – the heirs to the royal, and later to the imperial, throne. Its form is the outcome of numerous changes made to what was originally a modest house dating from 1663–9. The first extensions, designed in the late-Baroque style, were conducted by Philipp Gerlach in 1732 and 1733. Between 1856 and 1857 Johann Heinrich Strack added the second floor. These extensions were rebuilt following World War II.

The palace served the royal family until the abolition of the monarchy. From 1919 to 1937, it was used by the Nationalgalerie. Under Communist rule it was renamed Palais Unter den Linden and reserved for official government guests. It was here, on 31 August 1990, that the pact was signed paving the way for reunification.

Next to the palace, with the prestigious address of Unter den Linden 1, is where the Kommandantur, the official quarters of the city's garrison commander, once stood. Totally destroyed in the last days of World War II, the original façade was rebuilt in 2003 by the German media company Bertelsmann, as part of their Berlin headquarters.

Joined to the main palace by an overhanging passageway is the smaller Prinzessinnenpalais (Princesses' Palace), built for the daughters of Friedrich Wilhelm III.

Friedrichswerdersche Kirche (Schinkel-Museum) ⑭

Werderscher Markt. **Map** 7 B4, 16 E3. *Tel* 20 90 55 77. Ⓢ & Ⓤ *Friedrichstrasse.* 🚌 100, 147, 200, 348. ⏰ 10am–6pm daily. 📷 ♿

This picturesque church, designed by Karl Friedrich Schinkel and constructed between 1824 and 1830, was the first Neo-Gothic church to be built in Berlin. The small single-nave structure, with its twin-tower façade, resembles an English college chapel. Schinkel's original interior of the church was largely destroyed in World War II.

Following its reconstruction, the church was converted to a museum. It is currently used by the Nationalgalerie to house its permanent exhibition of sculptures from the late 16th to the mid 19th century. Highlights include a model of the famous group sculpture by Johann Gottfried Schadow, depicting the princesses Friederike and Luise (later Queen of Prussia).

Princesses Luise and Friederike in the Schinkel-Museum

Gendarmenmarkt ⓯

This is one of Berlin's most beautiful squares, created at the end of 17th century as a market square for the newly established Friedrichstadt. It is named after the Regiment Gens d'Armes who had their stables here. In 1950 it was renamed Platz der Akademie; after reunification the square reverted to its original name.

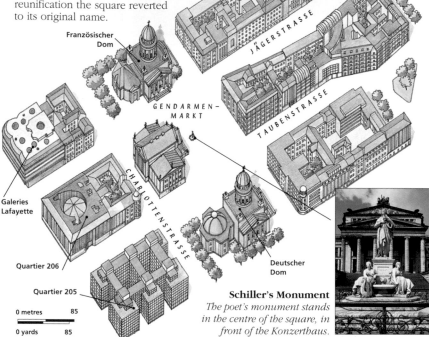

Französischer Dom

JÄGERSTRASSE

GENDARMEN- MARKT

TAUBENSTRASSE

CHARLOTTENSTRASSE

Galeries Lafayette

Quartier 206

Quartier 205

0 metres   85

0 yards   85

Deutscher Dom

Schiller's Monument
The poet's monument stands in the centre of the square, in front of the Konzerthaus.

Französischer Dom ⓰

FRENCH CATHEDRAL

Gendarmenmarkt 6. **Map** 7 A4, 16 D4. **Tel** 204 15 07. Ⓤ *Stadtmitte or Französische Strasse.* **Museum Tel** 22 91 760. ◯ *11am–5pm Tue–Sun.* 🖼 **Viewing Platform Tel** 20 62 872. ● *for renovation.* 🖼 **Church** ◯ *noon–5pm Tue–Sun (from 11am Sun).* 🛉 *Sun 10am.*

Although the two churches on the opposite sides of Schauspielhaus seem identical, they differ from each other quite considerably. Their only common feature is the front towers. The French cathedral was built for the Huguenot community, who found refuge in protestant Berlin following their expulsion from France after the revocation of the Edict of Nantes. The modest

Side elevation of the Französischer Dom, built for Huguenot refugees

church, built between 1701 and 1705 by Louis Cayart and Abraham Quesnay, was modelled on the Huguenot church in Charenton, France, which was destroyed in 1688. The main entrance, on the west elevation (facing

Charlottenstrasse), leads to an uncomplicated interior with a rectangular nave and semi-circular sections on both sides. It features a late-Baroque organ from 1754.

The structure is dominated by a massive, cylindrical tower which is encircled by Corinthian porticoes at its base. The tower and porticoes were designed by Carl von Gontard and added around 1785, some 80 years after the church was built. It houses the Huguenot Museum, which details the history of the Huguenots in France and Brandenburg. Well-educated and highly skilled, they played a crucial part in Berlin's rise as a city of science, craft and commerce. The French language they brought with them survives to this day in many words used in the Berlin dialect.

The interior of the Konzerthaus, formerly the Schauspielhaus

Konzerthaus 🕖

CONCERT HALL

Gendarmenmarkt 2. **Map** 7 A4, 16 D4. **Tel** 20 30 921 01. **U** *Stadtmitte.*

A late Neo-Classical jewel, this magnificent theatre building, known until recently as the Schauspielhaus, is one of the greatest achievements of Berlin's best-known architect, Karl Friedrich Schinkel. It was built between 1818 and 1821 around the ruins of Langhan's National Theatre, destroyed by fire in 1817. The portico columns were retained in the new design. Schinkel was responsible not only for the architectural structure but also for the interior design, right down to the door handles. Following bomb damage in World War II, it was reconstructed as a concert hall with a different interior layout. The exterior was restored to its former glory. The Konzerthaus is now home to the Berlin Symphony Orchestra.

The theatre façade includes a huge Ionic portico with a set of stairs that was only used by the middle classes (the upper classes entered via a separate entrance where they could leave their horse-drawn carriages). The whole building is richly decorated with sculptures

alluding to drama and music. These include statues of musical geniuses mounted on lions and panthers, as well as figures representing the Muses and a Bacchanal procession. The façade is crowned with the sculpture of Apollo riding a chariot pulled by griffins.

In front of the theatre stands a shining, white marble statue of Friedrich Schiller. It was sculpted by Reinhold Begas, and erected in 1869. Removed by the Nazis during the 1930s, the monument was finally returned to its rightful place in 1988. Schiller's head was copied by the sculptor from a bust of the poet created in 1794 by Johann Heinrich Dannecker. The statue is mounted on a high pedestal surrounded by allegorical figures representing Lyric Poetry, Drama, Philosophy and History.

Deutscher Dom 🕖

GERMAN CATHEDRAL

Gendarmenmarkt 1. **Map** 7 A4, 16 D4. **U** *Stadtmitte or Französische Strasse.* **Tel** 22 73 04 31. **Exhibition** ◻ Sep–May: 10am–6pm Wed–Sun (to 10pm Tue); Jun–Aug: 10am–7pm Wed–Sun.

The Cathedral at the southern end of the square, to the left of Konzerthaus, is an old German Protestant-Reformed church. It was designed by Martin Grünberg and built in 1708 by Giovanni Simonetti. The design was based on a five-petal shape, and in 1785 it acquired a dome-covered tower identical to that of the French cathedral. Burned down in 1945, the church was finally rebuilt in 1993. Its exterior was painstakingly reconstructed, including its sculpted decorations. The interior is now modern and has been adapted as an exhibition space. On display is *"Wege, Irrwege, Umwege"* ("Paths, Confusions, Detours"), an exhibition about Germany's parliamentary democracy.

Sculpture from the Deutscher Dom

Friedrichstadt-passagen 🕖

FRIEDRICHSTADT PASSAGES

Friedrichstrasse Quartiere 205, 206, 207. **Map** 6 F4, 15 C4. **U** *Französische Strasse or Stadtmitte.*

This group of passages is part of a huge development of luxury shops, offices, restaurants and apartments built in recent years along Friedrichstrasse.

Quartier 207 is the famous Galeries Lafayette, a branch of the French department store occupying a charming building designed by Jean Nouvel and constructed almost entirely of glass. The building's axis is formed by an inner courtyard, which is defined by two glass cones with their bases facing each other. The highly reflective glass panes, together with the multicoloured stands that are clustered around the structure, make an extraordinary impression on the visitor.

The next passage, Quartier 206, has offices and smart luxury boutiques, and is the work of the American design team Pei, Cobb, Freed & Partners. The building owes its alluring, but somewhat nouveau-riche appearance to the use of forms inspired by Art Deco architecture, including sophisticated details and expensive stone cladding.

The southernmost building in the complex, and the largest passage, is Quartier 205, which is the work of Oswald Mathias Ungers.

The exterior and main entrance of Quartier 206

Mohren-kolonnaden ⑳

Mohrenstrasse 37b and 40/41.
Map 6 F5, 15 B5. **U** *Mohrenstrasse*.

Designed by Carl Gotthard Langhans, these Neo-Classical arcades resting on twin columns were constructed in 1787. They originally surrounded a bridge that spanned the moat around the city of Berlin. The bridge has since been demolished, and the arcades have been incorporated into buildings of a much later architectural style located on Mohrenstrasse.

One of the original arcades known as the Mohrenkolonnaden

Spittelkolonnaden ㉑

Leipziger Strasse. **Map** 7 B5, 16 E5.
U *Spittelmarkt*.

In the vicinity of Spittelmarkt is a picturesque Baroque-Neo-Classical colonnade squeezed between several 20-storey tower blocks. These tower blocks were erected to obscure the view of the Axel Springer Publishers' building, which stood on the opposite side of the Berlin Wall.

A pair of such semicircular colonnades, designed by Carl von Gontard and built in 1776, originally surrounded Spittelmarkt. The southern one was demolished in 1929, and the northern one was destroyed during World War II.

A copy of one of the original Spittelkolonnaden in Leipziger Strasse

In 1979, a copy of one of the colonnades was erected in Leipziger Strasse, using elements from the original.

Museum für Kommunikation ㉒

MUSEUM OF TELECOMMUNICATIONS

Leipziger Strasse 16. **Map** 6 F5, 15 C5. **U** *Stadtmitte* 🚌 *148.*
Tel *20 29 40.* ⭘ *9am–5pm Tue–Fri, 11am–7pm Sat–Sun.* ⬤ *Mon.*

Founded in 1872 as the Post Office museum, this is the world's oldest establishment of its kind. A dozen or so years after it was founded, it moved into the corner of the huge building constructed for the main post office. The office wings, with their modest Neo-Renaissance elevations, contrast with the museum premises, which has a grand Neo-Baroque façade that is richly decorated with sculptures. The museum's rooms house exhibits that illustrate the history of postal and telecommunication services, including contemporary digital communications.

Ehemaliges Regierungsviertel ㉓

Wilhelmstrasse, Leipziger Strasse, Voss Strasse. **Map** 6 E5. **U** *Potsdamer Platz, Mohrenstrasse.*

Wilhelmstrasse, and the area situated to the west of it up to Leipziger Platz, was the former German government district, where the main departments had offices from the mid-19th century until 1945. The building at Voss Strasse No. 77 was once the Reich's Chancellery and Otto von Bismarck's office. From 1933, it served as the office of Adolf Hitler, for whom the building was specially extended by Albert Speer.

In the spring of 1945 the square was the scene of fierce fighting, and after World War II most of the buildings had to be demolished. Among those that survived are the former Prussian Landtag offices – the huge complex occupying the site between Leipziger and Niederkirchner Strasse. This building in the Italian Renaissance-style was designed by Friedrich Schulz, and constructed from 1892 to 1904. It consists of two segments: the one on the side of Leipziger Strasse (No. 3–4) once housed the upper chamber of the National Assembly (the Herrenhaus) and is now used by the Bundesrat. The building on the side of Niederkirchner Strasse (No. 5) was once the seat of the Landtag's lower chamber, and is now the Berliner Abgeordnetenhaus (House of Representatives).

The second surviving complex is the former Ministry of Aviation (Reichsluftfahrtministerium), at Leipziger Strasse No. 5, built for Hermann Göring in 1936 by Ernst Sagebiel. This awesome building is typical of architecture of the Third Reich.

Pariser Platz ㉔

Map 6 E3, 15 A3.
Ⓢ Unter den Linden. 🚌 100, 200.

This square, at the end of Unter den Linden, was created in 1734. Originally called Quarrée, it was renamed Pariser Platz after 1814, when the *Quadriga* sculpture from the Brandenburg Gate was returned to Berlin from Paris.

The square, enclosed on the west by the Brandenburg Gate, was densely built up until World War II. Most buildings, including the house of painter Max Liebermann, were destroyed in 1945.

Following reunification, the square was redeveloped. Twin houses designed by Josef Paul Kleihues now flank the Brandenburg Gate. On the north side of the square are the Dresdner Bank building and the French Embassy. On the south side are the US Embassy, the DG Bank head office and the Akademie der Künste (Academy of Fine Arts). To the east is the Adlon Hotel.

Brandenburger Tor ㉕

BRANDENBURG GATE

Pariser Platz. **Map** 6 E3, 15 A3.
Ⓢ Unter den Linden. 🚌 100, 200.

The Brandenburg Gate is the quintessential symbol of Berlin. This magnificent Neo-Classical structure, completed in 1795, was designed by Carl Gotthard Langhans and modelled on the entrance to the Acropolis in Athens. A pair of pavilions,

MAX LIEBERMANN (1849–1935)

One of the greatest German painters, Max Liebermann was also one of the most interesting and controversial figures of Berlin's élite circles at the start of the 20th century. A sensitive observer as well as an outstanding portraitist, Liebermann was famously stubborn – he could stand up even to the Kaiser himself. From 1920 he was president of the Akademie der Künste (Academy of Fine Arts), but in view of his Jewish origin he was removed from office in 1933. He died just two years later, alone, and his wife committed suicide to escape being sent to a concentration camp.

A frieze from the Brandenburg Gate

once used by guards and customs officers, frames its powerful Doric colonnade. The bas-reliefs depict scenes from Greek mythology, and the whole structure is crowned by the sculpture *Quadriga*, designed by Johann Gottfried Schadow. The *Quadriga* was originally regarded as a symbol of peace. In 1806, during the French occupation, it was dismantled on Napoleon's orders and taken to Paris. On its return in 1814, it was declared a symbol of victory, and the goddess received the staff bearing the Prussian eagle and the iron cross adorned with a laurel wreath.

The Brandenburg Gate has borne witness to many of

Berlin's important events, from military parades to celebrations marking the birth of the Third Reich and Hitler's ascent to power. It was here, too, that the Russian flag was raised in May 1945, and on 17 June 1953 that 25 workers demonstrating for better conditions were killed.

The gate, located in East Berlin, was restored between 1956 and 1958, when the damaged *Quadriga* was rebuilt in West Berlin. Until 1989 it stood watch over the divided city. Between 2000 and 2002 the Brandenburg Gate was meticulously restored.

Holocaust Denkmal ㉖

HOLOCAUST MEMORIAL

Ebertstrasse. **Map** 6 E3, 15 A3.
Tel 28 04 59 60. Ⓢ Unter den Linden.
🚌 100, 200. ⬜ 10am–8pm daily.

In 2003 the construction of a memorial for the Jews killed by the Nazis between 1933 and 1945 began. Designed by US architect Peter Eisenmann, it covers an area of 19,000 sq m (205,000 sq ft) next to the Brandenburg Gate. Above ground, an undulating field of concrete slabs is visible through which visitors can walk; beneath lies an information centre on the genocide.

Oskar Kokoschka's *Pariser Platz in Berlin* (1925–6), Nationalgalerie

The luxurious interior of the Adlon Hotel

Hotel Adlon ②

Unter den Linden 77. **Map** 6 E3,
6 E4, 15 A3, 15 B3. **Tel** 226 10.
⑤ Unter den Linden. 🚌 100, 200.

Considered to be the most
important society venue in
Berlin, the original Hotel Adlon
opened its doors to the public
in 1907. Its luxurious suites
were once used by the world's
celebrities, including Greta
Garbo, Enrico Caruso and
Charlie Chaplin. The hotel
suffered bomb damage in
World War II, and was demolished in 1945. A new building bearing the same name
was opened in a blaze of
publicity on 23 August 1997.

Today, it is once again the
best address in town. Comfort,
discretion and lavish interiors
featuring exotic timber, marble
and heavy silk, still tempt
visitors despite high prices.
Those who cannot afford to
stop for a night should at
least drop in for a cup of
coffee in the main hall. In this
hall stands the only authentic
remnant of the former Adlon
Hotel, an elegant black
marble fountain decorated
with elephants, which once
stood in the orangery.

Russische Botschaft ②

RUSSIAN EMBASSY

Unter den Linden 63/65. **Map** 6 F3, 15
B3. ⑤ Unter den Linden. 🚌 100, 200.

The monumental, white
Russian Embassy building is
an example of the Stalinist
"wedding cake" style, or

Zuckerbäckerstil. Built between 1948 and 1953, it was
the first postwar building
erected on Unter den Linden.
It is built on the site of a
former palace that had
housed the Russian
(originally Tsarist)
embassy from 1837.

The building is the
work of the Russian
architect Anatoli
Strizhevsky. This
structure, with its
strictly symmetrical
layout, resembles the
old Berlin palaces of
the Neo-Classical period.
The sculptures that
adorn it, however,
belong to an altogether
different era: the gods
of ancient Greece
and Rome have been
replaced by working-
class heroes.

Statue of a worker
on the Russian
Embassy building

Komische Oper ②

COMIC OPERA

Behrenstr. 55/57. **Map** 6 F4, 15 C3.
Tel 47 99 74 00. 🅄 Französische-
strasse. ⑤ Unter den Linden.
🚌 100, 147, 200, 348.

Looking at the modern
façade of this theatre it is
hard to believe that it hides
one of Berlin's most im-
pressive interiors. Originally
called the Theater Unter den
Linden, the theatre was built
in 1892 by the internationally
famous Viennese architectural
practice of Ferdinand Fellner
and Hermann Helmer. It has
served as a variety theatre
and as the German National
Theatre in the past, and has
only housed the Komische
Oper since World War II.
The postwar reconstruction
deprived the building of its
former façades but the
beautiful Viennese
Neo-Baroque interior
remained, full of
stuccoes and gilded
ornaments. Parti-
cularly interesting are
the expressive and
dynamically posed
statues on the pilasters
of the top balcony – the
work of Theodor Friedel.
The Komische Oper is
one of Berlin's three
leading opera comp-
anies. Its repertoire
consists mainly of
light opera.

Crowded balconies and the plush interior of the Komische Oper

S-Bahnhof Friedrichstrasse

Map 6 F2, 6 F3 & 15 C2.

One of the city's most famous urban railway stations, Bahnhof Friedrichstrasse used to be the border station between East and West Berlin. It was built in 1882 to a design by Johannes Vollmer. In 1925 a roof was added, covering the hall and the platforms.

The original labyrinth of passages, staircases and checkpoints no longer exists but it is possible to see a model of the station at the Stasi-Museum *(see p174)*. Now used as a theatre, the only remaining structure from the original station is the special pavilion once used as a waiting room by those waiting for emigration clearance. It earned the nickname Tränenpalast, the "Palace of Tears", as it is here that Berliners from different sides of the city would say goodbye to each other after a visit.

Admiralspalast ③

Friedrichstr. 101–102. **Map** 6 F2, 15 C1. **U** & **S** *Friedrichstrasse.*

The Admiralspalast was built in 1911 to house an indoor swimming pool and a bath above a natural hot spring. Designed by Heinrich Schweitzer, the main façade is punctuated by Doric half-columns and inlaid with bas-relief slabs made of Istrian marble. Quite different in style, the façade on Planck-strasse is also interesting. It was designed by Ernst Westphal and includes various exotic overlapping motifs.

The area around Friedrich-strasse was once well known for its excellent theatres, and in 1922 part of the Admirals-palast was converted to house the Metropol-Theater. It had specialized in light musical fare and closed in 1997. A new investor will give the whole building a facelift, restore the historic façade and reopen it as a complex reminiscent of the Roaring Twenties, with bars, a theatre and a restaurant.

A window of the Admiralspalast decorated with marble slabs

Part of the building is used by one of the best political cabarets in Berlin, Die Diestel, which hails from East Berlin.

Maxim Gorki Theater ③

Am Festungsgraben 2. **Map** 7 A3, 16 E2. **Tel** 20 22 11 15. **U** & **S** *Friedrichstrasse.* 🚌 100, 200, 348.

The Maxim Gorki theatre was once a singing school or *Sing-Akademie*. Berlin's oldest concert hall, it was built in 1827 by Karl Theodor Ottmer, who based his design on drawings by Karl Friedrich Schinkel. This modest Neo-Classical building, with its attractive façade resembling a Greco-Roman temple, was well known for the excellent acoustic qualities of its concert hall.

Many famous composer-musicians performed here, including violinist Niccolò Paganini and pianist Franz Liszt. In 1829, Felix Mendelssohn-Bartholdy conducted a performance of the *St Matthew*

Maxim Gorki Theater occupying the oldest concert hall in Berlin

Passion by Johann Sebastian Bach, the first since the composer's death in 1750. Following reconstruction after World War II, the building is now used as a theatre.

Palais am Festungs-graben (Museum Mitte) ③

FESTUNGSGRABEN PALACE (MITTE MUSEUM)

Am Festungsgraben 1. **Map** 7 A3, 16 E2. **Tel** 20 84 000. **S** *Friedrich-strasse.* 🚌 100, 200, 348. 🚃 6, 8. ⏰ 1–5pm Mon–Fri, 1–5pm Sat, 11am–5pm Sun.

The Palace in Festungsgraben is one of the few structures in this part of town that has maintained its original interior decor. Built as a small Baroque palace in 1753, it owes its present form to major extension work, carried out in 1864 in the style of Karl Friedrich Schinkel, by Heinrich Bürde and Hermann von der Hude.

The late Neo-Classical style of the building is reminiscent of Schinkel's later designs. The interior includes a magnificent double-height marble hall in the Neo-Renaissance style and modelled on the White Room in the former Stadtschloss *(see p71)*. In 1934 one of the ground-floor rooms was turned into a music salon, and many musical instruments were brought here from the 19th-century house (now demolished) of wealthy merchant and manufacturer Johann Weydinger (1773–1837).

MUSEUM ISLAND

The long island that nestles in the tributaries of the Spree river is the cradle of Berlin's history. It was here that the first settlements appeared at the beginning of the 13th century – Cölln is mentioned in documents dating back to 1237 and its twin settlement, Berlin, is mentioned a few years later (1244). Not a trace of Gothic and Renaissance Cölln is left now: the island's character was transformed by the construction of the Brandenburg

Bas-relief from the façade of the Berliner Dom

Electors' palace, which served as their residence from 1470. Over the following centuries, the palace was converted first into a royal and later into an imperial palace – the huge Stadtschloss. Although it was razed to the ground in 1950, some interesting buildings on the island's north side have survived, including the huge Berliner Dom (cathedral) and the impressive collection of museums that give the island its name – Museumsinsel.

SIGHTS AT A GLANCE

Museums and Galleries
Alte Nationalgalerie **7**
Altes Museum p75 **6**
Bodemuseum **10**
Galgenhaus **19**
Historischer Hafen Berlin **13**
Märkisches Museum **14**
Neues Museum **8**
Pergamonmuseum pp80–83 **9**

Streets, Squares and Parks
Lustgarten **5**
Märkisches Ufer **15**
Schlossplatz **1**

Historic Buildings
Berliner Dom pp76–7 **4**
Ermeler-Haus **16**
Gertraudenbrücke **17**
Marstall **11**
Nicolai-Haus **18**
Ribbeckhaus **12**
Schlossbrücke **3**

Other Buildings
Palast der Republik **2**

KEY

▢	Street-by-Street map *See pp72–3*
U	U-Bahn Station
S	S-Bahn Station
▣	Bus terminus

GETTING THERE

The easiest way to get to Museum Island and Schlossplatz is to walk from Hackescher Markt S-Bahn station, or to take a bus, either the 100, 157 or the 348. The Breite Strasse district is served by buses 147 and 257, while the south end of the island can be reached by U-Bahn line 2, going to Spittelmarkt, and by buses 142 and 147 to Märkisches Ufer.

0 metres   400
0 yards   400

◁ The elegant Bodemuseum, with the Fernsehturm (Television Tower) in the background

Street-by-Street: Museum Island

On this island are the pretty Lustgarten and the
Berliner Dom (Berlin Cathedral). It is also where you
will find some of the most important museums in
the east of the city. These include the Bodemuseum,
the Altes Museum, the Alte Nationalgalerie and the
splendid Pergamonmuseum, famous for its collection
of antiquities and visited by crowds of art-lovers
from around the world.

Bodemuseum
*The dome-covered rounded
corner of the building provides
a prominent landmark at the
tip of the island* ❿

Railway bridge,
also used by the
S-Bahn.

★ Pergamonmuseum
*The museum is famous
for its reconstruction of
fragments of ancient
towns, as well as the
original friezes from
the Pergamon altar* ❾

AM KUPFER-GRABEN

Alte Nationalgalerie
*The equestrian statue of King
Friedrich Wilhelm IV in front of
the building is the work of
Alexander Calandrelli* ❼

BODESTRASSE

Schlossbrücke
*Under the GDR regime this
unusual bridge was called
Marx-Engels-Brücke* ❸

| 0 metres | 100 |
| 0 yards | 100 |

Neues Museum
*The building, which
once housed a col-
lection of Egyptian
antiquities, is currently
in the final stages of
reconstruction* ❽

STAR SIGHTS

★ Pergamonmuseum

★ Altes Museum

★ Berliner Dom

KEY

━ ━ ━ Suggested route

★ Altes Museum
The corners of the central building feature figures of Castor and Pollux, heroes of Greek myth also known as the Dioscuri **6**

LOCATOR MAP
See Street Finder, maps 7 &16

Lustgarten
The 70-ton granite bowl was the biggest in the world when it was placed in the garden in 1828 **5**

★ Berliner Dom
The Neo-Baroque interior of the Berlin Cathedral features some extravagant late 19th-century furnishings **4**

BODESTRASSE

LUSTGARTEN

SSBRÜCKE

KARL-LIEBKNECHT STR.

SCHLOSSPLATZ

Palast der Republik
Originally the home of the East German parliament, this controversial building is to be torn down **2**

Schlossplatz
Excavations conducted here have unearthed the cellars of the demolished Stadtschloss **1**

Schlossplatz **1**

Map 7 B3, 16 F3. ⑤ *Hackescher Markt.* ▦ *100, 200, 348.*

This square was once the site of a gigantic residential complex known as Stadt-schloss (City Castle). Built in 1451, it served as the main residence of the Brandenburg Electors. It was transformed from a castle to a palace in the mid-16th century when Elector Friedrich III (later King Friedrich I) ordered its reconstruction in the Baroque style. The building works (1698–1716) were overseen initially by Andreas Schlüter and then by Johann von Göthe and Martin Heinrich Böhme.

The three-storey residence, designed around two court-yards, was the main seat of the Hohenzollern family for almost 500 years until the end of the monarchy. The palace was partly burned during World War II, but after 1945 it was provisionally restored and used as a museum. In 1950–51, despite protests, the palace was demolished and the square was renamed Marx-Engels-Platz under the GDR.

Now all that remains of the palace is the triumphal-arch portal that once adorned the façade on the Lustgarten side. This is now incorporated into the wall of the government building, the Staatsratgebäude, erected in 1964 on the square's south side. The building's décor features the remaining

The surviving Stadtschloss portal fronting a government building

original sculptures, including the magnificent atlantes by the famous Dresden sculptor Balthasar Permoser. Their inclusion, however, was not due to their artistic merit, but rather to their propaganda value: it was from the balcony of the portal that in 1918 Karl Lieb-knecht proclaimed the birth of the Socialist Republic *(see p28).*

In 1989 the square reverted to its original name. In 1993 a full-scale model of the palace was built out of cloth stretched over scaffolding. After a lenghty debate, it was decided not to rebuild the palace, instead the remaining fragments were incorporated into a new museum and conference complex.

Palast der Republik **2**

PALACE OF THE REPUBLIC

Map 7 B3, 16 F2. ⑤ *Hackescher Markt.* ▦ *100, 200, 348.*

Built on the site of the Stadtschloss in 1976, the Palast der Republik was once considered one of East Berlin's most prestigious buildings. Although it housed the GDR parliament, it was also acces-sible to the public. It boasted restaurants, a theatre, a discotheque, sports facilities and a large hall. In 1990 the discovery that asbestos had been used in its construction led to its closure. Now cleaned, the building awaits imminent demolition.

Schlossbrücke **3**

Map 7 B3, 16 E2. ⑤ *Hackescher Markt.* ▦ *100, 200, 348.*

This is one of the town's most beautiful bridges, connecting Schlossplatz with Unter den Linden. It was built in 1824 to a design by Karl Friedrich Schinkel, who was one of Germany's most influential architects *(see p187).* Statues were added to the top of the bridge's sparkling

Sculptures on the Schlossbrücke

granite pillars in 1853. These figures were also created by Schinkel and made of stunning white Carrara marble. The statues depict tableaux taken from Greek mythology, for instance Iris, Nike and Athena training and looking after their favourite young warriors. The wrought-iron balustrade is decorated with intertwined sea creatures.

Berliner Dom **4**

BERLIN CATHEDRAL

See pp76–7.

Lustgarten **5**

Map 7 B3, 16 E2. ⑤ *Hackescher Markt.* ▦ *100, 200, 348.*

The enchanting garden in front of the Altes Museum looks as though it has always been here, but in its present form it was established as recently as 1998 to 1999.

Used to grow vegetables and herbs for the Stadtschloss until the late-16th century, it became a real *Lustgarten* (pleasure garden) in the reign of the Great Elector (1620–88). However, its statues, grottoes, fountains and exotic vegetation were removed when Friedrich Wilhelm I (1688–1740), known for his love of military pursuits, turned the garden into an army drill ground.

Following the construction of the Altes Museum, the ground became a park, designed by Peter Joseph Lenné. In 1831 it was adorned with a monolithic granite bowl by Christian Gottlieb Cantian, to a design by Schinkel. The 70-ton bowl, measuring nearly 7 m (23 ft) in diameter, was intended for the museum rotunda, but was too heavy to carry inside.

After 1933, the Lustgarten was paved over and turned into a parade ground, remai-ning as such until 1989. Its current restoration is based on Lenné's designs.

Altes Museum ❻

The museum building, designed by Karl Friedrich Schinkel, is undoubtedly one of the world's most beautiful Neo-Classical structures, with an impressive 87-m (285-ft) high portico supported by 18 Ionic columns. Officially opened in 1830, this was one of the first purpose-built museums in Europe, built to house the royal collection of paintings and antiquities. Following World War II, the building was only used to display temporary exhibitions. Since 1998 the Altes Museum has housed parts of the Antikensammlung, a magnificent collection of Greek and Roman antiquities.

VISITORS' CHECKLIST

Am Lustgarten (Bodestrasse 1–3). **Map** 7 B3. **Tel** 20 90 55 77
Ⓢ *Hackescher Markt.* 🚌 *100, 200, 348.* ⏺ *10am–6pm Tue–Sun.* 🖼️📷🛗

Andochides' Amphora
The amphora is decorated with the figures of wrestlers, a common motif.

Pericles' Head
This is a Roman copy of the sculpture by Kresilas that stood at the entrance to the Acropolis in Athens.

Staircase

The monument-al colonnade
at the front of the building dominates the façade.

Main entrance

The stately rotunda is decorated with sculptures and ringed by a colonnade. Its design is based on the ancient Pantheon.

GALLERY GUIDE
The ground floor galleries house Greek and Roman antiquities; the first floor is used for temporary exhibitions.

Mosaic from Hadrian's Villa
(c.117–138)
This colourful mosaic depicts a battle scene between centaurs and a tiger and lion. The mosaic comes from a floor of Hadrian's Villa, near Tivoli on the outskirts of Rome.

KEY

☐	Greek and Roman antiquities
☐	Temporary exhibitions

Berliner Dom 4

The original Berliner Dom was based on a modest Baroque design by Johann Boumann. Built between 1747 and 1750 on the site of an old Dominican church, the cathedral included the original crypt of the Hohenzollern family, one of the largest in its kind in Europe. The present Neo-Baroque structure is the work of Julius Raschdorff and dates from 1894 to 1905. The central copper dome is some 98 m (321 ft) high. Following severe World War II damage, the cathedral has now been restored in a simplified form. The Hohenzollern memorial chapel, which had originally adjoined the northern walls of the cathedral, has been dismantled.

Royal crest of Friedrich III

Phil.d.Grossm.

Figures of the apostles

Philipp der Grossmütige (Philip the Magnanimous)
At the base of the arcade stand the statues of church reformers and those who supported the Reformation. The statue of Prince Philip the Magnanimous is the work of Walter Schott.

★ **Church Interior**
The impressive and richly-decorated interior was designed by Julius Raschdorff at the start of the 20th century.

Sauer's Organ
The organ, the work of Wilhelm Sauer, has an exquisitely carved case. The instrument contains some 7,200 pipes.

Main entrance

★ **Hohenzollern Sarcophagi**
The Imperial Hohenzollern family crypt, hidden beneath the floor of the cathedral, contains 100 richly decorated sarcophagi, including that of Prince Friedrich Ludwig.

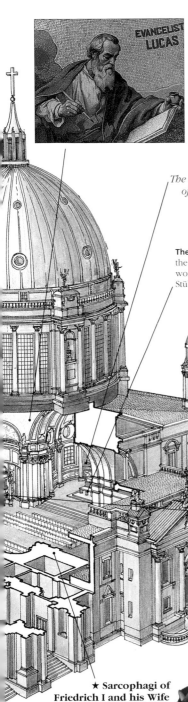

The Four Evangelists
Mosaics depicting the Four Evangelists decorate the ceilings of the smaller niches in the cathedral. They were designed by Woldemar Friedrich.

VISITORS' CHECKLIST

Am Lustgarten. **Map** 7 B3, 16 F2.
Tel 20 26 91 19. Ⓢ Hackescher
Markt. 🚌 100, 200, 348. ◻
9am–8pm (7pm in winter) Mon–
Sat, noon–8pm Sun. 🔊 ✝ Sun.

The Resurrection
The stained glass in the windows of the apses depict scenes from the life of Jesus. They are the work of Anton von Werner.

The main altar, saved from the previous cathedral, is the work of Friedrich August Stüler. It dates from 1820.

The Pulpit
This elaborate Neo-Baroque pulpit is part of the cathedral's ornate decor dating from the early 20th century.

★ **Sarcophagi of Friedrich I and his Wife**
Both of these were designed by Andreas Schlüter. The sculpture on Sophie Charlotte's sarcophagus depicts death.

STAR FEATURES

★ Church Interior

★ Hohenzollern Sarcophagi

★ Sarcophagi of Friedrich I and his Wife

Arnold Böcklin's *The Island of the Dead*, 1883, Alte Nationalgalerie

Alte Nationalgalerie ❼

OLD NATIONAL GALLERY

Bodestrasse 1–3. **Map** 7 B2, 16 E1.
Tel 20 90 55 77. ⑤ *Hackescher Markt, Friedrichstrasse.* 🚌 *100, 200, 348.* 🚊 *1, 2, 3, 4, 5, 6, 7, 13, 52, 53.* ⬜ *10am–6pm Tue–Sun (to 10pm Thu).*

The Nationalgalerie building was erected between 1866 and 1876 and designed by Friedrich August Stüler, who took into account the sketches made by Friedrich Wilhelm IV. The building is situated on a high platform reached via a double staircase. On the top stands an equestrian statue of Friedrich Wilhelm IV, the work of Alexander Calandrelli in 1886. The façade of the building is preceded by a magnificent colonnade, which becomes a row of half-columns higher up. The decorations are in keeping with the purpose of the building – the tympanum features Germania as patroness of art, while the top is crowned with the personification of the arts.

The museum was originally intended to house the collection of modern art that had been on display since 1861 in the Akademie der Künste *(see p67)*. After World War II the collection was split up. Part of it was shown in West Berlin, where the Neue Nationalgalerie was erected for this purpose

(see p126). This building was then renamed Alte (meaning Old) Nationalgalerie.

Following the reunification of Germany, the modern art collections were merged again. The current collection includes works of masters such as Adolph von Menzel, Wilhelm Leibl, Max Liebermann and Arnold Böcklin. Other works include paintings by the Nazarene Brotherhood and the French Impressionists. There is also no shortage of sculptures, including works by Christian Daniel Rauch, Johann Gottfried Schadow and Reinhold Begas. Two new exhibition halls now present paintings (formerly shown at the Schloss Charlottenburg) from the German Romantic era, as well as works by Caspar David Friedrich, Karl Friedrich Schinkel and Karl Blechen.

Neues Museum ❽

NEW MUSEUM

Bodestrasse 1–3. **Map** 7 B2, 16 E2. ⑤ *Hackescher Markt or Friedrichstrasse.* 🚌 *100, 200, 348.* 🚊 *1, 2, 3, 4, 5, 13, 53, 58.* ⬤ *until 2009.*

The Neues Museum was built on Museum Island in order to relieve the Altes Museum, which was already very

crowded. The building was erected between 1841 and 1855 to a design by Friedrich August Stüler. Until World War II it housed a collection of antiquities, mainly ancient Egyptian art. The monumental building's beautiful rooms were decorated to complement the exhibitions they contained. Wall paintings by Wilhelm von Kaulbach depicted key events in world history.

Façade statue, Neues Museum

In 1945 the building was badly damaged and it took a long time to decide if it would be feasible to rebuild it. Reconstruction work has started, based on designs by David Chipperfield. When the reconstruction is complete it will once again house the collection of Egyptian art, although the exact interior decor will not be restored. The building will serve not only as a venue for exhibitions, but it will also contain an information centre for the whole Museum Island (Museumsinsel) complex.

Pergamonmuseum ❾

See pp80–81.

Bodemuseum ⑩

Monbijoubrücke. (Bodestrasse 1–3).
Map 7 A2, 16 D1, 16 E1. **Tel** 20 90
55 77. Ⓢ Hackescher Markt or
Friedrichstrasse. 🚌 100, 200, 348.
⬤ until 2006.

The fourth museum building
on the island was erected
between 1897 and 1904. It was
designed by Ernst von Ihne to
fit the wedge-shaped end of
the island. The interior was
designed with the help of an
art historian, Wilhelm von
Bode, who was the director
of the Berlin state museums
at the time. The museum
displayed a rather mixed
collection that included some
Old Masters. Its original name,
Kaiser Friedrich Museum, was
changed after World War II.
Following the reassembling of
the Berlin collections, all of
the paintings were put in the
Kulturforum (see pp122–3),
while the Egyptian art and the
papyrus collection were
moved to the Ägyptisches
Museum (Egyptian Museum)
at Charlottenburg (see p164).
    Whilst the museum is being
refurbished part of its
outstanding coin collection is
on display. This includes
some of the world's oldest
coins, from Athens in the 6th
century BC, as well as Roman,
medieval and 20th-century
coins. When the museum
reopens fully in 2006 its other
collections will once again be
on show, including sculptures
by Tilman Riemenschneider,
Donatello, Gianlorenzo
Bernini and Antonio Canova.

Marstall ⑪

THE ROYAL STABLES

Schlossplatz/Breite Strasse 36–37.
Map 7 B3, C3, C4, 16 F3.
Ⓤ Spittelmarkt. 🚌 143, 148.

This huge complex, occupying the area between the
Spree and Breitestrasse, south
of Schlossplatz, is the old
Royal Stables block. The
wing on the side of Breite
Strasse is a fragment of the
old structure built in 1669. It
was designed by Michael
Matthias Smids and is the
only surviving early Baroque
building in Berlin. The wings
running along Schlossplatz
and the Spree river were built
much later, between 1898 and
1901. Although they were
designed by Ernst von Ihne,
these buildings are reminiscent
of the Berlin Baroque style –
probably because von Ihne
modelled them on designs by
Jean de Bodt from 1700.

Ribbeckhaus ⑫

RIBBECK'S HOUSE

Breite Strasse 35. **Map** 7 C4.
Ⓤ Spittelmarkt. 🚌 143, 148.

Four identical, picturesque
gables crown central Berlin's
only surviving Renaissance
building. The house was built
c.1624 for Hans Georg von
Ribbeck, a court counsellor,
who sold it shortly afterwards
to Anna Sophie of Brunswick.
The architect Balthasar Benzelt
converted the house for her
in 1629. After her death in

The Ribbeckhaus, central Berlin's
only surviving Renaissance building

1659, the house passed to her
nephew Elector Friedrich
Wilhelm. As crown property,
the building later housed
various state administrative
offices. When another storey
was added, the row of gables
was retained by royal decree.
    The house also has an
interesting late-Renaissance
portal, ornamented with the
date and coat of arms of the
first owners – von Ribbeck
and Katharina von Brösicke
his wife. This was replaced
in 1960 with a copy. Original
features of interest include the
beautiful wrought-iron grilles
on the ground-floor windows.

Historischer
Hafen Berlin ⑬

HISTORIC PORT OF BERLIN

Märkisches Ufer. **Map** 8 D4.
Tel 21 47 32 57. Ⓤ Märkisches Ufer.
Ⓢ Jannowitzbrücke. 🚌 240, 265.
⬤ 1 Apr–31 Oct: 2–6pm Tue–Fri,
11am–6pm Sat & Sun. 📷

Moored on the south shore
of Museum Island, in an area
called Fischerinsel, and
opposite the Märkisches Ufer
are several examples of boats,
barges and tug-boats which
operated on the Spree river at
the end of the 19th century.
These craft constitute an open-
air museum which was once
located in the Humboldt Port.
One of the boats is now used
as a summer café, while
another, the Renate Angelika,
houses a small exhibition
illustrating the history of
inland waterway transport.

The Bodemuseum designed by Ernst von Ihne

Pergamonmuseum ❾

The Pergamonmuseum was built between 1912
and 1930 to a design by Alfred Messels and
Ludwig Hoffmann. It houses one of the most
famous collections of antiquities in Europe, and
owes its name to the famous Pergamon Altar
which takes pride of place in the main hall. The
three independent collections – the Museum of
Antiquities (Greek and Roman), the Museum of
Near Eastern Antiquities and the Museum of
Islamic Art – are the result of intensive archaeological excavations by German expeditions to
the Near and Middle East at the end of the 19th
and beginning of the 20th century.

★ **Pergamon Altar** *(170 BC)*
*This scene, featuring the goddess
Athena, appears on the large
frieze illustrating a battle between
the gods and the giants.*

Roman Mosaic *(3rd
or 4th century AD)
This ancient mosaic was
found at Jerash, Jordan.
A second part of it is in
the collection of the Stark
Museum of Art, Texas.*

Non-exhibition
rooms

First
floor

The Goddesss Athena
*This enchanting Hellenistic
sculpture of the goddess
Athena is one of many
displayed in the museum.*

Ground
floor

Main
entrance

Assyrian Palace
*Parts of this beauti-
fully reconstructed
palace interior,
from the ancient
kingdom of Assyria,
date from the 12th
century BC.*

Aleppo Zimmer
(c.1603)
This magnificent panelled room comes from a merchant's house in the Syrian city of Aleppo.

GALLERY LAYOUT

The central section of the ground floor houses reconstructions of ancient monumental structures, and the left wing is devoted to the Antiquities of Greece and Rome. The right wing houses the Museum of Near Eastern Antiquities; the first floor of the right wing houses the Museum of Islamic Art.

Façade of the Mshatta Palace *(744 AD)*
This fragment is from the southern façade of the Jordanian Mshatta Palace, presented to Wilhelm II by Sultan Abdul Hamid of Ottoman in 1903.

★ Market Gate from Miletus *(c.120 AD)*
This gate, measuring over 16 m (52 ft) in height, opened on to the southern market of Miletus, a Roman town in Asia Minor.

★ Ishtar Gate from Babylon
(6th century BC)
Original glazed bricks decorate both the huge Ishtar gate and the impressive Processional Way that leads up to it.

KEY

- ☐ Antiquities (Antikensammlung)
- ☐ Near Eastern Antiquities (Vorderasiatisches Museum)
- ☐ Islamic Art (Museum für Islamische Kunst)
- ☐ Non-exhibition rooms

STAR EXHIBITS

- ★ Pergamon Altar
- ★ Market Gate from Miletus
- ★ Ishtar Gate from Babylon

Exploring the Pergamonmuseum

Opened in 1930, the Pergamonmuseum is the newest museum in the Museum Island complex and is one of Berlin's major attractions. The building was one of the first in Europe designed specifically to house big architectural exhibits. The richness of its collections is the result of large-scale excavations by German archaeologists at the beginning of the 20th century. Currently, the museum is at the heart of a redevelopment programme, due for completion in 2010, that will considerably increase the range of large-scale exhibits on display.

Bird from Mesopotamia

The Greek goddess Persephone, from Tarentum, 5th century BC

Restored entrance hall of the Athena temple from Pergamon, 2nd century BC

COLLECTION OF ANTIQUITIES

Berlin's collection of Greek and Roman antiquities (Antikensammlung) came into existence during the 17th century. Growing steadily in size, the collection was opened for public viewing in 1830, initially in the Altes Museum *(see p75)*, and from 1930 in the new, purpose-built Pergamonmuseum. The high-

light of the collection is the huge Pergamon Altar from the acropolis of the ancient city of Pergamon in Asia Minor (now Bergama, Turkey). It formed part of a larger architectural complex, a model of which is also on display in the museum. The magnificently restored altar is thought to have been built to celebrate victory in war and to have been commissioned by King Eumenes in 170 BC. Probably dedicated to the god Zeus and the goddess Athena, this artistic masterpiece was discovered in a decrepit state by German archaeologist Carl Humann who, after long negotiations, was allowed to transport the surviving portions of the altar to Berlin. The front section of the building was restored in the museum, together with the so-called small frieze, which once adorned the inside of the building, and fragments of the large frieze, which originally encircled the base of the colonnade. The large frieze has now been reconstructed around the interior walls of the museum and its theme is the Gigantomachy (the battle of the gods against the giants). The small frieze tells the story

of Telephos, supposed founder of the city and son of the hero Heracles. The frieze is an attempt to claim an illustrious ancestry for Pergamon's rulers.

The collection also contains fragments of other Pergamon structures from the same period, including part of the Athena temple. Also featured here are some excellent examples of Greek sculpture, both originals and Roman copies, as well as many statues of the Greek gods unearthed at Miletus, Samos and Nakosos, and various examples of Greek ceramic art.

Roman architecture is represented by the striking market gate from the Roman city of Miletus, on the west coast of Asia Minor. The gate dates from the 2nd century AD, and shows strong Hellenistic influences. Discovered by a German archaeological expedition, it was transported to Berlin where it was restored in 1903. Also on display are a number of magnificent Roman mosaics. A huge and impressive marble

Roman marble sarcophagus depicting the story of Medea, 2nd century AD

sarcophagus dates from the 2nd century AD and is decorated with delicate bas-relief carvings depicting the story of the Greek heroine Medea.

Glazed-brick wall cladding from the palace of Darius I in Susa, capital of the Persian Empire

MUSEUM OF NEAR EASTERN ANTIQUITIES

The collection now on display in the Museum of Near Eastern Antiquities (Vorderasiatisches Museum) was made up initially of donations from individual collectors. However, hugely successful excavations, begun during the 1880s, formed the basis of a royal collection that is one of the richest in the world. It features architecture, sculpture and jewellery from Babylon, Iran and Assyria.

One striking exhibit is the magnificent Ishtar Gate and the Processional Way that leads to it. They were built during the reign of Nebuchadnezzar II (604–562 BC) in the ancient city of Babylon. The original avenue was about 180 m (590 ft) long. Many of the bricks used in its reconstruction are new, but the lions – sacred animals of the goddess Ishtar (mistress of the sky, goddess of love and patron of the army) – are all originals. Although impressive in size, the Ishtar Gate has in fact not been reconstructed in full and a model of the whole structure shows the scale of

the original complex. Only the inner gate is on display, framed by two towers. Dragons and bulls decorate the gate, emblems of the Babylonian gods, Marduk, patron of the city, and Adad, god of storms.

The collection also includes pieces from the neighbouring regions of Persia, Syria and Palestine including a gigantic basalt sculpture of a bird from Tell Halaf and a glazed wall relief of a spear bearer from Darius I's palace in Susa. Other Mesopotamian peoples, including the Assyrians and the Cassians, are represented here too, as are the inhabitants of Sumer in the southern part of the Babylonian Empire with pieces dating from the 4th century BC.

MUSEUM OF ISLAMIC ART

The history of the Museum of Islamic Art (Museum für Islamische Kunst) begins in 1904 when Wilhelm von Bode launched the collection by donating his own extensive selection of carpets. He also brought to Berlin a 45-m (150-ft) long section of the façade of a Jordanian desert palace. The façade, covered with exquisitely carved limestone cladding, was presented to Kaiser Wilhelm II in 1903 by Sultan Abdul Hamid of Ottoman. The palace was part of a group of defence fortresses and residential buildings dating from the Omayyad period (AD661–750). These were probably built for the Caliph al-Walid II.

Another fascinating exhibit is a beautiful 13th-century *mihrab*, the niche in a

Brilliantly-glazed *mihrab* from a Kashan mosque built in 1226

mosque that shows the direction of Mecca. Made in the Iranian town of Kashan renowned for its ceramics, the *mihrab* is covered in lustrous metallic glazes that make it sparkle as if studded with sapphires and gold.

The collection's many vivid carpets come from as far afield as Iran, Asia Minor, Egypt and the Caucasus. Highlights include an early 15th-century carpet from Anatolia decorated with an unusual dragon and phoenix motif and, dating from the 14th century, one of the earliest Turkish carpets in existence.

Other rooms hold collections of miniature paintings and various objects for daily use. An interesting example of provincial Ottoman architecture is an exquisitely-panelled early 17th-century reception room, known as the Aleppo Zimmer, which was once part of a Christian merchant's house in the Syrian city of Aleppo.

17th-century carpet with flower motif from western Anatolia

The exterior of the Märkisches Museum, echoing a medieval monastery

Märkisches Museum ⓮

Am Köllnischen Park 5. **Map** 8 D4. **Tel** 308 660. Ⓤ Jannowitzbrücke, Märkisches Museum. Ⓢ Jannowitzbrücke. 🚌 147, 240, 265. 🕙 10am–6pm Tue, Thu–Sun; noon–8pm Wed. 🎼 Presentation of mechanical musical instruments 3pm Sun.

This architectural pastiche is a complex of red brick buildings that most resembles a medieval monastery. It was built between 1901 and 1908 to house a collection relating to the history of Berlin and the Brandenburg region, from the time of the earliest settlers to the present. Inspired by the brick-Gothic style popular in the Brandenburg region, architect Ludwig Hoffmann included references to Wittstock Castle and to St Catherine's Church in the city of Brandenburg. In the entrance hall, a statue of the hero Roland stands guard, a copy of the 15th-century monument in the city of Brandenburg. The main hall features the original Gothic portal from the Berlin residence of the Margraves of Brandenburg (see pp17–19), demolished in 1931. Also featured is a horse's head from the Schadow *Quadriga*, which once crowned the Brandenburg Gate (see p67). A further collection in the same building is devoted to the Berlin theatre during the period 1730 to 1933, including many posters, old programmes and stage sets. One of the galleries houses some charming old-time mechanical musical instruments, which can be heard playing during special shows.

The Märkisches Museum is a branch of the Stadtmuseum Berlin organization, and those who wish to find out more about the history of the city can visit other affiliated museums and monuments such as the Nikolaikirche (see pp90–91) and the Ephraim-Palais (see p91). Surrounding the museum is the Köllnischer Park, home to three brown bears, the official city mascots, and an unusual statue of Berlin artist Heinrich Zille.

Märkisches Ufer ⓯

Map 8 D4. Ⓤ Märkisches Museum. Ⓢ Jannowitzbrücke. 🚌 240, 265.

Once called Neukölln am Wasser, this street, which runs along the Spree river, is one of the few corners of Berlin where it is still possible to see the town much as it must have looked in the 18th and 19th centuries. Eight picturesque houses have been meticulously conserved here.

Two Neo-Baroque houses at No. 16 and No. 18, known as Otto-Nagel Haus, used to contain a small museum displaying paintings by Otto Nagel, a great favourite with the communist authorities. The building now houses the photographic archives for the

state museums of Berlin. A number of picturesque garden cafés and fashionable restaurants make this attractive area very popular with tourists.

The Neo-Classical exterior of the Ermeler-Haus

Ermeler-Haus ⓰

ERMELER HOUSE

Märkisches Ufer 10. **Map** 7 C4. Ⓤ Märkisches Museum. Ⓢ Jannowitzbrücke. 🚌 240, 265.

With its harmonious Neo-Classical façade, Märkisches Ufer No. 12 stands out as one of the most handsome villas in Berlin. This house was once the town residence of Wilhelm Ferdinand Ermeler, a wealthy merchant and shopkeeper, who made his money trading in tobacco. It originally stood on Fischerinsel on the opposite bank of the river, at Breite Strasse No. 11, but in 1968 the house was dismantled and reconstructed on this new site. The house was remodelled in 1825 to Ermeler's specifications, with a decor

Barges moored alongside Märkisches Ufer

that includes a frieze alluding to aspects of the tobacco business. Restorers have recreated much of the original façade. The Rococo furniture dates from about 1760 and the notable 18th-century staircase has also been rebuilt.

A modern hotel has been built to the rear of the house facing Wallstrasse, using Ermeler-Haus as its kitchens while the first-floor rooms are used for special events.

Gertrauden-brücke ⑰

ST GERTRUDE'S BRIDGE

Map 7 B4, 16 F4.
Ⓤ Spittelmarkt. 🚌 143, 147.

One of Berlin's more interesting bridges, this connects Fischer Island with Spittel-markt at the point where St Gertrude's Hospital once stood. The Gertrauden-brücke was designed by Otto Stahn and built in 1894.

Standing in the middle of the bridge is a bronze statue of the hospital's patron saint, St Gertrude, by Rudolf Siemering. A 13th-century Christian mystic, St Gertrude is shown here as a Benedictine abbess. Leaning over a poor youth she hands him a lily (symbol of virginity), a distaff (care for the poor), and a vessel filled with wine (love). The pedestal is surrounded by mice, a reference to the fact that Gertrude is patron saint of farmland and graves – both popular environments for mice.

Statue of St Gertrude

Nicolai-Haus ⑱

Brüderstr. 13. **Map** 7 B4, 16 F4. **Tel** 24 00 21 62. Ⓤ Spittelmarkt. 🚌 143, 148. ◯ by appointment only during renovation.

Built around 1710, the Nicolai-Haus is a fine example of Baroque architecture with the original, magnificent oak

staircase still in place. The house owes its fame, however, to its time as the home and bookshop of the publisher, writer and critic Christoph Friedrich Nicolai (1733–1811). Nicolai acquired the house around 1788 when he had it rebuilt to a Neo-Classical design by Karl Friedrich Zelter to become a bookshop and major German cultural centre.

One of the outstanding personalities of the Berlin Enlightenment, Nicolai was a great supporter of such talents as the Jewish philosopher Moses Mendelssohn (see p102) and the playwright Gotthold Ephraim Lessing (1729–81). Other regular literary visitors to the Nicolai-Haus at this period included Johann Gottfried Schadow, Karl Wilhelm Ramler and Daniel Chodowiecki, all of whom are commemorated with a wall plaque.

Between 1905 and 1935 the building housed a museum devoted to Gotthold Ephraim Lessing. Today the rear wing features a fine staircase from the Weydinger-Haus, demolished in 1935. Installed in the Nicolai-Haus in the late 1970s, the staircase previously stood in the nearby Ermeler Haus (see p84).

COLLN

An ancient settlement in the area called Fischerinsel at the southern end of Museum Island, the village of Cölln has now been razed almost to the ground. Not even a trace remains of the medieval St Peter's parish church. Until 1939, however, this working-class area with its tangle of narrow streets maintained a historic character and unique identity of its own. This vanished completely in the 1960s when most of the buildings were demolished, to be replaced with prefabricated tower blocks. A few historic houses, including Ermeler-Haus (see p84), were reconstructed elsewhere, but the atmosphere of this part of town has changed forever.

An engraving of old Cölln

East German fashion now on show in the Märkisches Museum (see p84)

Galgenhaus ⑲

GALLOWS HOUSE

Brüderstrasse 10. **Map** 7 B4, 16 F4. **Tel** 240 02 162. Ⓤ Spittelmarkt. 🚌 147, 148. ◯ 10am–4pm Tue–Sun. 📷

Local legend has it that an innocent girl was once hanged in front of this building, which dates from 1700. It was originally built as the presbytery of the now vanished church of St Peter. Redesigned in the Neo-Classical style around 1805, the front portal and one of the rooms on the ground floor are all that remain of the original Baroque structure.

Today the Galgenhaus houses an archive of historic photographs. These reveal the ways in which Berlin has developed over the years through changes in its buildings and monuments.

EAST OF THE CENTRE

This part of Berlin, belonging to the Mitte district, is the historic centre. A settlement called Berlin was first established on the eastern bank of the Spree river in the 13th century. Together with its twin settlement, Cölln, it grew into a town. This district contains traces of Berlin's earliest history, including the oldest surviving church (Marienkirche). In later centuries, it became a trade and residential district, but the Old Town (the Nikolaiviertel)

The organ-grinder at Gerichtslaube

survived until World War II. The GDR regime replaced the huge apartment buildings and department stores just to the north with a square, Marx-Engels-Forum, and built the Fernsehturm (television tower). Their redevelopment of the Nikolaiviertel was controversial – buildings were faithfully rebuilt but were grouped rather than being placed in their original locations. The area still offers cosy mews and alleys, which are surrounded by postwar high-rise blocks.

SIGHTS AT A GLANCE

Churches
Franziskaner Klosterkirche ⑮
Heiliggeistkapelle ⑩
Nikolaikirche ③
Marienkirche ⑪
Parochialkirche ⑰

Historic Buildings
Ephraim-Palais ⑥
Gaststätte "Zur letzten Instanz" ⑱
Gerichtslaube ⑦
Knoblauchhaus ④
Palais Podewils ⑯
Palais Schwerin and Münze ⑤
Rotes Rathaus ①
Stadtgericht ⑭
Stadtmauer ⑲

Others
Alexanderplatz ⑬
Fernsehturm p93 ⑫

Neptunbrunnen ⑨
Nikolaiviertel ②
Marx-Engels-Forum ⑧

KEY

▦	Street-by-Street map *See pp88–9*
🚆	Railway station
Ⓢ	S-Bahn station
Ⓤ	U-Bahn station

0 metres   400
0 yards   400

GETTING THERE

This part of the city is served by S-Bahn 3, 5, 7 and 9, with stations at Hackescher Markt, Alexanderplatz and Jannowitz-brücke. Alexanderplatz is the interchange for U-Bahn routes 2, 5 and 8. Buses 100 and 157 run along Karl-Liebknecht-Strasse; buses 142 and 257 along Grunerstrasse.

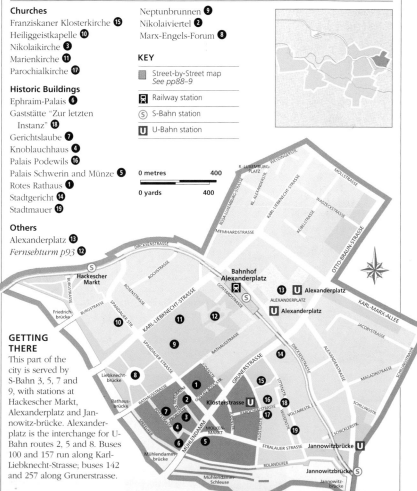

◁ **Detail from the Neptunbrunnen (Neptune Fountain)**

Street-by-Street: Nikolaiviertel

St Nicholas' Quarter, or the Nikolaiviertel, owes its name to the parish church whose spires rise above the small buildings in this part of town. The Nikolaiviertel is full of narrow alleys crammed with popular restaurants, tiny souvenir shops and small museums. The district was once inhabited by artists and writers, but now it is usually filled with tourists looking for a place to rest after an exhausting day of sightseeing – particularly in the summer. Almost every other house is occupied by a restaurant, inn, pub or café, so the area is quite lively until late at night.

Bear on façade of the Rathaus

Nikolaikirche
The church is now a museum, with its original furnishings incorporated into the exhibition ❸

Gerichtslaube
The replica arcades and medieval court-house now contain restaurants ❼

POSTSTRASSE

SPREEUFER

St George Slaying the Dragon
This statue once graced a courtyard of the Stadtschloss.

| 0 metres | 75 |
| 0 yards | 75 |

Knoblauchhaus
This Biedermeirer-style room is on the first floor of the building, which is one of the few to survive World War II damage ❹

★ Ephraim-Palais
A feature of this palace is the elegant façade. Inside there is also an impressive spiral staircase and balustrade ❻

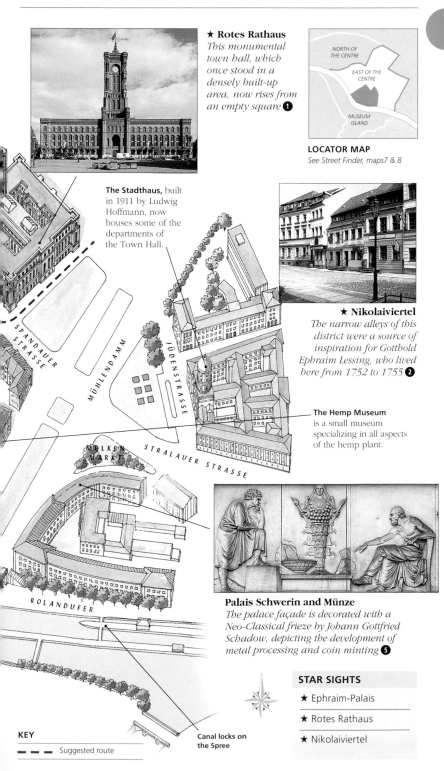

★ **Rotes Rathaus**
This monumental town hall, which once stood in a densely built-up area, now rises from an empty square ❶

LOCATOR MAP
See Street Finder, maps 7 & 8

The Stadthaus, built in 1911 by Ludwig Hoffmann, now houses some of the departments of the Town Hall.

★ **Nikolaiviertel**
The narrow alleys of this district were a source of inspiration for Gotthold Ephraim Lessing, who lived here from 1752 to 1755 ❷

The Hemp Museum is a small museum specializing in all aspects of the hemp plant.

Palais Schwerin and Münze
The palace façade is decorated with a Neo-Classical frieze by Johann Gottfried Schadow, depicting the development of metal processing and coin minting ❺

STAR SIGHTS

★ Ephraim-Palais

★ Rotes Rathaus

★ Nikolaiviertel

KEY
– – – Suggested route

Canal locks on the Spree

Red-brick walls giving the Red Town Hall its name

Rotes Rathaus ❶

RED TOWN HALL

Rathausstr. 15. **Map** 7 C3. *Tel* 90 26 0. **U** & **S** *Alexanderplatz.* **U** *Klosterstrasse.* 100, 143, 148, 200, 348. 9am–6pm Mon–Fri.

This impressive structure is Berlin's main town hall. Its predecessor was a much more modest structure and by the end of the 19th century, it was insufficient to the needs of the growing metropolis.

The present building was designed by Hermann Friedrich Waesemann, and the construction went on from 1861 until 1869. The architect took his main inspiration from Italian Renaissance municipal buildings, but the tower is reminiscent of Laon cathedral in France. The walls are made from red brick and it was this, rather than the political orientation of the mayors, that gave the town hall its name. The building has a continuous frieze known as the "stone chronicle", which was added in 1879. It features scenes and figures from the city's history and the development of its economy and science.

The Rotes Rathaus was badly damaged during World War II and, following its reconstruction (1951–58), it became the seat of the East Berlin authorities. The West Berlin magistrate was housed in the Schöneberg town hall (see p177). After the reunification of Germany, the Rotes Rathaus became the centre of authority, housing the offices of the mayor, the magistrates' offices and state rooms. The forecourt sculptures were added in 1958. These are by Fritz Kremer and depict Berliners helping to rebuild the city.

Nikolaiviertel ❷

Map 7 C3, C4. **U** & **S** *Alexanderplatz.* **U** *Klosterstrasse.* 100, 143, 148, 200, 348.

This small area on the bank of the Spree, known as the Nikolaiviertel (St Nicholas Quarter), is a favourite place for strolling, for both Berliners and tourists. Some of Berlin's oldest houses stood here until they were destroyed in World War II. The redevelopment of the whole area, carried out by the GDR government between 1979 and 1987, was an interesting, if somewhat controversial, attempt at recreating a medieval village. With the exception of one or two restored buildings, the Nikolaiviertel consists of newly built replicas of historic buildings.

The narrow streets of the Nikolaiviertel tempt the visitor with their small shops, as well as many cafés, bars and restaurants. One of the most popular is Zum Nussbaum, a historical inn that was once located on Fischer Island. The original building, dating from 1507, was destroyed but was subsequently reconstructed at the junction of Am Nussbaum and Propststrasse.

The interior of the Nikolaikirche, one of Berlin's oldest churches

Nikolaikirche ❸

Nikolaikirchplatz. **Map** 7 C3. *Tel* 24 00 20. **U** & **S** *Alexanderplatz.* **U** *Klosterstrasse.* 100, 142, 148, 157, 348. 10am–6pm Tue & Thu–Sun, noon–8pm Wed. &

The Nikolaikirche is the oldest sacred building of historic Berlin. The original structure erected on this site was started probably around 1230, when the town was granted its municipal rights. What remains now of this stone building is the massive base of the two-tower façade of the present church, which dates from c.1300. The presbytery was completed around 1402, but the construction of the main building went on until the mid-15th century. The result was a magnificent Gothic brick hall-church, featuring a chancel with an

Riverside buildings of the Nikolaiviertel

ambulatory and a row of low chapels. In 1877 Hermann Blankenstein, who conducted the church restoration works, removed most of its Baroque modifications and reconstructed the front towers.

Destroyed by bombing in 1945, the Nikolaikirche was eventually rebuilt in 1987. Today it houses an exhibition covering the history of Berlin, featuring items that escaped the ravages of war. The west wall of the southern nave contains Andreas Schlüter's monument to the goldsmith Daniel Männlich and his wife, which features a gilded relief portrait of the couple above a mock doorway.

Knoblauchhaus ❹

Poststr. 23. **Map** 7 C3. **Tel** 24 00 20.
Ⓤ & Ⓢ Alexanderplatz, Ⓤ Klosterstrasse. 🚌 100, 142, 148, 157, 348.
◘ 10am–6pm Tue & Thu–Sun,
noon–8pm Wed.

This small townhouse in Poststrasse is the only Baroque building in Nikolaiviertel that escaped damage during World War II. It was built in 1759 for the Knoblauch family which includes the famous architect, Eduard Knoblauch. His works include, among others, the Neue Synagoge (see p102).

The current appearance of the building is the result of work carried out in 1835, when the façade was given a Neo-Classical look. The ground floor houses a popular wine bar, while the upper floors belong to a museum. On the first floor it is possible to see the interior of an early 19th-century middle-class home, including a beautiful Biedermeier-style room.

Palais Schwerin and Münze ❺

Molkenmarkt 1–3. **Map** 7 C4.
Ⓤ & Ⓢ Alexanderplatz. Ⓤ Klosterstrasse. 🚌 100, 143, 148, 200, 348.

These two adjoining houses have quite different histories. The older one, at Molkenmarkt No. 2, is Palais

A fine example of German Baroque architecture, the Ephraim-Palais

Schwerin, which was built by Jean de Bodt in 1704 for a government minister, Otto von Schwerin. Despite subsequent remodelling, the palace kept its beautiful sculptured window cornices, the interior wooden staircase, and the magnificent cartouche featuring the von Schwerin family crest.

The adjoining house is the mint which was built in 1936. Its façade is decorated with a copy of the frieze that once adorned the previous Neo-Classical mint building in Werderscher Markt. The antique style of the frieze was designed by Friedrich Gilly and produced in the workshop of JG Schadow.

Ephraim-Palais ❻

Poststr. 16. **Map** 7 C3. **Tel** 24 00 20.
Ⓤ & Ⓢ Alexanderplatz. Ⓤ Klosterstrasse. 🚌 100, 143, 148, 200, 348.
◘ 10am–6pm Tue & Thu–Sun,
noon–8pm Wed.

The corner entrance of the Ephraim-Palais, standing at the junction of Poststrasse and Mühlendamm, used to be called "die schönste Ecke

Berlins", meaning "Berlin's most beautiful corner". This Baroque palace was built by Friedrich Wilhelm Diterichs in 1766 for Nathan Veitel Heinrich Ephraim, Frederick the Great's mint master and court jeweller.

During the widening of the Mühlendamm bridge in 1935 the palace was demolished, which may have been due in some part to the Jewish origin of its owner. Parts of the façade, saved from demolition, were stored in a warehouse in the western part of the city. In 1983 they were sent to East Berlin and used in the reconstruction of the palace, which was erected a few metres from its original site. One of the first floor rooms features a restored Baroque ceiling, designed by Andreas Schlüter. The ceiling previously adorned Palais Wartenberg, which was dismantled in 1889.

Currently Ephraim-Palais houses a branch of the Stadtmuseum Berlin (Berlin City Museum). It shows a series of temporary exhibitions on Berlin's local artistic and cultural history.

Frieze from the façade of the Münze (the Mint)

Gerichtslaube ➐

Poststrasse. 28. **Map** 7 C3.
Ⓤ & **Ⓢ** *Alexanderplatz.* **Ⓤ** *Klosterstrasse.* 🚌 *100, 143, 148, 200, 348.*

This small building, with its
sharply angled arcades, has
had a turbulent history.
It was built around 1280 as
part of Berlin's town hall in
Spandauer Strasse. The
original building was a single
storey arcaded construction
with vaults supported by a
central pillar. It was open on
three sides and adjoined the
shorter wall of the town hall.
A further storey was added
in 1485 to provide a hall to
which the magnificent lattice
vaults were added a few
decades later, in 1555.
    In 1692, Johann Arnold
Nering refurbished the town
hall in a Baroque style, but
left the arcades unaltered.
Then, in 1868, the whole
structure was dismantled to
provide space for the new
town hall, the Rotes Rathaus
(see p90). The Baroque part
was lost forever, but the
Gothic arcades and the first
floor hall were moved to the
palace gardens in Babelsberg,
where they were reassembled
as a building in their own
right *(see pp210–11).* When the
Nikolaiviertel was undergoing
restoration it was decided to
restore the court of justice as
well. The present building in
Poststrasse is only a copy of
a part of the former town
hall, erected on a different
site from the original one.
Inside is a restaurant
specializing in local cuisine.

Marx-Engels-Forum ➑

Map 7 C3, 16 F2. **Ⓢ** *Hackescher
Markt or Alexanderplatz.*
🚌 *100, 143, 148, 200, 348.*

This vast, eerily empty
square, stretching from the
Fernsehturm (television tower)
to the Spree river in the west,
was given the inappropriate
name Marx-Engels-Forum (it is
not really a forum). Devoid of
any surroundings, the only
features in this green square
are the statues of Karl Marx

**Statue of Karl Marx and Friedrich
Engels in Marx-Engels-Forum**

and Friedrich Engels. Marx sits
and Engels stands, seemingly
staring at the Fernsehturm.
The statues, added in 1986,
are by Ludwig Engelhart. The
base is decorated with bas-
reliefs showing the "old order"
at the rear, the "world revolution from Marx-Engels to the
present day" at the front, and
the "dignity and beauty of free
men" on the sides.

Neptunbrunnen ➒

NEPTUNE FOUNTAIN

Spandauer Str. (Rathausvorplatz).
Map 7 C3. **Ⓢ** *Hackescher Markt
or Alexanderplatz.* 🚌 *100, 143, 148,
200, 348.*

This magnificent fountain,
sparkling with cascades of
running water, provides a
splendid feature on the main
axis of the town hall building.
It was created in 1886 by
Reinhold Begas, to stand in
front of the southern wall of
the former Stadtschloss
(Berlin Castle). It was moved
to its present site in 1969.
    Begas, who designed it in
the Neo-Baroque style, was

**Neptune surrounded by goddesses
personifying Germany's rivers**

undoubtedly inspired by the
famous Roman fountains by
Bernini and the Latony fountain in Versailles. The statue
of Neptune, in a dynamic
pose and in the centre of the
fountain, is surrounded by
four figures representing
Germany's greatest rivers of
the time: the Rhine, the Vistula,
the Oder and the Elbe. The
naturalism of the composition
and the attention to detail,
such as the beautiful bronze
fish, crayfish, snails and
fishing nets, are noteworthy.

**The Gothic Chapel of the Holy
Spirit, seen from Spandauer Strasse**

Heiliggeistkapelle ➓

CHAPEL OF THE HOLY SPIRIT

Spandauer Strasse 1. **Map** 7 B2,
16 F2. **Ⓢ** *Hackescher Markt.*
🚌 *100, 143, 148, 200, 348.*

This modest Gothic structure is
the only surviving hospital
chapel in Berlin. It was built
as part of a hospital complex
in the second half of the 13th
century, but was subsequently
rebuilt in the 15th century.
The hospital itself was demolished in 1825, but the chapel
was retained. In 1906, it was
incorporated into a newly
erected College of Trade,
designed by Cremer and
Wolffenstein.
    The chapel is a fine example
of Gothic brick construction.
Its rather modest interior
features a 15th century star-
shaped vault. The supports
under the vault, or consoles,
are decorated with half-
statues of prophets and saints.

Marienkirche ⓫

See pp94–95.

Fernsehturm ⑫

The television tower, called by the locals *Telespargel*, or toothpick, remains to this day the city's tallest structure at 365 m (1,197 ft), and one of the tallest structures in Europe. The tower was built in 1969 to a design by a team of architects including Fritz Dieter and Günter Franke, with the help of Swedish engineering experts. However, the idea for such a colossal tower in Berlin originated much earlier from Hermann Henselmann (creator of the Karl-Marx-Allee development) in the Socialist-Realist style.

VISITORS' CHECKLIST

Panoramastrasse. **Map** 7 C2. **Tel** 242 33 33. Ⓢ & Ⓤ Alexanderplatz. 🚌 100, 157, 200, 348. ⬜ Mar–Oct: 9am–1am daily; Nov–Feb: 10am–midnight daily.

The television antenna is visible all over Berlin.

Viewing Platform
Situated inside a steel-clad giant sphere, the viewing platform is 203 m (666 ft) above the ground.

Television Tower
The slim silhouette of the Fernsehturm is visible from almost any point in Berlin. The ticket office and elevator entrance are located at the base of the tower.

Transmitter aerials

The metal sphere is covered with steel cladding.

Concrete structure rising to 250 m (820 ft)

The concrete shaft contains two elevators that carry passengers to the café and viewing platform.

The elevators are small, resulting in long queues at the base of the tower.

Tele-Café
One of the attractions of the tower is the revolving café. A full rotation takes about half an hour, so it is possible to get a bird's-eye-view of the whole city while sipping a cup of coffee.

View from the Tower
On a clear day the viewing platform offers a full view of Berlin. Visibility can reach up to 40 km (25 miles).

Marienkirche ⑪

St Mary's Church, or the Marienkirche, was first established
as a parish church in the second half of the 13th century.
Construction started around 1280 and was completed early
in the 14th century. During reconstruction works in 1380,
following a fire, the church was altered slightly but its overall
shape changed only in the 15th century when it acquired the
front tower. In 1790, the tower was crowned with a dome
designed by Carl Gotthard Langhans. The church was once
hemmed in by buildings, but today it stands alone in
the shadow of the Fernsehturm (Television Tower).
The early-Gothic hall design and the lavish decorative touches make this church one of the most
interesting in Berlin.

The Tower
*The dome that
crowns the tower
includes both
Baroque and Neo-
Gothic elements.*

Crucifixion (1562)
*This image of
Christ, flanked by
Moses and St John
the Baptist, was
painted in the
Mannerist style by
Michael Ribestein.*

Totentanz,
meaning "dance
of death", is the
name of a 22-m
(72-ft) long
Gothic wall
fresco, dating
from 1485.

Retable
*The central part of the
Gothic altar, dating
from 1510, features
figures of three
unknown monks.*

STAR FEATURES

★ Pulpit

★ Baptismal Font

**Main
entrance**

★ Pulpit
Carved from alabaster, this masterpiece by Andreas Schlüter, completed in 1703, is placed by the fourth pillar. The pulpit is decorated with bas-reliefs of St John the Baptist and the personifications of the Virtues.

VISITORS' CHECKLIST

Karl-Liebknecht-Str 8. **Map** 7 C2.
Tel 242 44 67. Ⓢ & Ⓤ Alexanderplatz. 🚌 100, 143, 148, 200, 348.
🕐 Oct–Mar: 10–4pm; Apr–Sep:
10–6pm daily. 📷 1pm Mon & Tue.

Von Röbel Family Tomb
This richly decorated Mannerist-Baroque tomb of Ehrentreich and Anna von Röbel was probably built after 1630.

Main Altar
The Baroque altar was designed by Andreas Krüger c.1762. The paintings, including Deposition from the Cross *in the centre;* Christ on the Mount of Olives *and* Doubting Thomas *on the sides, are the works of Christian Bernhard Rode.*

★ Baptismal Font
This Gothic font dating from 1437 is supported by three black dragons and decorated with the figures of Jesus Christ, Mary and the Apostles.

The magnificent interior of the Stadtgericht

Alexanderplatz ⑬

Map 8 D2. **U** & **S** *Alexanderplatz.*
🚌 *100, 143, 148, 200, 348.*

Alexanderplatz, or "Alex" as it is locally called, has a long history, although it would be difficult now to find any visible traces of the past. Once called Ochsenmarkt (oxen market), it was the site of a cattle and wool market. It was later renamed after Tsar Alexander I, who visited Berlin in 1805. At the time, the square boasted a magnificent monumental colonnade, which was designed by Carl von Gontard *(see pp176).*

With the passage of time, many houses and shops sprang up around the square, and a market hall and an urban train line were built nearby. "Alex" had become one of the town's busiest spots. Its frenzied atmosphere was captured by Alfred Döblin (1878-1957) in his novel, *Berlin Alexanderplatz.*

In 1929, attempts were made to develop the square, though only two office buildings were added – the Alexanderhaus and the Berolinahaus. These two, both by Peter Behrens, are still standing today.

World War II erased most of the square's buildings. It is now surrounded by characterless 1960s edifices, including the Forum Hotel (formerly Hotel Stadt Berlin) and the Fernsehturm *(see p93).* Alexanderplatz awaits its next transformation, which might happen soon: a winning design has been chosen from a competition for the square's redevelopment.

Stadtgericht ⑭

COURTS OF JUSTICE

Littenstrasse 13–17. **Map** 8 D3.
U & **S** *Alexanderplatz or*
U *Klosterstrasse.* 🚌 *148.*

This gigantic building, situated on a long stretch of Littenstrasse, does not seem particularly inviting, but its interior hides a true masterpiece of the Viennese Secession style of architecture.

At the time of its construction, the building was the largest in Berlin after the Stadtschloss *(see p74).* The Neo-Baroque structure, built between 1896 and 1905, was designed by Paul Thomer and Rudolf Mönnich, but its final shape is the work of Otto Schmalz. This maze-like complex, with its 11 inner courtyards, was partly demolished in 1969. What remains, however, is still worth seeing, especially the magnificent staircase in the form of overlying ellipses. The staircase is an example of Secession architecture at its boldest. The slim Neo-Gothic pillars and the Neo-Baroque balustrades further enhance the fairytale interior.

Franziskaner Klosterkirche ⑮

FRANCISCAN FRIARY CHURCH

Klosterstrasse 74. **Map** 8 D3.
U *Klosterstrasse.* 🚌 *148.*

These picturesque ruins surrounded by greenery are the remains of an early-Gothic Franciscan church. The Franciscan friars settled in Berlin in the early 13th century. Between 1250 and 1265 they built a church and a friary, which survived almost unchanged until 1945. The church was a triple-nave basilica with an elongated presbytery, widening into a heptagonal section that was added to the structure in c.1300. Protestants took over the church after the Reformation and the friary became a famous grammar school, whose graduates included Otto von Bismarck and Karl Friedrich Schinkel.

The friary was so damaged in World War II that it was subsequently demolished, while the church is gradually

Ruins of the Franziskaner Klosterkirche (Franciscan Friary Church)

being reconstructed. The giant Corinthian capitals, emerging from the grass near the church ruins, are from a portal from the Stadtschloss (Berlin Castle) *(see p74).*

Façade of the twice-restored Palais Podewils

Palais Podewils ⑯

PODEWILS PALACE

Klosterstrasse 68–70. **Map** 8 D3.
Ⓤ *Klosterstrasse.* 🚌 *148.*

This charming Baroque palace, set back from the street, was built between 1701 and 1704 for the Royal Court's counsellor, Caspar Jean de Bodt. Its owes its present name to its subsequent owner, a minister of state called von Podewils, who bought the palace in 1732.

After World War II, the palace was restored twice: in 1954 and then again in 1966 after it had been damaged by fire. The carefully reconstructed building did not lose much of its austere beauty, but the interior completely changed to suit its current needs. Today, the palace serves as a cultural centre that organizes concerts and theatre performances, including ballet.

Parochialkirche ⑰

PARISH CHURCH

Klosterstr. 67. **Map** 8 D3. *Tel* 247
59 10. Ⓤ *Klosterstrasse.* 🚌 *148.*
⭘ *10am–4pm Mon–Fri.*

This building was, at one time, one of most beautiful Baroque churches in Berlin. Johann Arnold

Nering prepared the initial design, with four chapels framing a central tower. Unfortunately, Nering died as construction started in 1695. The work was continued by Martin Grünberg, but the collapse of the nearly completed vaults forced a change in the design. Instead of the intended tower over the main structure, a vestibule with a front tower was built. The church was completed in 1703, but then, in 1714, its tower was enlarged by Jean de Bodt in order to accommodate a carillon.

World War II had a devastating effect on the Parochialkirche. The interior was completely destroyed, and the tower collapsed. Following stabilization of the main structure, the façade has been restored and the inside will be complete by 2004, with some reproduced historic elements set within a plain interior. During the summer, mass is held in the church.

Medallion from a headstone in the Parochialkirche

Gaststätte Zur letzten Instanz ⑱

INN OF THE LAST INSTANCE

Waisenstrasse 14–16. **Map** 8 D3.
Ⓤ *Klosterstrasse.* 🚌 *148.*

The small street at the rear of the Parochialkirche leads directly to one of the oldest inns in Berlin, Zur letzten Instanz, which translates as the Inn of the Last Instance. The inn occupies one of the four picturesque houses on Waisenstrasse – the only survivors of the whole row of houses that

once adjoined the town wall. Their history goes back to medieval times, but their present form dates from the 18th century. The houses are actually the result of an almost total reconstruction carried out after World War II. This was when one of the houses acquired its spiral Rococo staircase, which came from a dismantled house on the Fischerinsel.

The Zur letzten Instanz was first established in 1621 and initially specialized in serving alcoholic beverages. Interestingly, it was frequently patronized by lawyers. Today, however, the Zur letzten Instanz is one of Berlin's finest historic pub-restaurants frequented by all types of people, not just lawyers *(see p237).* Its interior is full of old memorabilia.

Stadtmauer ⑲

TOWN WALL

Waisenstrasse **Map** 8 D3.
Ⓤ & Ⓢ *Alexanderplatz or*
Ⓤ *Klosterstrasse.* 🚌 *148.*

The town wall that once surrounded the settlements of Berlin and Cölln was erected in the second half of the 13th century. The ring of fortifications, built from fieldstone and brick, was made taller in the 14th century. Having finally lost its military significance by the 17th century, the wall was almost entirely dismantled. Today, some small sections survive around Waisenstrasse, because they were incorporated into other buildings.

Remains of the Berlin's Stadtmauer (old town wall)

NORTH OF THE CENTRE

The area northwest of Alexanderplatz, bounded by Friedrichstrasse and Karl-Liebknecht-Strasse, is the former Spandauer Vorstadt, so called because one of its main streets, Oranienburger Strasse, led to Spandau. The eastern part of the area is known as Scheunenviertel (Barn Quarter). In 1672, the Great Elector moved the hay barns – a fire hazard – out of the city limits. From that time it became a refuge for Jews fleeing Russia and Eastern Europe, and by the 19th century it had become the well-established centre for Berlin's Jewish community. The area also

Detail from Postfuhramt

attracted artists, writers and political activists in the 1920s. Shops, hospitals, small factories and narrow streets of houses inhabited by workers and merchants gave the district its unique, lively character. After World War II the area gradually fell into decay. However, it has recently become fashionable again. Today, its newly restored houses, grand buildings and trendy restaurants stand side by side with dilapidated tenement blocks, shabby courtyards and buildings engulfed in scaffolding. The area is popular with tourists and Berliners alike, especially in the evenings.

SIGHTS AT A GLANCE

Streets and Parks
Alte and Neue
  Schönhauser Strasse ❿
Monbijoupark ❹
Oranienburger Strasse ❸
Sophienstrasse ❾

Churches and Synagogues
Neue Synagoge ❶
Sophienkirche ❽

Theatres
Berliner Ensemble ⓭
Deutsches Theater ⓮
Friedrichstadtpalast ⓬
Volksbühne ⓫

Museums
Brecht-Weigel-Gedenkstätte ⓱
Centrum Judaicum ❷

*Hamburger Bahnhof
  pp110–11* ⓳
Museum für Naturkunde ⓲

Cemeteries
Alter Jüdischer Friedhof ❼
*Dorotheenstädtischer Friedhof
  pp106–7* ⓰

Others
Charité ⓯
Gedenkstätte Grosse
  Hamburger Strasse ❻
Hackesche Höfe ❺

GETTING THERE
S-Bahn lines 3, 5, 7 and 9 run along the south of the area, with stops at Lehrter Stadtbahnhof, Friedrichstrasse and Hackescher Markt. S-Bahn lines 1 and 2 stop at Oranienburger Strasse. U-Bahn line 6 goes to Oranienburger Tor station, line 8 to Weinmeisterstrasse and line 2 to Rosa-Luxemburg-Platz.

KEY

Street-by-Street map
  See pp100–1

Ⓤ U-Bahn station

Ⓢ S-Bahn station

Tram stop

Bus stop

0 metres   600

0 yards   600

◁ **The first courtyard in Hackesche Höfe**

Street-by-Street: Scheunenviertel

Until World War II Scheunenviertel lay at the heart of Berlin's large Jewish district. During the 19th century the community flourished, its prosperity reflected in grand buildings such as the Neue Synagoge, which opened in 1866 in the presence of Chancellor Otto von Bismarck. Left to crumble for nearly 50 years after the double devastations of the Nazis and Allied bombing, the district has enjoyed a huge revival since the fall of the Wall. Recently cafés and bars have opened and visitors can expect to find some of the liveliest nightlife in East Berlin.

★ **Neue Synagoge**
Sparkling with gold, the recently-restored New Synagogue is now used again for services ❶

The Postfuhramt
was used originally as stables for the horses that delivered the post. Its ceramic-clad façade resembles a palace more than a post office.

Centrum Judaicum
Standing next to the Neue Synagoge, the Jewish Centre houses documents relating to the history and cultural heritage of the Berlin Jews ❷

Heckmann-Höfe
Today these lavishly restored yards, the most elegant in Berlin, attract visitors with a restaurant and fashionable clothes shops.

KEY

– – – Suggested route

STAR SIGHTS

★ Neue Synagoge

★ Hackesche Höfe

S-Bahn line

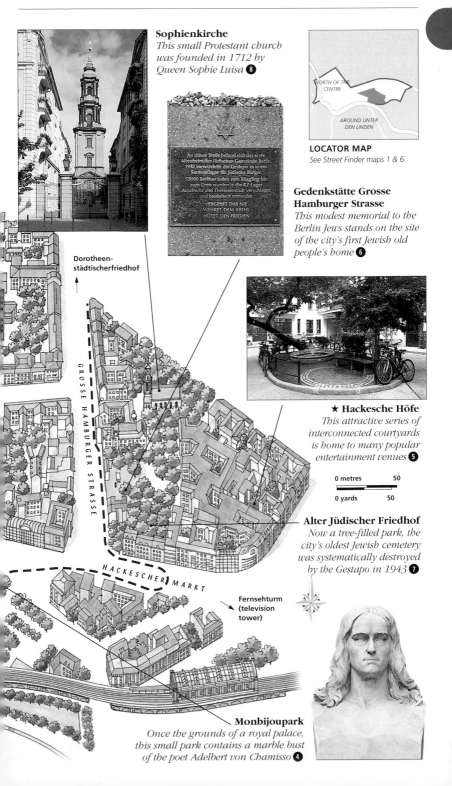

Sophienkirche
This small Protestant church was founded in 1712 by Queen Sophie Luisa **8**

LOCATOR MAP
See Street Finder maps 1 & 6

Gedenkstätte Grosse Hamburger Strasse
This modest memorial to the Berlin Jews stands on the site of the city's first Jewish old people's home **6**

Dorotheen-städtischerfriedhof

GROSSE HAMBURGER STRASSE

★ Hackesche Höfe
This attractive series of interconnected courtyards is home to many popular entertainment venues **5**

0 metres   50

0 yards   50

Alter Jüdischer Friedhof
Now a tree-filled park, the city's oldest Jewish cemetery was systematically destroyed by the Gestapo in 1943 **7**

HACKESCHER MARKT

Fernsehturm (television tower)

Monbijoupark
Once the grounds of a royal palace, this small park contains a marble bust of the poet Adelbert von Chamisso **4**

Neue Synagoge ❶

NEW SYNAGOGUE

Oranienburger Strasse 30. **Map** 7 A1.
Tel 880 28 316. Ⓢ Oranienburger
Strasse. 🚋 1, 6, 13. ⏰ 10am–
6pm Sun–Thu, 10am–2pm Fri.
🎦 ⚫ Jewish festivals. 📷

The building of the New
Synagogue was started in
1859 by architect Eduard
Knoblauch, and completed in
1866. The design was a highly
sophisticated response to the
asymmetrical shape of the
plot of land, with a narrow
façade flanked by a pair of
towers and crowned with a
dome containing a round
vestibule. A series of small
rooms opened off the
vestibule, including an ante-
room and two prayer rooms –
one large and one small. The
two towers opened onto a
staircase leading to the
galleries, and the main hall
had space for around 3,000
worshippers. An innovative use
of iron in the construction of
the roof and galleries put the
synagogue at the forefront of
19th-century civil engineering.

With its gilded dome, this
fascinating structure was
Berlin's largest synagogue, until
9 November 1938, when it
was partially destroyed during
the infamous *"Kristallnacht"*
(see pp28–9). The building
was damaged further by Allied
bombing in 1943 and was
finally demolished in 1958 by
government authorities.

Reconstruction started in
1988 and was completed with
due ceremony in 1995. The
front of the building is now
used for public exhibitions by
the Centrum Judaicum.

The Centrum Judaicum, centre for research into Jewish heritage

Centrum Judaicum ❷

JEWISH CENTRE

Oranienburger Strasse 28–30. **Map** 7
A1. **Tel** 880 28 316. Ⓢ Oranienburger
Strasse. 🚋 1, 6, 13. ⏰ 10am–8pm
(6pm in winter) Sun–Mon, 10am–6pm
Tue–Thu, 10am–2pm (2pm in winter)
Fri. 🎦 ⚫ Jewish festivals. 📷

The entrance to the Jewish
Centre is easy to recognize
thanks to the policemen
permanently stationed here.
All visitors must undergo a
strict security check involving
the use of a metal detector,
which is conducted by guards
who are polite but firm. The
Centrum Judaicum occupies
the former premises of the
Jewish community council,
and contains a library and
archives and a research centre
devoted to the history and
cultural heritage of the Berlin
Jews. Next door to the
Centrum, the restored rooms
of the Neue Synagoge are
used to exhibit material
relating to the local Jewish
community, including one of

the greatest of all Jewish
thinkers and social activists,
Moses Mendelssohn. Next to
the Centrum is the well-
known Oren restaurant, which
serves Jewish and Middle
Eastern cuisine *(see p238)*.

Oranienburger Strasse ❸

Map 6 F1, 7 A1 & 7 B2.
Ⓢ Oranienburger Strasse or
Hackescher Markt. 🚋 1, 6, 13.

Oranienburger Strasse is
home to many of Berlin's
most popular nightspots.
People of all ages flock here,
spending pleasant hours in
the area's numerous cafés,
restaurants and bars. The
district has traditionally been
a centre for alternative
culture, home to the famous
state-sponsored Tacheles
centre for the arts. The life
of the Tacheles centre may
now be coming to an end,
but many good art galleries
remain in this area. As you
stroll around the district it is
worth looking out for a

The Neue Synagoge with its
splendidly reconstructed dome

MOSES MENDELSSOHN (1729–1786)

One of the greatest German philosophers
of the 18th century, Moses Mendelssohn
arrived in Berlin in 1743 and was a
central figure in the Jewish struggle
for citizenship rights. About 50 years
later the first Jewish family was
granted full civic rights, however, it
wasn't until the Emancipation Edict of
1812 that Jewish men finally became full citizens. The
grandfather of composer Felix Mendelssohn-Bartholdy, he
is immortalized in the drama "Nathan der Weise" (Nathan
the Wise) by his friend Gotthold Ephraim Lessing.

number of interesting buildings, such as the one at Oranienburger Strasse No. 71–2, which was built by Christian Friedrich Becherer in 1789 for the Great National Masonic Lodge of Germany.

Monbijoupark ❹

MONBIJOU PARK

Oranienburger Strasse. **Map** 7 B2. Ⓢ *Oranienburger Strasse or Hackescher Markt.* 🚊 *1, 6, 13.*

This small park, situated between Oranienburger Strasse and the Spree river, was once the grounds of the Monbijou Palace. Damaged by bombing during World War II, the ruined palace was finally dismantled in 1960. A rare green space in this part of the city, the well-kept park makes a pleasant place to spend some time relaxing. It features a marble bust of the poet Adelbert von Chamisso, and there is also a swimming pool for children.

Hackesche Höfe ❺

Rosenthaler Strasse 40–41. **Map** 7 B1 7 B2. Ⓢ *Hackescher Markt.* 🚊 *1, 6, 13.*

Running from Oranienburger Strasse and Rosenthaler up as far as Sophienstrasse, the Hackesche Höfe (*Höfe* means yards) is a huge, early 20th-century complex. It is made up of an intricate series of nine interconnecting

One of the striking inner courtyards at the Hackesche Höfe

courtyards surrounded by tall and beautifully proportioned buildings. The development dates from 1906, and was designed by Kurt Berendt and August Endell, both of whom were outstanding exponents of the German Secession style.

Damaged during World War II, Hackesche Höfe has been restored recently to its original splendour. The first courtyard is especially attractive, featuring glazed facings with geometric designs decorated in fabulous colours. A whole range of restaurants, bars, art galleries, shops and restaurants can be found here, as well as offices and apartments on the upper floors. The complex also has its own theatre, the Hackesche Hoftheater, specializing in mime. For many Berliners the Hackesche Höfe has become something of a cult spot, and for visitors it is definitely a sight not to be missed.

Gedenkstätte Grosse Hamburger Strasse ❻

GROSSE HAMBURGER STRASSE MEMORIAL

Grosse Hamburger Strasse. **Map** 7 B1. Ⓢ *Hackescher Markt.* 🚊 *1, 6, 13.*

Until the years leading up to World War II, Grosse Hamburger Strasse was one of the main streets of Berlin's Jewish quarter. It was home to several Jewish schools, an old people's home and the city's oldest Jewish cemetery, established in 1672. The home was used during World War II as a detention centre for many thousands of Berlin Jews condemned to death in the camps at Auschwitz and Theresienstadt. The building was later destroyed, and in its place now stands a small monument representing a group of Jews being led to their deaths. A modest commemorative plaque is displayed nearby.

Nearby, at Grosse Hamburger Strasse No. 27, stands a Jewish school, originally founded in 1778 by Moses Mendelssohn. Rebuilt in 1906, the building was reopened as a Jewish secondary school in 1993. The empty space once occupied by house No. 15–16, which was destroyed by World War II bombing, is now an installation, *"The Missing House"* by Christian Boltanski, with plaques recording the names and professions of the former inhabitants of the house.

The Gedenkstätte Grosse Hamburger Strasse commemorating Berlin Jews murdered in the Holocaust

Alter Jüdischer Friedhof **7**

OLD JEWISH CEMETERY

Grosse Hamburger Strasse. **Map** 7 B2. Ⓢ *Hackescher Markt.* 🚊 *1, 6, 13.*

The Old Jewish Cemetery was established in 1672 and, until 1827 when it was finally declared full, it provided the resting place for over 12,000 Berliners. After this date Jews were buried in cemeteries in Schönhauser Allee and in Herbert-Baum-Strasse. The Alter Jüdischer Friedhof was destroyed by the Nazis in 1943, and in 1945 the site was turned into a park. Embedded in the original cemetery wall, a handful of Baroque *masebas* (or tombstones) continue to provide a poignant reminder of the past. A new *maseba* stands on the grave of the philosopher Moses Mendelssohn *(see p102)*, erected in 1990 by members of the Jewish community.

Tombstone of Moses Mendelssohn

Sophienkirche **8**

Grosse Hamburger Str. 29. **Map** 7 B1. **Tel** 308 79 20. Ⓢ *Hackescher Markt.* Ⓤ *Weinmeisterstrasse.* 🚊 *13, 53.* ◻ *May–Oct: 3–6pm Wed, 3–5pm Sat, 11:30am–1pm Sun.* ✝ *10am Sun.*

A narrow passageway and a picturesque gate take you through to this small Baroque church. Founded in 1712 by

Interior of the Sophienkirche with its original 18th-century pulpit

Eighteenth-century buildings along Sophienstrasse

Queen Sophie Luisa, this was the first parish church of the newly developed Spandauer Vorstadt area *(see p99)*. Johann Friedrich Grael designed the tower which was built between 1729 and 1735.

In 1892 the building was extended to include a new presbytery, though the church still retains its original Baroque character. A modest, rectangular structure, Sophienkirche is typical of its period, with the tower adjoining the narrower side elevation. The interior still contains a number of its original 18th-century furnishings, including the pulpit and the font.

Several gravestones, some from the 18th century, have survived in the small cemetery surrounding the church.

Sophienstrasse **9**

Map 7 B1. **Sammlung Hoffmann** Sophienstrasse 21. **Tel** 284 99 121. Ⓢ *Hackescher Markt.* Ⓤ *Weinmeisterstrasse.* 🚊 *13, 53.* ◻ *11am–4pm Sat, by appointment.* 📷

The area around Sophienstrasse and Gipsstrasse was first settled at the end of the 17th century. In fact, Sophienstrasse was once the main street of Spandauer Vorstadt. The area underwent extensive restoration during the 1980s. It was one of the

first parts of East Berlin in which renovation was chosen in favour of large-scale demolition and redevelopment. Now these modest but charming 18th-century Neo-Classical buildings are home to a number of different arts and crafts workshops, cosy bars, unusual boutiques and interesting art galleries.

One building with a particularly eventful history is Sophienstrasse No. 18. The house was erected in 1852, although its striking and picturesque, terracotta double doorway dates from the time of its extensive restoration. This was undertaken in 1904 by Joseph Franckel and Theodor Kampfmeyer on behalf of the Crafts Society. Founded in 1844, the Crafts Society moved its headquarters to Sophienstrasse in 1905. On 14 November 1918 the very same house was used as the venue for the first meeting of the Spartacus League *(see p132)*, which was later to become the Communist Party of Germany.

The main door of the house at Sophienstrasse No. 21 leads into a long row of interior courtyards running up as far as Gipsstrasse. In one of these courtyards is a private modern art gallery, the **Sammlung Hoffmann**, which can be reached by passing through a brightly-lit tunnel.

Alte and Neue Schönhauser Strasse ⑩

Map 7 B1, 7 C1. Ⓢ *Hackescher Markt.* Ⓤ *Weinmeisterstrasse.* 🚋 *1, 7.*

Alte Schönhauser Strasse is one of the oldest streets in the Spandauer Vorstadt district, running from the centre of Berlin to Pankow and Schönhausen. In the 18th and 19th centuries this was a popular residential area among wealthy merchants. The proximity of the neighbouring slum area of the Scheunen-viertel *(see pp100–3)* to the west, however, lowered the tone of the neighbourhood quite considerably.

For a long time, bars, small factories, workshops and retail shops were the hallmark of the neighbourhood around Alte Schönhauser Strasse. Small private shops survived longer here than in most other parts of Berlin, and until recently the largely original houses maintained much of their pre-1939 atmosphere.

Much has changed, however, since the fall of the Berlin Wall. Some of the houses have now been restored, and many old businesses have been replaced by fashionable new shops, restaurants and bars. Throughout the district, the old and the new now stand side by side. One poignant example is at Neue

The *Schwarzen Raben* restaurant on Neue Schönhauser Strasse

Schönhauser Strasse No. 14. This interesting old house in the German Neo-Renaissance style was built in 1891 to a design by Alfred Messel. The first-floor rooms were home to the first public reading-room in Berlin, while on the ground floor was a *Volkskaffeehaus,* a soup-kitchen with separate rooms for men and women. Here the poor of the neigh-bourhood could get a free bowl of soup and a cup of ersatz (imitation) coffee.

Today, ironically, the building is home to one of Berlin's most fashionable restaurants, the Schwarzen Raben *(see p239).*

Volksbühne ⑪

PEOPLE'S THEATRE

Rosa-Luxemburg-Platz. **Map** 8 D1. *Tel 24 06 55.* Ⓤ *Rosa-Luxemburg-Platz.* 🚌 *100, 200, 340, 348.* 🚋 *1, 7, 8.*

Founded during the early years of the 20th century, this theatre owes its existence to the efforts of the 100,000 members of the Freie Volks-bühne (Free People's Theatre Society). The original theatre was built to a design by Oskar Kaufmann in 1913, a time when the Scheunen-viertel district was undergoing rapid redevelopment. During the 1920s the theatre became famous thanks to the director Erwin Piscator (1893–1966), who later achieved great acclaim at the Metropol-Theater on Nollendorfplatz.

Destroyed during World War II, the theatre was eventually rebuilt during the early 1950s to a new design by Hans Richter.

The eye-catching façade of the Friedrichstadtpalast theatre complex

Friedrichstadt-palast ⑫

FRIEDRICHSTADT PALACE

Friedrichstrasse 107. **Map** 6 F2. *Tel 23 26 23 26.* Ⓤ *Oranienburger Tor.* Ⓢ *Oranienburger Strasse or Friedrichstrasse.* 🚌 *147.* 🚋 *1, 53.*

Multi-coloured glass tiles and a pink, plume-shaped neon sign make up the gaudy but eye-catching façade of the Friedrichstadt-palast. Built in the early 1980s, this gigantic theatre complex specializes in revues and variety shows. Nearly 2,000 seats are arranged around a huge podium, used by turns as a circus arena, a swimming pool and an ice-rink. In addition, a further huge stage is equipped with every technical facility. There is also a small cabaret theatre with seats for 240 spectators.

The original and much-loved Friedrichstadtpalast suffered bomb damage during World War II, and was later condemned and replaced with the existing version. Built as a market hall, the earlier building was later used as a circus ring. In 1918 it became the Grosse Schau-spielhaus, or Grand Playhouse, opening on 28 November 1919 with a memorable production of Aeschylus' *The Oresteia* directed by the extraordinary Max Reinhardt *(see p108).*

The building itself was legendary, its central dome supported by a forest of columns and topped with an Expressionist, stalactite-like decoration. An equally fantastical interior provided seating for 5,000 spectators.

Dorotheenstädtischer Friedhof ⓖ

This small cemetery, established in 1763, is the final resting place of many famous Berlin citizens. It was enlarged between 1814 and 1826, but in 1899, following the extension of Hannoversche Strasse, the southern section of the cemetery was sold and its graves moved. Many of the monuments are outstanding works of art, coming from the workshops of some of the most prominent Berlin architects, including Karl Friedrich Schinkel *(see p187)* and Johann Gottfried Schadow. A tranquil, tree-filled oasis, the cemetery is reached via a narrow path, leading from the street, between the wall of the French Cemetery and the Brecht-Weigel-Gedenkstätte house *(see p109).*

Copy of Schadow's Martin Luther

★ Johann Gottfried Schadow (1764–1850)
Schadow created the famous Quadriga, which adorns the Brandenburg Gate.

Friedrich August Stüler (1800–1865)
Damaged during World War II, the grave of this famous architect was rebuilt in a colourful, post-modernist style.

Heinrich Mann (1871–1950)
This famous German novelist died in California but was buried in Berlin. The portrait is the work of Gustav Seitz.

Bertolt Brecht (1898–1956)
The grave of this famous playwright is marked with a rough stone. Beside him rests his wife, the actress Helene Weigel.

Hermann Wentzel (1820–1889)
This architect designed his own tombstone; the bust was carved by Fritz Schaper.

Main entrance

Friedrich Hoffmann
(1818–1900)
The tomb of this engineer, best known as the inventor of the circular brick-firing kiln, takes the form of a colonnade faced with glazed bricks.

VISITORS' CHECKLIST

Chausseestrasse 126. **Map** 6 F1.
Tel 461 72 79. 832 51 01.
Zinnowitzerstrasse or Oranienburger Tor. 340. 6, 13, 50. May–Aug: 8am–8pm; Sep–Apr: 8am until dusk.

★ Karl Friedrich Schinkel
(1781–1841)
Schinkel was the most prominent German architect of his time, and the creator of many of Berlin's best-loved buildings.

Georg Wilhelm Friedrich Hegel
(1770–1831)
Probably the greatest German philosopher of the Enlightenment era, Hegel worked for many years as a professor at Berlin University.

BIRKENALLEE

Luther's statue
is a copy of the monument designed by JG Schadow.

Chapel

Johann Gottlieb Fichte
(1762–1814)
A well-known philosopher of the Enlightenment era, Fichte was also the first Rector of Berlin University.

STAR FEATURES

★ JG Schadow

★ KF Schinkel

0 metres   20
0 yards   20

Bertolt Brecht's monument in front of the Berliner Ensemble

Berliner Ensemble ⑬

Bertolt-Brecht-Platz 1. **Map** 6 F2.
Tel 28 40 81 55. ⑤ & Ⓤ
Friedrichstrasse. 🚌 147. 🚊 1, 50.

Designed by Heinrich Seeling in the Neo-Baroque style and built from 1891 to 1892, this theatre has been witness to many changes in Berlin's cultural life. First known as the Neues Theater am Schiffbauerdamm, it soon became famous for staging important premieres. In 1895 it put on the first performance of *The Weavers*, by Gerhart Hauptmann. Later on, the theatre was acclaimed for its memorable productions by Max Reinhardt. These included Shakespeare's *A Midsummer Night's Dream* in 1905 which, for the first time, used a revolving stage and real trees as part of the set. In 1928 the theatre presented the world premiere of Bertolt

Brecht's *The Threepenny Opera*. The building was destroyed during World War II and subsequently restored with a much simpler exterior, but its Neo-Baroque interior, including Ernst Westphal's decorations, survived intact. After 1954 the theatre returned to prominence with the arrival of the Berliner Ensemble under the directorship of Bertolt Brecht and his wife, the actress Helene Weigel. The move from its former home, the Deutsches Theater, to the new venue was celebrated in November 1954, by staging the world premiere of *The Caucasian Chalk Circle*, written by Brecht in 1947. After Brecht's death his wife took over running the theatre, maintaining its innovative tradition.

Deutsches Theater ⑭

Schumannstrasse 13A. **Map** 6 E2.
Tel 28 44 12 25. **Kammerspiele**
Ⓤ Oranienburger Tor. 🚌 147.

The building currently used by the theatre was designed by Eduard Titz and built between 1849 and 1850 to house the Friedrich-Wilhelm Städtisches Theater. In 1883, following substantial recon-struction, it was renamed Deutsches Theater and opened with Friedrich Schiller's *Intrigue and Love*. The theatre became famous under its next director, Otto Brahm, and it was here that Max Reinhardt began his career as an actor, before

eventually becoming director from 1905 until 1933. On Reinhardt's initiative the theatre's façade was altered and in 1906 the adjacent casino was converted into a compact theatre – the Kammerspiele. At the time, the first-floor audi-torium was decorated with a frieze by Edvard Munch (now in the Neue Nationalgalerie).

Another famous figure associated with the Deutsches Theater was Bertolt Brecht who, until 1933, wrote plays for it; after World War II he became the director of the Berliner Ensemble, whose first venue was the Deutsches Theater. Brecht's debut as director was his play, *Mother Courage and Her Children*.

Elegant 19th-century façade of the Deutsches Theater

Charité ⑮

Schumannstrasse 20–21. **Map** 6 E1, E2.
Tel 450 53 61 56. Ⓤ Oranienburger Tor.
🚌 147. 🕐 10am–5pm Tue, Thu–Sun, 10am–7pm Wed.

This huge building complex near Luisenstrasse contains the Charité hospital. Germany's oldest teaching hospital, it was first established in 1726 and has been attached to the Humboldt University (*see p60*) since its foundation in 1810. The oldest buildings of the current complex date back to the 1830s. Over the years, Charité has been associated with many famous German doctors and scientists who worked here, including Rudolf Virchow and Robert Koch.

In 1899 Virchow founded the Museum of Pathology, which occupied purpose-built premises next to the Institute of Pathology. Its collection consisted of some 23,000 specimens, which were also available for public viewing.

MAX REINHARDT (1873–1943)

This actor and director became famous as one of the 20th century's greatest theatre reformers. He worked in Berlin, first as an actor in the Deutsches Theater, and then from 1905 as its director. As well as setting up the Kammerspiele, he produced plays for the Neues Theater am Schiffbauerdamm (renamed the Berliner Ensemble) and the Schumann Circus (later to become the Friedrichstadtpalast), which was converted specially for him by Hans Poelzig. His experimental productions of classic and modern works brought him world-wide fame. Forced to emigrate because of his Jewish origins, he left Germany in 1933 and settled in the United States, where he died in 1943.

Although many artifacts were destroyed in World War II, the museum itself has survived and was reopened in 1999.

Dorotheenstädt-ischer Friedhof ⑯

See pp106–107.

Brecht-Weigel-Gedenkstätte ⑰

BRECHT-WEIGEL MEMORIAL

Chausseestrasse 125. **Tel** *283 057 044.* **Map** *6 E1.* **U** *Zinnowitzer Strasse or Oranienburger Tor.* 🚌 *340.* 🚊 *6, 13, 50.* ○ *10am–noon Tue–Fri, also 5–7pm Thu, 9:30am–2pm Sat, 11am–6pm Sun.* 🎟 *compulsory. Every half hour (every hour on Sun).* ● *Mon, public hols.* 📷

Brachiosaurus skeleton in the Museum für Naturkunde

Bertolt Brecht, one of the greatest playwrights of the 20th century, was associated with Berlin from 1920, but emigrated in 1933. After the war, his left-wing views made him an attractive potential resident of the newly created German socialist state. Lured by the promise of his own theatre he returned to Berlin in 1948, with his wife, actress Helene Weigel. Working as the director of the Berliner Ensemble until his death, he concentrated mainly on the production of his plays.

In 1953 he moved into a first-floor apartment at Chausseestrasse 125 and lived here until his death in 1956. He is buried in Dorotheen-städtischer Friedhof *(see pp106–7).* His wife lived in the second-floor apartment, and after Brecht's death moved to the ground floor. She also founded an archive of Brecht's works which is located on the second floor of the building.

Museum für Naturkunde ⑱

NATURAL HISTORY MUSEUM

Invalidenstrasse 43. **Map** *6 E1.* **Tel** *20 93 85 91.* **U** *Zinnowitzer Strasse.* 🚌 *147, 245.* ○ *9:30am–5pm Tue–Fri, 10am–6pm Sat & Sun.* 📷

One of the biggest natural history museums in the world, the collection here contains over 60 million exhibits. Occupying a purpose-built Neo-Renaissance building, constructed between 1883 and 1889, the museum has been operating for over a century, and although it has undergone several periods of extension and renovation, it has maintained its unique old-fashioned atmosphere.

The highlight of the museum is the world's largest original dinosaur skeleton which is housed in the glass-covered courtyard. This colossal 23-m (75-ft) long and 12-m (39-ft) high brachiosaurus was discovered in Tanzania in 1909 by a German fossil-hunting expedition. Six other smaller reconstructed dinosaur skeletons and a replica of the fossilized remains of an archaeopteryx, thought to be the prehistoric link between reptiles and birds, complete this fascinating display.

The adjacent rooms feature extensive collections of colourful shells and butterflies, as well as stuffed birds and mammals. Particularly popular are the dioramas – scenes of stuffed animals set against the background of their natural habitat. A favourite with young children is Bobby the Gorilla, who was brought to Berlin Zoo in 1928 as a 2-year old and lived there until 1935. The museum also boasts an impressive collection of minerals and meteorites.

Bertolt Brecht's study in his former apartment

Hamburger Bahnhof ⑲

This museum is situated in a specially adapted Neo-Renaissance building that was formerly the Hamburg Railway station, which dates from 1847. Following extensive refurbishment by Josef Paul Kleihues, it was opened to the public in 1996. The neon installation surrounding the façade is the work of Dan Flavin. The museum has works by Joseph Beuys, contemporary art donated by the Neue Nationalgalerie and, until 2011, a continually changing selection from the world-renowned Flick Collection of art from the second half of the 20th century. The result is one of the best modern art museums in Europe, which features film, video, music and design alongside painting and sculpture.

★ **Richtkräfte** (1974–77)
Joseph Beuys' work – often a record of his thoughts – created an archive of the artist's vision.

Untitled (1983)
This is a fine example of Anselm Kiefer's work, which often attempts to come to terms with Germany's past.

GALLERY GUIDE
The gallery has over 10,000 sq m (108,000 sq ft) of exhibition space. The west wing contains works by Beuys and the main hall is used for special installations. The Rieck-hallen shows selected works from the Flick Collection in rotation.

First floor

Rieckhallen

Ground floor

Genova (1980)
In this painting, Sandro Chia contrasts a finely-drawn Renaissance palace with a colourful sky full of movement and two mysteriously floating figures.

Main entrance

Untitled (1983)
Keith Haring uses a simple means of expression, one that is reminiscent of graffiti, comic book art and woodblock prints.

Untitled (1990)
This painting is a fine example of Cy Twombly's distinctive style, characterized by apparently random scrawls and scribbles, rejecting traditional composition.

VISITORS' CHECKLIST

Invalidenstrasse 50/51. **Map** 6 D1.
Ⓢ *Lehrter Stadtbahnhof.* 🚌 *245, 340.* **Tel** *20 90 55 66.* ⏲ *10am– 6pm Tue–Fri, 11am–6pm Sat & Sun.* ⦿ *1 Jan, Tue following Easter and Whitsun, 24, 25 & 31 Dec.* 🍴 ♿ 🛗 ⛰ 📷 **www**.hamburgerbahnhof.de

Bourgeois Bust – Jeff and Ilona (1991)
The Rococo-style marble bust by Jeff Koons depicts himself with his wife at the time, Ilona, better known as La Cicciolina. The sculpture is deliberately pretentious and tawdry.

Second floor

Not Wanting to Say Anything About Marcel (1969)
John Cage created this work after the death of his friend, the famous artist Marcel Duchamp.

★ **Mao** (1973)
This well-known portrait by Andy Warhol initially elevated the Chinese communist leader to the rank of pop icon.

First Time Painting (1961)
This work by American artist Robert Rauschenberg was created while he worked with John Cage at Black Mountain College.

KEY

	Exhibitions
	Flick Collection

STAR EXHIBITS

★ Mao

★ Richtkräfte

TIERGARTEN

Once a royal hunting estate, the Tiergarten became a park in the 18th century. In the 19th century a series of buildings, mostly department stores and banks, was erected at Potsdamer Platz. During World War II many of these buildings were destroyed. The division of Berlin changed the character of the area. The Tiergarten area ended up on the west side of the Wall, and later regained its glory with the creation of the Kulturforum and the Hansaviertel. The area around Potsdamer Platz fell in East Berlin, and became a wasteland. Since reunification, however, this area has witnessed exciting development. Together with the new government offices near the Reichstag, this ensures that the Tiergarten area is at the centre of Berlin's political and financial district.

The Caller, on Strasse des 17 Juni

SIGHTS AT A GLANCE

Museums and Galleries
Bauhaus-Archiv ⓮
Bendlerblock (Gedenkstätte Deutscher Widerstand) ⓬
Gemäldegalerie pp122–5 ❽
Kunstbibliothek ❻
Kunstgewerbemuseum pp118–21 ❹
Kupferstichkabinett ❺
Musikinstrumenten-Museum ❷
Neue Nationalgalerie ❾

Districts, Squares and Parks
Diplomatenviertel ⓯
Grosser Stern ⓱
Hansaviertel ⓳

Potsdamer Platz pp128–31 ❿
Regierungsviertel ㉒
Tiergarten ⓰

Historic Buildings
Haus der Kulturen der Welt ㉑

Philharmonie und Kammermusiksaal ❸
Reichstag ㉓
Shell-Haus ⓫
Schloss Bellevue ⓴
Staatsbibliothek ❼
St-Matthäus-Kirche ❼
Villa von der Heydt ⓭

Monuments
Siegessäule ⓲
Sowjetisches Ehrenmal ㉔

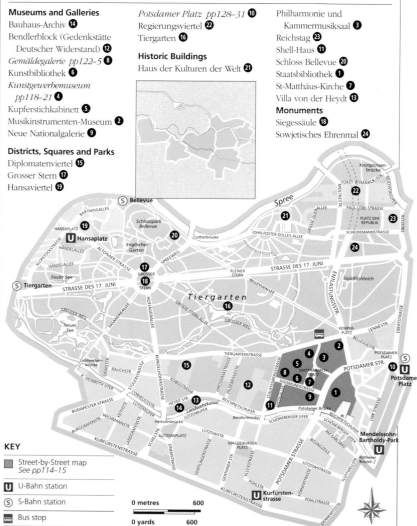

KEY

▨	Street-by-Street map See pp114–15
Ⓤ	U-Bahn station
Ⓢ	S-Bahn station
	Bus stop

0 metres   600
0 yards   600

◁ **One of the many charming stretches of water in the Tiergarten**

Street-by-Street: Around the Kulturforum

Sculpture by Henry Moore

The idea of creating a new cultural centre in West Berlin was first mooted in 1956. The first building to go up was the Berlin Philharmonic concert hall, built to an innovative design by Hans Scharoun in 1961. Most of the plans for the various other components of the Kulturforum were realized between 1961 and 1987, and came from such famous architects as Ludwig Mies van der Rohe. The area is now a major cultural centre which attracts millions of visitors every year.

★ Kunstgewerbe-museum
Among the collection at the Museum of Arts and Crafts you can see this intricately carved silver and ivory tankard, made in an Augsburg workshop in around 1640 ❹

Kupferstichkabinett
The large collection of prints and drawings owned by this gallery includes this portrait of Albrecht Dürer's mother ❺

★ Gemäldegalerie
Among the most important works of the Old Masters exhibited in this gallery of fine art is this Madonna in Church *by Jan van Eyck (circa 1425)* ❽

Kunstbibliothek
The Art Library boasts a rich collection of books, graphic art and drawings, many of which are displayed in its exhibition halls ❻

REICHPIETSCHUFER

LANDWEHRKANAL

STAR SIGHTS

★ Gemäldegalerie

★ Kunstgewerbe-museum

★ Philharmonie

KEY

– – – Suggested route

Neue Nationalgalerie
Sculptures by Henry Moore and Alexander Calder stand outside this streamlined building, designed by Ludwig Mies van der Rohe ❾

★ Philharmonie
Its outside covered in a layer of golden aluminium, the Berlin Philharmonic concert hall is known all over the world for its superb acoustics ❸

LOCATOR MAP
See Street Finder maps 4, 5 & 6

Musikinstrumenten-Museum
This harpsichord is part of a collection of musical instruments dating from the 16th to 20th centuries ❷

St-Matthäus-Kirche
This picturesque 19th-century church stands out among the modern buildings of the Kulturforum ❼

SCHAROUNSTRASSE

POTSDAMER STRASSE

MATTHÄI-KIRCH PLATZ

SMUNDSTRASSE

POTSDAMER STRASSE

0 metres 50
0 yards 50

Staatsbibliothek
Hans Scharoun designed this public lending and research library built in 1978 ❶

The main reading room in the Staatsbibliothek

Staatsbibliothek ❶

STATE LIBRARY

Potsdamer Strasse 33. **Map** 6 D5.
Tel 266 23 03. Ⓢ & Ⓤ *Potsdamer Platz.* 🚌 *129, 148, 200, 348.*
◖ *9am–9pm Mon–Fri, 9am–7pm Sat.*

An unusual-shaped building with an east facing gilded dome, the Staatsbibliothek is home to one of the largest collections of books and manuscripts in Europe and is fondly referred to by Berliners as the Stabi. After World War II, East and West Berlin each inherited part of the pre-war state library collection and the Staatsbibliothek was built to house the part belonging to West Berlin. The building itself was designed by Hans Scharoun and Edgar Wisniewski and constructed between 1967 and 1978.

It is a building where the disciplines of function and efficiency took precedence to that of form. The storerooms hold about five million volumes; the hall of the vast reading room is open plan, with an irregular arrangement of partitions and floor levels; general noise and the sound of footsteps is muffled by fitted carpets, making the interior a very quiet and cosy place in which to work.

The library itself houses more than four million books, and an excellent collection of manuscripts. In recent years the Staatsbibliothek has been formally linked to the Staatsbibliothek on Unter den Linden *(see p61)*.

Musikinstrumen-ten-Museum ❷

MUSEUM OF MUSICAL INSTRUMENTS

Tiergartenstrasse 1. **Map** 6 D5.
Tel 25 48 11 78. Ⓢ & Ⓤ *Potsdamer Platz or* Ⓤ *Mendelssohn-Bartholdy-Park.* 🚌 *129, 148, 200, 348.*
◖ *9am–5pm Tue–Fri, 10am–5pm Sat–Sun.* **Wurlitzer Organ demonstration** *noon Sat.* 📷
♿ 🚻 🅿

Hidden behind the Philharmonie, in a small building designed by Edgar Wisniewski and Hans Scharoun between 1979 and 1984, the fascinating Museum of Musical Instruments houses over 750 exhibits in a collection dating from 1888. Intriguing displays enable you to trace each instrument's development from the 16th century to the present day. You can marvel at the harpsichord of Jean Marius, once owned by Frederick the Great, and the violins made by Amati and Stradivarius.

Most spectacular of all is the silent-film era cinema organ, a working Wurlitzer dating from 1929. With a range of sounds that extends even to loco-motive impressions, the Saturday demonstrations of its powers attract enthusiastic crowds. However, during the the week the sounds of exhibited instruments can be heard on tapes. The museum also has an excellent archive and library open to the public.

Philharmonie und Kammer-musiksaal ❸

PHILHARMONIC AND CHAMBER MUSIC HALL

Herbert-von-Karajan-Str. 1. **Map** 6 D5.
Tel 25 48 81 32. Ⓢ & Ⓤ *Potsdamer Platz or* Ⓤ *Mendelssohn-Bartholdy-Park.* 🚌 *129, 148, 200, 348.*
Home to one of the most renowned orchestras in Europe, this unusual building is among the finest postwar architectural achievements in Europe. The Philharmonie, built between 1960 and 1963 to a design by Hans Scharoun, pioneered a new concept for concert hall interiors. The orchestra's podium occupies the central section of the pentagonal-shaped hall, around which are galleries for the public, designed to blend into the perspective of the five corners.

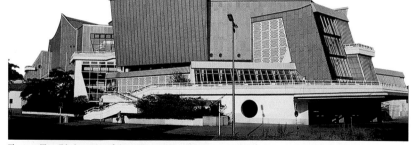

The tent-like gilded exterior of the Philharmonie and Kammermusiksaal

The exterior reflects the interior and is reminiscent of a circus tent. The gilded exterior was added between 1978 and 1981.

The Berlin orchestra was founded in 1882, and has been directed by such luminaries as Hans von Bülow, Wilhelm Furtwängler, the controversial Herbert von Karajan, who led the orchestra from 1954 until his death in 1989, and Claudio Abbado. The current director is Sir Simon Rattle. The orchestra attained renown not only for the quality of its concerts but also through its prolific symphony recordings.

Between the years 1984 to 1987 the Kammermusiksaal, which was designed by Edgar Wisniewski on the basis of sketches by Scharoun, was added to the Philharmonie. This building consolidates the aesthetics of the earlier structure by featuring a central multi-sided space covered by a fanciful tent-like roof.

Kunstgewerbe-museum ❹

MUSEUM OF ARTS AND CRAFTS

See pp118–121.

Kupferstich-kabinett ❺

PRINT GALLERY

Matthäikirchplatz 8. **Map** 5 C5. **Tel** 20 90 55 66. Ⓢ & Ⓤ Potsdamer Platz or Ⓤ Mendelssohn-Bartoldy-Park. 🚍 129, 148, 200, 348. **Exhibitions** 10am–6pm Tue–Fri, 11am–6pm Sat–Sun. 🎨 ♿ 🖼 🛗 📹 🍴 🚫

The print collections of galleries in the former East and West Berlin were united in 1994 in this building located in the Kulturforum. These displays originate from a collection started by the Great Elector in 1652, which has been open to the public since 1831. Despite wartime losses it has an imposing breadth and can boast around 2,000 engraver's plates, over 520,000 prints and at least 80,000 drawings and watercolours.

Edvard Munch's *Girl on a Beach*, a coloured lithograph

Unfortunately, only a small fraction of these delicate treasures can be even briefly exposed to daylight. Therefore the museum does not have a permanent exhibition, only galleries with temporary displays of selected works. For those with a special interest, items in storage can be viewed in the studio gallery by prior arrangement.

The collection includes work from every renowned artist from the Middle Ages to contemporary times. Well represented is the work of Botticelli (including illustrations for Dante's *Divine Comedy*), Dürer, Rembrandt and the Dutch Masters, Watteau, Goya, Daumier, and painters of the Brücke art movement.

Kunstbibliothek ❻

ART LIBRARY

Matthäikirchplatz 6. **Map** 5 C5. **Tel** 20 90 55 55. Ⓢ & Ⓤ Potsdamer Platz or Ⓤ Mendelssohn-Bartoldy-Park. 🚍 129, 148, 200, 348. **Exhibits** 10am–6pm Tue–Fri, 11am–6pm Sat, Sun. **Library** 2–8pm Mon, 9am–4pm Tue–Fri. 🎨

The Kunstbibliothek is not only a library with a wide range of publications about the arts, it is also a museum with a huge collection of posters, advertisements and an array of other forms of design. Worth seeing is a display on the history of fashion, as well as a vast collection of items of architectural interest. The

latter includes around 30,000 original plans and drawings by architects such as Johann Balthasar Neumann, Erich Mendelssohn and Paul Wallot.

The exhibitions can be seen in the reading and studio rooms, although parts of the collection are also exhibited in the library's own galleries.

St-Matthäus-Kirche ❼

ST MATTHEW'S CHURCH

Matthäikirchplatz. **Map** 5 C5. **Tel** 262 12 02. Ⓢ & Ⓤ Potsdamer Platz or Ⓤ Mendelssohn-Bartoldy-Park. 🚍 129, 148, 200, 348. 🕐 noon–6pm Tue–Sun, and for services.

St Matthew's Church once stood in the centre of a small square surrounded by buildings. After bomb damage in World War II, the structure was restored, making it the focal point of the Kulturforum. The church was originally built between 1844 and 1846 to a design by Friedrich August Stüler and Hermann Wentzel in a style based on Italian Romanesque temples.

Each of the three naves is covered by a separate two-tier roof, while the eastern end of the church is closed by a semi-circular apse. The exterior of the church is covered in a two-tone brick façade arranged in yellow and red lines. Ironically, this picturesque church with its slender tower now creates quite an exotic element among the many ultramodern and sometimes extravagant buildings of the Kulturforum complex.

The colourful exterior of the St-Matthäus-Kirche

Kunstgewerbemuseum ❹

The Museum of Arts and Crafts holds a rich collection embracing many genres of craft and decorative art, from the early Middle Ages to the modern day. Goldwork is especially well represented, as are items made from other metals during the Middle Ages. Among the most valuable exhibits is a collection of medieval goldwork from the church treasuries of Enger near Herford, and the Guelph treasury from Brunswick. The museum also takes great pride in its collection of late-Gothic and Renaissance silver from the civic treasury in the town of Lüneberg. There are also fine examples of Italian majolica, and 18th- and 19th-century German, French and Italian glass, porcelain and furniture.

Meissen porcelain figure

★ Domed Reliquary (1175–80)
From the Guelph treasury in Brunswick, the figures in this temple-shaped reliquary are made from walrus ivory.

Main entrance

Minneteppich (c.1430)
The theme of this famous tapestry is courtly love. Amorous couples, accompanied by mythical creatures, converse on topics such as infidelity, their words extending along the banners they hold.

★ Goblet (c.1480)
This glass Gothic goblet was made in Venice and is decorated with scenes from the lives of Adam and Eve.

Lüneburg Lion (1540)
From the civic treasury in Lüneburg, this gold-plated silver jug in the form of a lion was crafted in the workshop of Joachim Worm.

Basement

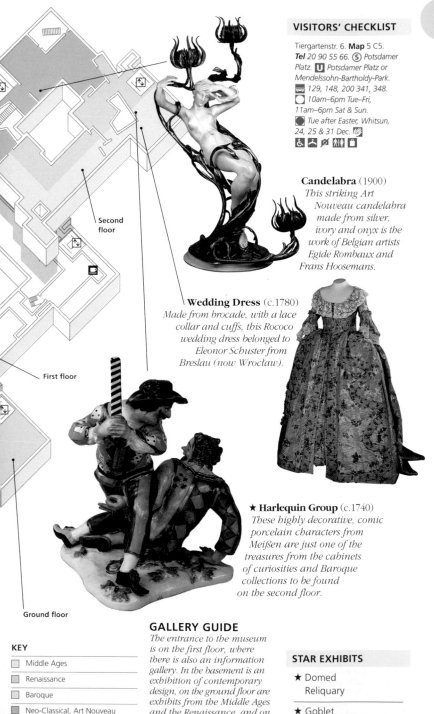

VISITORS' CHECKLIST

Tiergartenstr. 6. **Map** 5 C5.
Tel 20 90 55 66. Ⓢ *Potsdamer
Platz.* Ⓤ *Potsdamer Platz or
Mendelssohn-Bartholdy-Park.*
🚌 *129, 148, 200 341, 348.*
🕙 *10am–6pm Tue–Fri,
11am–6pm Sat & Sun.*
🌑 *Tue after Easter, Whitsun,
24, 25 & 31 Dec.*

Candelabra (1900)
*This striking Art
Nouveau candelabra
made from silver,
ivory and onyx is the
work of Belgian artists
Egide Rombaux and
Frans Hoosemans.*

Wedding Dress (c.1780)
*Made from brocade, with a lace
collar and cuffs, this Rococo
wedding dress belonged to
Eleonor Schuster from
Breslau (now Wrocław).*

★ **Harlequin Group** (c.1740)
*These highly decorative, comic
porcelain characters from
Meißen are just one of the
treasures from the cabinets
of curiosities and Baroque
collections to be found
on the second floor.*

Second floor

First floor

Ground floor

GALLERY GUIDE
*The entrance to the museum
is on the first floor, where
there is also an information
gallery. In the basement is an
exhibition of contemporary
design, on the ground floor are
exhibits from the Middle Ages
and the Renaissance, and on
the second floor are handi-
crafts from the Renaissance
through to Art Nouveau.*

KEY

- ☐ Middle Ages
- ☐ Renaissance
- ☐ Baroque
- ☐ Neo-Classical, Art Nouveau
- ☐ 20th-century
- ☐ Temporary exhibitions

STAR EXHIBITS

- ★ Domed
  Reliquary
- ★ Goblet
- ★ Harlequin Group

Exploring the Kunstgewerbemuseum

Opened in 1867, the Museum of Arts and Crafts was the first of its kind in Germany. It was housed initially in the Martin-Gropius-Bau (*see p140*), then, from 1919 to 1939 it occupied the Stadtschloss (*see p74*), and in 1940 it was moved to Schloss Charlottenburg (*see pp160–61*). The current building, designed by Rolf Gutbrod especially to house the collection, was built between 1978 and 1985. A part of the collection is also now on show in the Schloss Köpenick (*see p175*).

Pendant of the suffering of Christ

northern Germany, acquired by the museum in 1874. Made of gold-plated silver, the set is the work of the skilled metalworkers of the town; some take the form of lions. Also notable are the works of the Nürnberg master craftsmen, above all the renowned Wenzel Jamnitzer and his nephew Christoph Jamnitzer.

As a result of the 16th-century fashion for *Kunstkammern*, or curiosity cabinets, the collection also includes rare examples of naturalistic and exotic creations from other cultures, as well as some unusual technical equipment. Look out for a few pieces from the Pommersche Kunstschrank (curio cabinet), made for a 16th-century Pomeranian prince, Phillip II, as well as a display of 17th-century clocks and scientific instruments.

MIDDLE AGES

A large part of this collection is devoted to sacred art, much of it originating from church treasuries. A fine 8th-century reliquary in the shape of a burse (the container used in the Roman Catholic mass to hold the white linen cloth on which the bread and the wine are placed), comes from the treasury of a church in Enger in Westphalia. More reliquaries, many in the form of crosses, date from the 11th and 12th centuries. Two of the most interesting are the Heinrichskreuz, a gift to the cathedral in Basel from the Roman Emperor Heinrich II, and the Welfenkreuz, which comes from the Guelph treasury in Brunswick. Also from the latter comes a beautiful domed reliquary in the form of a small temple, and a portable altarpiece decorated with enamelwork, produced around 1150 by the craftsman Eilbertus of Cologne.

Exhibits from the Gothic period (12th to 16th centuries) include the stunning reliquary of St George of Elbing, made around 1480. Also fascinating are examples of secular art from this period, including caskets, vessels, a mirror, a knight's amulet and the renowned Minneteppich. This tapestry depicts a number of love scenes, and is designed to hang on the wall above a seat as a decorative means of keeping out draughts.

11th-century reliquary cross

RENAISSANCE

The arts and crafts of the Renaissance period are well represented here. Especially valuable is a collection of Italian majolica, a type of pottery glazed in bright metallic oxides, imported into Tuscany from Majorca in the 15th century. Majolica workshops flourished during the 16th century, and many, including those of Faenza, Cafaggiolo and Urbino, are on show here. Other interesting exhibits in this section are the 15th- and 16th-century Venetian glass, porcelain decorated with enamel work from Limoges in central France, and fine furniture and tapestry collections.

The highlight of the collection is a set of 32 magnificent, richly decorated goblets, bowls and jugs from the civic treasury at Lüneburg in

BAROQUE

Treasures from the Baroque period include an exquisite collection of German and Bohemian glass. A few of the pieces are made from so-called "ruby glass", a technique that was pioneered by Johann Kunckel in the second half of the 17th century.

A varied and rich collection of 18th-century ceramics includes some German faïence work, with amusingly decorated jugs and tankards. The porcelain display begins with a series of Böttger ceramics, the result of some of the very first European

16th-century tapestry entitled *The Triumph of Love*

Desk-board (c.1610–17) from the Pommersche Kunstschrank

various World Fairs that occurred at this time. Of note are the frosted glass vases by French artist Emile Gallé, and pieces by the American Louis Comfort Tiffany, creator of the Favrile style of iridescent stained glass. Also displayed are pieces by the legendary René Lalique, including jewellery and glassware.

An interesting diversion is offered by two entertaining pieces of furniture, both dating from 1885, by the Italian designer, Carlo Bugatti. Taking inspiration from Native American, Islamic and Far Eastern art, Bugatti made unique and spectacular use of rare woods and delicate inlays.

experiments in porcelain production, undertaken by Johann Friedrich Böttger with the assistance of Ehrenfried Walther von Tschirnhaus.

Among some of the finest works from a variety of European factories, the porcelain from the Meißen factory is particularly well represented, with several pieces by one of the most famous Meißen modellers and designers, Johann Joachim Kändler.

Also on show is a fascinating selection of artifacts from the Königliche Porzellan-Manufaktur (Royal Porcelain Factory) in Berlin *(see p133)* which is well-known for its porcelain pieces depicting views of the city.

The collection of porcelain is complemented by a display of silver dishes produced in European work-shops at the same period.

NEO-CLASSICAL REVIVAL AND ART NOUVEAU

A comprehensive collection of late-18th and early-19th century Neo-Classical artifacts includes porcelain from some of the most famous European and Russian factories, French and German silver, as well as comprehensive exhibitions of glassware and furniture.

The Revival movement in central European art and

crafts took place during the second half of the 19th century and is well represented here. A high standard of craftsmanship is seen in the sophisticated Viennese glass and jewellery. The collection also includes furniture made from papier-mâché. This interesting technique was first applied to furniture in England around 1850 and involves a wooden or wire frame which is covered in layers of paste and paper. Decorative techniques include painting and inlaying with mother-of-pearl.

The Secessionist and Art Nouveau movements of the 1890s and 1900s are represented by various artists including Henri van der Velde and Eugène Gaillard. Many pieces were acquired at the

Baroque clock by Johann Gottlieb Graupner (1739)

THE 20TH CENTURY

The years between the two World Wars were a time of mixed trends in the decorative arts. On the one hand the traditions of the 19th-century Historical movement were continued, while on the other many artists were developing a completely new perspective on both form and decoration.

Art Nouveau vase, Emile Gallé (1900)

This part of the museum includes pieces that embody both approaches, but the strongest emphasis is placed on the innovative Art Deco style. Notable examples include a small porcelain tea service by Gertrud Kant, and a silver coffee set decorated with inlaid ebony, designed by Jean Puiforcat.

The museum's unique 20th-century collection has been continually updated since 1945, aiming to document developments in 20th- and 21st-century decorative arts. On display are a wide range of ceramics, furniture by well-known designers, and a variety of items in daily use.

Gemäldegalerie

The Gemäldegalerie collection is exceptional in the consistently high quality of its paintings. Unlike those in many other collections, they were chosen by specialists who, from the beginning of the 19th century, systematically acquired pictures to ensure that all the major European schools of painting were represented. Originally part of the Altes Museum collection

Woman in a Bonnet by Rogier van der Weyden

(see p75), the paintings achieved independent status in 1904 when they were moved to what is now the Bodemuseum (see p79). After the division of Berlin in 1945, part of the collection was kept in the Bodemuseum, while the majority ended up in the Dahlem Museum (see pp178–9). Following reunification, with the building of a new home as part of the Kulturforum development, this unique set of paintings has finally been united again.

★ **Cupid Victorious** (1602)
Inspired by Virgil's Omnia vincit Amor, Caravaggio depicted a playful god, trampling over the symbols of Culture, Fame, Knowledge and Power.

Madonna with Child (c.1477)
A frequent subject of Sandro Botticelli, the Madonna and Child depicted here are surrounded by singing angels holding lilies, symbolizing purity.

Birth of Christ (c.1480)
This beautiful religious painting is one of the few surviving paintings on panels by Martin Schongauer.

Circular lobby leading to the galleries

Portrait of Hieronymus Holzschuher (1529)
Albrecht Dürer painted this affectionate portrait of his friend, who was the mayor of Nuremberg.

Main entrance

The Glass of Wine
(c.1658–61)
Jan Vermeer's carefully composed picture of a young woman drinking wine with a young man gently hints at the relationship developing between them.

VISITORS' CHECKLIST

Stauffenbergstr. 40.
Map 5 C5. *Tel 20 90 55 66.*
Ⓢ & Ⓤ *Potsdamer Platz.*
Ⓤ *Mendelssohn-Bartholdy-Park.*
🚌 *129, 148, 200, 348.*
🕐 *10am–6pm Tue–Sun (to 10pm Thu).* 🔴 *first Tue after Easter and Whitsun, 1 May, 24, 25 & 31 Dec.* 🅿 🍴 🛗 🎧
👫 ♿ 🚫 📷

Love in the French Theatre
This picture has a companion piece called Love in the Italian Theatre *(see p23). Both are the work of French painter, Jean-Antoine Watteau.*

★ Portrait of Hendrickje Stoffels (1656–7)
This portrait of Rembrandt's lover, Hendrickje Stoffels, is typical in that the painter focuses on the subject and ignores the background.

GALLERY GUIDE

The main gallery contains over 900 masterpieces grouped according to their country of origin and period. The educational gallery on the lower floor houses 13th–18th-century European paintings and another digital gallery.

KEY

- ☐ 13th–16th-century German painting
- ☐ 14th–16th-century Dutch and French painting
- ☐ 17th-century Flemish and Dutch painting
- ☐ 18th-century French, English and German painting
- ☐ 17th–18th-century Italian painting, 17th-century German, French and Spanish painting
- ☐ 13th–16th-century Italian painting
- ☐ 16th–18th-century miniatures
- ☐ Digital gallery
- ☐ Non-exhibition space

STAR EXHIBITS

- ★ Cupid Victorious
- ★ Portrait of Hendrickje Stoffels
- ★ Dutch Proverbs

★ Dutch Proverbs (1559)
Pieter Bruegel managed to illustrate more than 100 proverbs in this painting.

Visiting the Gemäldegalerie

The Gemäldegalerie's Modern building was designed by Heinz Hilmer and Christoph Sattler and its exhibition space offers a superb environment in which to view the paintings. The pictures are gently lit by the diffused daylight that streams in from above, while the walls are covered in light-absorbing fabric. The vast hall which occupies the centre of the building allows the visitor to take a break from sightseeing at any time. The hall, with a futuristic sculpture by Walter de Maria set in a water-filled pool, provides an ideal setting for a few moments of quiet contemplation and rest.

Frans Hals' portrait, *Malle Babbe* or *Crazy Babette* (c.1629–30)

Hans Holbein's *Portrait of Georg Gisze* (1532)

GERMAN PAINTING

German paintings are exhibited in several areas of the gallery. The first group comprises art from the 13th–16th centuries. A fine body of religious paintings and altar-pieces contains a historic 13th-century rectangular altarpiece from Westphalia. Other religious artifacts include the side panels of the 15th-century *Wurzach Altar*, ascribed to Hans Multscher, which vividly depict the torment of Christ and the life of the Virgin Mary. A real rarity is the *Nativity* by Martin Schongauer. Often thought of primarily as an engraver, he was one of the most significant painters of the late 15th century but few of his paintings have survived.

Another artist known for his engravings as well as paintings, Albrecht Dürer was a major figure in Renaissance art in northern Europe. His works displayed here include *Madonna with the Siskin*, painted in 1506 while he was visiting Italy, and two later portraits of Nürnberg patriarchs. There are also exhibits by Hans Süss von Kulmbach, Hans Baldung Grien and Albrecht Altdorfer. Among the many works by Lucas Cranach the Elder is the delightful *Fountain of Youth*, from which old women emerge young and beautiful, while men regain their youth through amorous liaisons with the women. Another excellent painting in this collection is a portrait of the Danzig merchant Georg Gisze, painted by Hans Holbein the Younger at a time when both men were living in London. 17th- and 18th-century paintings, including the works of Adam Elsheimer and Johann Heinrich Tischbein, are on show elsewhere.

DUTCH AND FLEMISH PAINTING

The gallery with Dutch and Flemish paintings begins with the captivating canvases of Jan van Eyck. In addition to his precise portraits, you can see here the celebrated *Madonna in a Church*. The high quality of paintings is maintained with the works of Petrus Christus and Rogier van der Weyden. Among the pictures by Hugo van der Goes, the most prized is *The Adoration of the Magi*, once the centre panel of a triptych.

The collection has four paintings by Hans Memling, and also the small *Madonna with Child* painted by one of his pupils, Michel Sittow. There is a large group of paintings by Gerard David, Jan Gossaert and Joos van Cleve. Try to keep an eye out for a modest picture by Hieronymus Bosch called *St John on Patmos*. One of the most outstanding paintings of the collection is Pieter Bruegel the Elder's *Dutch Proverbs*. However, in order to fully appreciate the mastery and humour in this work, make sure you use the accompanying board which explains all the one hundred or so proverbs illustrated here.

Within the large collection of excellent Flemish paintings you can marvel at the Baroque vitality and texture evident in the canvases of friends and

Salomon van Ruysdael's *Riders and Cattle* (1656)

sometime collaborators Petrus Paulus Rubens, Jacob Jordaens, Jan Brueghel the Elder and Frans Snyders. The exceptional portraits of Anton van Dyck, who painted complex, psychologically revealing studies, are indicative of the artist at the height of his powers.

The gallery of 17th-century Dutch paintings probably holds the richest collection in the museum. Included among these are the portraits by Frans Hals, which perfectly illustrate his enormous artistic talents. Excellent examples of his varied work are the vigorous *Malle Babbe (c.1629–30)* – a portrait of the "crazy Babette" of Haarlem.

In fact, all the most famous Dutch painters are represented here but, of course, the works of Jan Vermeer and the master, Rembrandt, attract the greatest amount of interest. The works of Rembrandt include the paintings *Samson and Delilah, Susanna and the Two Elders,* and *Joseph and the Wife of Potiphar.* It is also worth taking time to view the *Man in the Golden Helmet,* a sad yet noble painting originally attributed to Rembrandt. Carbon dating has shown it to be the work of members of his studio. It is a magnificent tribute to his skill as a teacher.

Jean Baptiste Siméon Chardin's The Draughtsman (1737)

FRENCH, ENGLISH AND SPANISH PAINTING

The collection of French art can be found in various parts of the gallery. Paintings of the 15th and 16th century are exhibited alongside Dutch paintings of that era. The oldest works date from the

Titian's Venus with the Organ Player (1550–52)

beginning of the 15th century, and the *Madonna with Child,* dating from c.1410, is one of the oldest preserved works of art painted on a canvas. One of the most valuable French works is by Jean Fouquet, entitled *Étienne Chevalier with Saint Stephen.* Comprising half of the *Diptych of Melun* this is one of Fouquet's few non-miniature paintings.

Nicolas Poussin, the mainspring of the French Classical tradition, and Claude Lorrain, famous for his idealized landscapes, represent 17th-century French painting. Eighteenth-century painting is strongly represented by the canvases of Jean-Antoine Watteau, Jean Baptiste Siméon Chardin and François Boucher.

Two areas in which this collection is less complete are Spanish and English painting. Nevertheless, there is a portrait by Diego Velázquez which is worth seeing, while the English pictures include good portraits by rivals Sir Joshua Reynolds and Thomas Gainsborough.

Sir Joshua Reynolds' Portrait of Lady Sunderlin (1786)

ITALIAN PAINTING

The collection of Italian paintings is fairly comprehensive. There are exemplary works by 14th-century masters, including *Laying the Body to Rest in the Grave* by Giotto and parts of *Scenes from the Life of St Humilitas* by Pietro Lorenzetti. Paintings by Piero della Francesca, Fra Angelico, Masaccio, Andrea del Verrocchio, Sandro Botticelli, and Antonio del Pollaiuolo all represent the 15th century. In this collection you will also find later works by Raphael, including the *Madonna di Casa Colonna,* and the *Madonna di Terranuova,* painted after Raphael's arrival in Florence around 1505. There is also a collection of works by the Venetian Renaissance painter, Giovanni Bellini.

Indeed, the Venetian school in general is well represented: *Portrait of a Young Man* by Giorgione is a vibrant and colourful study; there is also Titian's *Venus and the Organ Player* and Tintoretto's *Virgin and the Child Adored by Saints Mark and Luke.* It is worth comparing Caravaggio's *Cupid Victorious,* whose provocative and distinctly human sexuality contrasts with the spiritual orthodoxy of *Heavenly and Earthly Love,* by Giovanni Baglione. Similar in style, the two paintings convey opposing ideologies. Cardinal Giustiani, whose brother owned Caravaggio's controversial canvas, commissioned the latter painting. Works by Giovanni Battista Tiepolo, Francesco Guardi and Antonio Canaletto represent the art of 18th-century Venice.

Karl Schmidt-Rottluff's *Farm in Daugart* **(1910), Neue Nationalgalerie**

Neue Nationalgalerie ❾

NEW NATIONAL GALLERY

Potsdamer Strasse 50. **Map** 5 C5.
Tel *20 90 55 66.* 🚇 & Ⓢ *Potsdamer Platz or* 🚇 *Mendelssohn-Bartholdy-Park.* 🚌 *129, 148, 200, 341, 348.* ⬜ *10am–6pm Tue–Fri (to 10pm Thu), 11am–6pm Sat & Sun.* 📷 ♿

The magnificent collection of modern art housed in the Neue Nationalgalerie has a troubled history. The core of the collection consisted of 262 paintings that belonged to banker JHW Wagener. In the late 1860s, when Wagener died, he bequeathed them to Crown Prince William, who housed them in the National-galerie on Museum Island.

However, in 1937, a Nazi programme of cultural cleansing meant that many of the works in the collection, which had grown to include paintings by Monet, Manet and Renoir, were confiscated.

After World War II the Berlin municipal authority decided to rebuild the collection and authorized the construction of a suitable building in West Berlin to house it. A commission was given to the elder statesman of modern architecture, the 75-year-old Mies van der Rohe. The result was the first museum in what would later become known as the Kulturforum. The new

national gallery is a striking, minimalist building with a flat steel roof over a glass hall, which appears to float in mid-air supported only by six slender interior struts. The permanent collection is in the basement of the museum, while the spacious ground-level glass hall plays host to temporary exhibitions.

The collection of the Neue Nationalgalerie comprises largely 20th-century art, but begins with artists of the late 19th century, such as Edvard Munch, Ferdinand Hodler and Oskar Kokoschka. German movements, such as Die Brücke, are well represented, with pieces by Ernst Ludwig Kirchner (notably his *Potsdamer Platz*) and Karl Schmidt-Rottluff.

As well as the Bauhaus movement, represented by Paul Klee and Wassily

Kandinsky, the gallery shows works by exponents of a crass realism, such as Otto Dix and Georg Grosz. The most celebrated artists of other European countries are also included in the collection – Pablo Picasso, Ferdinand Léger, and the Surrealists Giorgio de Chirico, Salvador Dalí, René Magritte and Max Ernst. Post-World War II art is represented by the works of Barnett Newman and Frank Stella, among many others. The sculpture garden houses a variety of important works, both figurative and abstract.

Following reunification, a number of new works have been added to the collection. The most recent of these are displayed in the Hamburger Bahnhof branch *(see pp110–11)* of the museum.

Potsdamer Platz ❿

See pp128–131.

Shell-Haus ⓫

Reichpietschufer 60. **Map** 11 C1.
🚇 *Mendelssohn-Bartholdy-Park.* 🚌 *129, 341.*

This is undoubtedly a gem for lovers of the architecture developed during the period between World Wars I and II. This modernist office block was designed by Emil Fahren-kamp. Built from 1930 to 1931, it was one of the first buildings in Berlin to use a steel-frame construction.

The most eye-catching wing extends along Landwehrkanal with a zig-zag elevation; from a height of five storeys it climbs upwards in a series of steps, finishing up ten storeys high.

Damaged during World War II, Shell-Haus went through several stages of restoration and several incarnations, including as headquarters of the German navy and as a military hospital. Beautiful proportions and original design place the structure among the finest of Berlin's buildings of its era.

The impressive exterior of the Shell-Haus office building

The German State Naval Office, now part of the Bendlerblock complex

Bendlerblock (Gedenkstätte Deutscher Widerstand) ⑫

Stauffenbergstrasse 13–14.
Map 5 B5, 5 C5. **Tel** 26 99 50 00.
Ⓤ *Mendelssohn-Bartholdy-Park.*
129, 341. ◯ 9am–6pm Mon–Fri
(to 8pm Thu), 10am–6pm Sat & Sun.
◑ 1 Jan, 24, 25 & 31 Dec.

The collection of buildings known as the Bendlerblock was originally built during the Third Reich as an extension to the German State Naval Offices. During World War II these buildings were the headquarters of the Wehrmacht (German Army). It was here that a group of officers planned their famous and ultimately unsuccessful assassination attempt on Hitler on 20 July 1944. When the attempt led by Claus Schenk von Stauffenberg failed, he and his fellow conspirators were quickly rounded up and arrested. The death sentences on these men were passed at the Plötzensee prison *(see*

p186). General Ludwig Beck was forced to commit suicide, while Stauffenberg, Friedrich Olbricht, Werner von Haeften and Ritter Mertz von Quirnheim were shot in the Bendlerblock courtyard.

A monument commemorating this event, designed by Richard Scheibe in 1953, stands where the executions were carried out. On the upper floor of the building there is an exhibition documenting the history of the German anti-Nazi movements.

Villa von der Heydt ⑬

Von-der-Heydt-Strasse 18. **Map** 11
B1. Ⓤ *Nollendorfplatz.* 100,
129, 187, 341.

This fine villa, built in a late-Neo-Classical style, is one of the few surviving reminders that the southern side of the Tiergarten was one of the most expensive and beautiful residential areas of Berlin.

Designed by Hermann Ende and GA Linke, the villa was built from 1860 to 1862. The neatly manicured gardens and railings around the villa are adorned with busts of Christian Daniel Rauch and Alexander von Humboldt. The statues, by Reinhold Begas, originally lined the Avenue of Triumph in the Tiergarten before being moved here. After restoration in 1967, the villa became the headquarters of one of the most influential cultural bodies, the Stiftung Preussischer Kulturbesitz (Foundation of Prussian Cultural Heritage).

The captivating, streamlined buildings of the Bauhaus-Archiv

Bauhaus-Archiv ⑭

Klingelhöferstrasse 14. **Map** 11 A1.
Tel 254 00 20. Ⓤ *Nollendorfplatz.*
100, 129, 187, 341.
◯ 10am–5pm Wed–Mon.

The Bauhaus school of art, started by Walter Gropius in 1919, was one of the most influential art institutions of the 20th century. The belief of the Bauhaus group was that art and technology should combine in harmonious unity.

Originally based in Weimar, and from 1925 in Dessau, this school provided inspiration for numerous artists and architects. Staff and students included Mies van der Rohe, Paul Klee, Wassily Kandinsky, Theo van Doesburg and László Moholy-Nagy. The school moved to Berlin in 1932, but was closed down by the Nazis in 1933.

After the war, the Bauhaus-Archiv was relocated to Darmstadt. In 1964 Walter Gropius designed a building to house the collection, but it was never realized. The archive was moved to Berlin in 1971 and the design had to be adapted to the new site. Because the maestro was no longer alive, the project was taken over by Alexander Cvijanovic. The gleaming white building with its distinctive glass-panelled gables was built between 1976 and 1979 and houses the archive, library and exhibition halls for temporary displays.

Neo-Classical façade of the elegant Villa von der Heydt

Potsdamer Platz ⑩

To experience the vibrant energy of the new Berlin, there is no better place to visit than Potsdamer Platz. During the Roaring Twenties it was Europe's busiest plaza and a bustling entertainment centre, but during World War II it was bombed into a mountain of rubble. After the war, the square was left as a derelict wide open space, a no-man's-land beside the Berlin Wall. With reunification, the square was redeveloped by various international business concerns, such as DaimlerChrysler and Sony, and became Berlin's largest building project. Today, a phoenix has risen from the ashes. Berlin's old hub is once again a dynamic centre, a jewel of modern architecture created by architects such as Renzo Piano, Helmut Jahn and Arata Isozaki.

View of modern-day Potsdamer Platz

Beisheim Center
Lenné-, Bellevue- and Ebertstrasse
Otto Beisheim, the founder and owner of the Metro retail chain, and one of Europe's wealthiest entrepreneurs, has created a glass and steel monument on Potsdamer Platz – the Beisheim Center. Completed in 2004, the two elegant high-rise towers on the northern edge of the square encompass several de luxe apartments. The largest was sold for around $5 million, to an American émigrée returning to her home city, and is probably Berlin's most expensive apartment. The center also incorporates a luxurious Ritz-Carlton and an elegant Marriott hotel.

The building was designed by the Berlin architectural team Hilmer, Sattler & Albrecht, although parts of the building were also created by architect David Chipperfield. The sandstone appearance of the small 19-floor skyscrapers, with receding façades on the upper levels, is meant to be a modern reinterpretation of New York's Rockefeller Center.

Filmmuseum Berlin
Potsdamer Strasse 2 (at Sony Center).
Tel 30 09 030. ☐ 10am–6pm Tue-Sun, 10am–8pm Thu. 📷 Ⓟ ☐
In a city once famous for its world-class film industry, the new film museum takes visitors backstage to Hollywood and the historic UFA (Universal Film AG) film studios.

Located in the Sony Center and run by the Freunde der Deutschen Kinemathek, a non-profit-making association for film-lovers, the museum chronicles the development of cinema from the first silent movie hits to the latest science-fiction productions. However, the main focus is on German films from the glorious UFA days in the 1920s, when Germany's leading film company produced one smash hit after another at the Babelsberg studios *(see p205)*. Films such as *The Cabinet of Dr Caligari*, directed by Friedrich Wilhelm Murnau (1888–1931), or *M* and *Metropolis* by Fritz Lang (1890–1976) are presented with costumes, set sketches, original scripts, models and photos. The Nazi era, when film making became a propaganda machine, is particularly interesting, and the museum documents the life and work of the actor Kurt Gerron, who died in Auschwitz, as well as other exhibits relating to the uses of propaganda in film.

One of the treasure-troves of the museum is the collection of personal effects of the Berlin-born diva Marlene Dietrich (1901–1992). The exhibition presents her gowns, personal correspondence and complete luggage set. A unique item is a minute cigarette case, given to her as a gift by the director Josef von Sternberg (1894–1969), bearing the inscription: "To Marlene Dietrich, woman, mother and actress as there never was one before". Also on display are personal possessions from German film and television stars such as Heinz Rühmann (1902–1994) and Hans Albers (1891–1960).

The museum features a range of exhibitions with changing themes and special film programmes.

Façade of the Filmmuseum Berlin

Arkaden, one of Berlin's favourite shopping centres

Potsdamer Platz Arkaden

Alte Potsdamer Str. 7. *Tel* 25 59 270. ☐ *10am–8pm Mon–Sat.* **CinemaxX** *Potsdamer Str. 5. Tel Programme info: 25 92 21 11; reservations: (0180) 524 63 62 99.*

This entertainment and shopping complex is hugely popular with visitors. Spread over three floors, the building includes around 140 shops, restaurants and boutiques. The basement houses a food court with many budget eateries offering regional specialities from all over Germany, as well as several grocery shops.

Berlin's largest cinema, the **CinemaxX**, is nearby. With 19 screens it can accommodate up to 3,500 filmgoers. Current Hollywood blockbusters and foreign-language films are shown regularly.

Stella Musical Theater Berlin

Marlene-Dietrich-Platz 1. *Tel* (018 0) 544 44. ☐ *8pm daily.* **Spielbank Berlin** *Marlene-Dietrich-Platz 1. Tel* 25 59 90. ☐ *3pm–3am daily.*

Situated in a square dedicated to the famous actress Marlene Dietrich, Berlin's largest musical stage is housed in the modern Stella Musical Theater, designed by Renzo Piano as part of the DaimlerChrysler Quartier *(see pp130–1)*. For a long time it has shown the German version of the Broadway hit musical *Cats*. Other crowd-pulling musicals are planned over the next few years.

The exclusive Adagio nightclub is located in the basement of this building and Berlin's most popular casino, **Spielbank Berlin**, can also be found here. As well as offering roulette and Black Jack, an entire floor is given over to a wide variety of slot machines.

A large blue, bubble-like sculpture – *Balloon Flower* by the American artist Jeff Koons, adorns the square in front of the building.

The theatre complex is also the main forum for the Berlinale, Berlin's world-renowned film festival held throughout the city each February *(see p51)*.

***Balloon Flower* by Jeff Koons**

HISTORIC POTSDAMER PLATZ

Potsdamer Platz first evolved from a green park in 1831 and was named after one of the city's gates, the Potsdamer Tor, located to the east of today's square. Thanks to a new railway station of the same name, where the city's first ever train made its maiden journey in 1838, the square developed into a major traffic hub at the intersection of Potsdamer Strasse and other thoroughfares. Later an underground train line, along with a total of 31 tram and bus lines, added to the traffic chaos here. At the beginning of the 20th century it became the centre of Berlin's celebrated nightlife, with legendary, huge entertainment venues such as Haus Vaterland and the Café Josty (a meeting place for famous artists including author Theodor Fontane

and painter Adolph von Menzel), as well as several luxury hotels. Germany's first radio transmission was broadcast in 1923 at the Vox Haus. The square was almost destroyed by Allied bombardments during the final Battle of Berlin in April 1945. It became a vast open space in the shadow of the Berlin Wall where Western tourists, standing on high observation platforms, could peek over the wall. The empty square featured in Wim Wenders' 1987 hit film, *Wings of Desire*.

Development commenced in 1992, and Potsdamer Platz rose to become Europe's largest construction site where a total of $25 billion has been invested.

Bustling Potsdamer Platz in the 1930s

Sony Center

Potsdamer Strasse 2. ○ *24 hrs.*

The Sony Center, designed by the German-American architect Helmut Jahn, is Berlin's most exciting new architectural complex. Built between 1996 and 2000, the glitzy steel and glass construction covers a breathtaking 4,013 sq m (43,195 sq ft).

The piazza at the heart of the Center has become one of Berlin's most popular attractions. Set under a soaring tent-like roof, it is dominated by a pool with constantly changing fountains where the water sprays high above the pool, then falls back to rise again in a different location. The light and airy piazza is surrounded by the offices of Sony's European headquarters, as well as apartment complexes, several restaurants, cafés and shops including the Sony style store. There is also the Cinestar *(see pp264–5)*, a huge multiplex cinema with eight different screens, in addition to the Filmmuseum Berlin *(see p128)*. At the rear of the building is the blue-domed IMAX cinema which shows nature and science films on imposing 360° screens.

Inside the Sony Center is the small but magnificent **Kaisersaal**, a historic architectural gem that is set behind a glass façade. This dining hall, one of the city's finest but private function locations, was once part of the Grand Hotel Esplanade. The epitome of luxury in pre-war Berlin, it was almost

Interior of the cupola of the Sony Center, designed by Helmut Jahn

destroyed during World War II. When the site was sold to Sony by the City of Berlin in the early 1990s, the Berlin magistrate stipulated that the Kaisersaal, stairways, bathrooms and several other smaller rooms should be restored and integrated into the Sony Center. The historic ensemble originally stood some 46 m (150 ft) away and was carefully moved on air cushions to its present location in 1996. The fully restored Kaisersaal is dominated by a portrait of Kaiser Wilhelm II, the last German emperor, whose frequent visits to the original hotel gave this hall its name, although he never actually dined in this particular room.

Replica traffic lights, DaimlerChrysler Quartier

DaimlerChrysler Quartier

Around Alte Potsdamer Strasse.
Panorama Punkt observation platform Potsdamer Platz 1.
Tel 25 29 43 72. ○ *11am–7:30pm Tue–Sun.*

This vast complex was built between 1993 and 1998 and comprises 19 modern buildings, all designed in different styles according to an overall plan by architects Renzo Piano and Christoph Kohlbecker. The buildings form a long, narrow column of modern architectural jewels leading south from Potsdamer Platz all the way down to the Landwehr Canal.

Standing on either side of Alte Potsdamer Strasse, the red-brick high-rise block and its sister building opposite mark the entrance to this city quarter, and were designed by Berlin architect Werner Kollhoff. The western skyscraper is topped by a 96-m (315-ft) high observation platform called **Panorama Punkt** (Panorama Point). It offers a breathtaking view which can be reached via Europe's fastest elevator.

The green traffic-light tower in front of the DaimlerChrysler Quartier is a replica of the first automatic traffic light in Berlin, which was erected on the same spot in 1924. In

The glass façade of the Kaisersaal, part of the Sony Center

prewar days, Potsdamer Platz was an intricate crossing of several major streets and avenues, making it Europe's busiest traffic junction at the time.

At the southern end of this complex is yet another high-rise tower block, the **Debis-Haus** (formerly the Daimler-Chrysler software subsidiary). This 90-m (295-ft) high, 22 floor, yellow and green skyscraper is topped by a striking green cube and was designed by Renzo Piano and Hans Kollhoff *(see p45)*. A captivating sculpture by Jean Tinguely, entitled *Meta-Maxi*, adorns its soaring atrium. The sculpture is powered by 16 engines and symbolizes the constant movement of time.

Various works of art were commissioned for this complex and these can be seen throughout the public areas.

The red-brick office block of the DaimlerChrysler House

Leipziger Platz

Leipziger Platz, a small square just east of Potsdamer Platz, is currently undergoing major reconstruction. Completion of this historic site is planned for late 2005. The original octagonal but rather bland square was created between 1732 and 1734 and later renamed Leipziger Platz in commemoration of the Battle of Leipzig in 1813 (the first decisive defeat of Napoleon). In the 19th century, the architects Karl-Friedrich Schinkel (1781–1841) and Peter Joseph Lenné (1879–1866) transformed the square into an architectural gem with beautifully land-scaped gardens, surrounded by some of the most elegant city palaces and mansions in the whole of Berlin.

At the beginning of the 20th century the modern buildings, most notably the Kaufhaus Wertheim by Alfred Messel (1853–1909) built in 1905, made Leipziger Platz one of the major, and more fashionable, shopping districts in pre-war Berlin.

Unfortunately, there are no historic remnants left. The new buildings will have a modern look but will be restricted to a maximum height of only 35 m (115 ft), the same height as the original buildings. They will house various shops and restaurants, the Canadian Embassy and further international company headquarters.

Haus Huth

Alte Potsdamer Strasse 5.
Tel 25 94 14 20. ◻ 11am–6pm daily. **Sammlung DaimlerChrysler Contemporary** ◻ as Weinhaus Huth. 🖪 6pm daily.

The only historic building on Potsdamer Platz to escape destruction in World War II was the grey limestone building of the Haus Huth. Originally a restaurant and wine shop, it was one of the first buildings in Berlin to be erected with a steel frame, intended to support the weight of the wine. It was designed by architects Conrad Heidenreich and Paul Michel in 1912. After the war, it stood alone on the vast

Rauschenberg's sculpture *Riding Bikes*, with Weinhaus Huth in the background

eroded square. Today however, the offices of the famous car manufacturers DaimlerChrysler are located here, along with the Diekmann im Haus Huth restaurant, a small café and Hardy's, an upmarket wine shop.

Haus Huth is also home to the **Sammlung DaimlerChrysler Contemporary**, a small exhibition featuring the latest additions to the corporation's collection of 20th-century art, which mostly consists of abstract and geometric paintings by German and international artists.

The best view of the building is from its south side where a jubilant, bright light installation by Robert Rauschenberg called *Riding Bikes* can be found.

The historic Haus Huth on Leipziger Platz

Diplomatenviertel ⓯

DIPLOMATIC QUARTER

Map 4 F5, 5 A5, B5, C5.
Ⓤ *Nollendorfplatz.* 🚌 *100, 129, 187, 341.*

Although a number of consulates existed in the Tiergarten area as early as 1918, the establishment of a diplomatic district along the southern edge of the Tiergarten, between Stauffenbergstrasse and Lichtensteinallee, did not take place until the period of Hitler's Third Reich between 1933 and 1945. During the years 1938 to 1943 large embassies representing the Axis Powers, Italy and Japan, were built here.

Despite the fact that these monumental buildings were designed by a number of different architects, the Fascist interpretation of Neo-Classicism and the influence of Albert Speer as head architect meant that the group was homogenous, if bleak. Many of the buildings did not survive World War II bombing.

A new diplomatic area has now emerged along Tiergartenstrasse. The Austrian embassy designed by Hans Hollein stands at the junction of Stauffenbergstrasse, next door to the embassies of Turkey and the Republic of South Africa. At Tiergartenstrasse Nos. 21–3 the pre-World War II Italian embassy still stands, while next door is a copy of the first Japanese embassy. Between Klingelhöferstrasse and Rauchstrasse stands an imposing complex of five embassies. Completed in 1999, these represent Norway, Sweden, Denmark, Finland and Iceland.

One of many tranquil areas within the Tiergarten

Tiergarten ⓰

Map 4 E4, 5 A3, 6 D3. Ⓢ *Tiergarten or Bellevue.* 🚌 *100, 187, 200, 341.*

This is the largest park in Berlin. Situated at the geographical centre of the city it occupies a surface area of more than 200 ha (495 acres). Once a forest used as

the Elector's hunting reserve, it was transformed into a landscaped park by Peter Joseph Lenné in the 1830s. A half-kilometre Triumphal Avenue was built in the eastern section of the park at the end of the 19th century, lined with statues of the country's rulers and statesmen.

World War II inflicted huge damage on the Tiergarten, including the destruction of the Triumphal Avenue, many of whose surviving monuments can now be seen in the Lapidarium *(see p144)*. Replanting, however, has now restored the Tiergarten which is a favourite meeting place for Berliners. Its avenues are now lined with statues of figures such as Johann Wolfgang von Goethe and Richard Wagner.

By the lake known as Neuer See and the Landwehrkanal are memorials to the murdered leaders of the Spartacus movement, Karl Liebknecht and Rosa Luxemburg *(see p28)*. Also worth finding is a collection of gas lamps, displayed near the Tiergarten S-Bahn station.

Grosser Stern ⓱

GREAT STAR

Map 5 A4. Ⓢ *Bellevue.* 🚌 *100, 187, 341.*

This vast roundabout at the centre of the Tiergarten has five large roads leading off it in the shape of a star. At its centre is the enormous Siegessäule (Triumphal Column). Surrounding it are various monuments brought over from the nearby Reichstag

building *(see pp134–5)* during the late 1930s. At the same period the Strasse des 17 Juni was widened to twice its size, the square surrounding the roundabout was enlarged and much of the existing statuary removed.

In the northern section of the square stands a vast bronze monument to the first German Chancellor, Otto von Bismarck (1815–98). Around it stand allegorical figures, the work of late-19th-century sculptor Reinhold Begas. Other statues represent various national heroes including Field Marshal Helmuth von Moltke (1800–91), chief of the Prussian general staff between the years 1858 and 1888, who won the Franco-German war.

Monument to Otto von Bismarck at the Grosser Stern

Siegessäule ⓲

TRIUMPHAL COLUMN

Grosser Stern. **Map** 5 A4. **Tel** 391 29 61. Ⓢ *Bellevue.* 🚌 *100, 187, 341.* ⏰ *Apr–Oct: 9:30am–6:30pm daily; Nov–Mar: 9:30am–5:30pm daily.*

The triumphal column is based on a design by Johann Heinrich Strack, and was built to commemorate victory in the Prusso-Danish war of 1864. After further Prussian victories in wars against Austria (1866) and France (1871), a gilded figure by Friedrich Drake representing Victory, known as the "Goldelse", was added to the top. The monument originally stood in front of the Reichstag building, but was moved to its present location by the Nazi government in 1938. The base is decorated with bas-reliefs commemorating battles, while higher up the column a mosaic frieze by Anton von Werner depicts the founding of the German Empire in 1871. An observation terrace at the top of the monument offers magnificent vistas over Berlin.

Siegessäule (Triumphal Column)

Hansaviertel ⑲

Map 4 E3, E4, F3. Ⓢ *Bellevue.*
🚌 *123, 341.* **Akademie der Künste**
Hanseatenweg 10. *Tel 39 07 60.*
⭕ *11am–8pm Tue–Sun.* 🈵

This area to the west of Schloss Bellevue is home to some of the most interesting

---

KONIGLICHE PORZELLAN-MANUFAKTUR

Established in 1763, the Königliche Porzellan-Manufaktur (Royal Porcelain Factory) was soon producing items of the highest artistic quality, competing with the products of the older Meissen factory in Saxony. The Berlin factory is particularly renowned for its Neo-Classical urns and plates decorated with views of the city. Large collections of porcelain with the markings KPM can be seen at the Ephraim-Palais *(see p 91),* in the Kunstgewerbemuseum *(see pp118–21)* and at the Belvedere within the grounds of Schloss Charlottenburg *(see pp160–61).* It is also worth visiting the factory, located at Wegelystrasse 1, which is still producing porcelain, and includes a sales gallery and exhibition hall.

Neo-Classical vase with a view of the Gendarmenmarkt

---

modern architecture in Berlin, built for the 1957 Internationale Bauausstellung (International Architectural Exhibition). Taking on a World War II bomb site, prominent architects from around the world designed 45 projects, of which 36 were realized, to create a varied residential development set in an environment of lush greenery. The list of distinguished architects involved in the project included Walter Gropius (Händelallee Nos. 3–9), Alvar Aalto (Klopstockstrasse Nos. 30–32) and Oskar Niemeyer (Altonaer Strasse Nos. 4–14). The development also includes a school, a commercial services building and two churches.

In 1960, a new headquarters for the **Akademie der Künste** (Academy of Arts) was built at Hanseatenweg No. 10. Designed by Werner Düttmann, the academy has a concert hall, an exhibition area, archives and a library. In front of the main entrance is a magnificent piece, *Reclining Figure,* by eminent British sculptor Henry Moore.

Schloss Bellevue ⑳

BELLEVUE PALACE

Spreeweg 1. **Map** 5 A3. Ⓢ *Bellevue.*
🚌 *100, 187.* ⬤ *to the public.*

This captivating palace with its dazzlingly white Neo-Classical façade is now the official residence of the German Federal President. Built in 1786 to a design by Philipp Daniel Boumann for the Prussian Prince August Ferdinand, the palace served as a royal residence until 1861. In 1935 it was refurbished to house a Museum of German Ethnology. Refurbished again in 1938, it became a hotel for guests of the Nazi government.

Following bomb damage during World War II, the palace was carefully restored to its former glory, with the oval ballroom rebuilt to a design by Carl Gotthard Langhans. The palace is set within an attractive park laid out to the original late-18th-century design, though unfortunately the picturesque garden pavilions did not survive World War II.

Imposing façade of Schloss Bellevue, now the official Berlin residence of the German President

Haus der Kulturen der Welt or "pregnant oyster" as it is also known

Haus der Kulturen der Welt ㉑

HOUSE OF WORLD CULTURE

John-Foster-Dulles-Allee 10.
Map 5 C3. **Tel** 39 78 70.
Ⓢ *Unter den Linden.* 🚌 *100.*
⬜ **Exhibitions** *9am–8pm Tue–Sun.*

This former congress hall's squat structure and parabolic roof has given rise to its affectionate nickname "the pregnant oyster". Built between 1956 and 1957 to a design by the American architect Hugh Stubbins, it was intended as the American entry in the international architecture competition "Interbau 1957", (from which the Hansaviertel apartment blocks originated). It soon became a symbol of freedom and modernity in West Berlin during the Cold War, particularly when compared to the GDR-era monumental buildings of Karl-Marx-Allee in East Berlin *(see pp172–3).* However, its concept outran current technologies and the roof failed to withstand the test of time, as the building partially collapsed in 1980.

After reconstruction it was re-opened in 1989, with a change of purpose. It is now used to bring world cultures to a wider German audience, and stages various events and performances to this effect. It is known for its jazz festivals in particular *(see pp48–51).*

Standing nearby is the black tower of the Carillon built in 1987 to commemorate the 750th anniversary of Berlin. Suspended in the tower is the largest carillon in Europe, comprising 67 bells. Daily at noon and 6pm, the bells give a brief computer-controlled concert.

Regierungsviertel ㉒

GOVERNMENT DISTRICT

Map 6 D2, E2. Ⓢ *Unter den Linden.* 🚌 *100, 248.*

This bold concept for a new government district in keeping with a 21st-century capital was the winning design in a competition held in 1992. Construction of the complex began in 1997 and was completed in 2003. Axel Schultes and Charlotte Frank's grand design proposed a rectangular site cutting across the meander of the Spree river just north of the Reichstag.

While many of the buildings have been designed by other architects, their plans fitting within the overall concept, Schultes and Frank designed the Bundeskanzleramt, situated opposite the Riechstag, which is the official residence of German Chancellor.

The offices – Alsenblock and Luisenblock – are the work of Stephan Braunfels, as is the office Dorotheenblöcke, built by a consortium of five architects. The whole project will be complemented by an ultra-modern, integrated transport system which will include a road tunnel under the Tiergarten and a vast subterranean railway station – Berlin Hauptbahnhof. The architects responsible for the station project are Mainhard von Gerkan, Oswald Mathias Ungers and Max Dudler.

Reichstag ㉓

Platz der Republik. **Map** 6 D3, E3.
Ⓢ *Unter den Linden.* 🚌 *100, 248.*
Tel *227 32 152.* **Dome** ⬜ *8am–midnight daily (last admission 10pm).*
Assembly Hall ⬜ *by appointment only.* 🎧 *noon Tue, 10am Sat (in English).* ● *1 Jan, 24, 26 & 31 Dec.*

Built to house the German Parliament, the Reichstag was intended as a symbol of national unity and to showcase the aspirations of the new German Empire, declared in 1871. The Neo-Renaissance design by Paul Wallot captured the prevailing spirit of German optimism. Constructed between the years 1884 and 1894 it was funded by money paid by the French as wartime reparations.

On 23 December 1916, the inscription *"Dem Deutschen Volke"* ("To the German People") was added to the façade. The Reichstag became a potent symbol to the German populace; this power would be exploited in the years to come.

In 1918 Philipp Scheidemann declared the formation of the

The Bundeskanzleramt, the official residence of the Federal Chancellor

The Reichstag crowned by a dome designed by Sir Norman Foster

Weimar Republic from the building. The next time the world heard about the Reichstag was on the night of 28 February 1933, when a fire destroyed the main hall. The Communists were blamed, accelerating a political witch-hunt driven by the Nazis, who subsequently came to power.

With the onset of World War II, the building was not rebuilt. Yet its significance resonated beyond Germany, as shown by the photograph of the Soviet flag flying from the Reichstag in May 1945, which became a symbol of the German defeat.

Rebuilding work undertaken between 1957 and 1972 removed the dome and most of the ornamentation. As well as providing a meeting-place for the lower house of the German Bundestag (Parliament), the Reichstag also made a spectacular back-drop for huge festivals and rock concerts, much to the annoyance of the East German authorities.

On 2 December 1990, the Reichstag was the first meeting-place of a newly-elected Bundestag following German reunification. On 23 June 1995 the artist Christo and his wife Jeanne-Claude wrapped the Reichstag in glistening fabric – an artistic statement that lasted for two weeks.

The latest phase of rebuilding was between 1995 and 1999 to a design by Sir Norman Foster that transforms the Reichstag into a modern meeting hall crowned with an elliptical dome with a viewing gallery. The first parliamentary meeting in the new building took place on 19 April 1999.

Sowjetisches Ehrenmal ㉔

MONUMENT TO SOVIET SOLDIERS

Strasse des 17 Juni. **Map** 6 D3.
Ⓢ *Unter den Linden.* 🚌 *100, 248.*

This huge monument near the Brandenburg Gate was unveiled on 7 November 1945, on the anniversary of the start of the October Revolution in Russia. Flanked by the first two tanks into the city, the monument commemorates over 300,000 Soviet soldiers who perished in the battle for Berlin at the end of World War II. The vast column was made from marble taken from the headquarters of the Chancellor of the Third Reich, when it was being dismantled. The column was designed by Nicolai Sergiejev, while the imposing figure on top, a soldier cast in bronze, is the work of Lew Kerbel. This monument is also a cemetery for around 2,500 Soviet casualties. Following the partition of Berlin, the site ended up in the British sector, but formed a kind of non-territorial enclave to which Soviet soldiers posted to East Berlin had access.

The sculpture of a Soviet soldier atop the Sowjetisches Ehrenmal

BERLIN'S BRIDGES

Despite wartime damage, Berlin's bridges are still well worth seeing. The Spree river and the city's canals have some exemplary architecture on their banks, while many of the bridges were designed and decorated by famous architects and sculptors. Probably the most renowned bridge is the Schlossbrücke designed by Karl Friedrich Schinkel *(see p74)*. Further south along the Kupfergrabenkanal, the Schleusenbrücke dates from c.1914, and is decorated with reliefs of the early history of the city's bridges and sluices. The next bridge, heading south, is the Jungfernbrücke dating from 1798, which is the last drawbridge in Berlin. The next bridge along is the Gertraudenbrücke *(see p85)*. Where Friedrichstrasse crosses the Spree river is the Weiden-dammer Brücke, originally built in 1695-7 and subsequently rebuilt in 1923, with an eagle motif decorating its balustrade. On the Spree near the Regierungsviertel is the magnificent Moltkebrücke (1886–91). The bridge is guarded by a huge griffin wielding a shield adorned with the Prussian eagle, while cherubs dressed in a military fashion hold up lamps. On the arches of the bridges are portraits of leaders designed by Karl Begas.

Ornamental feature of a bear on the Liebknechtbrücke

KREUZBERG

The area covered in this chapter is only a part of the suburb of the same name. The evolution of Kreuzberg began in the late 19th century when it was a working-class area. After World War II unrepaired buildings were abandoned by those who could afford to move, leaving a population of artists, foreigners, the unemployed and members of a variety of sub-cultures.

Detail from the Martin-Gropius-Bau façade

Kreuzberg is now an area of contrasts, with luxury apartments next to dilapidated buildings. Some parts of Kreuzberg are mainly Turkish, while others are inhabited by affluent young professionals. The district's attractions are its wealth of restaurants and Turkish bazaars, as well as an interesting selection of nightclubs, cinemas, theatres and galleries.

SIGHTS AT A GLANCE

Museums
Berlinische Galerie ❺
Checkpoint Charlie ❹
Deutsches Technikmuseum Berlin ❾
Jüdisches Museum ❻
Lapidarium ❽
Martin-Gropius-Bau ❷
Topographie des Terrors ❸

Historic Buildings
Anhalter Bahnhof ❶
Flughafen Tempelhof ⓭
Riehmers Hofgarten ⓫

Squares, Parks and Cemeteries
Friedhöfe vor dem Halleschen Tor ❿
Mehringplatz ❼
Viktoriapark ⓬

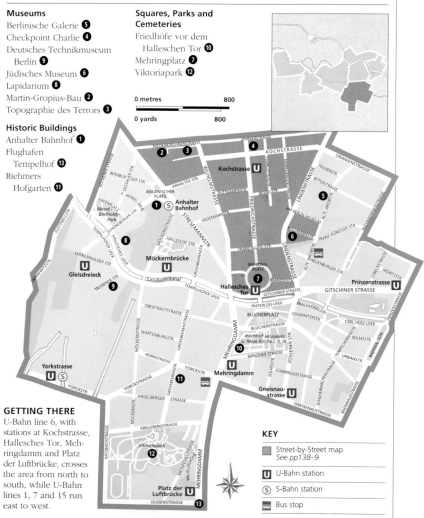

GETTING THERE
U-Bahn line 6, with stations at Kochstrasse, Hallesches Tor, Mehringdamm and Platz der Luftbrücke, crosses the area from north to south, while U-Bahn lines 1, 7 and 15 run east to west.

KEY

▨	Street-by-Street map *See pp138–9*
Ⓤ	U-Bahn station
Ⓢ	S-Bahn station
🚏	Bus stop

◁ **The magnificent 24-metre waterfall in Viktoriapark, Kreuzberg**

Street-by-Street: Mehringplatz and Friedrichstrasse

The areas north of Mehringplatz are the oldest sections of Kreuzberg. Mehringplatz, initially called Rondell, together with the Oktogon (Leipziger Platz) and the Quarré (Pariser Platz), were laid out in 1734 as part of the enlargement of Friedrichstadt. World War II totally changed the character of this area. It is now full of modern developments such as the Friedrichstadt Passagen – a huge complex of shops, apartments, offices, galleries and restaurants. Only a few buildings recall the earlier splendour of this district.

★ Checkpoint Charlie
This small hut marks the place of the notorious border crossing between East and West Berlin ❹

Topographie des Terrors
A shocking exhibition detailing Nazi crimes is housed within the former Gestapo and SS headquarters ❸

Martin-Gropius-Bau
This interesting, multi-coloured Neo-Renaissance building was once home to the Kunstgewerbemuseum (see pp118–21) ❷

KOCHSTRASSE

FRIEDRICHSTRASSE

WILHELMSTRASSE

PUTTKAMERSTRASSE

HEDEMANNSTRASSE

Deutsches Technikmuseum ◀

0 metres	150
0 yards	150

STAR SIGHTS

★ Checkpoint Charlie

★ Jüdisches Museum

Haus am Checkpoint Charlie
Butterflies on a piece of the Berlin Wall mark the entrance to this museum.

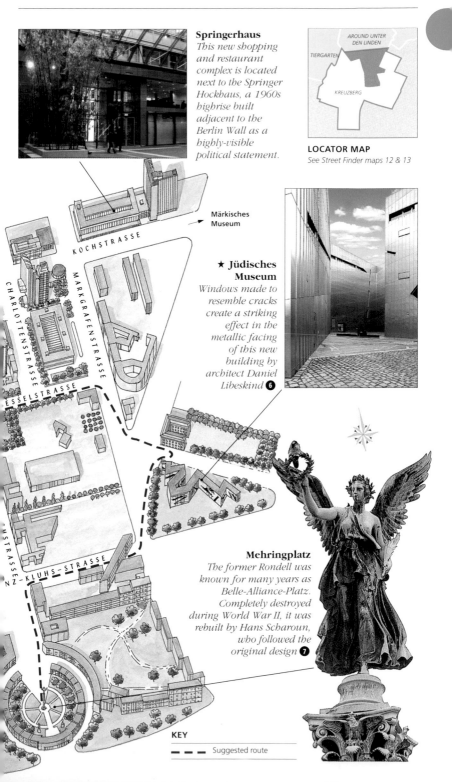

Springerhaus
This new shopping and restaurant complex is located next to the Springer Hochhaus, a 1960s highrise built adjacent to the Berlin Wall as a highly-visible political statement.

LOCATOR MAP
See Street Finder maps 12 & 13

AROUND UNTER DEN LINDEN

TIERGARTEN

KREUZBERG

KOCHSTRASSE

Märkisches Museum

★ Jüdisches Museum
Windows made to resemble cracks create a striking effect in the metallic facing of this new building by architect Daniel Libeskind ⑥

CHARLOTTENSTRASSE

MARKGRAFENSTRASSE

ESSELSTRASSE

KLUHS-STRASSE

Mehringplatz
The former Rondell was known for many years as Belle-Alliance-Platz. Completely destroyed during World War II, it was rebuilt by Hans Scharoun, who followed the original design ⑦

KEY

- - - Suggested route

Anhalter Bahnhof ❶

Askanischer Platz 6–7. **Map** 12 E1.
Ⓢ *Anhalter Bahnhof.* 🚌 *129, 248, 341.*

Only a tiny fragment now remains of Anhalter Bahnhof (Hitchhiker Station), once Berlin's largest and Europe's second largest railway station.

The hugely ambitious structure was designed by Franz Schwechten and constructed in 1880. The station was intended to be the largest and most elegant in Europe in order to impress official visitors to the capital of the German Empire. Some of the most famous people to alight at Anhalter Bahnhof were the Italian king Umberto, who was welcomed by Kaiser Wilhelm II himself, and the Russian tsar Nicholas. From here trains travelled to Dresden, Vienna, Rome and Athens. The station was taken out of public use in 1943 after its roof was destroyed by Allied bombing. Only the front portico remains, crowned by still-damaged sculptures and the hole that housed a large electric clock, as well as fragments of its once glorious façade. On the vast grounds behind it is the tent-like entertainment venue Tempodrom *(see p269).*

Martin-Gropius-Bau ❷

Stresemannstrasse 110. **Map** 12 E1.
Tel *25 48 60.* ◻ *10am–8pm Wed–Mon.* Ⓢ & Ⓤ *Potsdamer Platz.* 🚌 *129, 248, 341.*

The innovative Martin-Gropius-Bau was originally built to fulfil the requirements of an arts and crafts museum. It was designed by Martin Gropius with the participation of Heino Schmieden and constructed in 1881. The building is in a style reminiscent of an Italian Renaissance palace, with a magnificent glazed interior courtyard, an impressive atrium and unusual, richly

Exhibition documenting Nazi crimes at the Topographie des Terrors

decorated elevations. Located between the windows are the crests of German cities, and within the friezes are reliefs illustrating the different arts and crafts. In the plaques between the windows of the top storey are beautiful mosaics containing allegorical figures representing the cultures of different eras and countries.

From 1922 Martin-Gropius-Bau accommodated the Museum of Ethnology, but after World War II the building was abandoned and left in ruins. Although plans for an inner-city motorway threatened it until the 1970s, a reconstruction programme eventually commenced in 1981, led by architects Winnetou Kampmann and Ute Westroem. This was followed in 1999 by a further refurbishment, and since then the building has housed a changing series of exhibitions on art, photography and architecture.

Allegorical mosaic on display in the Martin-Gropius-Bau

Topographie des Terrors ❸

Stresemannstrasse 110 (entrance on Niederkirchner Strasse). **Map** 6 F5, 12 F1. **Tel** *25 48 67 03.* Ⓢ & Ⓤ *Potsdamer Platz.* Ⓤ *Potsdamer Platz.* 🚌 *129, 248, 341.*
◻ *May–Sep: 10am–8pm daily; Oct–Apr: 10am–6pm daily.* 📷

During the Third Reich Prinz-Albrecht-Strasse was probably the most frightening address in Berlin. In 1934, three of the most terrifying Nazi political departments had their headquarters in a block between Stresemann-, Wilhelm-, Anhalter-, and Prinz-Albrecht-Strasse (now Niederkirchner Strasse), making this area the government district of National Socialist Germany.

The Neo-Classical Prinz-Albrecht palace at Wilhelmstrasse No. 102 became the headquarters of Reinhard Heydrich and the Third Reich's security service (SD). The arts and crafts school at Prinz-Albrecht-Strasse No. 8 was occupied by the head of the Gestapo, Heinrich Müller, while the Hotel Prinz Albrecht at No. 9 became the headquarters of the Schutzstaffel or SS, with Heinrich Himmler in command. It was from the buildings in this area of the city that decisions about the Germanization of the occupied territories were made, as well as plans on the genocide of European Jews. After World War II, the buildings were pulled down. In 1987, however, in some surviving cellars that were once torture cells, an exhibition was mounted that documented Nazi crimes.

A preserved section of the Berlin wall runs alongside the grounds of the Topographie des Terrors at Niederkirchner Strasse.

Checkpoint Charlie ❹

Friedrichstrasse 43–45. **Map** 7 A5. **Tel** 253 72 50. **U** Kochstrasse. 🚌 129. **Haus am Checkpoint Charlie** ⭕ 9am–10pm daily. 📷

A Alpha, B Bravo, C Charlie. Not many people remember that the name of this notorious border crossing between the American and Soviet sectors stemmed from the word that signifies the letter C in the international phonetic alphabet.

Between 1961 and 1990, Checkpoint Charlie was the only crossing point for foreigners between East and West Berlin. During that time, it represented a symbol of both freedom and separation for the many East Germans trying to escape from the DDR's Communist regime.

Little remains of the former crossing point, which was witness to a number of dramatic events during the Cold War, including a tense two-day standoff between Russian and American tanks in 1961.

In 1990, the checkpoint was formally closed with an official ceremony attended by the foreign ministers of the four occupying powers: the US, Great Britain, France and the Soviet Union.

Today, there are no longer any gates, barriers or barbed wire to be seen; instead there is a replica checkpoint booth, complete with sand bags and the famous, huge sign on the old Western side that reads "You are leaving the American Sector".

Also on Friedrichstrasse are two large photographs of an

The replica booth at the former Checkpoint Charlie

American and a Russian soldier, that form part of a well-known series by the Berlin photographer Frank Thiel. His portraits of four Allied soldiers commemorate the departure of the Allies.

One of the original watchtowers is worth visiting at the museum nearby – **Haus am Checkpoint Charlie**. The museum's rich collection details Cold War border conflicts, and the construction of the Berlin Wall. Of special interest are the exhibits connected with the escape attempts of East Germans to the West. The ingenuity and bravery of these escapees is astonishing, using devices such as secret compartments built into cars, and specially constructed suitcases.

A separate exhibition illustrates the peaceful campaigns carried out in the name of democracy in a number of totalitarian countries.

Berlinische Galerie ❺

Alte Jakobstrasse 124–28. **Map** 7 C5. **Tel** 78 90 26 00. **U** Kochstrasse. 🚌 129, 143, 240, 341. ⭕ noon–8pm Mon–Sat, 10am–6pm Sun. 📷

Newly reopened, the city's museum for modern art, design and architecture is one of the finest regional museums in the country. Themed exhibitions, which are regularly changed, draw upon its huge collection of German, East European and Russian paintings, photographs, graphics and architectural artefacts.

One of the highlights is the 5,000-strong painting collection, which covers all the major art movements from the late 19th century until today. It includes works by Max Liebermann, Otto Dix, Georg Baselitz, Alexander Rodtschenko, Iwan Puni and Via Lewandowsy.

The museum's collection of sketches, prints and posters encompasses the Berlin Dadaists George Grosz, Hanna Höch and Werner Heldt, as well as works by Ernst Ludwig Kirchner and Hanns Schimansky.

Amongst the architectural items held by the Galerie are drawings and models for buildings that were never built, offering fascinating glimpses into how the city might have looked. A fine example is the shell-like Expressionist Sternkirche (Star Church), designed by Otto Bartning in 1922.

Kühn Malvessi's *Letter Field* in front of the Berlinische Galerie

Jüdisches Museum Berlin ⑥

The Jewish Museum designed by Daniel Libeskind, a Polish-Jewish architect based in the United States, is an exciting and imaginative example of late 20th-century architecture. The plan, shape, style, and interior and exterior arrangement of the building are part of a complicated philosophical programme to illustrate the history and culture of Germany's Jewish community, and the repercussions of the Holocaust. The exhibition has gathered together many artifacts, such as books and photographs, to bring the memories and stories of Jewish life alive. The long, narrow galleries with slanting floors and sharp zig-zagging turns are designed to evoke the feeling of loss and dislocation. These are interspersed by "voids" that represent the vacuum left behind by the destruction of Jewish life.

★ Moses Mendelssohn's Glasses
These glasses are on show in the section entitled "Moses Mendelssohn and the Enlightenment", which details the philosopher's fight for religious tolerance in a time when Jews possessed no civil rights.

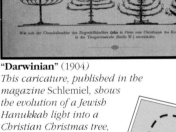

"Darwinian" (1904)
This caricature, published in the magazine Schlemiel, *shows the evolution of a Jewish Hanukkah light into a Christian Christmas tree, implying that the wish of many Jews was to assimilate with Germans.*

Rural Jews and Court Jews

At the Heart of the Family

STAR SIGHTS

★ Moses Mendelssohn's Glasses

★ Daniel Libeskind's Design

★ Garden of Exile and Emigration

Same Responsibilities – Same Rights?

MUSEUM GUIDE

Entrance to the museum is via an underground path from the Berlinische Galerie next door. Stairs lead up to the start of the exhibition which is divided into 14 sections, taking visitors through German Jewish history and culture from early history, through the Middle Ages and up to the present day.

VISITORS' CHECKLIST

Lindenstrasse 9–14. **Map** 13 A2. **Tel** 25 99 33 00. **U** *Hallesches Tor* or *Kochstrasse.* 143, 240, 248. ☐ 10am–10pm Mon, 10am– 8pm Tue–Sun. ● *Jewish hols and 24 Dec.* 🎧 📷 *in German: 11am, 2pm (English too), 3pm Sat & Sun.* **www**.jmberlin.de

Entrance to exhibition via underground tunnel

German Jews and Jewish Germans

Persecution – Resistance – Extermination

Exit

★ **Daniel Libeskind's Design**
The extraordinary zinc-clad, jagged structure of the museum is likened to a deconstructed Star of David, and attracted over 350,000 visitors to the museum in the two years before the exhibitions were installed.

Electric Iron AEG

An iron made by one of Germany's largest electrical companies, founded by Emil Rathenau, forms part of the collection celebrating the dominant position of Jews in trade and industry in Berlin throughout the late 19th and early 20th centuries.

East and West

KEY

☐	Beginnings
■	Middle Ages
☐	1500–1800
☐	Tradition and Change
■	1850–1933
■	Modern Judaism and Urban Life
☐	1914–1933
☐	1933–1945
■	The Present
■	Non-exhibition space
--	Suggested Route

★ **Garden of Exile and Emigration**
Comprising 49 tilted pillars to represent the foundation of the state of Israel in 1948 plus one for Berlin, the garden also symbolizes the forced exile of Germany's Jews.

A representation of Peace, by Albert Wolff, in Mehringplatz

Mehringplatz ❼

Map 13 A2. **U** *Mehringplatz.* 🚌 *248, 341.*

Mehringplatz was planned in the 1830s, when the boundaries of the city were extended. Its original name was Rondell, meaning round-about. This was an appropriate name as Wilhelmstrasse, Friedrichstrasse and Linden-strasse all converged here.

Mehringplatz was the work of Philipp Gerlach then, in the 1840s, Peter Joseph Lenné designed the decoration of the square. At the centre is the Column of Peace, designed by Christian Gottlieb Cantian, commemorating the Wars of Liberation in 1815. The column is crowned by the figure of Victory by Christian Daniel Rauch. Two sculptures were added in the 1870s: *Peace* by Albert Wolff; and *Clio* (the Muse of History) by Ferdinand Hartzer. In the 19th and early 20th centuries the area was fashionable and populated with politicians, diplomats and aristocrats. The current buildings date from the 1970s.

Lapidarium ❽

Hallesches Ufer 78. **Map** 12 E2. **Tel** *25 48 63 05.* ⬤ *by appointment only.* **U** *Mendelssohn-Bartholdy-Park.*

This interesting building, decorated with an enchan-ting Oriental-style chimney, was once Berlin's pumping station. It was built from 1873 to 1876 and designed by Hermann Blankenstein. The original steam pumps have

survived to this day and can be seen during a visit. The Lapidarium contains numerous sculptures, some of which have been replaced by copies for conservation purposes. Virtually all the sculptures that once decorated the Avenue of Victory in the Tiergarten, known as "Puppenallee", are housed here. These majestic statues of celebrated warriors and rulers stand side by side in their robes and weapons, only slightly diminished by the loss of many heads, arms and other body parts.

Deutsches Technikmuseum Berlin ❾

Trebbiner Strasse 9. **Map** 12 E2. **Tel** *90 25 40.* **U** *Gleisdreieck.* 🚌 *129, 341.* ⬤ *9am–5:30pm Tue–Fri, 10am–6pm Sat–Sun.* ♿ 🖼

The Technical Museum was first established in 1982 with the intention of grouping more than 100 smaller, specialized collections under one roof. The current collection is arranged on the site of the former trade hall, the size of which allows many of the museum's exhibits, such as locomotives, aircraft, boats, water towers and storerooms, to be displayed full-size and in their original condition.

Of particular interest in the collection are the dozens of locomotives and railway car-riages from different eras as well as the vintage cars. There are also exhibitions dedicated to flying, the history of paper manufacture, printing, weaving,

electro-technology and com-puter technology. There are also two windmills, a brewery and an old forge. The section called Spectrum is especially popular with children as it allows them to conduct "hands-on" experiments.

Friedhöfe vor dem Halleschen Tor ❿

Mehringdamm, Blücher-, Baruther & Zossener Strasse. **Map** 13 A3. **U** *Mehringdamm.* 🚌 *140, 341.* ⬤ *10am–5pm daily.*

Beyond the city walls, next to the Hallesches Tor, four neighbouring cemeteries were established in 1735. A number of famous people are buried here. Among the beautiful gravestones are the greatest of Berlin's artists, including the composer Felix Mendelssohn-Bartholdy, architects Georg Wenzeslaus von Knobelsdorff, David Gilly and Carl Ferdinand Langhans, portraitist Antoine Pesne and the writer, artist and composer ETA Hoffmann.

Riehmers Hofgarten ⓫

Yorckstr. 83–86, Grossbeerenstr. 56–57 & Hagelberger Strasse 9–12. **Map** 12 F4. **U** *Mehringdamm.* 🚌 *119, 140.*

Riehmers Hofgarten is the name given to the 20 or so exquisite houses arranged around a picturesque garden in the area bordered by the

Headstone in the picturesque Friedhöfe vor dem Halleschen Tor

Renaissance-style façade in Riehmers Hofgarten

streets Yorck-, Hagelberger and Grossbeerenstrasse. These houses were built between 1881 and 1892 to the detailed designs of Wilhelm Riehmer and Otto Mrosk. These respected architects created this unique group of houses, not only designing intricate, Renaissance-style façades but also giving equal splendour to the elevations overlooking the courtyard garden. The streets of Riehmers Hofgarten have been carefully restored and Yorckstrasse also has quite a few cafés. Next to Riehmers Hofgarten is the church of St Bonifaz, which was designed by Max Hasak. Adjacent to the church is a similar complex of houses built in an impressive Neo-Gothic style.

To experience the authentic atmosphere of old Kreuzberg, you need to go no further than Bergmannstrasse. Here, entire districts of 19th-century houses have been restored to their original state. The atmosphere is further enhanced by antique streetlamps, a pedestrianized street, and bars and galleries. This is also true for Marheinekeplatz, where there is a lively covered market.

Viktoriapark ⓬

Map 12 E4, E5, F5. **U** *Platz der Luftbrücke.* 104, 140.

This rambling park, with several artificial waterfalls, short trails and a small hill, was designed by Hermann Machtig and built between 1884 and 1894. The Neo-Gothic Memorial to the Wars of Liberation at the summit of the hill is the work of Karl Friedrich Schinkel, created

between 1817 and 1821. The monument commemorates the Prussian victory against Napoleon's army in the Wars of Liberation. The cast-iron tower is well ornamented. In the niches of the lower section are 12 allegorical figures by Christian Daniel Rauch, Friedrich Tieck and Ludwig Wichmann. Each figure symbolizes a battle and is linked to a historic figure – either a military leader or a member of the royal family.

Flughafen Tempelhof ⓭

Platz der Luftbrücke. **Plan** 12 F5. **U** *Platz der Luftbrücke.* 104, 119, 184, 341.

Situated beyond Kreuzberg, the Tempelhof airport was once Germany's largest. Built in 1923, the structure was enlarged during the Third Reich. The building is typical of Third Reich architecture, even though the eagles that decorate the buildings predate the Nazis. The additions to the original structure were designed by Ernst Sagebiel and completed in 1939.

In 1951, a monument was added in front of the airport. Designed by Edward Ludwig, it commemorates the airlifts of the Berlin Blockade. The three spikes on the top symbolize the air corridors used by Allied planes. The names of those who lost their lives during the Blockade appear on the plinth.

THE BERLIN BLOCKADE (1948–9)

On 24 June 1948, as a result of rising tensions between East Germany and West Berlin, Soviet authorities blockaded all the roads leading to West Berlin. In order to ensure food and fuel for the residents, US General Lucius Clay ordered that provisions be flown into the city. British and American planes made a total of 212,612 flights, transporting almost 2.3 million tons of goods, among which were parts of a power station. In April 1949, at the height of the airlifts, planes were landing every 63 seconds. The blockade ended in May, 1949. Although the airlifts were successful, there were casualties: 70 airmen and 8 ground crew lost their lives.

Allied plane bringing supplies during the Berlin Airlift

AROUND KURFÜRSTENDAMM

The eastern area of the Charlottenburg region, around the boulevard known as Kurfürstendamm, was developed in the 19th century. Luxurious buildings were constructed along Kurfürstendamm (the Ku'damm), while the areas of Breitscheidplatz and Wittenbergplatz became replete with hotels and department stores. After World War II, with the old centre (Mitte) situated in East Berlin,

Sculpture from the Jüdisches Gemeindehaus

Charlottenburg became the centre of West Berlin. Traces of wartime destruction were removed very quickly and this area was transformed into the heart of West Berlin, and dozens of new company headquarters and trade centres were built. The situation changed after the reunification of Berlin, and although many tourists concentrate on Mitte, the heart of the city continues to beat around Kurfürstendamm.

SIGHTS AT A GLANCE

Museums
Käthe-Kollwitz-Museum ❿
Newton-Sammlung ❻

Streets and Squares
Fasanenstrasse ❾
Kurfürstendamm ❹
Savignyplatz ⓫
Tauentzien-
    strasse ⓮

Parks
Zoologischer
  Garten ❶

Historic Buildings
Europa-Center ❷
Jüdisches Gemeindehaus ❽
KaDeWe ⓯
*Kaiser-Wilhelm-Gedächtnis-
    Kirche pp152–3* ❸
Ludwig-Erhard-Haus ❺
Technische Universität ⓭
Theater des Westens ❼
    Universität der Künste ⓬

KEY

▨	Street-by-Street map *pp148–9*
🚉	Railway station
Ⓢ	S-Bahn station
Ⓤ	U-Bahn station
🚌	Bus station

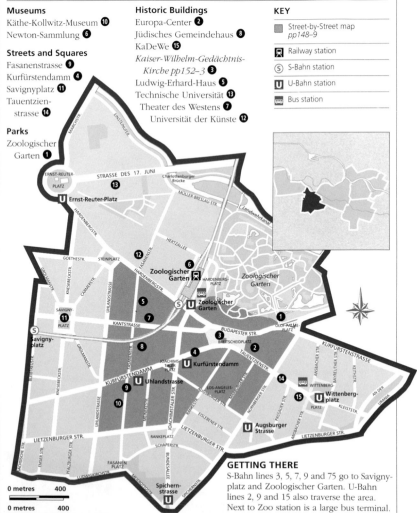

GETTING THERE

S-Bahn lines 3, 5, 7, 9 and 75 go to Savigny-platz and Zoologischer Garten. U-Bahn lines 2, 9 and 15 also traverse the area. Next to Zoo station is a large bus terminal.

0 metres   400

0 metres   400

◁ **Mosaic depicting a standard-bearer inside the Kaiser-Wilhelm-Gedächtnis-Kirche**

Street-by-Street: Breitscheidplatz and Ku'damm

The area surrounding the eastern end of the
Ku'damm, especially Tauentzienstrasse and
Breitscheidplatz, is the centre of the former
West Berlin. Thirty years ago this ultramodern
district, full of department stores and office
blocks, attracted visitors from all over the world.
Today, although the area still retains its unique
atmosphere, it is becoming overshadowed by
Potsdamer Platz and the arcades of Friedrichstrasse. However, nowhere else in Berlin is
there a place so full of life as Breitscheidplatz,
a department store with such style as KaDeWe,
or streets as refined as Fasanenstrasse.

Kant-Dreieck
*This building,
containing only
right angles,
was designed
by Josef Paul
Kleihues. The
"sail" on the
roof makes it
instantly
recognizable.*

Jüdisches Gemeindehaus
*Some of the remaining
fragments of the old
synagogue have been
incorporated into the
façade of this building* ⓼

Literaturhaus
contains a charming
café and a good
bookshop.

**Käthe-Kollwitz-
Museum**
*The museum is
housed in one of the
charming villas on
Fasanenstrasse* ⓾

Fasanenstrasse
*This tranquil street features
some of the most expensive
shops in Berlin* ⓽

Ku'damm
*A stroll along the Ku'damm is a
stroll into the heart of Berlin,
and an essential part of any
visit to the city* ❹

STAR SIGHTS

★ Kaiser-Wilhelm-
   Gedächtniskirche

★ Zoologischer
   Garten

KEY

 — — — Suggested route

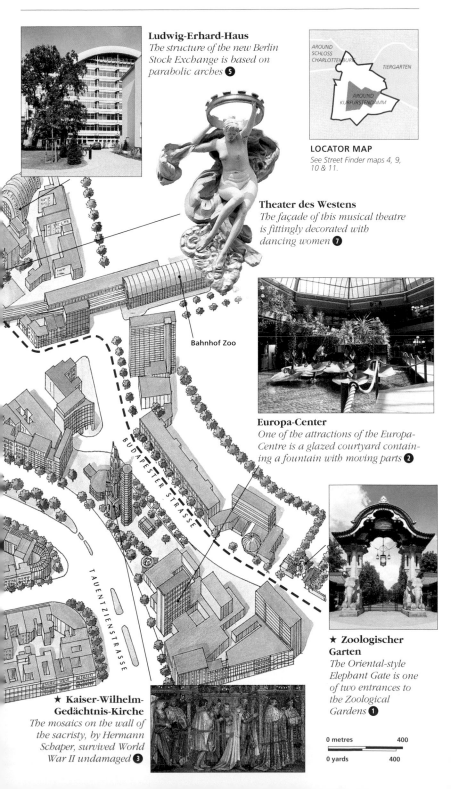

Ludwig-Erhard-Haus
The structure of the new Berlin Stock Exchange is based on parabolic arches **5**

LOCATOR MAP
See Street Finder maps 4, 9, 10 & 11.

Theater des Westens
The façade of this musical theatre is fittingly decorated with dancing women **7**

Bahnhof Zoo

Europa-Center
One of the attractions of the Europa-Centre is a glazed courtyard containing a fountain with moving parts **2**

★ **Zoologischer Garten**
The Oriental-style Elephant Gate is one of two entrances to the Zoological Gardens **1**

★ **Kaiser-Wilhelm-Gedächtnis-Kirche**
The mosaics on the wall of the sacristy, by Hermann Schaper, survived World War II undamaged **3**

0 metres	400
0 yards	400

Bao-Bao, one of the star attractions at the Zoologischer Garten

Zoologischer Garten ❶

ZOOLOGICAL GARDEN

Hardenbergplatz 8 or Budapester Strasse 34. **Map** 4 E5, 10 E1. **Tel** 25 40 10. Ⓢ & Ⓤ Zoologischer Garten. 🚌 100, 109, 110, 145, 146, 149, 200, 204, 245, 249, X-10, X-34. ◯ Apr–Sep: 9am–6:30pm daily; Oct: 9am–6pm daily; Nov–Mar: 9am–5pm daily. ♿

The Zoological Garden is one of Berlin's greatest attractions. It is part of the Tiergarten and dates from 1844, which makes this zoo one of the oldest in Germany. You can enter from Hardenbergplatz through the Lion's Gate, and from Budapester Strasse through the decorative Oriental-style Elephant Gate.

The zoo offers a number of attractions, including the monkey house, which contains a family of gorillas, and a darkened pavilion for nocturnal animals. The hippopotamus pool has a glazed wall that enables visitors to observe these enormous animals underwater. The aquarium, one of the largest in Europe, contains sharks, piranhas and unusual animals from coral reefs. There is also a huge terrarium with an overgrown jungle that is home to a group of crocodiles. Some of the best-loved animals at the zoo are the giant pandas – Bao-Bao and Yan-Yan.

Europa-Center ❷

Breitscheidplatz. **Map** 10 E1. Ⓢ & Ⓤ Zoologischer Garten. 🚌 100, 109, 119, 146, 200, 219, X-9.

The Europa-Center stands on the site of the legendary Romanisches Café, a famous meeting place for Dada artists in the 1920s. The current building was established in 1965, and since that time it has been one of the largest complexes of its type in the whole of Germany. Designed by Helmut Hentrich and Hubert Petschnigg, the Europa-Center is a group of low-rise buildings housing a trade centre, numerous restaurants and pubs. The uninspiring edifice of the deluxe Palace Hotel (see p226) has been incorporated into the centre, as well as a 22-storey office block.

Around the Center are dotted some amusing fountains, including the "Flow of Time Clock", designed by Bernard Gitton. Seconds, minutes and hours are measured in vials and spheres of green liquid. The Europa-Center also houses the political cabaret Die Stachelschweine and Berlin's largest tourist information centre (see pp278–9).

Kaiser-Wilhelm-Gedächtnis-Kirche ❸

See pp152–3.

Kurfürstendamm ❹

Map 9 A2, B2, C3, 10 D1. Ⓤ Kurfürstendamm. 🚌 109, 119, 129, 219.

This is undoubtedly one of the most elegant streets in Berlin. The wide avenue was established in the 1880s on the site of a former track that led to the Grunewald forest. It was quickly populated with imposing buildings and grand hotels. In the 20 years between World Wars I and II, the Ku'damm (as it is popularly called) was renowned for its great cafés, visited by famous writers, directors and painters.

After World War II, the damaged houses were replaced with modern buildings, but this did not change the essential character of this fine street. During the Cold War years it became a symbol of free-market consumerism and the main shopping street in West Berlin. Today, elegant shops and cafés with pretty summer gardens continue to attract a chic crowd.

Ludwig-Erhard-Haus ❺

Fasanenstrasse 83–84. **Map** 4 D5. Ⓢ & Ⓤ Zoologischer Garten. 🚌 145, 149, 245, X-9, X-39.

The distinctive curve of this innovative new building houses the headquarters of the Berlin stock exchange as well as a trade and industry centre. Completed in 1998, Ludwig-Erhard-Haus is the creation of British architect Nicholas Grimshaw and has been compared to the skin of an armadillo, a giant skeleton and the ribbing of a shell.

The main structure of the building is composed of 15 elliptical arches, which extend above the roof and down through the glass walls on each side of the building.

A fountain representing Earth, outside the Europa-Center

Newton-Sammlung 6

Jebensstrasse 2. **Map** 4 D5. *Tel* 20 90 55 66. Ⓢ & Ⓤ *Zoologischer Garten.* ◯ *10am–6pm Tue–Wed Fri–Sun, 10am–10pm Thu.* ♿

After his death in 2004, the society and art photographer Helmut Newton (1931–2004) bequeathed his life's work to the city of Berlin. Newton, who was born and received his first training as a photographer in Berlin, became one of the 20th-century's most well-known photographers with his images of nudes and portraits of the rich and famous.

The museum plans to broaden its collections to eventually serve as the city's museum of photography. Currently, it exhibits selections of Newton's work, including his early fashion and nude photography as well as self-portraits and landscapes.

The façade of the Theater des Westens on Kantstrasse

Theater des Westens 7

Kantstrasse 9–12. **Map** 10 D1. *Tel* (0180) 44 44. Ⓢ & Ⓤ *Zoologischer Garten.* 🚌 149, X-34.

The Theater des Westens, one of the most picturesque of all Berlin's theatres, was built in 1896 to a design by Bernhard Sehring. The composition of its façade links Neo-Classical elements with Palladian and Art Nouveau details. The interior of the theatre has been designed in a splendid Neo-Baroque style, while the back and the sections that houses the stage have been rebuilt

within a Neo-Gothic structure, incorporating the decorative elements of a chess set.

From its very beginning the theatre catered for lighter forms of musical entertainment. Operettas and vaudeville were staged here, followed by musicals such as *Les Miserables*. Some of the world's greatest stars have appeared on the stage here, including Josephine Baker, who performed her famous banana dance in 1926. Near the theatre is the renowned Delphi cinema and popular jazz club Quasimodo.

Jüdisches Gemeindehaus 8

JEWISH COMMUNITY HOUSE

Fasanenstrasse 79/80. **Map** 10 D1. Ⓤ *Uhlandstrasse or Kurfürstendamm.* 🚌 109, 119, 129, 149, 219, X-10, X-34.

The Jewish community has its headquarters in this building, constructed on the site of a synagogue that was burned down during *Kristallnacht* on 9 November 1938 *(see p29)*. The original synagogue was designed by Ehenfried Hessel in a Romanesque-Byzantine style and built in 1912. The ruins of the synagogue were removed only in the mid-1950s. The new building,

The entrance of the Jüdisches Gemeindehaus

designed by Dieter Knoblauch and Heinz Heise, was constructed in 1959. The only reminders of the splendour of the former synagogue are the portal at the entrance to the building and some decorative fragments on the façade.

Inside there are offices, a school, a kosher restaurant called Arche Noah and a prayer room covered by three glazed domes. At the rear there is a courtyard with a place of remembrance. There is also an emotive statue at the front of the building, depicting a broken scroll of the Torah (the holy book of Jewish Law).

GERMAN CINEMA

The 1920s were a boom time for the arts, and German cinema gained prominence throughout the world with the rise of Expressionism. The opening of the UFA film studios in 1919 in Babelsberg *(see p205)* was a milestone in the development of German cinema. The studios became the heart of the film industry and rivalled Hollywood as a centre for innovation. Many famous films were produced

Marlene Dietrich in the well-known film *The Blue Angel*

here, including the Expressionist masterpiece *The Cabinet of Dr Caligari* (1920) by Robert Wiene, Ernst Lubitsch's *Madame Dubarry* (1919) with Pola Negri and *Nosferatu* (1922) by Friedrich Murnau. Other films released by the studios were Fritz Lang's *Doctor Mabuse* (1922) and his futuristic film *Metropolis* (1927). In April 1930, the studios premiered Josef von Sternberg's *The Blue Angel* featuring the young Marlene Dietrich in the lead role. After Hitler came to power many directors and actors left Germany.

Kaiser-Wilhelm-Gedächtnis-Kirche ❸

This church-monument is one of Berlin's most famous landmarks, surrounded by a lively crowd of street traders, buskers and beggars. The vast Neo-Romanesque church was designed by Franz Schwechten. It was consecrated in 1895 but was destroyed by bombs in 1943. After World War II the ruins were removed, leaving only the massive front tower at the base of which the Gedenkhalle (Memorial Hall) is situated. This hall documents the history of the church and contains some of the original ceiling mosaics, marble reliefs and liturgical objects from the church. In 1961, Egon Eiermann designed a new octagonal church in blue glass and a new freestanding bell tower.

Bell Tower
The new hexagonal bell tower stands on the site of the former main nave of the destroyed church.

Kaiser's Mosaic
Kaiser Heinrich I is depicted here in this elaborate mosaic, sitting on his throne.

Rose window

Mosaic Decoration
Original mosaics remain on the arches and the walls near the staircase. These feature the Dukes of Prussia among the other decorative elements.

Walls of reinforced concrete and blue-coloured glass form a dense grid.

Main Altar
The vast figure of Christ on the Cross is the work of Karl Hemmeter.

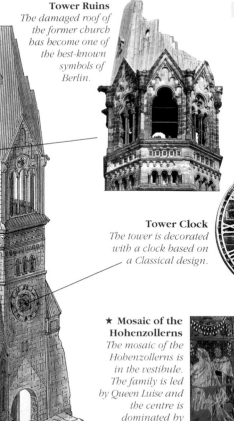

Tower Ruins
The damaged roof of the former church has become one of the best-known symbols of Berlin.

VISITORS' CHECKLIST

Breitscheidplatz. **Map** 10 D1.
Tel 218 50 23. Ⓢ & Ⓤ
Zoologischer Garten or
Ⓤ Kurfürstendamm.
🚌 100, 119, 129, 146, 200,
219, X-9. ⬜ **Church**
9am–7pm daily. **Gedenkhalle**
10am–4pm Mon–Sat. 🔔 10am
& 6pm Sun. 🖼

Tower Clock
The tower is decorated with a clock based on a Classical design.

★ Mosaic of the Hohenzollerns
The mosaic of the Hohenzollerns is in the vestibule. The family is led by Queen Luise and the centre is dominated by Kaiser Wilhelm I.

Orthodox Cross
This cross was a gift from the Russian Orthodox bishops from Volokolamsk and Yuryev, given in memory of the victims of Nazism.

Figure of Christ
This vast sculpture by Hermann Schaper once decorated the church altar. It survived World War II damage.

Main entrance

★ Coventry Crucifix
This modest cross was fashioned from nails found in the ashes of Coventry Cathedral, England. The Cathedral was destroyed during German bombing raids in 1940.

STAR SIGHTS

★ Mosaic of the Hohenzollerns

★ Coventry Crucifix

Fasanenstrasse – one of the most elegant streets in Berlin

Fasanenstrasse ❾

Map 9 C2, 10 D1, 10 D3.
Ⓤ *Uhlandstrasse.* 🚌 *109, 119, 129, 219, 249, X-10.*

The discreet charm of Fasanenstrasse, particularly between Lietzenburger Strasse and Kurfürstendamm, has attracted the most exclusive designer shops in the world. Well maintained buildings, *fin-de-siècle* villas set in tranquil gardens and elegant shop windows of jewellers, art galleries and fashion shops will all entice you to take an afternoon stroll along this street.

It is worth seeing the villas at No. 23–5, which are called the Wintergarten-Ensemble. The first one, No. 23, dates from 1889. Tucked away in a garden, the villa is home to the Literaturhaus, which organizes interesting exhibitions and readings. It has an excellent café that extends into a conservatory. At No. 24 is the Käthe-Kollwitz museum, and No. 25, built in 1892 by Hans Grisebach, accommodates an auction house and art gallery.

Käthe-Kollwitz-Museum ❿

Fasanenstrasse 24. **Map** 9 C2.
Tel 882 52 10. Ⓤ *Uhlandstrasse or Kurfürstendamm.* 🚌 *109, 119, 129, 219, 249, X-10.* ⏰ *11am–6pm Wed–Mon* 📷 🔲

This small private museum provides a unique opportunity to become acquainted with the work of Käthe Kollwitz (1867–1945). Born in Königsberg, the artist settled in Berlin where she married a doctor who worked in Prenzlauer Berg, a working-class district *(see p170)*. Her drawings and sculptures portrayed the social problems of the poor, as well as human tragedy and suffering. She frequently took up the theme of motherhood and war after losing a son and grandson in World Wars I and II.

The museum exhibits her work, including sculptures, posters and drawings, as well as letters and photographs.

Mother and Child, from the Käthe-Kollwitz-Museum

Savignyplatz ⓫

Map 9 C1. Ⓢ *Savignyplatz.* 🚌 *149.*

Savignyplatz is enclosed on the south side by the arcade of a railway viaduct, which appears in the film *Cabaret* by Bob Fosse. During the day the square does not look interesting – there are no remarkable historic buildings, only carefully tended greenery and flower beds. However, the area around the square truly comes alive at night. The dozens of cafés and restaurants fill up, while in summer the entire edge of the square and neighbouring streets turn into one big garden filled with tables and umbrellas. People come from outlying districts to visit popular restaurants and cafés such as Zwiebelfisch, Dicke Wirtin, or XII Apostel *(see p240)*. The arcades in the viaduct contain many cafés and bars. One section of the arcades has been taken up by the Bücherbogen bookshop *(see p254)*.

Universität der Künste ⓬

UNIVERSITY OF THE ARTS

Hardenbergstrasse 32–33 and Fasanenstrasse 1b. **Map** 4 D5.
Ⓢ *Zoologischer Garten or* Ⓤ *Ernst-Reuter-Platz.* 🚌 *145, 245, X-9.*

The Universität der Künste was originally called Preussische Akademie der Künste, which was established in 1696. It continued a long tradition of teaching artists in Berlin and has been headed by well-known figures including Johann Gottfried Schadow and Anton von Werner. As a result of a number of reforms between 1875 and 1882, the Academy was divided into two separate colleges. A complex of buildings was erected for them on Hardenbergstrasse and Fasanenstrasse. The Neo-Baroque buildings were constructed between 1897 and 1902 to a design by Heinrich Keyser and Karl von Grossheim.

After World War II, only two large buildings, both with decorative façades, survived. On the Hardenbergstrasse side was the Hochschule für Bildende Künste (College for Fine Art), while on the Fasanenstrasse side was the Hochschule für Musik und Darstellende Kunst (College for Music and Performing Arts). Unfortunately, the concert hall did not survive. A new one was built in 1955, designed by Paul Baumgarten.

Bas-relief sculpture on the façade of the Hochschule der Künste

A small *fin-de-siècle* building that looks like a castle, at Hardenbergstrasse No. 36, is a college for religious music which belongs to this group of college buildings.

Technische Universität ⓭

TECHNICAL UNIVERSITY

Strasse des 17 Juni 135. **Map** 3 C4. Ⓤ *Ernst-Reuter-Platz.* 🚌 *145, 245, X-9.*

The vast area that lies to the east of Ernst-Reuter-Platz along the Strasse des 17 Juni is occupied by the buildings of the Technische Universität. Officially called Technische Hochschule Berlin (TUB), it was established in 1879 after the unification of the School of Crafts and the renowned Bauakademie. From its inception the Technische Universität had five different departments, which were all housed, from 1884, in a Neo-Renaissance building designed by Richard Lucae, Friedrich Hitzig and Julius Raschdorff. After World War II, the ruined front wing was rebuilt as a flat block without any divisions, while the rear wings and three internal courtyards retained their original appearance.

It is worth continuing along Strasse des 17 Juni towards the colonnade of the Charlottenburger Tor (or gate), dating from 1908. The colonnade is ornamented with the figures of Friedrich and Sophie Charlotte holding a model of Schloss Charlottenburg *(see pp160–1)* in their hands. Beyond the gate and to the right, on the island, is an unusual green building with a gigantic pink pipe. This is the centre that monitors water currents and caters to the needs of seagoing vessels.

Tauentzienstrasse ⓮

Map 10 E1. Ⓤ *Wittenbergplatz.* 🚌 *119, 129, 146, 219.*

This is one of the most important streets for trade and commerce in this part of Berlin. The shops are not as expensive or as elegant as on Kurfürstendamm – but they attract more visitors for this reason. One of the highlights of the street is the unusual façade of the department store Peek & Clopenburg. Designed by Gottfried Böhm, the walls of the building are covered with transparent, gently slanting and undulating "aprons".

Other highlights include the central bed of colourful flowers as well as an interesting sculpture entitled *Berlin*. Created by Brigitte and Martin Matschinsky-Denninghoff, the sculpture was erected near Marburger Strasse in 1987 on the occasion of the 750th anniversary of Berlin.

KaDeWe ⓯

Tauentzienstrasse 21–24. **Map** 10 E2. *Tel 21 21 00.* Ⓤ *Wittenbergplatz.* 🚌 *119, 129, 146, 185, 219.* ◯ *10am–8pm Mon–Fri, 9:30am–8pm Sat.*

Kaufhaus des Westens, or KaDeWe, as it is popularly known, is the largest department store in Europe. It was built in 1907 to a design by Emil Schaudt, but it has been extended several times from the original building. From the very beginning KaDeWe was Berlin's most exclusive department store with a comprehensive collection of goods for sale and with a slogan that ran "In our shop a customer is a king, and the King is a customer".

After World War II, KaDeWe effectively became the symbol of the economic success of West Berlin. You can buy everything here, however, the main attraction must be the gourmet's paradise, with the largest collection of foodstuffs in the whole of Europe. Here there are exotic fruits and vegetables, live fish and seafood, 100 varieties of tea, more than 2,400 wines and a host of other gastronomic delights. KaDeWe also has a restaurant, the Wintergarten.

The sculpture *Berlin*, symbolizing the former divided Berlin

AROUND SCHLOSS CHARLOTTENBURG

The area surrounding Schloss Charlottenburg is one of the most enchanting regions of the city, full of greenery and attractive buildings dating from the end of the 19th century. Originally a small settlement called Lützow, it was only when Elector Friedrich III (later King Friedrich I) built his wife's summer retreat here at the end of the 17th century *(see p21)* that this town attained significance. Initially called Schloss

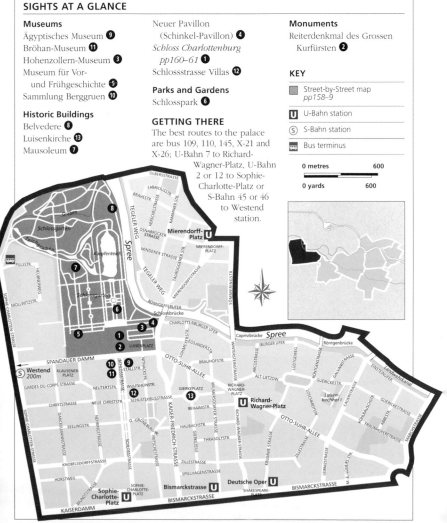

Urn at Schloss Charlottenburg

Lietzenburg, the palace was renamed Schloss Charlottenburg after the death of Queen Sophie Charlotte. By the 18th century Charlottenburg had become a town, and was for many years an independent administration, inhabited by wealthy people living in elegant villas. It became officially part of Berlin in 1920, and despite World War II and the ensuing division of the city, the central section of this area has kept its historic character.

SIGHTS AT A GLANCE

Museums
Ägyptisches Museum **9**
Bröhan-Museum **11**
Hohenzollern-Museum **3**
Museum für Vor-
    und Frühgeschichte **5**
Sammlung Berggruen **10**

Historic Buildings
Belvedere **8**
Luisenkirche **13**
Mausoleum **7**

Neuer Pavillon
    (Schinkel-Pavillon) **4**
Schloss Charlottenburg
    pp160–61 **1**
Schlossstrasse Villas **12**

Parks and Gardens
Schlosspark **6**

GETTING THERE
The best routes to the palace are bus 109, 110, 145, X-21 and X-26; U-Bahn 7 to Richard-Wagner-Platz, U-Bahn 2 or 12 to Sophie-Charlotte-Platz or S-Bahn 45 or 46 to Westend station.

Monuments
Reiterdenkmal des Grossen
    Kurfürsten **2**

KEY

▨	Street-by-Street map *pp158–9*
Ⓤ	U-Bahn station
Ⓢ	S-Bahn station
🚌	Bus terminus

0 metres	600
0 yards	600

The façade of Schloss Charlottenburg, originally the summer residence of Elector Friedrich III

Street-by Street: Around the Schloss

The park surrounding the former royal summer residence in Charlottenburg is one of the most picturesque places in Berlin. Visitors are drawn here by the meticulous post-war rebuilding of this luxury Baroque complex and outlying structures, whose marvellous interiors were once home to Prussian nobles. The wings of the palace and its pavilions house interesting exhibitions. After a stroll in the beautiful park, you can take refreshment in the Kleine Orangerie.

Detail from the main gate

★ Schloss Charlottenburg
The central section of the palace is called Nering-Eosanderbau, in honour of the architects who designed the building ❶

Museum für Vor- und Frühgeschichte
The museum is housed in a pavilion which served formerly as the court theatre, designed by Carl Gotthard Langhans ❺

Monument to the Great Elector
The momument to the Great Elector was funded by his son King Friedrich I and designed by Andreas Schlüter ❷

Kleine Orangerie

Hohenzollern-Museum
This museum is planned for the new wing of the palace and will house a selection of precious items from the royal collection ❸

KEY

– – – Suggested route

Mausoleum
In the Neo-Classical mausoleum built for Queen Luise, members of the royal family are laid to rest 🥈

LOCATOR MAP
See Street Finder map 2.

Belvedere
In 1960 Karl Bobeck created the group of statues that surmount the Belvedere, in imitation of the original figures which were designed by Johann Eckstein 🥉

Palace Park
A French-style park, laid-out in a geometric pattern, extends behind the palace 🥈

★ **Neuer Pavillon**
In front of the western elevation of this pavilion are two granite columns (1840), topped by statues of Victory, the work of Christian Daniel Rauch 🥈

0 metres   150

0 yards   150

STAR SIGHTS

★ Schloss Charlottenburg

★ Neuer Pavillon

Schloss Charlottenburg ❶

The palace in Charlottenburg was intended as a summer home for Sophie Charlotte, Elector Friedrich III's wife. Construction began in 1695 to a design by Johann Arnold Nering. Between 1701 and 1713 Johann Friedrich Eosander enlarged the palace, crowning it with a cupola and adding the orangery wing. Subsequent extensions were undertaken by Frederick the Great (Friedrich II), who added the Neuer Flügel, designed by Georg Wenzeslaus von Knobelsdorff, between 1740 and 1746. Restored to its former elegance following World War II, its collection of richly decorated interiors is unequalled in Berlin.

GALLERY GUIDE

The ground floor of the main building must be visited by guided tour. The upper floor and the Neuer Flügel, containing the private apartment of Frederik the Great, can be visited independently.

First floor

Ground floor

★ **Porzellankabinett**
This exquisite mirrored gallery has walls lined from top to bottom with a fine display of Japanese and Chinese porcelain.

Schlosskapelle
Only parts of the pulpit in the court chapel are original to the palace. All the other furniture and fittings, including the royal box, are reconstructions.

Main entrance

Façade
The central section of the palace is the oldest part of the building, and is the work of Johann Arnold Nering.

Cupola
The palace's tall, Baroque cupola completes the perspective from Schlossstrasse.

Fortuna
A new sculpture by Richard Scheibe crowns the palace, replacing the original statue destroyed during World War II.

VISITORS' CHECKLIST

Luisenplatz. **Map** 2 E2.
Altes Schloss (Nering-Eosanderbau) *Tel* 32 09 12 75.
U *Richard-Wagner-Platz & Sophie-Charlotte- Platz.*
S *Westend.* 109, 145, 210, X-21. ☐ *9am–5pm Tue–Fri, 10am–5pm Sat & Sun.* compulsory on ground floor only.
Neuer Flügel (Knobels-dorff-Flügel) *Tel* 32 09 12 02.
☐ *10am–6pm Tue–Fri, 11am–6pm Sat & Sun.*

KEY

- ☐ Official reception rooms
- ☐ Apartments of Sophie-Charlotte
- ☐ Neuer Flügel or Knobelsdorff-Flügel exhibition space
- ◼ Friedrich Wilhelm II's summer apartments
- ☐ Mecklenburg apartments
- ☐ Apartments of Friedrich Wilhelm IV
- ☐ Friedrich Wilhelm II's winter apartments
- ☐ Frederick the Great's apartments

Ahnengalerie
This long gallery, lined with huge oil paintings and decorated with oak-panelling, was completed in 1713.

Weisser Saal

Goldene Galerie

Neuer Flügel
The new wing holds the elegant apartments and exquisite furniture of Frederick the Great.

Entrance to Neuer Flügel

★ Gersaint's Shop Sign (1720)
An avid collector of French painting, Frederick the Great bought this and other fine canvases by Antoine Watteau for his collection.

The Monument to the Great Elector standing in front of Schloss Charlottenburg

Reiterdenkmal des Grossen Kurfürsten ❷

MONUMENT TO THE GREAT ELECTOR

Luisenplatz. **Map** 2 E2. 🚇 *Richard-Wagner-Platz & Sophie-Charlotte-Platz.* Ⓢ *Westend.* 🚌 *109, 145, 210, X-21.*

The statue of the Great Elector (Friedrich Wilhelm) is the finest in Berlin and was paid for by his son, Elector Friedrich III (later King Friedrich I). Designed by Andreas Schlüter to be cast in one piece, the statue was started in 1696 but not finished until 1703. It was initially erected near the former Berlin palace, by Lange Brücke (now called Rathausbrücke). The statue was moved to safety during World War II but ironically, on the return journey, the barge transporting the monument sank in the port of Tegel.

In 1949 the statue was retrieved intact from the water and erected in the courtyard of Schloss Charlottenburg. However, it lacked the original base which was left behind in East Berlin, so a copy was commissioned. The original base finally ended up in the Bodemuseum topped with a replica of the statue.

The statue portrays the Great Elector as a warrior in ancient armour (albeit wearing a 17th-century wig) mounted on horseback, triumphant over the figures of prisoners of war around the base. The base itself is decorated with patriotic reliefs of allegorical scenes. One scene depicts the kingdom surrounded by figures representing History, Peace and the Spree river; another shows the kingdom protected by embodiments of Faith, Bravery (in the form of Mucius Scaevola) and Strength (represented by the figure of Hercules).

Hohenzollern-Museum ❸

Luisenplatz (Schloss Charlottenburg–Neuer Flügel). **Map** 2 E2. **Tel** 20 90 55 66. 🚇 *Richard-Wagner-Platz & Sophie-Charlotte-Platz.* Ⓢ *Westend.* 🚌 *109, 145, 210.* ⬛ *until 2005 for the installation of the new collection.*

Built between 1740 and 1746, the new wing of Schloss Charlottenburg used to house the popular Galerie der Romantik. The main part of this collection of Romantic paintings has now been

returned to the Alte National-galerie *(see p78)*. The rest have been moved to the Neuer Pavillon. In its place, a new museum that will bring together precious items from the Hohenzollern family collection, including paintings, craft objects and furniture, is due to open in late 2005.

Neuer Pavillon (Schinkel-Pavillon) ❹

Luisenplatz (Schlosspark Charlottenburg). **Map** 2 F2. **Tel** 32 09 11. 🚇 *Richard-Wagner-Platz & Sophie-Charlotte-Platz.* Ⓢ *Westend.* 🚌 *109, 210, X-21.* ⬛ *10am–5pm Tue–Sun.* 🎟

This charming Neo-Classical pavilion, with its clean lines and first-floor balcony, was built for Friedrich Wilhelm III and his second wife, Princess Auguste von Liegnitz. During a visit to Naples, the king stayed in the Villa Reale del Chiamonte and was so impressed that he commissioned Karl Friedrich Schinkel to build him something similar. The pavilion was completed for the king's birthday on 3 August 1825. Schinkel designed a two-storey structure with a central staircase and ranged the rooms around it in perfect symmetry. Pillared galleries, on the first floor, added variety to the eastern and western elevations. A cast iron balcony runs around the entire structure.

The display inside the pavilion reveals the original splendour and atmosphere of

The Neuer Pavillon which was modelled on a Neapolitan villa

the aristocratic interiors, enhanced with pictures and sculptures of the period. The prize picture is a renowned panorama of Berlin dated 1834, painted by Eduard Gärtner from the roof of the Friedrichs-werdersche Kirche *(see p63)*.

The painting collection has recently been enhanced through the addition of works from the old Galerie der Romantik. These include landscapes by Casper David Friedrich. You can also admire the paintings of Karl Friedrich Schinkel, who was not only a great architect but also a fine painter of fabulous architectural fantasies.

Urn (c.800 BC) from the Museum für Vor- und Frühgeschichte

Museum für Vor- und Frühgeschichte ❺

MUSEUM OF PRE- AND EARLY HISTORY

Luisenplatz (Schloss Charlotten-burg–Theater). **Map** 2 E2. *Tel 20 90 55 66.* Ⓤ *Richard-Wagner-Platz & Sophie-Charlotte-Platz.* Ⓢ *Westend.* 🚌 *109, 145, 210, X-21.* ⏰ *10am–6pm Tue–Fri, 11am– 6pm Sat & Sun.* ♿

Originally used as the court theatre, this Neo-Classical pavilion was designed by Carl Gotthard Langhans and added to the orangery wing of Schloss Charlottenburg between 1787 and 1791. It now holds a museum that documents the development of early cultures and civilizations. The evolution of mankind from prehistoric times, through the Stone Age, Bronze Age and Iron Age up to medieval times is portrayed by means of dioramas, skulls (real and imitation) and a

large display of pottery, tools, weapons and artifacts. A similar wealth of archaeological finds charts the growth of Celtic, Germanic, Slavic, Baltic and even Sumerian civilizations.

The museum's best display is a magnificent collection from the ancient city of Troy, donated in 1881 by Heinrich Schliemann. The collection contains an array of tools and pottery on the second floor, and a spectacular collection of gold jewellery known as "The Treasure of Priam". Some of the exhibits are replicas, the originals having disappeared after World War II. Many originals, however, are now in the Pushkin Museum, Moscow.

Schlosspark ❻

PALACE PARK

Luisenplatz (Schloss Charlottenburg). **Map** 2 D1. Ⓤ *Richard-Wagner-Platz & Sophie-Charlotte-Platz.* Ⓢ *Westend.* 🚌 *109, 145, 210, X-21.*

This extensive royal park surrounding Schloss Charlottenburg *(see pp160–61)*, criss-crossed with tidy gravel paths, is a favourite place for Berliners to stroll at the weekend. The park is largely the result of reconstruction work carried out after World War II, when 18th-century prints were used to help reconstruct the varied layout of the original grounds. Immediately behind Schloss Charlottenburg is a French-style Baroque garden, made to a strict geometrical design with a vibrant patchwork of flower beds, carefully trimmed shrubs and ornate fountains adorned with replicas of antique sculptures. Further away from the

palace, beyond the curved carp lake, is a less formal English-style landscaped park, the original layout of which was created between 1819 and 1828 under the direction of the renowned royal gardener, Peter Joseph Lenné.

Mausoleum ❼

Luisenplatz (Schlosspark Charlotten-burg) **Map** 2 D2. *Tel 32 09 14 46.* Ⓤ *Richard-Wagner-Platz & Sophie-Charlotte-Platz.* Ⓢ *Westend.* 🚌 *109, 145, 210.* ⏰ *Apr–Oct: 10am–noon 1–5pm Tue–Sun.* ♿

Queen luise, the beloved wife of Friedrich Wilhelm III, was laid to rest in this dignified, modest building, set among the trees in Schloss-park. The mausoleum was designed by Karl Friedrich Schinkel, in the style of a Doric portico-fronted temple.

In the original design, the queen's sarcophagus was housed in the crypt while the tombstone (actually a ceno-taph sculpted by Christian Daniel Rauch) stood in the centre of the mausoleum. After the death of Friedrich Wilhelm in 1840, the mausoleum was refurbished; an apse added and the queen's tomb moved to one side, leaving room for her husband's tomb, also designed by Rauch. The second wife of the king, Princess Auguste von Liegnitz, was also buried in the crypt of the mausoleum, but without a tombstone.

Between the years 1890 and 1894, the tombs of Kaiser Wilhelm I and his wife, Auguste von Sachsen-Weimar, were added to the crypt. Both monuments are the work of Erdmann Encke.

French-style garden in the Schloss Charlottenburg park

The Belvedere's Baroque flourishes and clean Neo-Classical lines

Belvedere ⓐ

Spandauer Damm (Schlosspark Charlottenburg). **Map** 2 E1. **Tel** *32 09 14 45.* Ⓤ *Richard-Wagner-Platz & Sophie-Charlotte-Platz.* Ⓢ *Westend.* 🚌 *109, 145, 210.* 🕐 *Apr–Oct: 10am–5pm Tue–Sun; Nov–Mar: noon–4pm Tue–Fri, noon– 5pm Sat & Sun.* 🖼

The Belvedere is a summerhouse in the Schlosspark which served as a tea pavilion for Friedrich Wilhelm II and, in times of war, as a watchtower. It dates from 1788 and was designed by Carl Gotthard Langhans. The architect mixed Baroque and Neo-Classical elements, giving the building an oval central structure with four straight-sided annexes. The building is crowned by a low dome topped with a sculpture of three cherubs dragging a basket of flowers.

Ruined during World War II, the summer-house was reconstructed between 1956 and 1960 and adapted to serve as exhibition space. The exhibition is a large collection of porcelain from the Berlin Königliche Porzellan-Manufaktur (Royal Porcelain Workshop), which has pieces from the Rococo period up to late Biedermeier, including some outstanding individual items.

Ägyptisches Museum ⓑ

EGYPTIAN MUSEUM

Schlossstrasse 70. **Map** 2 E3. **Tel** *20 90 55 60.* Ⓤ *Richard-Wagner- Platz & Sophie-Charlotte-Platz.* Ⓢ *Westend.* 🚌 *109, 145, 210, X-21.* 🕐 *10am–6pm Tue–Sun.*

The two pavilions on either side of Schlossstrasse were intended as officers' barracks for the Kings's Garde du Corps. Built between the years 1851 and 1859 by Friedrich August Stüler, they were inspired by a design by King Friedrich Wilhelm IV. The eastern pavilion joins the stable block and now houses the collection of the Egyptian Museum. Numerous sculptures, sarcophagi, murals and architectural fragments of various eras are on display, including the *Berlin Green Head*, a 4th-century BC head carved from green stone. The greatest attraction, however, is the fascinating collection from the 19th century archaeological digs by Richard Lepsius and

Ludwig Borchardt in Tell el-Amarna. This was the capital of Egypt during the era of the reign of Amenhotep IV, a Pharaoh in the 14th century BC, also called Akhenaten. He revolutionized Egyptian religion, introducing the cult of the god Aton, and also brought about a radical change in the basic principles of representative arts. In a break from previous traditions he and his wife, Nefertiti, are depicted with broad hips and swollen stomachs. While the Pharaoh is plainly depicted, the queen's face is beautiful, as can be seen from the other representations in the museum. The most renowned is the delicate, long-necked *Nefertiti Bust*, carved from limestone and carefully painted. This delightful exhibit was discovered in 1912 in the workshop of the ancient Egyptian sculptor Thutmosis.

Sammlung Berggruen ⓒ

Schlossstrasse 1. **Map** 2 E3. **Tel** *20 90 55 60.* Ⓤ *Richard-Wagner-Platz & Sophie-Charlotte-Platz.* Ⓢ *Westend.* 🚌 *109, 145, 210, X-21.* 🕐 *10am–6pm Tue–Sun.*

Heinz Berggruen assembled this tasteful collection of art dating from the late 19th and first half of the 20th century. Born and educated in Berlin, he emigrated to the US in 1936, spent most of his life in Paris, but finally entrusted his collection to the city of his birth. The museum opened in 1996, in what was once the west pavilion of the barracks using space freed up by moving the Antikensammlung to Museum Island *(see p75)*. The exhibition halls were modified according to the designs of Hilmer and Sattler, who also designed the layout of the Gemäldegalerie. The Sammlung

Figure from Ägyptisches Museum (c.660 BC)

Pablo Picasso's *Woman in a Hat* (1939), Sammlung Berggruen

Berggruen is particularly well-known for its large collection of quality paintings, drawings and gouaches by Pablo Picasso. In addition to these, the museum displays more than 20 works by Swiss artist Paul Klee and paintings by other major artists from that time. The exhibition is supplemented by some excellent sculptures, particularly those of Henri Laurens and Alberto Giacometti.

Bröhan-Museum ⑪

Schlossstrasse 1a. **Map** 2 E3. *Tel* 32 69 06 00. **U** *Richard-Wagner-Platz & Sophie-Charlotte-Platz.* **S** *Westend.* 🚌 *109, 145, 210, X-21.* 🕐 *10am–6pm Tue–Sun.* ● *24 & 31 Dec.* 📷

Located in a late-Neo-Classical building which, like the Sammlung Berggruen, was formerly used as army barracks, is this small but interesting museum. The collection of decorative arts was amassed by Karl H Bröhan, who from 1966 collected works of art from the Art Nouveau (Jugend-stil or Secessionist) and Art Deco styles. The paintings of the artists particularly connected with the Berlin Secessionist movement, such as Karl Hagermeister and Hans Baluschek, are especially well represented. Alongside the paintings there are fine examples of other media and crafts: furniture, ceramics, glassware, silverwork and textiles.

Art Deco vase, Brohan-Museum

THE GREAT ELECTOR (1620–88)

The Elector Friedrich Wilhelm was one of the most famous rulers of the Hohenzollern dynasty. He inherited the position of Elector of Brandenburg in 1640. Brandenburg-Prussia, founded in 1618, was subject to the Polish crown. One of his first duties was to rebuild the region after the devastation of the 30 Years' War *(see p21)* and in 1660 he wrested the territory from Poland. During the course of his reign, Berlin became a powerful city. Rich families from all over Europe, fleeing persecution in their own land, chose to settle in Berlin – wealthy Dutch merchants, Huguenots from France and Jews from Vienna following the Edict of Potsdam (1685).

Each of the main halls features an individual artist, but often using an array of artistic media. There is also a display of furniture by Hector Guimard, Eugène Gaillard, Henri van de Velde and Joseph Hoffmann, glasswork by Emile Gallé, and porcelain from the best European manufacturers.

Schlossstrasse Villas ⑫

Schlossstrasse 65–67. **Map** 2 E3. **U** *Sophie-Charlotte-Platz.* 🚌 *210.*

Most of the historic villas and buildings that once graced Schlossstrasse no longer exist. However, careful restoration of a few villas enables the visitor to get a feel for what the atmosphere must have been like at the end of the 19th century. It is worth taking a stroll down Schlossstrasse to look at three of the renovated villas — No. 65, No. 66 and especially No. 67. The latter villa was built in 1873, in a Neo-Classical style to a design by G Töbelmann. After World War II the building was refurbished to return it to its former splendour. The front garden, however, a characteristic of the area, was only returned to its original state in 1986, when several villas had their gardens restored.

If you continue the walk down the nearby Schustehrusstrasse, there is an interesting school building at No. 39–43 linked to the Villa Oppenheim since the end of the 19th century. In the same area another school building on Nithackstrasse has survived. Built between 1913 and 1914, its sides are covered in pretty terracotta decorations.

Luisenkirche ⑬

LUISE CHURCH

Gierkeplatz. **Map** 2 F3. *Tel* 341 90 61. **U** *Richard-Wagner-Platz & Sophie-Charlotte-Platz.* 🚌 *109, 145, X-9.* 🕐 *during Sunday service (10 & 11:30am).*

This small church has undergone a series of re-designs and refurbishments in its lifetime. The original plans by Philipp Gerlach were first adapted by Martin Böhme, before the church was built (1713–16). Its Baroque styling was removed in the next course of rebuilding, undertaken by Karl Friedrich Schinkel from 1823 to 1826, when the church was renamed in memory of Queen Luise, who died in 1810. The most recent refurbishment took place after the church suffered major damage during World War II.

The shape of the church is based on a traditional Greek cross, with a tower at the front. The interior fixtures and fittings are not the originals, and the elegant stained-glass windows were only made in 1956.

FURTHER AFIELD

Coat of Arms on the Oberbaumbrücke

Berlin is an extensive city with a totally unique character, shaped by its history. Up until 1920 the actual city of Berlin consisted only of the districts which now comprise mainly Mitte, Tiergarten, Wedding, Prenzlauer Berg, Friedrichshain and Kreuzberg. It was surrounded by satellite towns and villages, which for many years had been evolving independently. Each of these had its own administrative centre, parish church, and individual architecture.

In 1920, as part of great administrative reforms, seven towns were incorporated into Berlin, along with 59 communes, and 27 country estates. This reform effected the creation of an entirely new city occupying around 900 sq km (348 sq miles), with a population that had expanded to 3.8 million.

In this way the range of the metropolis extended to small towns with medieval origins, such as Spandau.

Private estates and palaces, such as Britz and Niederschönhausen, were absorbed into Berlin. So were many old villages, such as Marienfelde with its 13th-century church. Suburban housing developments full of luxury villas were also incorporated.

Over the last hundred years the faces of many of these places have changed. Modern housing developments have arisen together with industrial centres, although the character of individual areas has remained intact. Thanks to this diversity, a stay in Berlin is like visiting many cities simultaneously. A short journey by S-Bahn enables you to travel from a metropolitan city centre of the 21st century to the vast forests of the Grunewald or the beach at Wannsee. You can explore everything from Dahlem's tranquil streets lined with villas to Spandau with its Renaissance citadel and vast Gothic church of St Nicholas.

MAP OF GREATER BERLIN

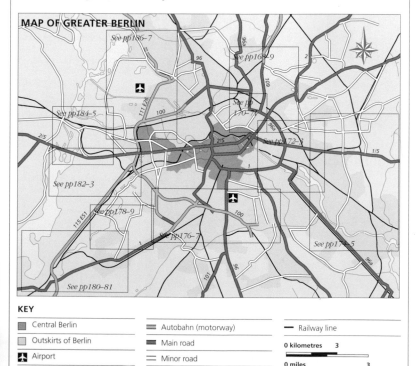

KEY

■ Central Berlin	▬ Autobahn (motorway)
□ Outskirts of Berlin	▬ Main road
✈ Airport	▬ Minor road

— Railway line

0 kilometres 3

0 miles 3

◁ **The tranquil Botanischer Garten in Southwest Berlin** *(see p177)*

Northeast Berlin

In the northeast of Berlin, but still within the Mitte district, a fragment of the Berlin Wall has survived; this has been earmarked as a place of remembrance. Further east extends Prenzlauer Berg *(see pp170–71)*, currently the most fashionable area for alternative youth culture. In the southern part of Pankow is the Baroque palace of Niederschönhausen. From here it is also worth setting off to see the Weissensee district, which has one of the largest Jewish cemeteries in Europe.

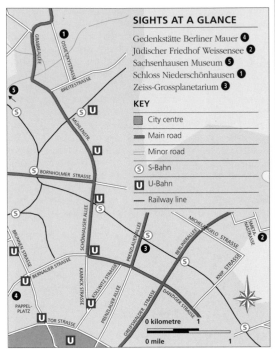

SIGHTS AT A GLANCE

Gedenkstätte Berliner Mauer ❹
Jüdischer Friedhof Weissensee ❷
Sachsenhausen Museum ❺
Schloss Niederschönhausen ❶
Zeiss-Grossplanetarium ❸

KEY

▦	City centre
▬	Main road
═	Minor road
Ⓢ	S-Bahn
Ⓤ	U-Bahn
▬	Railway line

The property remained in the hands of the Prussian royal family for the next hundred years. Among those who resided here were Princess Auguste von Liegnitz, following the death of her husband, King Friedrich Wilhelm III.

After World War II the rebuilt palace was occupied by the president of the German Democratic Republic, Wilhelm Pieck. In 1990 Round Table discussions were held here and the treaty to reunify Germany was signed here on 3 October that year.

Make time for a stroll through the vast park, which has kept the character bestowed by Peter Joseph Lenné in the 1820s.

Jüdischer Friedhof Weissensee ❷

Herbert-Baum-Strasse 45. ☐ 925 08 33. ☐ 8am–4pm (5pm in summer) Sun– Thu, 8am–3pm Fri. Ⓢ Greifs-walder Strasse, then ▦ 2, 3, 4, 13, 23, 24.

This extensive Jewish cemetery is the final resting place for more than 115,000 Berliners, many of whom were victims of Nazi persecution. The cemetery was established in 1880 according to a design by Hugo Licht.

By the main entrance is a place of remembrance for the victims of the Holocaust, with plaques bearing the names of the concentration camps. Buried here are renowned figures from Berlin's Jewish cultural and commercial past. Among others here rest the publisher Samuel Fischer and the restaurateur Berthold Kempinski.

Some tombstones are outstanding works of art, such as that of the Panowsky family, designed by Ludwig Hoffmann, or the Cubist tombstone of Albert Mendel, designed by Walter Gropius.

In 1999 Weissensee cemetery was desecrated in an act of anti-Semitic vandalism. More than 100 headstones were kicked over and some were smeared with swastikas.

Schloss Niederschönhausen ❶

Ossietzkystrasse Ⓢ Pankow. ▦ 52. ▦ 107, 155, 250, 255, X-33. **Schloss** ◉ closed to public. **Park** ☐ 8am–8pm daily.

This palace, located in an extensive and picturesque park, belonged to the von Dohna family during the 17th century. Ownership of the estate passed to the Elector Friedrich III in 1691, for whom Johann Arnold Nering designed the palace. In 1704 it was extended to a design by Johann Friedrich Eosander von Göthe, who added side wings. The palace was home to Queen

Christine, estranged wife of Frederick the Great, between 1740 and 1797. In 1763 further extensive refurbishment was undertaken by architect Johann Boumann.

A section of the garden elevation of Schloss Niederschönhausen

Silvery dome of the Zeiss-Grossplanetarium

Zeiss-Gross-planetarium ❸

Prenzlauer Allee 80 (Ernst-Thälmann-Park) *Tel 42 18 45 12 (reservations).* Ⓢ *Prenzlauer Allee, then* 🚋 *1.* ◻ *call for details.* ▨

The silvery dome visible from afar is the huge planetarium, built in the grounds of a park dedicated to the memory of the inter-war communist leader Ernst Thälmann, who died at Buchenwald concentration camp. The foyer of the planetarium houses an exhibition of optical equipment and various accessories produced by the renowned factory of Carl-Zeiss-Jena.

Gedenkstätte Berliner Mauer ❹

Bernauer Strasse 111. Ⓢ *Nordbahn-hof.* Ⓤ *Bernauer Strasse.* 🚌 *147, 245.* **Wall Documentation Center** *Tel 464 10 30.* ◻ *10am–5pm Wed–Sun.* ▨ *2pm Sat & Sun.*

On the night between 12 and 13 August 1961 the East German authorities decided to close the border around the western sectors of Berlin. Initially the Berlin Wall *(die Mauer)* consisted simply of rolls of barbed wire. However, these were soon replaced by a 4-m (13-ft) wall safeguarded by a second wall made from reinforced concrete. This second wall was topped with a thick pipe to prevent people from reaching the top of the Wall with their fingers.

Along the Wall ran what was known as a "death zone", an area controlled by guards with dogs. Where the border passed close to houses, the inhabitants were relocated, while windows on to the "western" street were bricked up. Along the border with West Berlin there were 293 watch towers and 57 bunkers. Later, there were alarms, too.

On 9 November 1989, with the help of Soviet leader Mikhail Gorbachev, the Berlin Wall was finally breached. Dismantling it took much longer, however, with more than a million tons of rubble to be removed.

Only small fragments of the Wall have survived. One of these, along Bernauer Strasse between Acker- and Berg-strasse, is now an official place of remembrance.

During the Wall's 28-year existence, about 5,000 people managed to escape into West Berlin; a total of 192 people were killed by the Eastern border guards while attempting to do so.

Sachsenhausen Museum ❺

Strasse der Nationen 22, Oranienburg. *Tel 03301/2000.* Ⓢ *Oranienburg, then* 🚌 *804.* ◻ *Apr–Sep: 8:30am–6pm Tue–Sun; Oct–Mar: 8:30am–4:30pm Tue–Sun.* 🖥 www. sachsenhausen.brandenburg.de

Built by the Nazis in 1936, the concentration camp at Sachsenhausen was liberated in 1945 by the Russians. Up to 200,000 people were incarcerated in this camp during its nine-year existence. However, when the Soviet Army entered Sachsenhausen, there were only 3,000 inmates in the camp, mostly women and sick people.

The iron gate at the entrance bears a sign that reads *"Arbeit macht frei"* ("Work will set you free"), and indeed, many early prisoners were released upon demonstrating that they had learned how to be "good German citizens". By 1939, however, fewer prisoners were being released. It is estimated that over 30,000 people died in the camp, killed by hunger, disease or mass extermination.

Sachsenhausen is now a museum. Each area of the camp hosts a relevant exhibit – for example, the one in the former infirmary focuses on medicine and racism under the Nazi regime. Other exhibits illustrate the daily life of the prisoners, or the way Sachsenhausen worked as a Soviet Special Camp between 1945 and 1950, when it housed Nazi functionaries and political undesirables.

Former entrance to the Sachsenhausen Prison Camp

Prenzlauer Berg

Once one of the most impoverished and densely populated working-class districts of Berlin, the 19th-century tenement houses in Prenzlauer Berg are now occupied by students, young families, artists and an increasing number of West Berliners looking for more affordable apartments. Even during communist times, this area was known for its independent art and nightlife scene which still thrives today around Kollwitzplatz, along the beautifully restored Husemannstrasse and the Kastanienallee, and in former factories in the vicinity.

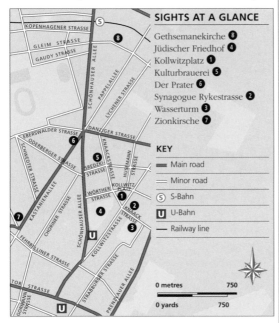

SIGHTS AT A GLANCE

Gethsemanekirche **8**
Jüdischer Friedhof **4**
Kollwitzplatz **1**
Kulturbrauerei **5**
Der Prater **6**
Synagogue Rykestrasse **2**
Wasserturm **3**
Zionkirsche **7**

KEY

— Main road
— Minor road
Ⓢ S-Bahn
Ⓤ U-Bahn
— Railway line

0 metres 750
0 yards 750

Kollwitzplatz **1**

Ⓤ *Senefelderplatz.*

This green square is named after the German painter and sculptress Käthe Kollwitz (1867–1945), who once lived nearby. It was here that the socially engaged artist observed and painted the daily hardships of the working-class people living in overcrowded tenements. One of her sculptures stands on the square which is now the major nightlife hub of the district, with numerous trendy bars, restaurants and shops that extend into the surrounding streets, primarily along Kollwitzstrasse. Käthe Kollwitz's work can be seen at the Käthe-Kollwitz-Museum *(see p154).*

Synagogue Rykestrasse **2**

Rykestrasse 53. **Tel** 88 02 80 *by appointment only.* Ⓤ *Senefelderplatz.*

This small synagogue is one of the few reminders of old Jewish life in Berlin, and one of the few in Germany left almost intact during the Nazi terror regime. Built in 1904, the red-brick synagogue has a basilica-like nave with three aisles and certain Moorish features. Thanks to the fact that it was built inside a huge tenement area, Nazi SA troops did not set it on fire during the "*Kristallnacht*" pogrom on 9 November 1938, when hundreds of other synagogues were razed to the ground. Despite being hit by bombs

during World War II, the synagogue has since been restored to its original glory and can now be visited by appointment.

Wasserturm **3**

Knaackstrasse/Belforter Strasse. Ⓤ *Senefelderplatz.*

The unofficial symbol of the district is a 30 m (98 ft) high water tower, standing high on the former mill hill in the heart of Prenzlauer Berg. It was here that some of the windmills, once typical in Prenzlauer Berg, turned and ground grain, providing flour for the city's population. The distinctive brick water tower was built in 1874 by Wilhelm Vollreng and served as a water reservoir for the country's first running water system. Later, the tower was transformed into an apartment complex. In the 1930s, the basement served as a *wildes Konzentrationslager*, a makeshift jail, where Nazi SA troops held and tortured Communist opponents. This dark period is commemorated by a plaque.

The giant Wasserturm looming high in Knaackstrasse

Jüdischer Friedhof **4**

Schönhauser Allee 22–25. **Tel** 925 08 33. Ⓤ *Senefelderplatz.* ⬤ *8am–4pm Mon–Thu, 8am–1pm Fri.* ⬤ *day before Jewish holidays after 1pm and Jewish holidays.*

This small Jewish cemetery is hidden behind thick walls on Schönhauser Allee, but the serene atmosphere, with tall trees and thick undergrowth

Gravestones in the peaceful Jüdischer Friedhof

between the gravestones, is a welcome oasis for many visitors. The cemetery was laid out in 1827, even though the oldest gravestone dates back to the 14th century. It served as Berlin's second largest Jewish cemetery after the Jüdischer Friedhof Weissensee *(see p168)*. Among the many prominent Berliners resting here are the painter Max Liebermann (1847–1935), the composer and musical director of the Staatsoper Unter den Linden; Giacomo Meyerbeer (1791–1864); and the author David Friedländer (1750–1834).

Kulturbrauerei ❺

Schönhauser Allee 36–39. **Tel** 44 31 51 00. Ⓤ *Eberswalder Strasse.* 🚋 20, 50, 53. **Sammlung Industrielle Gestaltung** ☐ *Varies for each exhibition. Telephone to check.*

This vast Neo-Gothic, industrial red and yellow brick building is the former Schultheiss brewery, Berlin's most famous brewery, built by Franz Schwechten in 1889–1892. Now housing the Kulturbrauerei, the vast complex with several courtyards has been revived as a cultural and entertainment centre with theatres, restaurants and cafés, a cinema, as well as artists' ateliers. Inside the Kulturbrauerei, the **Sammlung Industrielle Gestaltung** (Collection of Industrial Design) features changing exhibitions on East German industrial product designs.

Der Prater ❻

Kastanienallee 7–9. **Tel** 24 06 55. Ⓤ *Eberswalder Strasse.* 🚋 50, 53.

Der Prater has been one of Berlin's best known entertainment institutions for more than a century. The building, along with its quiet courtyard, was constructed in the 1840s and later became the city's largest beer garden *(see p249)*. It now not only houses a restaurant, but also stages a wide variety of pop, rock and folk concerts.

Zionskirche ❼

Zionskirchplatz. **Tel** 449 21 91. Ⓤ *Senefelderplatz, Rosenthaler Platz.* 🚋 13, 50, 53. ☐ *Apr–Oct: 8am–6pm Wed, 11–7pm Thu, noon–4pm Sun; Nov–Mar: 8–4pm Wed, 8–4pm Sun.*

Located in the square of the same name, Zionsplatz, this Protestant church was built between 1866 and 1873 – a tranquil oasis in the middle of this lively district. Both the square and the church have always been centres of political opposition.
During the Third Reich, resistance groups against the Nazi regime congregated at the church, and when the communists were in power in East Germany the alternative "environment library" (an information and documentation centre) was established here. Church and other opposition groups active here played a decisive role in the transformation of East Germany in 1989–90.

Kulturbrauerei tower

Gethsemanekirche ❽

Stargader Strasse 77. **Tel** 44 57 745. Ⓤ & Ⓢ *Schönhauser Allee.* 🛈 *11am Sun.*

The quaint little area surrounding this Neo-Gothic red-brick church is one of the most intact original communities to be found anywhere in Berlin.
The neighbourhood is dominated by the Protestant Gethsemanekirche, which dates back to 1890. The church was one of several built on the order of Emperor Wilhelm II, who wanted to increase religious worship among the mostly Social Democratic working-classes living in Prenzlauer Berg and other areas. The building was designed by August Orth (1828–1911), one of the period's most important architects of churches and railway stations.
The Protestant community here is proud to have pioneered civil rights movements, and hosted political Anti-Nazi rallies from 1933–45. The congregation also questioned the socialist regime after World War II, while the church itself served as an assembly hall for peaceful opponents in October 1989. On 2 October that year, the praying crowd was brutally attacked by the East German secret service police, marking the start of the Communist regime's demise.
Today, the square is surrounded by beautiful restored buildings, housing many sidewalk restaurants, cafés and quaint little shops.

Entrance to the red-brick Gethsemanekirche

Friedrichshain and Treptow

Both these districts are situated to the southeast of Mitte and provide excellent opportunities for walks amid some spectacular remnants of Berlin's most recent history. Visitors can see the official face of the German Democratic Republic, as shown in the Socialist Realist architecture of Karl-Marx-Allee, and the Soviet ideals of nationalism in the huge monument to the Red Army in Treptower Park. A sharp contrast is provided by stark reminders of a less glorious past – the Berlin Wall, East Side Gallery and the grim watchtower on the border.

The park has undergone frequent redesigns in its history including, during World War II, the construction of two large bunkers. After the war, the site was covered with a mound of earth.

Between the years 1969 and 1973 a sports and games area was established in the park, although there is still plenty of room for leisurely strolls.

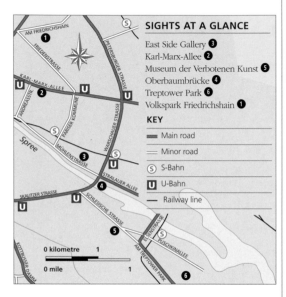

SIGHTS AT A GLANCE

East Side Gallery ❸
Karl-Marx-Allee ❷
Museum der Verbotenen Kunst ❺
Oberbaumbrücke ❹
Treptower Park ❻
Volkspark Friedrichshain ❶

KEY

■	Main road
─	Minor road
Ⓢ	S-Bahn
Ⓤ	U-Bahn
─	Railway line

0 kilometre 1

0 mile 1

Fragment of Socialist Realist decoration from Karl-Marx-Allee

Karl-Marx-Allee ❷

Map 8 F3. Ⓤ *Strausberger Platz or Weberwiese.*

The section of Karl-Marx-Allee between Strausberger Platz and Frankfurter Tor is effectively a huge open-air museum of Socialist Realist architecture. The route to the the east, leading on to Poland and Moscow, was named Stalinallee in 1949 and chosen as the site for the construction showpiece of the new German Democratic Republic. The avenue was widened to 90 m (300 ft) and in the course of the next ten years, huge residential tower blocks and a row of shops were built on it. The designers, led by Hermann Henselmann, succeeded in combining three sets of architectural guidelines. They used the style known in the Soviet Union as "pastry chef" according to the precept: "nationalistic in form but socialist in content", and linked the whole work to Berlin's own traditions. Hence there are motifs taken from famous Berlin architects Schinkel and Gontard, as well as from the renowned Meissen porcelain.

The buildings on this street, renamed Karl-Marx-Allee in 1961, are now considered historic monuments. The buildings have been cleaned up and the crumbling details are gradually being restored.

Volkspark Friedrichshain ❶

Am Friedrichshain/Friedenstrasse. **Map** 8 F1. 🚌 *142, 200, 348.*

This extensive park complex of Friedrichshain, with its picturesque nooks and crannies, was one of Berlin's first public parks. It was laid out in the 1840s on the basis of a design by Peter Joseph Lenné, with the idea of creating an alternative Tier-garten for the inhabitants of the eastern districts of the city.

The greatest attraction of the park is the Fountain of Fairy Tales – Märchenbrunnen by Ludwig Hoffmann, built from 1902 until 1913. It is a spectac-ular feature, in a Neo-Baroque style with fountain pools made from Tivoli stone, decorated with small statues of turtles and

other animals. The fountain is surrounded by well-known characters from the fairy tales by the Brothers Grimm.

Neo-Baroque Märchenbrunnen in Volkspark Friedrichshain

East Side Gallery ❸

Mühlenstrasse. Ⓢ *&* Ⓤ *Warschauer Strasse.* Ⓢ *Hauptbahnhof.* 🚌 *142.*

Since 1990, this 1300-m (one mile) section of the Berlin Wall, running along Mühlen-strasse between Hauptbahnhof and Oberbaumbrücke, has been known as the East Side Gallery. A huge collection of graffiti is on display here, comprising the work of 118 different artists from 21 countries. This expansive display was organized by the Scottish artist Chris MacLean.

Oberbaumbrücke ❹

Ⓢ *&* Ⓤ *Warschauer Strasse* Ⓤ *Schlesisches Tor.* 🚌 *265.*

This pretty bridge crossing the Spree river was built from 1894 to 1896 to a design by Otto Stahn. It is actually made from reinforced concrete, but the arches are covered with red brick. The most decorative element of the bridge is a Neo-Gothic arcade which supports a line of the U-Bahn. The central arch of the bridge is marked by a pair of cren-ellated Neo-Gothic towers.

The bridge was not open to traffic for 12 or so years prior to reunification, as it linked districts from opposing sides of the Berlin Wall. Only pedestrians with the relevant documents were able to use this bridge. After reunification and renovation, it was returned to full working order.

The picturesque Neo-Gothic archway of Oberbaumbrücke

Museum der Verbotenen Kunst ❺

MUSEUM OF FORBIDDEN ARTS

Im Schlesischen Busch (Puschkinallee/ Schlesische Strasse.) Ⓤ *Schlesisches Tor.* Ⓢ *Treptower Park.* 🚌 *265. Park* 🕐 *Apr–Oct: noon–6pm Sat, Sun.*

In a neglected park near the former Berlin Wall stands the only remaining watchtower in the border control system that divided East and West Berlin.

The upper floor has been preserved as it was during the Cold War years, when it was used by border guards to monitor the Wall. While it is possible to visit the park, you will need to telephone ahead to find out when the tower is open to the public.

Museum der Verbotenen Kunst in the last remaining watchtower

Treptower Park ❻

Archenhold-Sternwarte, Alt-Treptow 1. Ⓢ *Treptower Park.* 🚌 *166, 167, 265.* **Archenhold Sternwarte** *Tel 53 48 080.* 📷 *2–4:30pm Wed–Sun.*

The vast park in Treptow was laid out in the 1860s on the initiative and design of Johann Gustav Meyer. In 1919 it was where revolutionaries Karl Liebknecht, Wilhelm Pieck and Rosa Luxemburg assembled 150,000-strong group of striking workers.

The park, however, is best known for the colossal monu-ment to the Red Army. Built between 1946 and 1949, it stands on the grave of 5,000

Gigantic wreath commemorating the Red Army in Treptower Park

Soviet soldiers killed in the battle for Berlin in 1945. The gateway is marked by a vast granite sculpture of a grieving Russian Motherland surroun-ded by statues of Red Army soldiers. This leads to the mausoleum, topped by an 11-m (35-ft) high figure of a soldier rescuing a child and resting his mighty sword on a smashed swastika. The whole scheme was the work of architect Jakow Białopolski and sculptor Jewgien Wuczeticz.

In the farthest section of the park it is worth going to see the astronomical observatory, **Archenhold Sternwarte**, built for a decorative arts exhibition held here in 1896. Given a permanent site here in 1909, the observatory was used by Albert Einstein for a lecture on the Theory of Relativity in 1915. It is also home to the longest refracting telescope in the world (21-m or 70-ft), and a small planetarium.

Beyond Treptower Park lies another park, Plänterwald, while the Spree river provides an ideal place for a riverside stroll or maybe a trip in one of the rowing or pedal boats.

At the beginning of the 19th century, Berliners flocked to the banks of the Spree to enjoy themselves at the weekend. However, from the many dance halls and restaurants, only one historic building has remained – Zenner. This can trace its history back as far as the 17th century.

The small Insel der Jugend can be reached via the Abtei-brücke, an ornamental bridge built by French prisoners of war in 1916. The island was once home to an abbey, but it now houses a fashionable arts complex and nightclub.

Southeast Berlin

An expedition to Berlin's furthest corners, Lichtenberg and Hohenschönhausen, provides an occasion to visit shocking museums documenting the work of the German Democratic Republic's security services (Stasi). However, you can just as easily stroll through the zoological garden in the park at the Baroque Schloss Friedrichsfelde or enjoy a leisurely break in Köpenick, which has retained the atmosphere of a small town.

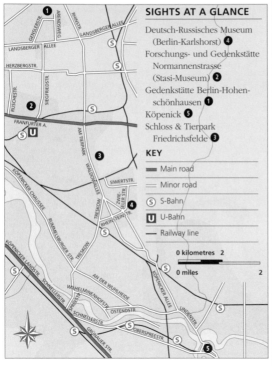

SIGHTS AT A GLANCE

Deutsch-Russisches Museum
(Berlin-Karlshorst) **4**
Forschungs- und Gedenkstätte
Normannenstrasse
(Stasi-Museum) **2**
Gedenkstätte Berlin-Hohen-
schönhausen **1**
Köpenick **5**
Schloss & Tierpark
Friedrichsfelde **3**

KEY

■ Main road
 Minor road
Ⓢ S-Bahn
Ⓤ U-Bahn
── Railway line

0 kilometres   2

0 miles   2

Gedenkstätte Berlin-Hohen-schönhausen **1**

Genslerstrasse 66. **Tel** 9860 82 30.
Ⓢ Landsberger Allee, then ⊟ 5, 6,
7, 17. 🚌 256. ◯ 9am–6pm daily.
🏛 (in German) 11am, 1pm daily
(also 3pm Sat & Sun).

This museum was established in 1995 within the former custody building of the Stasi – the dreaded security service of the GDR. The custody building was part of a huge complex built in 1938. In May 1945 the occupying Russian authorities created a special transit camp here, in which they interned war criminals

who were subsequently transported to Siberia. Shortly thereafter they started to bring anyone under political suspicion to the camp. During this time more than 20,000 people passed through here.

From 1946 this group of buildings was refashioned into the custody area for the KGB (Soviet Secret Service), and in 1951 it was given over for the use of the Stasi.

During a visit to the complex you can see prisoners' cells and interrogation rooms, two of which have no windows and are lined with rubber. Housed in the cellars was the "submarine" – a series of cells without daylight for the most "dangerous" suspects.

Forschungs- und Gedenkstätte Normannenstrasse (Stasi-Museum) **2**

Ruschestrasse 103 (Haus 1).
Tel 553 68 54. Ⓤ Magdalenen-
strasse. ◯ 11am–6pm Mon–Fri,
2–6pm Sat & Sun. 🏛

Under the German Democratic Republic, this huge complex of buildings at Ruschestrasse housed the Ministry of the Interior. It was here that the infamous Stasi (GDR secret service) had its headquarters. The Stasi's "achievements" in infiltrating its own community were without equal in the Eastern bloc.

Since 1990 one of the buildings has housed a museum that displays photographs and documents depicting the activities of the Stasi. You can see a model of the headquarters, and equipment used for bugging and spying on citizens suspected of holding an unfavourable view of the political regime. You can also walk around the office of infamous Stasi chief Erich Mielke. A "big-brother"-like figure, Mielke's legacy of suffering still lives on in the memory of millions of German citizens.

Stasi chief Erich Mielke's office at the Stasi Museum

Schloss & Tierpark Friedrichsfelde **3**

Am Tierpark 125. Ⓤ Tierpark. **Tel** 66
63 50 35. 🚌 296, 396. **Schloss** ◯
Apr–Oct: 10am–6pm Tue–Sun;
Nov–Mar: noon–4pm Sat & Sun.
Tierpark Tel 51 53 10. ◯ 9am–6pm
daily (or until dusk in winter). 🏛

This charming Baroque palace was built for the Dutchman Benjamin von Raule around 1695, to a

The façade of Schloss Friedrichsfelde

design by Johann Arnold Nering. Under successive owners, it underwent major renovations. In 1719 it was redesigned by Martin Heinrich Böhme, and again in 1786 this time to designs by Peter Biron. It was this renovation which gave the residence its current appearance.

The well-balanced structure, typical of the style during the transition from Baroque to Neo-Classical, was extensively restored in the 1970s. It now houses a museum of interiors, and is chiefly furnished with 18th- and 19th-century pieces. The palace's park was re-designed into the zoological garden of East Berlin in 1957.

Deutsch-Russisches Museum (Berlin-Karlshorst) ❹

Zwieseler Strasse 4/Rheinsteinstrasse
Tel 50 15 08 10. Ⓢ Karlshorst.
🚌 26, 27, 28. 🚋 396.
🕐 10am–6pm Tue–Sun.

This building was erected in the 1930s as the casino of the Wehrmacht (armed services of the Third Reich). It was here on the night of 8 May 1945 that Hitler's successor Grossadmiral Karl Dönitz, Field Marshal Wilhelm Keitel, Admiral Hans Georg von Friedeburg and General Hans-Jürgen Stumpff signed the unconditional surrender of Germany's armed forces. You can visit the renowned hall in which the surrender was signed, the office of Marshal Zhukov, and see an exhibition documenting the history of World War II.

Köpenick ❺

Kunstgewerbemuseum Tel 20 90 55 60. Ⓢ Spindlersfeld, then 🚌 167, 169 or Ⓢ Köpenick, then 🚋 169, 360, 369. 🚋 60, 61, 62, 63, 68.

Köpenick is much older than Berlin. Already in the 9th century AD this island contained a fortified settlement called Kopanica. It was inhabited by Slavs from the Łaba river region, which in the 12th century was ruled by Duke Jaksa, who was waging a war against the Ascanian Albrecht the Bear over Brandenburg (*see p19*). From the late 12th century Köpenick belonged to the Margrave of Brandenburg, also an Ascanian. In about 1240 a castle was built, around which a town began to evolve, though over the years it lost out in importance to Berlin. Craftsmen settled here, and after 1685 a large colony of Huguenots also settled here. In the 19th century Köpenick

Part of the town hall's Neo-Gothic façade

A reconstructed drawing room dating from 1548 in Köpenick's Kunstgewerbemuseum

recreated itself as an industrial town. Despite wartime devastation it has retained its historic character. There are no longer any 13th-century churches, which in the years 1838 to 1841 were replaced by buildings in the style of Schinkel, nevertheless it is worth strolling around the old town. By the old market square and the neighbouring streets, such as Alt Köpenick and Grünstrasse, modest houses have survived which recall the 18th century, next to buildings from the end of the 19th century.

At Alt Köpenick No. 21 is a vast brick town hall built in the style of the Brandenburg Neo-Renaissance between the years 1901 and 1904 by Hans Schütte and Hugo Kinzer. It was here on 16 October 1906 that a famous swindle took place. Wilhelm Voigt dressed himself in a Prussian officer's uniform and proceeded to arrest the mayor and then fraudulently empty everything from the city treasury. This incident became the inspiration for a comedy, *The Captain from Köpenick* by Carl Zuckmayer, which is still popular.

Köpenick's greatest attraction is a magnificent palace on the island in the southern part of town. It was built between 1677 and 1681 for the heir to the throne Friedrich (later King Friedrich I), to a design by the Dutch architect Rutger van Langfeld. The three-storey Baroque building that resulted was extended to a design by Johann Arnold Nering, but until 1693 only part of the extension was completed: the chapel, entrance gate and a small gallery wing.

In 2004 the **Kunstgewerbemuseum** *(see pp118–21)* opened a series of Renaissance and Baroque rooms in the Köpenick palace. This collection also includes some examples of magnificent furniture.

Southwest Berlin

An excursion to Britz provides a chance to visit one of the few surviving manor houses in the suburbs of Berlin, Schloss Britz. In Schöneberg you can see the town hall from which President Kennedy gave his famous speech, and visit the grave of Berlin-born actress and singer, Marlene Dietrich. The Botanical Gardens are great for those who enjoy a stroll through cultivated and wild gardens, but you should allow at least half a day.

Neo-Classical Königskolonnaden, gateway to the Kleistpark

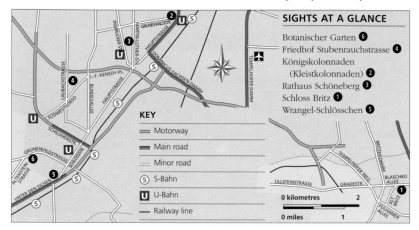

SIGHTS AT A GLANCE

Botanischer Garten ❻
Friedhof Stubenrauchstrasse ❹
Königskolonnaden
(Kleistkolonnaden) ❷
Rathaus Schöneberg ❸
Schloss Britz ❶
Wrangel-Schlösschen ❺

KEY

━━━ Motorway
━━━ Main road
─── Minor road
Ⓢ S-Bahn
Ⓤ U-Bahn
─── Railway line

0 kilometres   2

0 miles   1

Schloss Britz ❶

Alt-Britz 73. *Tel 60 97 92 30.*
Ⓤ *Parchimer Allee.* 🚌 *144, 174, 181.*
⏰ *2–6pm Tue–Thu, 2–8pm Fri, 11am–6pm Sat & Sun.* 🎟 *compulsory.*

Originally a small manor house built in 1706 for Sigismund von Erlach, Schloss Britz was extended to its current size between 1880 and 1883 to a design by Carl Busse. It is a one-storey palace with a modest Neo-Classical aspect adorned with Baroque statues at the front and a tower on the garden side. As well as housing a permanent museum, the building is often used as a venue for concerts and temporary exhibitions. The palace displays furnishings from the *Gründerzeit* – the years after the founding of the German Empire in 1871. The 19th-century interiors are excellent but it is also worth strolling through the park, where there is a bust of one of the former owners, Rüdiger von Ilgen, which once stood in the Tiergarten.

Next to the palace is a housing estate called Hufeisensiedlung (Horseshoe Colony), built in the late 1920s to a design by Bruno Taut and Bruno Schneidereit. The architects' aim was to create spacious and affordable housing for Berliners.

Schloss Britz's Neo-Classical façade

Königskolonnaden (Kleistkolonnaden) ❷

Potsdamer Strasse **Map** 11 B4.
Ⓤ *Kleistpark.* 🚌 *148, 187, 348.*

A short walk north of U-Bahn Kleistpark, the unremarkable architecture of Potsdamer Strasse suddenly transforms dramatically. Leading to the park, the elegant sandstone Königskolonnaden captivates the passer-by with its Baroque ornamental sculptures. The royal colonnade, designed by Carl von Gontard and built between 1777 and 1780, once graced the route from Königsstrasse to Alexanderplatz. In 1910, to protect it from traffic, it was moved to this new site.

The huge Kammergericht at the far boundary of the park was built between 1909 and 1913 to a design by Carl Vohl, Rudolf Mönnich and Paul Thömer. The site of the notorious Nazi Volksgericht or "People's Court", it was also used to try members of the failed July 1944 Bomb Plot against Hitler (*see p127*).

Rathaus Schöneberg ❸

SCHONEBERG TOWN HALL

John-F-Kennedy-Platz.
Ⓤ *Rathaus Schöneberg.*

The gigantic building with a tower is the Schöneberg town hall, built between 1911 and 1914. From 1948 to 1990 it was used as the main town hall of West Berlin. Here, on 26 June 1963, the US President John F Kennedy gave his famous speech. More than 300,000 Berliners assembled to hear the young president say "*Ich bin ein Berliner*" – "I am a Berliner", intended as an expression of solidarity from the democratic world to a city defending its right to freedom.

While Kennedy's meaning was undoubtedly clear, pedants were quick to point out that, strictly speaking, he said "I am a small doughnut".

Rathaus Schöneberg – the site of President Kennedy's speech

Friedhof Stuben-rauchstrasse ❹

STUBENRAUCHSTRASSE CEMETERY

Stubenrauchstrasse/Südwestkorso.
Ⓢ & Ⓤ *Bundesplatz.* 🚌 348.

This small cemetery in the shadow of a motorway achieved renown in 1993 as the burial place of Marlene Dietrich, who died on 6 May. Born Maria Magdalena von Losch in 1901, she grew up at Leberstrasse No. 65 in Schöneberg. For a few years she struggled to make a career as an actress, playing small parts.

The pleasantly cultivated spaces of the Botanischer Garten

In 1929 she was discovered in Berlin by Hollywood director Josef von Sternberg who was filming *The Blue Angel*, based on Heinrich Mann's novel *Professor Unrat*. The ensuing role of Lola took Marlene to the height of fame. She sang only once more in Berlin, giving a concert at the Titania-Palast in 1960. Although she died in Paris, she was laid to rest in the city of her birth.

Wrangel-Schlösschen ❺

Schlossstrasse 48. *Tel* 63 21 39 24.
Ⓤ *Rathaus Steglitz.* 🚌 148, 170, 185, 277, 280, 283, 285.

This compact Neo-Classical palace derives its name from Field Marshal Wrangel, the building's mid-19th century owner. However, the house was built much earlier, in 1804, following a design by Heinrich Gentz. The simplicity and clarity of its details make it a prime example of early Neo-Classical architecture. It currently houses the cultural centre for the district of Steglitz.

Botanischer Garten ❻

BOTANICAL GARDEN

Unter den Eichen 5–10 & Königin-Luise-Strasse 6–8. *Tel* 83 85 01 00.
Ⓤ *Dahlem-Dorf.* Ⓢ *Botanischer Garten.* 🚌 101, 148. ⬜ daily; Nov–Jan: 9am–4pm; Feb: 9am–5pm; Mar & Oct: 9am–6pm; Apr & Aug: 9am–8pm; May–Jul: 9am–9pm; Sep: 9am–7pm. **Museum** ⬜ 10am–6pm daily. 🖼

The Botanical Garden is one of the most beautiful places in Berlin. The expansive park was created towards the end of the 19th century and has a romantic character with gentle hills and picturesque lakes. Of particular interest is the 19th-century palm house, designed by Alfred Koerner. The new greenhouses were built from 1984 to 1987 to a design by Engelbert Kremser. The most popular plants are the exotic species such as the orchids and cacti. By the entrance on the Königin-Luise-Platz side is the Botanisches Museum, home to an excellent collection of plant specimens.

COUNTRY CHURCHES

The establishment of Greater Berlin in 1920 swallowed up nearly 60 villages, some of which were older than the city itself. Now they have evolved into large residential estates, and many of the parish churches (more than 50) have survived. The most treasured, dating from the 13th century, can be seen in the south of Berlin, for instance in Britz by Backbergstrasse, Buckow (Alt-Buckow) or in Mariendorf (Alt Mariendorf). The oldest church, dating from the 13th century, has survived in Marienfelde (Alt Marienfelde).

St Anna's in Dahlem   Wittenau   Marienfelde

Dahlem

Dahlem is first mentioned in 1275 and it remained a small village surrounded by private estates until the 19th century. Retaining its Gothic parish church and its manor house, Dahlem was transformed into an affluent, tranquil city suburb with grand villas and a clutch of museums, designed by Bruno Paul, at the beginning of the 20th century. The district was confirmed as a major cultural and educational centre after World War II with the establishment of the Freie Universität and the completion of the museum complex. The Botanischer Garten also sits on the borders of Dahlem *(see p177)*.

the more recent Nordamerika Ausstellung (Exhibition of Native North American Cultures).

Highlights from the collections include bronzes from Benin at the Museum of African Art, gold Inca jewellery at the Museum of Ethnology, and Japanese woodcuts and Buddhist cave paintings from Chinese Turkestan at the Museum of Far Eastern Art. Opened in 1999, the Exhibition of Native North American Cultures includes a collection of 600 ceremonial objects.

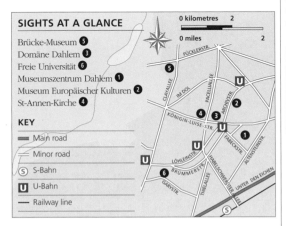

SIGHTS AT A GLANCE

Brücke-Museum ⑤
Domäne Dahlem ③
Freie Universität ⑥
Museumszentrum Dahlem ①
Museum Europäischer Kulturen ②
St-Annen-Kirche ④

KEY

— Main road
⟋ Minor road
Ⓢ S-Bahn
Ⓤ U-Bahn
— Railway line

0 kilometres 2
0 miles 2

An East Prussian carpet from the Museum Europäischer Kulturen

Museum Europäischer Kulturen ②

MUSEUM OF EUROPEAN CULTURE

Im Winkel 6. *Tel* 83 90 12 87.
Ⓤ *Dahlem Dorf.* 🚌 *110, 183, X-11, X-83.* ◯ *10am–6pm Tue–Fri, 11am–6pm Sat & Sun.* 🎧

This ethnographic museum specializes in European folk art and culture, documenting the daily life of its inhabitants. It hosts long-running but temporary exhibitions, often in conjunction with museums from other European countries. Among the exhibits you can expect to see are earthenware items, costumes, jewellery, toys and tools.

Museumszentrum Dahlem ①

Lansstrasse 8. *Tel* 20 90 55 66.
Ⓤ *Dahlem Dorf.* 🚌 *110, 183, X-11, X-83.* **Museum für Indische Kunst, Museum für Ostasiatische Kunst, Ethnologisches Museum** *(formerly Museum für Völkerkunde),* **Museum für Kunst Afrikas & Nordamerika Ausstellung** ◯ *10am–6pm Tue–Fri, 11am–6pm Sat & Sun.* 🎧

Dahlem's first museums were built between 1914 and 1923. After World War II, with many of Berlin's collections fragmented, a large miscellany of art and artifacts was put on display here. In the 1960s the museums were extended considerably: the new Museumszentrum was created to rival East Berlin's Museum Island. Reunification in 1990 meant the collections could be reunited and reorganized. Paintings were moved to the Kulturforum *(see pp122–5)*, and sculptures to the Bode-museum *(see p79)*. Five

museums are now housed at Dahlem: the Ethnologisches Museum (Museum of Ethnology); the Museum für Indische Kunst (Museum of Indian Art); the Museum für Ostasiatische Kunst (Museum of Far Eastern Art); the Museum für Kunst Afrikas (Museum for African Art) and

Japanese woodcut from the Museum für Ostasiatische Kunst

Domäne Dahlem ③

DAHLEM CITY FARM

Königin-Luise-Str. 49. *Tel* 66 63 000.
Ⓤ *Dahlem Dorf.* 🚌 *110, 183, X-11, X-83.* ◯ *10am–6pm Tue–Sun.* 🎧 *(museum only).*

Domäne Dahlem, a manor house and farming estate, is a rare oasis of country life in the Berlin suburbs. The Baroque house was built for Cuno Johann von Wilmersdorff

The combined museum and working farm of Domäne Dahlem

around 1680 and still retains its original character. Part of the Stadtmuseum Berlin (Museum of the City of Berlin), the manor house boasts period interiors, while the 19th-century farm buildings hold a collection of agricultural tools. Also on show is a large and varied collection of beehives.

Domäne Dahlem is a farm and a museum with a garden, workshops and farm animals. Festivals and markets are held here with demonstrations of rural crafts and skills – you can learn how to shoe a horse or milk a cow, or, if you prefer, you can just relax with a glass of cold beer.

Gothic St-Annen-Kirche dating back to the 14th century

St-Annen-Kirche ❹

Königin-Luise-Strasse/Pacelliallee. **Tel** 841 70 50. **U** Dahlem Dorf. 110, 183, X-11, X-83. 11am–1pm Sat–Sun.

At the centre of a small leafy cemetery stands the Gothic 14th-century St-Annen-Kirche. The church was built initially with a plain roof. The chancel was completed in the 15th century, the vaulting in the 17th century and the tower was added in the 18th century.

Inside the church, 14th-century wall paintings depict scenes from the life of St Anna, alongside items of ecclesiastical furnishings. These include a 15th-century painting called *The Crucifixion* and 11 late-Gothic figures of saints.

Brücke-Museum ❺

Bussardsteig 9. **Tel** 831 20 29. 115. 11am–5pm Wed–Mon.

One of the more interesting museums dedicated to 20th-century art is hidden away on a leafy, tranquil street lined with picturesque villas. The elegant Functionalist building was built by Werner Düttmann in 1966 to 1967. The museum houses a collection of German Expressionist painting linked to the artistic group known as Die Brücke, which originated in Dresden in 1905 and was based in Berlin from 1910. The members of this group included Karl Schmidt-Rottluff, Emil Nolde, Max Pechstein, Ernst Ludwig Kirchner and Erich Heckel. The collection is based on almost 80 works by Schmidt-Rottluff bequeathed to the town in 1964. The collection quickly grew, thanks to donations and acquisitions. In addition to displaying other works of art contemporary to Die Brücke (which was disbanded in 1913), there are also some paintings from the later creative periods of these artists, as well as works of other closely associated artists.

Nearby, at Käuzchensteig No. 8, lie the foundation's headquarters, established in the former studio of the sculptor Bernhard Heliger. The garden, which borders the Brücke-Museum, has a display of his metal sculptures.

A Bernhard Heliger sculpture outside the Brücke-Museum

Freie Universität ❻

Henry-Ford-Bau Garystrasse 35–39. **U** Thielplatz. 111.

The Free University was established on 4 December 1948 on the initiative of a group of academics and activists, led by Ernst Reuter. This was a reaction to the restrictions introduced at the Humboldt-Universität in the Soviet sector and further evidence of the competition between the two halves of the city. The new university was initially located in rented buildings. It was only thanks to the American Ford Foundation that the university's Henry-Ford-Bau, housing the rector's office, the auditorium and the library, was built. Designed by Franz Heinrich Sobotka and Gustav Müller, and built from 1951 to 1954, the building is distinguished by its fine proportions.

Henry-Ford-Bau, the rector's office and library at the Freie Universität

Zehlendorf

With nearly half of Zehlendorf covered by forests, lakes and rivers, the region has a quiet, rustic atmosphere that belies the fact that it is a mere 20 minutes away from the hustle and bustle of a huge metropolis. The area is dotted with picture-postcard villas and small settlements where life carries on at an unchanging, slow pace. It is worth taking a walk *(see pp208–211)* to see the stunning lakeside summer residences and royal parks, Pfaueninsel and Klein Glienicke, which are located in the furthest corner of this district.

Reconstructed medieval settlement at the Museumdorf Düppel

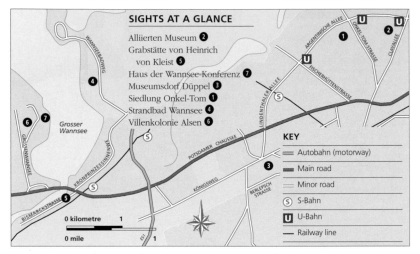

SIGHTS AT A GLANCE

Alliierten Museum ❷
Grabstätte von Heinrich
   von Kleist ❺
Haus der Wannsee-Konferenz ❼
Museumsdorf Düppel ❸
Siedlung Onkel-Tom ❶
Strandbad Wannsee ❹
Villenkolonie Alsen ❻

KEY

▬▬	Autobahn (motorway)
▬	Main road
—	Minor road
Ⓢ	S-Bahn
Ⓤ	U-Bahn
—	Railway line

Siedlung Onkel-Tom ❶

Argentinische Allee. Ⓤ *Onkel-Toms-Hütte.*

This housing estate, known as "Uncle Tom's Estate", represents one of the most interesting urban architectural achievements of the Weimar Republic. It was built from 1926 to 1932, to a design by

**The Siedlung (estate) Onkel-Tom,
built between 1926 and 1932**

Bruno Taut, Hugo Häring and Otto Rudolf Salvisberg. Their primary intention was to solve the city's housing shortage by building large developments that were both pleasant to live in and fairly inexpensive. This project in Zehlendorf was the realization of the English concept of garden cities. The result is an enormous housing estate comprising single- and multiple-family houses. It is set in lush greenery on the borders of Grunewald and accommodates nearly 15,000 people.

Alliierten-museum ❷

Clayallee 135. **Tel** *818 19 90.*
Ⓢ *Zehlendorf, then* 🚌 *115.*
Ⓤ *Oskar-Helene-Heim.* ◻ *10am–6pm Thu–Tue.* 📷 *by appointment.*

In the heart of the former US military sector of Berlin is the Allied Museum, which combines exhibition space with open-air grounds.

A fascinating exhibition of everyday objects, military memorabilia, photographs and films explains life during the Cold War and the story of Berlin and its inhabitants between 1945 and 1994.

Museumsdorf Düppel ❸

Clauerstrasse 11. **Tel** *802 66 71.*
Ⓢ *Mexikoplatz or* Ⓤ *Krumme Lanke,
then* 🚌 *211, 629.* ◻ *3 April–3 Oct:
3–6pm Thu, 10am–4pm Sun.* 📷

A visit to the Museumsdorf Düppel takes the visitor on a trip back in time. A reconstruction of a medieval village has been made on the site of a 13th-century settlement, discovered in the 1940s. It is a living village surrounded by still cultivated gardens and fields, where traditional breeds of pigs and sheep are raised in the sheds and pigsties.

On Sundays the village puts on displays of traditional

crafts. Here you can see how primitive saucepans and tools were fashioned; how wool was spun, dyed and woven; and how baskets were made.

Strandbad Wannsee ❹

Wannseebadweg. Ⓢ *Nikolassee.* 🚌 *218.*

The vast picturesque lake of Wannsee, situated on the edge of Grunewald, is a principal destination for Berliners who are looking for some kind of recreation. Here you can take part in water sports, enjoy a lake cruise, bathe, or simply enjoy relaxing on the shore. The most developed part is the southeastern corner of the lake. Here, near S-Bahn Wannsee, there are yachting marinas and harbours, while further north is one of the largest inland beaches in Europe – Strandbad Wannsee. It has been in use since the beginning of the 20th century, and was developed between 1929 and 1930 by the construction of a complex of changing rooms, shops and cafés on top of man-made terraces.

On sunny summer days, sun-worshippers completely cover the sandy shore, while the lake is filled with yachts and windsurfers. It is also quite pleasant to take a walk around Schwanenwerder island. It has many elegant villas, one of which, Inselstrasse No. 24/26, was built for Axel Springer, the German newspaper publisher.

Grabstätte von Heinrich von Kleist ❺

GRAVE OF HEINRICH VON KLEIST

Bismarckstrasse (near No. 3). Ⓢ *Wannsee.* 🚌 *114, 116, 211, 216, 316, 318.*

A narrow street running from Königstrasse at the viaduct of the S-Bahn Wannsee leads to the spot where the playwright Heinrich von Kleist committed suicide. On 21 November 1811 he shot his companion Henriette Vogel and then turned the pistol on himself. They are both buried here. A stone marks the location of their grave, on which flowers are left by well-wishers.

Villenkolonie Alsen ❻

Am Grossen Wannsee. Ⓢ *Wannsee,* then 🚌 *114.*

This clutch of villas forms a delightful holiday resort – the oldest of its kind in Berlin. The villas are thought to be the most beautiful, not just because of their picturesque lakeside location, but also because of the quality of their architecture.

Strolling along Am Grossen Wannsee, it is worth looking at the villa at No. 39/41, known as Haus Springer. It was designed by Alfred Messel in 1901 and is covered with shingles which reflect contemporary American designs.

Sculptures by Stuart N. R. Wolfe, Haus der Wannsee-Konferenz

At No. 42 stands a villa that was designed by Paul Baumgarten in 1909 for the painter Max Liebermann, who spent many summers here painting.

Haus der Wannsee-Konferenz ❼

Am Grossen Wannsee 56/58. *Tel 805 00 10.* Ⓢ *Wannsee, then* 🚌 *114.* ⚪ *10am–6pm daily.*

This is one of the most beautiful of the luxury Alsen holiday villas, and yet the most abhorrent. Designed by Paul Baumgarten between 1914 and 1915, it is in the style of a small Neo-Baroque palace with an elegant portico. In 1940 the villa was sold to the Nazi SS. On 20 January 1942, a meeting took place between Richard Heydrich and 14 other officers from the secret service and the SS, among them Adolf Eichmann. It was then that the decision was taken about "the final solution on the question of Jews". Their plans for the outright extermination of 11 million Jews embraced the whole of Europe, including Great Britain and neutral countries.

Since 1992 this has been a museum and place of remembrance. An exhibition depicts the history of the Holocaust with some shocking documents and photographs from the ghettos and extermination camps. For security reasons, the gate to the villa is always locked, and to enter the park you have to announce yourself through the intercom.

Boarding point for lake cruises on the Wannsee

Western Berlin

West of Charlottenburg, beyond the city ring road, stretches an area notable for its striking Funkturm (Radio Tower) and Internationales Congress Centrum, as well as a number of large exhibition centres. After World War II, a residential estate of villas was built here, one of which belonged to the sculptor Georg Kolbe and now houses a museum of his works. A radio station has its recording studios in a very large building nearby; its plain, almost boring looking façade hides one of Berlin's most beautiful art deco interiors.

The futuristic exterior of the Internationales Congress Centrum

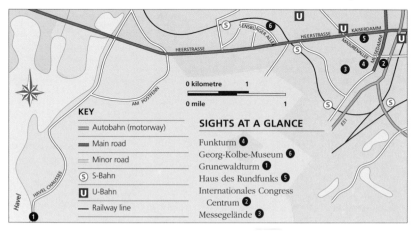

KEY

▰▰	Autobahn (motorway)
▬▬	Main road
═══	Minor road
Ⓢ	S-Bahn
Ⓤ	U-Bahn
━━	Railway line

SIGHTS AT A GLANCE

Funkturm ❹
Georg-Kolbe-Museum ❻
Grunewaldturm ❶
Haus des Rundfunks ❺
Internationales Congress Centrum ❷
Messegelände ❸

Grunewaldturm ❶

Havelchaussee. 🚌 218.

The neo-gothic tower built on a hill at the edge of the Havel river is one of the most prominent features of the area. This type of tower became popular in Germany during the 19th century as a way of commemorating important events or people. The Grunewaldturm was built in 1899 on the centenary of the birth of Wilhelm I. After 1871, he was the first Emperor of the Second Reich, and the tower was initially named "Kaiser-Wilhelm-Turm". The 56-m (185-ft) tower was designed by Franz Schwechten and is made of red brick with plaster details. The tower is made all the more striking by the green background provided by the surrounding leafy trees.

Currently used as an observation tower, the view from the top of this structure is well worth climbing the 204 steps for. There is a popular restaurant in the base of the tower and above, in the domed hall, is a marble statue of the Emperor that was designed by Ludwig Mansel.

The impressive red-brick Neo-Gothic Grunewaldturm

Internationales Congress Centrum ❷

Messedamm 19. Ⓢ Witzleben. Ⓤ Kaiserdamm. 🚌 104, 149, 218, X-34, X-49.

This silver futuristic structure stands on a peninsula of land, surrounded on two sides by a continuous stream of fast moving cars. The Internationales Congress Centrum (ICC) marked yet another stage in the rivalry between East and West Berlin – it was built in reply to the East's Palast der Republik.

Constructed between 1973 and 1979, to a design by Ralf Schüler and Ursulina Schüler-Witte, the building is a mass of angular aluminium shapes that disguise its well thought-out construction. The conference area is separate from the concert halls, for good sound-proofing. One of the most modern buildings of its type in the world, it has a state-of-the-art electronic security system and an advanced means of co-ordinating and directing the several thousand people who come here to attend various meetings and conferences. More than 80 rooms and halls enable the venue to host a variety of events, from rock concerts for up to 5,000 spectators to a small artistic workshop or seminar. The building also has a roof garden, where you can rest during intervals. In front of the main entrance stands *Alexander the Great in front of Ekbatana*, by French sculptor Jean Ipoustéguy (born 1920).

Monumental façade of the Ehren-halle part of the Messegelände

Messegelände ❸

Hammarskjöldplatz. Ⓢ *Witzleben.* Ⓤ *Kaiserdamm.* ▦ *104, 149, 204, 219.*

The pavilions of the vast exhibition and trade halls which lie south of Hammarsk-jöldplatz cover more than 160,000 sq m (1,700,000 sq ft). Many of the international events organized here, including the food and agricultural fair Grüne Woche, are among the largest events of their kind in Europe. Even so, the exhibition areas are constantly enlarged and updated.

The original exhibition halls on this site were built before World War I, but nothing of these buildings remains. The oldest part is the Funkturm and the group of pavilions which surround it. The huge building at the front – Ehren-halle – was built in 1936 to a design by Richard Ermisch, and is one of the few surviving buildings in Berlin designed in a Fascist architectural style.

The straight motorway that lies at the rear of the halls, in the direction of Nikolassee, is the famous Avus, the first German autobahn, built in 1921. It was adapted for motor racing, and became Germany's first car-racing track. It was here that the world speed record was broken before World War II. Now it forms part of the autobahn system.

Funkturm ❹

Hammarskjöldplatz. *Tel 30 38 0.* Ⓢ *Messe Nord.* Ⓤ *Kaiserdamm.* ▦ *104, 139, 149, 218, X-21.* **Observation Terrace** ◯ *10am–11pm Tue–Sun, 10am–9pm Mon.*

The radio tower, resembling Paris' Eiffel tower, has become one of Berlin's most recognizable landmarks. Built in 1924 to a design by Heinrich Straumer, it rises 150 m (500 ft) into the air. It now operates as both an air-traffic control tower and a radio mast. Visitors can enjoy views on the observation terrace at 125 m (400 ft), or dine at the Funkturm's lofty restaurant at 55 m (180 ft).

Haus des Rundfunks ❺

Masurenallee 8–14. Ⓢ *Witzleben.* Ⓤ *Theodor-Heuss-Platz.* ▦ *104, 149, 218, X-34, X-49.*

This building's depressing, flat, brick-covered façade hides an interior of startling beauty. The huge edifice was constructed as a radio station between 1929 and 1931 to a design by Hans Poelzig. The building has a triangular shape, with three studio wings radiating from the central five-storey hall. The impressive Art Deco interiors, which are spectacularly lit from above, are enhanced by geometrically-patterned rows of balconies and large, pendulous,

Clean, geometric shapes in the Art Deco lobby, Haus des Rundfunks

octagonal lamps. They represent one of the finest architectural achievements of this era in Berlin.

From the studio concert hall, concerts are often broadcast on radio SFB.

Fountain in the garden of the sculptor Georg Kolbe's villa

Georg-Kolbe-Museum ❻

Sensburger Allee 25. *Tel 304 21 44.* Ⓢ *Heerstrasse.* ▦ *149, X-34, X-49.* ◯ *10am–5pm Tue–Sun.*

One of the most renowned German sculptors, Georg Kolbe (1877–1947) bequeathed the house in which he lived and worked almost his entire life to the city of Berlin. The villa was built by the Swiss architect, Ernst Reutsch, between 1928 and 1929 in a Functionalist style. Extended a few years later by the architect Paul Lindner, it was given an old-fashioned styling with rooms that open onto a large hall. Kolbe also left the city 180 of his sculptures, as well as his own art collection, which includes works by the Expressionist painter Ernst Ludwig Kirchner and the sculptor Wilhelm Lehmbruck. Visiting here is not only a rare chance to get to know Kolbe's works but also an opportunity to see his house and workshop, which display the tools and various devices for lifting a heavy or large sculpture.

Northwest Berlin

A visit to this part of the city provides a chance to see the grandeur of the Olympia-Stadion, which was inspired by the monumental architecture of ancient Rome. Nearby stands the monolithic Le Corbusier Haus, once regarded as the model for future housing. The historic town of Spandau has some pretty medieval streets and a well-preserved Renaissance citadel. A number of original timber-framed houses remain and are well worth seeing, along with the Gothic St-Nikolai-Kirche.

500 two-storey apartments with integral services, such as a post office, shops, a sports hall and nursery school. The structure fell short of Le Corbusier's aspirations as financial pressure meant the estate lacked some service elements; in addition, structural alterations changed the building's proportions from the original plans.

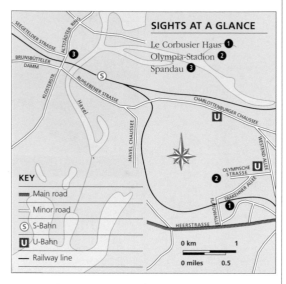

SIGHTS AT A GLANCE

Le Corbusier Haus **1**
Olympia-Stadion **2**
Spandau **3**

KEY

- Main road
- Minor road
- S S-Bahn
- U U-Bahn
- Railway line

0 km   1
0 miles   0.5

Two sculptures of athletes decorating the Olympia-Stadion

Olympia-Stadion **2**

Olympischer Platz. **Tel** 25 00 23 22.
S & U Olympia-Stadion. 218.
for tours: 10am–7pm in summer, 10am–6pm in winter. **Exhibition** 10am–6pm Wed, Sun.

The Olympia-Stadion, or Reichssportfeld, as it was originally known, was built for the 1936 Olympic Games in Berlin. It was designed by Werner March in the Nazi architectural style and was inspired by the architecture of ancient Rome. The Olympia-Stadion was immortalized in the final scenes of István Szabó's classic film *Mephisto*. To the west lie the Maifeld and the Waldbühne. The former is an enormous assembly-ground surrounded by grandstands and fronted by the Glockenturm, a 77-m (250-ft) tower, while the latter is an open-air amphitheatre. To the north are swimming pools and sports grounds. This complex was used for the Berlin Olympics.
    The stadium was modernized and reopened in 2004. An exhibit in an adjoining building chronicles its history.

Le Corbusier Haus **1**

Reichssportfeldstrasse 16.
S Olympia-Stadion. 218.

This apartment building by Le Corbusier, on a hill near the site of the Olympia-Stadion, was this architect's entry to the 1957 Interbau Exhibition (*see p133*). Following World War II, there was a housing shortage all over Europe, especially in the bomb-damaged cities. Le Corbusier's innovative design for what he called a *Unité d'Habitation* was his attempt to create fully self-sufficient housing estates in answer to this problem. He built three of these complexes, the most famous being in Marseilles. For his Berlin design, Le Corbusier wanted to build over

Le Corbusier Haus, by the renowned French architect

Interior of the Gothic St-Nikolai-Kirche in Spandau

Spandau ❸

Zitadelle Spandau Am Juliusturm.
Tel 354 94 42 00. 🅄 *Zitadelle.*
⬭ *9am–5pm Tue–Fri, 10am–5pm Sat & Sun.* 📷

Spandau is one of the oldest towns within the area of greater Berlin, and it has managed to retain a distinct character for itself. Evidence of the earliest settlement dates back to the 8th century, although the town of Spandau was only granted a charter in 1232. The area was spared the worst of the World War II bombing, so there are still some interesting sights to visit.

The heart of the town is a network of medieval streets with a picturesque market square and a number of original timber-framed houses; in the north of Spandau sections of town wall still stand, dating from the 15th century. In the centre of town is the magnificent Gothic St-Nikolai-Kirche dating from the 15th century. The church holds many valuable ecclesiastical furnishings, such as a splendid Renaissance stone altar from the end of the 16th century, a Baroque pulpit from around 1700 which came from a royal palace in Potsdam, a Gothic baptismal font and many epitaphs.

Crowned black Prussian eagle

A castle was first built on the site of the Zitadelle Spandau (citadel) in the 12th century, but today only the 36-m (120-ft) Juliusturm (tower) remains. In 1560 the building of a fort was begun here, to a design by Francesco Chiaramella da Gandino. It took 30 years to bring to completion, however, and most of the work was supervised by architect Rochus Guerrini, Graf zu Lynar. Though the citadel had a jail, Rudolf Hess, Spandau's most infamous resident, was incarcerated a short distance away in a military prison after the 1946 Nuremberg trials. In 1987 the former deputy leader of the Nazi party died, and the prison was torn down.

The Hohenzollern coat of arms above the main gate of the citadel

ZITADELLE SPANDAU

This magnificent and perfectly proportioned 16th-century citadel stands at the confluence of the Spree and Havel rivers. Both the main citadel and its various 19th-century additions are still in excellent condition. The "Iron Chancellor", Otto von Bismarck *(see p24)*, moved the gold treasure of the Reichskriegsschatz (Imperial War Fund) here in 1874, where it remained until 1919. The citadel now holds museums of local history, and an observation terrace on the crenellated Juliusturm (tower).

KEY

Bastion Kronprinz ①
Bastion Brandenburg ②
Palace ③
Main gate ④
Bastion König ⑤
Bastion Königin ⑥
Juliusturm ⑦
Ravelin Schweinekopf ⑧

Northern Berlin

Beyond the Tiergarten lie the AEG-Turbinenhalle, designed by Peter Behrens, and the Gedenkstätte Plötzensee, a sombre memorial to those executed for their supposed crimes against the Third Reich. Further north past the airport, the Tegel area contains the picturesque Schloss Tegel and the IBA-Viertel, an unusually colourful, modern housing estate designed by a team of architects. It is worth taking a cruise boat to Tegel and linking together sight-seeing in this area and a visit to Spandau with a relaxing voyage along the Havel river.

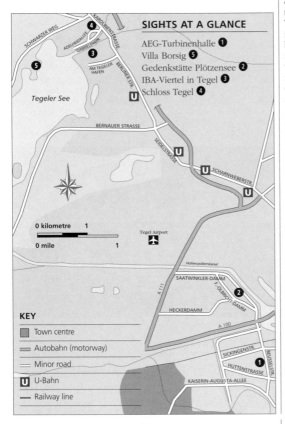

SIGHTS AT A GLANCE

AEG-Turbinenhalle **1**
Villa Borsig **5**
Gedenkstätte Plötzensee **2**
IBA-Viertel in Tegel **3**
Schloss Tegel **4**

KEY

- ▨ Town centre
- ══ Autobahn (motorway)
- — Minor road
- Ⓤ U-Bahn
- — Railway line

AEG-Turbinen-halle **1**

Huttenstrasse 12–16.
Ⓤ *Turmstrasse, then* 🚌 *227.*

This building is one of the most important textbook examples of modern architecture dating from the beginning of the 20th century. It was commissioned by the electronics company, AEG, in 1909 and designed by Peter Behrens in conjunction with Karl Bernhardt. It was among the earliest structures not to incorporate any element, decorative or otherwise, that reflected previous architectural styles. A huge hangar of a building, it has enormous windows and stretches 123 m (400 ft) down Berlichingenstrasse. The principal design imperative for this structure was to maintain a streamlined profile, while making no effort to disguise the materials used in its construction.

Gedenkstätte Plötzensee **2**

PLOTZENSEE MEMORIAL

Hüttigpfad. **Tel** *344 32 26.*
Ⓤ *Jakob-Kaiser-Platz, then* 🚌 *123.*
🕐 *Mar–Oct: 9am–5pm; Nov–Feb: 9am–4pm.*

A narrow street leads from Saatwinkler Damm to the site where nearly 2,500 people convicted of crimes against the Third Reich were hanged. The Gedenkstätte Plötzensee is a simple memorial in a brick hut, which still has the iron hooks from which the victims were suspended. The main figures in the unsuccessful assassination attempt against Hitler, on July 20 1944, were executed in Bendlerblock *(see p127)*, although the remainder of the conspirators were killed here. Count Helmut James von Moltke, one of the leaders of the German resistance movement, was also executed here. The count organized the Kreisauer Kreis – a political movement which gathered together and united German opposition to Hitler and the Third Reich.

Memorial to concentration camp victims at Gedenkstätte Plötzensee

IBA-Viertel in Tegel **3**

Karolinenstrasse & Am Tegeler Hafen. Ⓤ *Alt Tegel.*

The development around the southern edge of the port of Tegel is an essential stop for lovers of modern, and

The elegant Neo-Classical façade of Schloss Tegel

particularly post-modern, architecture. This complex developed out of the IBA (Internationale Baustellung) building exhibition in 1987. Over 30 architects were involved in this project, although the main designers were Charles Moore, John Ruble and Buzz Yudell. Within this complex stands the Humboldt-Bibliothek, which draws on Neo-Classical themes. In 1997 a monument was established to the eminent scientists Wilhelm and Alexander von Humboldt in front of this library.

Running the length of Am Tegeler Hafen street is a large housing estate where each unit has been designed by a different architect. For instance, at No. 8, the house by Stanley Tigerman recalls a style popular in Hanseatic architecture, while the red house at No. 10, designed by Paolo Portoghesi, looks as though it has been cracked lengthwise in two.

To the north, the IBA-Viertel estate borders another modern building, the Hotel Sorat, carefully built around the remaining section of an old windmill that was once part of the Humboldt estate.

Schloss Tegel 4

Adelheidallee 19–21. **Tel** 434 31 56. **U** Alt Tegel. **[bus]** 124, 133, 222. **◯** May–Sep: Mon (but due to renovation works **Tel** 434 31 56 to confirm). **[cam]** compulsory (10am, 11am, 3pm, 4pm Mon).

Schloss Tegel is one of the most interesting palace complexes in Berlin. In the 16th century there was already a manor house on this site, which in the second half of the 17th century was rebuilt into a hunting lodge for the Elector Friedrich Wilhelm. In 1766 the ownership of the property passed to the Humboldt family, and between the years 1820 and 1824, Karl Friedrich Schinkel thoroughly rebuilt the palace, giving it its current style.

There are tiled bas-reliefs decorating the elevations on the top floor of the towers. These were designed by Christian Daniel Rauch and depict the ancient wind gods. Some of Schinkel's marvellous interiors have survived, along with several items from what was once a large collection of antique sculptures. The palace is still private property, owned by descendants of the Humboldt family, but guided tours are offered on Mondays.

It is also worth visiting the park. On its western limits lies the Humboldt family tomb designed by Schinkel and decorated with a copy of a splendid sculpture by Bertel Thorwaldsen; the original piece stands inside the palace.

Villa Borsig 5

Reiherwerder. **U** Alt Tegel. **[bus]** 124, 133, 222, 224, then a 15-minute walk.

This villa sits on a peninsula which cuts into the Tegeler See and is reminiscent of Schloss Sanssouci in Potsdam. It was built much later, however, between 1911 and 1913. It was designed by Alfred Salinger and Eugen Schmohl, for the Borsig family, one of the wealthiest industrialist families in Berlin. This villa is particularly picturesque when observed from the lake, so it is worth looking out for it while cruising in a boat.

The Villa Borsig façade viewed from the garden

KARL FRIEDRICH SCHINKEL (1781–1841)

Schinkel was one of the most renowned German architects; even today his work forms an essential element of the architectural landscape of Berlin. He graduated from the Berlin Bauakademie, and for many years held a high-profile position in the Prussian Building Ministry. He was equally skilled in producing both Neo-Classical and Neo-Gothic designs. In Berlin and Potsdam he designed a few dozen buildings – palaces, civic buildings and churches, many of which still stand today. He also excelled at painting and even designed scenery for the opera house on Unter den Linden, among others. You can admire his paintings in the Galerie der Romantik in Schloss Charlottenburg. Schinkel's creativity had a truly enormous influence on the next generation of architects working in Prussia.

GREATER
BERLIN

POTSDAM

Potsdam is an independent city bordering Berlin. It is also the capital of Brandenburg, with almost 140,000 inhabitants. The first historical reference to Potsdam dates from AD 993. The town blossomed in the 1600s, during the era of the Great Elector *(see p20)*, and then again during the 18th century. Potsdam suffered very badly during World War II, particularly on the nights of 14 and 15 April 1945, when the Allies bombed the town's centre. Today, despite its

Sculpture from Park Sanssouci

wartime losses, Potsdam is one of the most interesting cities in Germany. Tourists flock to see the royal Park Sanssouci and palaces such as the Marmorpalais and Schloss Cecilienhof. It is also worth strolling around Neuer Garten and the historic area around the Rathaus. The Russian colony of Alexandrowka, the Holländisches Viertel, the film studios of Babelsberg and Babelsberg park *(see pp210–211)* also rate among the attractions of Potsdam.

SIGHTS AT A GLANCE

Historic Buildings
Altes Rathaus ㉑
Bildergalerie ⑪
Chinesisches Teehaus ⑥
Communs ③
Historische Mühle ⑫
Marmorpalais ⑯
Neue Kammern ⑨
Neues Palais pp194–5 ①
Orangerie ⑦
Römische Bäder ⑤
Schloss Cecilienhof ⑮
Schloss Charlottenhof ④
*Schloss Sanssouci
    pp200–1* ⑩

Wasserwerk Sanssouci ㉔

Historic Areas
Alexandrowka ⑬
Holländisches Viertel ⑰

Churches
Französische Kirche ⑲
Friedenskirche ⑧
Nikolaikirche ⑳
Peter und Paul Kirche ⑱

Parks and Theme Parks
Filmpark Babelsberg ㉖

Neuer Garten ⑭
Park Sanssouci ②
Telegrafenberg ㉕

Museums
Marstall (Filmmuseum) ㉒
Potsdam-Museum ㉓

KEY

▒	Street-by-Street map pp192–3
🚉	Railway station
Ⓢ	S-Bahn Station

0 metres   750
0 yards   750

GETTING THERE

S-Bahn 7 goes to Potsdam from Berlin. From Potsdam station, bus 606 goes to Neues Palais and trams 94, 96 and X-98 go to the centre of town. Bus 695 travels between Park Sanssouci and Neuer Garten.

◁ **Colonnaded cloister at the Friedenskirche**

Street-by-Street: Park Sanssouci

Flower-filled urn, Park Sanssouci

The enormous Park Sanssouci, covering an area of 287 hectares, is among the most beautiful palace complexes in Europe. The first building to be constructed was Schloss Sanssouci, the summer palace of Frederick the Great. It was built between 1745 and 1747 on the site of an orchard. Over the years, Park Sanssouci was expanded and enriched by the addition of other palaces and pavilions. Allow yourself at least a whole day to enjoy the park fully.

Communs
This house for the palace staff has an unusually elegant character, and is situated next to a pretty courtyard ❸

★ Neues Palais
This monumental building of the New Palace, constructed between 1763 and 1769, is crowned by a massive dome ❶

Römische Bäder
The Roman baths include a mock-Renaissance villa and a suite of Roman-style rooms ❺

0 metres	200
0 yards	200

STAR SIGHTS

★ Neues Palais

★ Schloss Sanssouci

Schloss Charlottenhof
This Neo-Classical palace gained its name from Charlotte von Gentzkow, the former owner of the land on which the palace was built ❹

Park Sanssouci
The extensive parkland is made up of several gardens. The one near the Orangerie is called the Lustgarten (pleasure garden) ❷

Orangerie
This Neo-Renaissance palace, the largest in the park, was built in the mid-19th century to house foreign royalty and guests ❼

Neue Kammern
This Rococo pavilion was once the orangerie of the Sanssouci Palace, but was rebuilt as a guest house ❾

★ **Schloss Sanssouci**
A beautifully terraced vineyard creates a grand approach to Schloss Sanssouci, the oldest building in the complex ❿

Bildergalerie
Built between 1755 and 1764, this pavilion houses an art gallery. It is Germany's oldest purpose-built museum building ⓫

Chinesisches Teehaus
The small Rococo-style Chinese Tea House features an exhibition of exquisite Oriental porcelain ❻

Friedenskirche
The Neo-Romanesque Church of Peace is modelled on the Basilica of San Clemente in Rome ❽

Neues Palais ●

This imposing Baroque palace, on the main avenue in Park Sanssouci, was built at the request of Frederick the Great. The initial plans were prepared in 1750 by Georg Wenzeslaus von Knobelsdorff. However, construction only began in 1763, after the Seven Years' War *(see p21)*, to a design by Johann Gottfried Büring, Jean Laurent Le Geay and Carl von Gontard. The result was a vast two-storey building, decorated with hundreds of sculptures and more than 200 richly adorned rooms, which together make up one of Germany's most beautiful palaces.

Cabinet from the study

The Schlosstheater
was completed in 1768, and designed by JC Hoppenhaupt.

Façade
The entrance to the Neues Palais is through the gate on the western façade. The imposing gate is flanked by stone sentry boxes.

Study
This Rococo-style study was part of Frederick the Great's personal apartment.

Upper Gallery
The Rococo interior, with a beautiful inlaid floor, is decorated with Italian paintings.

STAR FEATURES

★ Marmorsaal

★ Grottensaal

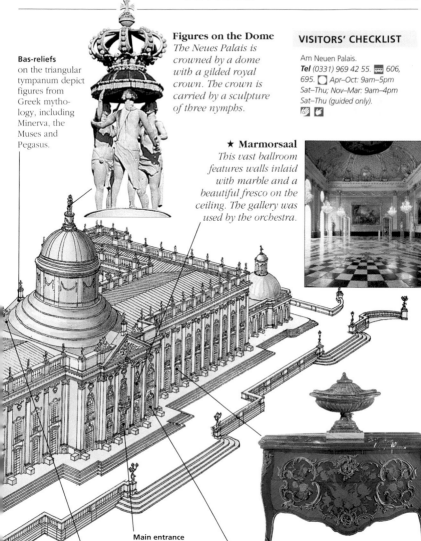

Bas-reliefs
on the triangular tympanum depict figures from Greek mythology, including Minerva, the Muses and Pegasus.

Figures on the Dome
The Neues Palais is crowned by a dome with a gilded royal crown. The crown is carried by a sculpture of three nymphs.

VISITORS' CHECKLIST

Am Neuen Palais.
Tel *(0331) 969 42 55.* 🚌 606, 695. ⬜ *Apr–Oct: 9am–5pm Sat–Thu; Nov–Mar: 9am–4pm Sat–Thu (guided only).*
♿ ⬜

★ Marmorsaal
This vast ballroom features walls inlaid with marble and a beautiful fresco on the ceiling. The gallery was used by the orchestra.

Main entrance

Commode
This Rococo commode was designed by JF Spindler in c.1765. It is located in the Red Room in the Duke's Apartments.

★ Grottensaal
The walls of this unusual grotto-style room are lined with semi-precious stones, coral and shells as well as man-made stalactites.

Upper Vestibule
This elegant room was designed by Carl von Gontard. The walls are covered with Silesian marble and the ceiling depicts Venus and the Graces.

Park Sanssouci ❷

Schopenhauerstrasse/ Zur Historischen Mühle. ▥ *612, 614, 695.*

This vast park, covering some 287 ha (700 acres), was established in 1725 on the site of an orchard. However, it was only transformed into an enormous landscaped park when construction work began on Schloss Sanssouci *(see pp200–1).* Today, the park is made up of smaller gardens dating from different eras, each of which has been maintained in the original style. At the foot of Schloss Sanssouci is the oldest section of the park, containing the Dutch garden, a number of fountains and the French-style Lustgarten (pleasure garden), with a symmetrical layout and lovely rose beds. Surrounding Friedenskirche is the Marly-garten, created in the mid-19th century by Ludwig Persius.

The eastern part of the park is called the Rehgarten, a beautifully landscaped park in the English style, designed by Peter Joseph Lenné, and established on the site of former hunting grounds. This park extends right up to the Neues Palais. To the south, surrounding the small palace,

extends the Charlottenhof Park, also designed by Lenné. In the northern section of the park, next to the Orangerie, is the Nordischer Garten and the Paradiesgarten.

The range of different garden styles makes a simple stroll through this park particularly pleasant. There are also a large number of sculptures, columns, obelisks and grottoes for the visitor to explore. The perspectives that suddenly open up across the park, and the picturesque groupings of trees, are also beautiful.

Communs ❸

Am Neuen Palais. ▥ *606, 695.*

This area of the park consists of a pair of two-storey pavilions linked by a semi-circular colonnade. They are unusually elegant buildings considering they were used for servants' quarters and the palace kitchens. However, they also served to screen from view the cultivated fields that extended past the park from the palace.

The Communs were built between 1766 and 1769 by Carl von Gontard, to a design by Jean Laurent Le Geay. The

Elegant façade of the Communs, the servants' quarters

buildings are enclosed by an elegant courtyard reflected in the style of the buildings. The kitchen was in the south pavilion, linked to the palace by an underground passage-way, and the north pavilion accommodated the servants of the king's guests. Today, the rectors' offices of the University of Potsdam are located here in the Communs.

Schloss Charlottenhof ❹

CHARLOTTENHOF PALACE

Geschwister-Scholl-Strasse (Park Charlottenhof). **Tel** *(0331) 969 42 28.* ▥ *605, 606, 610, X-5.* 🚃 *94, 96.* ◯ *15 May–15 Oct: 10am–5pm Tue–Sun.*

This small Neo-Classical palace is located in the southern extension of Park Sanssouci, Park Charlottenhof. It was designed by Karl Friedrich Schinkel in 1829 for the heir to the throne, later King Friedrich Wilhelm IV. This small one-storey building was built in the style of a Roman villa. The rear of the palace has a portico that opens out onto the garden terrace.

Some of the wall paintings which were made in the so-called Pompeiian style, designed by Schinkel, are still in place. The most interesting part of the interior is the blue-and-white-striped Humboldt Room, also called the Tent Room due to its resemblance to a tent. The palace is sur-rounded by a picturesque landscaped park designed by Peter Joseph Lenné.

One of the many sculptures on display in Park Sanssouci

Römische Bäder ❺

ROMAN BATHS

Lenné-Strasse (Park Charlottenhof).
Tel (0331) 969 42 24. 🚌 606.
🚋 94, 96. ⭕ 15 May–15 Oct:
10am–5pm Tue–Sun.

This picturesque group of pavilions, situated by the edge of a lake, forms the Roman Baths, which actually served as accommodation for the king's guests. It was designed by Karl Friedrich Schinkel, with the involvement of Ludwig Persius, between 1829 and 1840. At the front is the gardener's house, which is adjacent to an asymmetrical low tower in the style of an Italian Renaissance villa. In the background, to the left, extends the former bathing pavilion, which is currently used for temporary exhibitions. All of the pavilions are arranged around an internal garden planted with a multi-coloured carpet of shrubs. A closer look will reveal that many of these colourful plants are actually vegetables.

Spring of water, Römische Bäder

Chinesisches Teehaus ❻

CHINESE TEAHOUSE

Ökonomieweg (Rehgarten).
Tel (0331) 969 42 22. 🚌 606.
🚋 94, 96. ⭕ 15 May–15 Oct:
10am–5pm Tue–Sun.

The lustrous, gilded pavilion that can be seen glistening from a distance is the Chinese Teahouse. Chinese art was

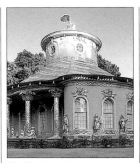

The Chinesisches Teehaus, now housing a collection of porcelain

popular during the Rococo period – people wore Chinese silk, rooms were wallpapered with Chinese designs, furniture was lacquered, drinks were served in Chinese porcelain, and Chinese pavilions were built in gardens.

The Chinesisches Teehaus was built in Park Sanssouci between 1754 and 1756 to a design by Johann Gottfried Büring. It is circular in shape with a centrally located main hall surrounded by three studies. Between each of these are pretty *trompe l'oeil* porticos. Ornaments, together with gilded figures of Chinese gentlemen and ladies, surround the pavilion. Originally the Chinesisches Teehaus served as a tea room and a summer dining room. Today, it houses a collection of porcelain.

Orangerie ❼

Maulbeerallee (Nordischer Garten).
Tel (0331) 96 94 280. 🚌 695.
⭕ 15 May–15 Oct: 10am–5pm
Tue–Sun. **Observation terrace**
1 Apr–14 May: 10am–5pm Sat–Sun;
15 May–15 Oct: 10am–5pm
Tue–Sun.

Towering above the park is the Orangerie, designed in the Italian Renaissance style and crowned by a colonnade. The Orangerie was built to house guests, not plants. It was constructed between 1851 and 1860 by Friedrich August Stüler, on the initiative and direction of Friedrich Wilhelm IV. The final design was partly based on the plans of Ludwig Persius. It served as a guest residence for the king's sister and her husband Tsar Nicholas I. The rooms were grouped around the Raphael Hall, which was based on the Regia Hall in the Vatican and decorated with copies of the works of Italian artist Raphael. It is also worth climbing up to the observation terrace, from where the view extends over Potsdam.

Friedenskirche ❽

Allee nach Sanssouci (Marlygarten).
Tel (0331) 97 40 09. 🚌 695. 🚋 94,
96. ⭕ May–Oct: 10am–6pm daily;
Nov–Apr: 10am–noon Sun.

Close to Schloss Sanssouci is Friedenskirche, or the Church of Peace. The foundation stone was laid by King Friedrich Wilhelm IV in 1845 and the church was completed in 1848. Designed by Ludwig Persius, Friedrich August Stüler and Ludwig Hesse, the church is based on San Clemente in Rome.

Inside, the vaulted ceiling of the apse is almost completely covered by an enchanting 12th-century mosaic depicting the figure of Christ as a judge. This Byzantine mosaic was originally located in the church of San Capriano on the island of Murano in Venice, Italy. Next to the church is a colonnaded atrium and a mausoleum containing the tombs of Friedrich Wilhelm I, Friedrich Wilhelm IV and Kaiser Friedrich III.

Long flight of stairs leading to the Renaissance-style Orangerie

Neue Kammern ❾

NEW CHAMBERS

Zur Historischen Mühle (Lustgarten).
Tel (0331) 969 42 06. 🚌 612, 614,
695. ⬤ mid-May–mid-Oct: 10am–
5pm Tue–Sun; Apr–mid-May: 10am–
5pm Sat–Sun. 🎫 🖾

The Neue Kammern contains
residential apartments. It is the
mirror image of the Bildergalerie and was originally
built as an orangery in 1747 to
a design by Georg Wenzeslaus
von Knobelsdorff. In 1777
Frederick the Great (Friedrich
II) ordered the building to be
remodelled as guest accommodation. The architect, Georg
Christian Unger, left the
elegant Baroque exterior of
the orangery largely
untouched and instead
concentrated on converting
the interior. As well as the
sumptuous guest suites, the
new design included four
elegant halls. The best of
these is the Ovidsaal, with its
rich reliefs and marble floors.
The interior décor has been
maintained in Frederick's
Rococo style. The building
also houses a collection of
Meissen figurines.

Schloss Sanssouci ❿

See pp200–201.

Detail of Caravaggio's *Doubting
Thomas*, **in the Bildergalerie**

Bildergalerie ⓫

Zur Historischen Mühle. **Tel** (0331)
969 42 02. 🚌 695. ⬤ mid-May–
mid-Oct: 10am–5pm Tue–Sun. 🖾

The picture gallery housed in
the building adjacent to
Schloss Sanssouci is the first
purpose-built gallery in
Germany. It was constructed
between 1755 and 1764 to a
design by JG Büring. The
garden elevation reveals an
allegorical tableau
representing Art, Education
and Crafts, while busts of
renowned artists have been
placed in the windows.
    The gallery contains an
exhibition of Baroque
paintings once owned by
Frederick the Great, although
part of the collection can be
found in the Gemäldegalerie
(see pp122–5). Highlights

include Caravaggio's *Doubting Thomas* and Guido Reni's
Cleopatra's Death, as well as
a number of canvases by
Rubens and van Dyck.

Historische Mühle ⓬

HISTORIC WINDMILL

Zur Historischen Mühle. **Tel** (0331)
969 42 84. 🚌 695. ⬤ Apr–Oct:
10am–6pm daily; Nov–Mar:
10am–4pm Sat & Sun. 🖾

A mill has been located here
since the early 18th century,
although this is actually a
reconstruction, dating from
1993. According to local
legend, the old windmill was
so noisy that Frederick the
Great ordered it to be dismantled. However, a court
upheld the miller's cause and
the mill stayed. In 1790 a new
windmill was built in its place,
which lasted until 1945. The
mill currently houses a museum
of mechanical windmills.

Alexandrowka ⓭

Russische Kolonie Allee/ Puschkinallee.
🚊 90, 92, 95, X-91. 🚌 604, 609,
650, 692, 697.

A trip to Alexandrowka takes
the visitor into the world of
Pushkin's stories. Wooden
houses made from logs,

A Russian-style wooden house in the settlement of Alexandrowka

decorated with carved motifs and set in their own gardens, create a very pretty residential estate. Although they appear to be picturebook, traditional Russian houses, they were constructed in 1826 under the direction of a German military architect called Captain Snethlage. What is interesting is that the estate was created for the singers of a Russian choir. The choir was set up in 1812 to entertain the troops and was recruited from over 500 Russian prisoners of war, who had fought with Napoleon. In 1815, when the Prussians and the Russians joined forces, the choir was retained by Friedrich Wilhelm III.

Peter Joseph Lenné was responsible for the overall appearance of the estate, and it was named Alexandrowka after the Tsarina, the Prussian Princess Charlotte. It is based on the shape of the cross of St Andrew inscribed within an oval. In all, 12 houses were built here, as well as an outhouse which now contains a small museum. Some of the dwellings are still owned by the descendants of the choir. To the north of this estate stands the Russian Orthodox church of Alexander Nevski (1829).

Schloss Cecilienhof, summer residence of the Hohenzollern family

layout was created by Peter Joseph Lenné in 1816. It is a Romantic park ornamented with numerous pavilions and sculptures. The charming Marmorpalais stands beside the lake, while the northern section contains the early 20th-century Schloss Cecilienhof. Elsewhere you can see the red and green gardeners' houses, the pyramid-shaped ice house and a Neo-Gothic library pavilion completed in 1794.

Schloss Cecilienhof ⑮

Am Neuen Garten. **Tel** *(0331) 969 42 44*. 🚌 *692, 695*. ⏱ *Apr–Oct: 9am– 5pm; Nov–Mar: 9am–4pm Tue–Sun.*

The Cecilienhof residence played a brief but important part in history because it was here that the 1945 Potsdam

Conference took place. Built between 1914 and 1917, the palace is the most recent of the Hohenzollern dynasty buildings and was designed by Paul Schultze-Naumburg in the style of an English country manor. It is a sprawling, asymmetrical building with wooden beams making a pretty herringbone pattern on its walls. The gatehouse passageways leading to the courtyards are decorated with Baroque reliefs.

The palace was the Hohenzollern family residence after they lost the crown; the family remained in Potsdam until February 1945. It now functions as a first-class hotel and restaurant, where history lovers can relax amid carefully tended shrubbery. Most of the historic furnishings used during the famous Potsdam conference are on display.

Orange growing in the Neuer Garten's Marmorpalais

Neuer Garten ⑭

NEW GARDEN

Am Neuen Garten. 🚌 *692, 695*.

Running along the edge of Heiliger See, on what was once the site of palace vineyards, is a park laid out between 1787 and 1791. It was landscaped originally by Johann August Eyserbeck on the instructions of Friedrich Wilhelm II, while the current

THE POTSDAM CONFERENCE OF 1945

On 17 July 1945 the heads of government for Great Britain (Winston Churchill, later represented by Clement Attlee), the United States (Harry Truman) and the Soviet Union (Joseph Stalin) met in Schloss Cecilienhof to confirm the decisions made earlier that year at Yalta. The aim of both conferences was to resolve the problems arising at the end of World War II. They decided to abolish the Nazi Party, to limit the size of the German militia and monitor it indefinitely, and also to punish war criminals and establish reparations. They also revised the German borders and arranged the resettlement of Germans from Poland. The conference played a major part in establishing the political balance of power in Europe, which continued for the next 45 years.

Attlee, Truman and Stalin at Cecilienhof

Schloss Sanssouci ⑩

The name Sanssouci is French for "without a care" and gives a good indication of the flamboyant character of this enchanting Rococo palace, built in 1745. The original sketches, made by Friedrich II (Frederick the Great) himself, were finalized by Georg Wenzeslaus von Knobelsdorff. The glorious interiors were designed by Knobelsdorff and Johann August Nahl. The king clearly loved this palace, as his final wishes were that he should be buried here, near the tomb of his Italian greyhounds. He was actually interred in the Garnisonkirche, Potsdam, but his final wishes were carried out in 1991.

Bacchanalian Figures
The carved male and female bacchanalian figures on the pilasters are the work of Friedrich Christian Glume.

The colonnade frames the view of the artificial ruins on the hill.

The wings were added to the building between 1841 and 1842.

Voltaire Room
This room, located in the Damenflügel (Ladies' wing), is decorated with naturalistic carvings of birds, flowers and fruit.

Domed Roof
The oxidized green dome covers the Marmorsaal. It is decorated with Baroque sculptures.

Marmorsaal
The imposing marble hall is decorated with pairs of columns made from Carrara marble. Frederick the Great wanted this room to be loosely based on the Pantheon in Rome.

STAR SIGHTS

★ Fêtes Galantes by Antoine Watteau

★ Konzertzimmer

Arbour
The palace design is completed by picturesque arbours and pergolas decorated with sun motifs.

VISITORS' CHECKLIST

Zur Historischen Mühle. **Tel** (0331) 969 41 90. 🚌 612, 614, 650, 695. 🚃 94, 96, X-98. ⬜ 1 Apr–31 Oct: 9am–5pm Tue–Sun; 1 Nov–31 Mar: 9am–4pm Tue–Sun. **Damenflügel** 15 May–15 Oct: 10am–5pm Sat–Sun. 📷 📹 compulsory.

★ Fêtes Galantes (c. 1715)
The real jewels in the palace are the enchanting paintings by Antoine Watteau. He was one of Frederick the Great's favourite artists.

Weimar Urn (1785)
This Neo-Classical urn from the Berlin company KPM (see p133) is a copy of the original urn, which was presented to the Duchess of Weimar.

★ Konzertzimmer
The walls of the salon are decorated with paintings by Antoine Pesne, based on Greek mythology.

Bibliothek
The library of Frederick the Great contains about 2,100 books. The walls are lined with cedar panelling to create a contemplative atmosphere.

Marmorpalais

MARBLE PALACE

Am Ufer des Heiligen Sees (Neuer Garten). *Tel (0331) 969 42 46.* 692, 695. ◯ *1 Apr–31 Oct: 10am–5pm Tue–Sun; 1 Nov–31 Mar: 10am–4pm Sat–Sun.*

The Marmorpalais is situated on the edge of the lake in Neuer Garten *(see p199)*, a park northeast of the centre of Potsdam. This small palace is a beautiful example of early Neo-Classical architecture. The palace owes its name to its façade, which is lined with Silesian marble.

The square main body of the palace was the initiative of King Friedrich Wilhelm II. The original building was completed in 1791 to a design by Carl von Gontard, under the direction of Carl Gotthard Langhans. The single-storey building had small rooms around a central staircase, but this turned out to be too small, and in 1797 it was extended. An extra floor and two projecting wings were added. This gave the Marmorpalais the character of a Palladian villa.

The main part of the palace contains Neo-Classical furnishings from the late 1700s, including furniture from the workshops of Roentgen and porcelain from Wedgwood, the English firm. The interiors of the wings date from slightly later, from the 1840s. The concert hall in the right hand wing is particularly beautiful. King Friedrich Wilhelm II died in this palace in 1797.

Neo-Classical Marmorpalais, with its inlaid marble façade

The historic Dutch district known as the Holländisches Viertel

Holländisches Viertel

DUTCH QUARTER

Friedrich-Ebert-/Kurfürsten-/Hebbel-/ Gutenbergstr. 138, 604, 606, 638, 639, 692, 695. 92, 95, X-91.

Just as amazing as the Russian district of Alexandrowka *(see pp198–9)* is this Dutch district. The area is popular with tourists, with numerous shops, galleries, cafés and beer cellars, especially along the central Mittelstrasse.

Dutch workers, invited by Friedrich Wilhelm I, arrived in Potsdam at the beginning of the 18th century. Between 1733 and 1742 a settlement was built for them, comprising 134 gabled houses arranged in four groups, according to plans by Johann Boumann the Elder. They were built from small red bricks, and finished with stone and plaster details. These houses are typically three-storey, with picturesque roofs and gables.

Peter und Paul Kirche

Bassinplatz. *Tel (0331) 230 79 90.* 618, 750, 780. 90, 92, 93, 96, X-91, X-98. ✝ *10am Sun.*

This 19th-century church was the first large Catholic church built in Potsdam, at the initiative of Friedrich Wilhelm IV. The first designs came from Friedrich August Stüler, but the final version is the work of Wilhelm Salzenberg. The church was built in 1870, in the shape of a Neo-

Romanesque cross. Its slender tower is a copy of the campanile of San Zeno Maggiore in Verona, Italy. Inside are three beautiful paintings by Antoine Pesne.

The colonnaded portico of the Französische Kirche

Französische Kirche

FRENCH CHURCH

Bassinplatz. *Tel (0331) 29 12 19.* 618, 750, 780. 90, 92, 93, 96, X-91, X-98. ◯ *noon– 5pm daily.*

This church, reminiscent of the Pantheon in Rome, was built especially for the Hugenots in 1752. Following their expulsion from France, they were given the option of settling in Prussia in 1685 *(see p21)*. Those who settled in Potsdam initially benefited from the hospitality of other churches, then eventually the Französische Kirche was built for them. It was designed by Johann Boumann the Elder in the shape of an ellipse. The front elevation is supported by a grand columned portico. The side niches, which are the entrances of the church, are decorated with the allegorical figures of Faith and Knowledge. The interior dates from the 1830s and is based on designs by Karl Friedrich Schinkel.

Nikolaikirche ⑳

Am Alten Markt. *Tel (0331) 270 86 02.* 🚌 *604, 609, 692.* 🚊 *90, 92, 93, 96, X-90, X-91, X-98.* ⏰ *2–5pm Mon, 10am–5pm Tue–Sat, 11:30am–5pm Sun.*

This imposing church, built in a late Neo-Classical style, is the most beautiful church in Potsdam. It was designed in 1830 by Karl Friedrich Schinkel and the building work was overseen by Ludwig Persius. The main body of the church is based on a square cross, with a semicircular presbytery.

It was decided only in the 1840s to crown the church with a vast dome, supported on a colonnaded tambour (wall supporting a dome). Schinkel had envisaged this from the beginning of the project, but it was not included in the orders of the king. Initially it was thought that the dome would be supported by a wooden structure, though ultimately it was built using iron between 1843 and 1848, according to a design by Persius and Friedrich August Stüler. The interior decoration and the furnishings of the church date back to the 1850s, and in the main area of the church they were based on the earlier designs by Schinkel.

In front of the church stands an obelisk built between 1753

and 1755 to a design by Georg Wenzeslaus von Knobelsdorff. Initially it was decorated by medallions depicting the portraits of Prussian rulers, but during the post-World War II restorations, they were replaced with portraits of renowned Prussian architects.

Altes Rathaus ㉑

OLD TOWN HALL

Am Alten Markt. 🚌 *604, 609, 692, 694.* 🚊 *90, 92, 93, 96, X-90, X-91, X-98.*

This elegant, colonnaded building, located on the eastern side of Alter Markt, is the old town hall. Designed by Johann Boumann the Elder, it was built in 1753 on the site of an earlier building that served a similar purpose. The uppermost storey, which features an ornamental attic roof, is decorated with the crest of Potsdam and allegorical sculptures. At the summit of the small tower are two gilded figures

Atlas at Altes Rathaus

of Atlas, each carrying a globe of the earth. The Altes Rathaus is currently used as a cultural centre. The interior of the neighbouring mid-18th century building was also refurbished, and a glassed- in passageway was built, linking the two buildings.

The Potsdam Royal Palace was located at one time on the west side of Alter Markt. It was a massive two-storey building with three wings. There was also an elegant courtyard and a superb gateway crowned by a tower. The palace was built in 1662 on the site of a former castle, on the initiative of the Great Elector. Over the following years the palace was greatly enlarged and modernized for members of the royal family, including Frederick the Great (Friedrich II). After a bombing raid in 1945 the palace remained in ruins for many years, but the East German Government decided finally to pull down the remains in 1960. A temporary theatre now occupies the site.

POTSDAM TOWN GATES

The city of Potsdam was enclosed by a wall in 1722. This wall did not serve a defensive purpose – it was supposed to contain criminals and stop soldiers deserting. When the borders of the town were extended in 1733, new districts were also enclosed by the wall. There was a total of five city gates, of which three have survived. Jägertor has survived in its original condition and dates from 1733. Featuring solid, wide pillars, the gate is crowned with a group of sculptures depicting hunting dogs attacking a deer. Nauener Tor was redesigned in 1755 by Johann Gottfried Büring and, interestingly, it is one of the earliest examples of Neo-Gothic design occurring outside Great Britain. The most imposing of the gates is the Brandenburger Tor. It was rebuilt in 1770 in a Neo-Classical style to commemorate victory in the Seven Years' War *(see p21).* The designers, Gontard and Unger, gave it the appearance of an ancient triumphal arch. At the very top is a number of different groups of sculptures. These include figures from Greek mythology, such as Hercules and Mars.

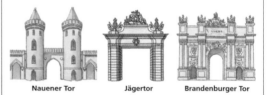

Nauener Tor   **Jägertor**   **Brandenburger Tor**

Nikolaikirche's imposing exterior, with its green, weathered dome

Stately building of the Marstall (Filmmuseum)

Marstall (Filmmuseum) ㉒

Am Lustgarten. *Tel (0331) 27 18 10.*
☐ *10am–6pm daily.* 🎫 🚌 *601, 603, 692, 694.* 🚊 *90, 92, 93, 96, X-91, X-98.*

This Baroque pavilion, once used as a royal stables, hence the name Marstall, is the only remaining building of a former royal residence. It was first established in 1714 by refashioning the orangery built by Johann Nering in 1685. In 1746 it was extended and refashioned once more, according to a design by the architect GW von Knobelsdorff. It suffered extensive damage in World War II and in 1977, after major restoration, it was converted to a film museum. As well as temporary exhibitions, this museum documents the history and work of the Babelsberg studios, Germany's earliest film studios. Exhibits include old projectors, cameras and other equipment as well as props used in some of the most famous German films.

Potsdam-Museum ㉓

Breite Strasse 8–12. *Tel (0331) 289 19 51.* ☐ *10am–5pm Tue–Sun.* 🎫 🚌 *695, X-5.*

The Potsdam-Museum's collection embraces natural science and historical exhibits equally, including a display illustrating the geography and nature of the Havel river basin. In the main building, the history of Potsdam is documented up until 1900 and the exhibition continues in two smaller buildings, called the Hiller-Brandt's Häuser (houses). These were built in

1769 by Georg Christian Unger and were a deliberate copy of Inigo Jones's Banqueting House on Whitehall, London.

Cherubs decorating the façade of the Potsdam-Museum

Wasserwerk Sanssouci ㉔

Breite Strasse. *Tel (0331) 969 42 02.* ☐ *15 May–15 October: 10am–5pm Sat–Sun.* 🚌 *606, 695.* 🚊 *94, 96, X-98.*

Although Potsdam once boasted a Russian and a Dutch community, the remarkable mosque was not built to serve the needs of an Islamic community. Rather, it was built to disguise the special steam pump that serviced the fountains in Park Sanssouci. This Moorish-style building, with its slender minaret and Oriental dome, was designed by Ludwig Persius in 1842. The dome does not serve any useful purpose, although within the minaret there is a huge chimney. While visiting the mosque you can see the preserved steam-powered machinery manufactured by the Borsig company.

Telegrafenberg ㉕

Albert-Einstein-Strasse. Ⓢ *Potsdam Hauptbahnhof.* **Einsteinturm**
🎦 *(0331) 29 17 41.* ☐ *by appointment only.* 🎫 *compulsory.*

The buildings on the Telegrafenberg are considered to be some of the best 20th-century structures in the world and attract many admirers of modern architecture. The hill received its current name in 1832, when an optical telegraph station linking Berlin and Koblenz was built here. In the late 19th century, various educational institutes were located here, including the Institute of Astrophysics, for which the complex of buildings in yellow brick was built.

The meandering avenues lead to a picturesque clearing where the small Einsteinturm (Einstein's Tower) breaks through the surrounding trees. Specially designed to observe the solar system, the tower was intended to provide information that would support Einstein's Theory of Relativity. It was built in 1920 by Erich Mendelsohn and is regarded as one of the finest architectural examples of German Expressionism. Its fantastical appearance was intended to show what could be achieved with reinforced concrete. However, the costs of the complicated form limited the use of concrete, and above the first storey the building is made from brickwork covered in plaster.

Moorish Wasserwerk Sanssouci, complete with minaret

Filmpark Babelsberg ㉖

This amazing theme park was laid out on the site of
the film studios where Germany's first films were
produced in 1912. From 1917 the studio belonged to
Universum-Film-AG (UFA), which produced some of the
most renowned films of the silent era, such as *Metropolis*
(see p151). Nazi propaganda films were also made here.
The studio is still operational today, although part of the
complex is open to visitors. Expect to see the sets from
old films, special effects at work and stuntmen in action.

VISITORS' CHECKLIST

August-Bebel Strasse 26–53
(entrance in Grossbeeren Strasse).
Tel (0331) 721 27 50. 📠 690,
696. Ⓢ Griebnitzsee. ◯ mid-
Mar–early Nov: 10am–6pm daily.
🖥 www.filmpark.de

Sandmann
*Sandmann is a character from an animated
television series. Sandmann has entertained
children in East Germany from
1959 to the present day.*

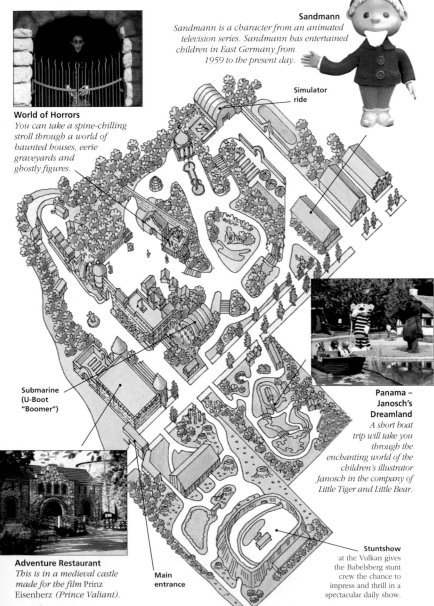

World of Horrors
*You can take a spine-chilling
stroll through a world of
haunted houses, eerie
graveyards and
ghostly figures.*

Simulator
ride

**Panama –
Janosch's
Dreamland**
*A short boat
trip will take you
through the
enchanting world of the
children's illustrator
Janosch in the company of
Little Tiger and Little Bear.*

Submarine
(U-Boot
"Boomer")

Adventure Restaurant
*This is in a medieval castle
made for the film* Prinz
Eisenherz *(Prince Valiant).*

**Main
entrance**

Stuntshow
at the Vulkan gives
the Babelsberg stunt
crew the chance to
impress and thrill in a
spectacular daily show.

THREE GUIDED WALKS

Berlin is full of enchanting parks, gardens, lakes and interesting monuments, and one of the best ways to enjoy them is by going on a guided walk. The three walks suggested in this chapter provide for relaxation far from the hustle and bustle of the city centre. The first takes you onto the picturesque Pfaueninsel (Peacock Island), which at the end of the 18th century was refashioned into a romantic English-style park with garden pavilions and an enchanting little palace. After visiting the island you can pay a short visit to Nikolskoe – a Russian-style *dacha* (country house) built for the future Tsar Nicholas I and his wife, the daughter of King Friedrich Wilhelm III. The second walk begins in Berlin and takes you first through the grounds of the Klein Glienicke Park, which was laid out in the 1820s for Prince Karl of Prussia. This route continues across the former border between East and West Germany, in an area which is now part of Potsdam. There you can visit the Romantic-era park of Babelsberg, and the Neo-Gothic palace designed for Prince Wilhelm by Karl Friedrich Schinkel. The third walk, around the forest called Grunewald, takes you initially through a deluxe villa resort of the late 19th century, and then along forest paths to the Grunewaldsee. On the shores of this lake stands an enchanting hunting lodge. From there you can continue walking to the Brücke-Museum. Because each of these three walks leads you across unpaved paths, remember to wear comfortable shoes.

Statue at Klein Glienicke

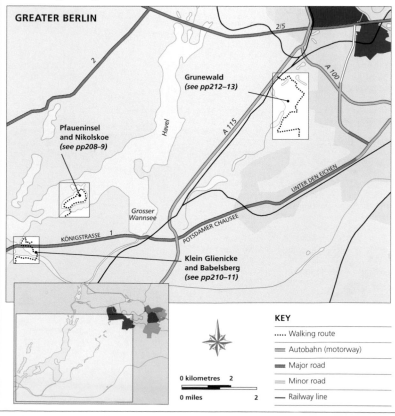

◁ **A picturesque corner of the Neo-Gothic Babelsberg palace**

Pfaueninsel and Nikolskoe

This walk takes you around Pfaueninsel (Peacock Island). This picturesque park, now a nature reserve, was laid out in 1795 according to a design by Johann August Eyserbeck. Its final form, which you see today, is the work of the renowned landscape architect Peter Joseph Lenné. This pleasant, relaxing walk allows you to explore several interesting sights, and to encounter the peacocks for which the island is named. Afterwards you can have refreshments at the lakeside, or head straight to Nikolskoe, the location of one of Berlin's finest restaurants.

Statue at the small palace

James's Well, deliberately built to resemble a picturesque ruin

One of the colourful peacocks on Pfaueninsel (Peacock Island)

Around Pfaueninsel

At the jetty ① you board a small passenger ferry which takes you to the island in a few minutes. After disembarking, follow the path which leads to the left. It continues along the edge of the island, gently uphill to the Castellan's House ② and further on to the Swiss House, dating from 1830, in which the gardener lived. Continue along the path to the extensive clearing with a picturesque flower garden, beyond which is the small romantic palace of Schloss Pfaueninsel ③. Dating from 1794, it was designed by

Johann Gottlieb Brendel for Friedrich Wilhelm II and his mistress Wilhelmine Encke (the future Countess Lichtenau). The palace was built of wood, with a façade (hidden away) fashioned in the form of a ruined medieval castle. The façade was visible from Neuer Garten in Potsdam. The cast-iron bridge which links the towers was built in 1807. During the summer months you can go inside the palace to see its furnishings from the 18th and 19th centuries.

After leaving the palace follow the path that leads along the edge, passing by the kitchen pavilion ④ on the left, which is set amid greenery. At the next junction turn gently right into the depths of the island. You will pass by the James's Well ⑤ which was built to resemble an ancient ruin, and cross a meadow heading towards a small wood which contains the Kavalierhaus ⑥. This building was used to provide the

royal household with accommodation. At the front of the house, Karl Friedrich Schinkel installed an authentic façade from a late Gothic house brought over from Danzig (now Gdansk) in Poland. From here you proceed further in the same

KEY

- ••• Suggested route
- – – Ferry route
- 🚢 Ferry boarding point

0 metres   200
0 yards   200

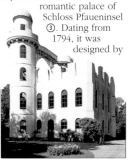

The Neo-Gothic Schloss Pfaueninsel designed by Johann Brendel

direction, and emerge again in a large clearing. To the left you can marvel at the Parschenkessel bay ⑦ in the distance, surrounded by dead trees on which cormorants nest. Take the path on the left to the Neo-Gothic Dairy ⑧

Guests on the terrace of the Blockhaus Nikolskoe in summer

mausoleum in Schlosspark Charlottenburg (see p163) in 1829. The path leads further along the edge of the lake, while on the right side among the trees you pass the stone commemorating Johannes Kunckel, an alchemist who lived on Pfaueninsel in the 17th century. In his quest to uncover how to make gold he, in fact, discovered a method of producing ruby-coloured glass. Carry on further through the forest, passing the Gothic Bridge ⑪, and then take the path to the right up towards the hill of the Aviary ⑫, home to multi-coloured parrots and pheasants. From here you continue towards the tall column of a Fountain ⑬ designed by Martin Friedrich Rabe in 1824. Next, walk onward to the jetty, passing the market gardens with their hothouses on the way.

From the Jetty to Nikolskoe
Once you've taken the little ferry back to the mainland, head off to the right, going

TIPS FOR WALKERS

Beginning of the walk: the jetty for the ferry to Pfaueninsel.
Length: 4.4 km (2.7 miles).
Duration: 2.5–3 hours.
Getting there: bus 216 or 316 from S-Bahn Wannsee; or ferry from Wannsee or Potsdam.
Stops: There are no cafés or restaurants on Pfaueninsel itself. By the jetty on the mainland is "Wirtshaus zur Pfaueninsel", a little place to eat with a summer beer garden. In Nikolskoe is a restaurant with a terrace called "Blockhaus Nikolskoe".

south. When you come to the fork take the left hand path leading gently uphill. This leads to the church of Saints Peter and Paul ⑭, which rises above a large terrace from where there are pretty views of Pfaueninsel. The church was built between the years 1834 and 1837, according to a design by Friedrich August Stüler. The small, orderly, body of the church is fronted by a tower crowned by an onion-shaped dome, which reflects Russian Orthodox sacral architecture. This links to the adjacent Blockhaus "Nikolskoe" ⑮, a Russian-style wooden *dacha* (country house), built in 1819 by the architect Snethlage, who created the Alexandrowka estate in Potsdam. The *dacha* was a present from King Friedrich Wilhelm III to his daughter and son-in-law, the future Tsar Nicholas I. Following a fire in 1985 the *dacha* was reconstructed, and it currently houses a restaurant. Nearby you will find a bus-stop where you can catch buses back to the S-Bahn Wannsee.

Havel

and the Dutch House ⑨. This was a cow shed and dates from 1802, while the Dairy is an artificial ruin of a medieval abbey dating from 1795. From here take the path along the edge of the lake heading south; you can marvel at the wonderful views. To the right by the edge of the forest you can see Luisentempel ⑩ in the form of a Greek temple. Its sandstone portico at the front was moved to the island from the

The little ferry on the Havel river which takes passengers to Pfaueninsel

Klein Glienicke and Babelsberg

A griffin in Klein Glienicke

This guided walk takes you through an area covered by two interesting palace-park complexes – Klein Glienicke and Babelsberg. They were built originally for members of the royal family during the mid-19th century. The buildings of Klein Glienicke were designed by Schinkel, Persius and von Arnim in a Neo-Classical style. Peter Joseph Lenné created the charming park in which they are located. Babelsberg has a more romantic park that was completed by Hermann von Pückler-Muskau. It is maintained in a completely different style, with regal Neo-Gothic pavilions.

Mosaic from the Klosterhof in the gardens of Klein Glienicke

Around Klein Glienicke

The walk begins by the main gate leading into the park. The southern section of the park has the feel of an Italianate Arcadian garden. Soon on the left you will see the Stibadium ①, a roofed pavilion designed by Ludwig Persius. Nearby you can marvel at the imposing Fountain of Lions ②, decorated with gilded figures of these royal beasts. The fountain stands on the axis of the palace ③ which was built in 1825, according to a design

by Karl Friedrich Schinkel for Prince Karl of Prussia. During summer weekends you can visit the palace between 10am and 5pm. Beyond the symmetrical, Neo-Classical building extends an irregular cluster of buildings, grouped around a courtyard with a veranda, which include a pergola and staff cottages. You pass by the palace and approach the Coach House ④, designed by Schinkel but refurbished several times. This now houses the Coach House restaurant (see p243).

Beyond the Coach House you can see the orangery and greenhouses built by Persius. A path leads in the direction of the lake, but on the way it is worth diverting to the right to the Klosterhof ⑤, a mock monastery with pavilions, also by Persius. In the walls of these buildings are numerous Byzantine and Romanesque architectural elements from Italy. Further to the north extends a second "wild" section of the park created to resemble an alpine and Carpathian landscape, with man-made waterfalls, planks

for crossing the water, and hunting lodges. You can return in the direction of the lake and go up to the Casino ⑦, which once contained guest apartments. From here a path extending along the lake takes you to the Grosse Neugierde ⑧, a circular pavilion with a roof supported by Doric columns, based on the Athenian monument to Lysikrates from the 4th century BC. From here there are beautiful views across the Havel river and Glienicker Brücke ⑨, known paradoxically as the bridge of unity under the East German

The reconstructed Gothic Gerichts-laube (arcaded courthouse)

Babelsberg's Neo-Gothic Flatow-turm dating from 1853 to 1856

contain original Roman and Byzantine fragments.

From Klein Glienicke to Babelsberg

On leaving the park you cross to the other side of Potsdamer Chaussee and proceed along Mövenstrasse, passing the massive building of the Jagd-schloss Glienicke ⑪ on the right. Located on the site of an earlier hunting lodge, its Neo-Mannerist appearance is the result of a massive rebuilding process undertaken in 1889 by Albert Geyer, on behalf of Prince Friedrich Leopold. It now houses an international meeting centre as well as an academy of folk art. Passing the Jagdschloss you turn right into Waldmüller-strasse, then right again into Lankestrasse, which leads you to the bridge linking Glienicke with Babelsberg.

Around Schloss Babelsberg

From the bridge you head right towards the engine house ⑫, designed by Persius to look like a medieval castle with a tall tower covering the chimney. From here you head towards Schloss Babelsberg ⑬, designed by Karl Friedrich Schinkel for the future Kaiser Wilhelm I of Germany. The palace was built between 1833 and 1835 in a Neo-Gothic style and shows the influence of English architecture on Schinkel. This beautiful, irregular building with many

towers and bay windows is one of Schinkel's greatest works. Visitors can go inside.

From here, take the path leading along the edge of the Havel to the so-called Kleines Schloss ⑭. Another Neo-Gothic palace, although much smaller in scale, this was where ladies of the court once resided. It now houses a café.

From here you proceed further to the edge of the lake, taking the left branch to the Neo-Gothic stable ⑮, and further to the Gerichtslaube (Gothic arcaded courthouse) ⑯ which was moved here from Berlin. The final sight on this walk is the Flatowturm ⑰, a Neo-Gothic tower dating from 1853 to 1856, from which there are marvellous views of the surrounding area. From here follow the path to the park exit at Grenzstrasse. Turning left, you reach the bus stop for the No. 690 and No. 691 which go to S-Bahn Babelsberg station.

TIPS FOR WALKERS

Beginning of the walk: bus stop at Klein Glienicke. *Length:* 4.2 km (2.6 miles). *Duration:* 3 hours. *Getting there:* bus 116 from S-Bahn station Wannsee or ferry from Wannsee or Potsdam. *Stops:* Café at Park Babelsberg; Coach House at Klein Glienicke. *Schloss Babelsberg* ☐ but no regular times due to restoration work. *Tel* (0331) 969 42 50 for latest information.

regime. The border with West Berlin ran across this bridge, where the exchange of spies was conducted during the Cold War. You return via a path along the wall of the main gate, passing the Kleine Neugierde ⑩, a pavilion serving as a tea room. This was built in the form of an ancient temple, and its walls

0 metres 300
0 yards 300

KEY

••• Suggested route

⊠ Ferry boarding point

The Neo-Gothic Schloss Babelsberg, designed by KF Schinkel

Grunewald

This walk leads initially through one of Berlin's most elegant residential areas, established in 1889. Once the haunt of politicians, wealthy industrialists, renowned artists and academics, some villas now serve as the headquarters of academic institutes. This walk continues through the forest to a small hunting lodge with an interesting art collection, and ends at the edge of the Grunewald in a residential estate of elegant villas, home of the Brücke-Museum.

The elegant villa at Winklerstrasse No. 11

From Bahnhof Grunewald to Hagenstrasse

From the S-Bahn Grunewald station follow the signs to "Grunewald (Ort)". Be sure to take a close look at the station itself ① – this picturesque wooden framed building was built in 1899. The station has a dark past, though, as Berlin's Jews were transported from here to the concentration camps. From the square in front of the station go along Winklerstrasse, which turns left. Along the way you will pass stunningly beautiful villas. The Neo-Classical house at No. 15, dating from 1899, was home to architect Ewald Becher ②. Not much further on the same side of the road, at No. 11, is a villa dating from 1906 ③. It was designed by Hermann Muthesius, who transplanted onto German soil the style of English rustic building. On the right at No. 12 is Villa Maren, dating from 1897, an example of a Neo-Renaissance building in the style of an Italian palazzo with *sgraffito* decorations ④. The villa at No. 8–10,

dating from 1902, boasts costly stone elevations, which fan out richly with decorations in the German Renaissance style ⑤. By this villa turn right into Hasensprung, which leads across the bridge decorated with running hares, dividing Diana-see from Königssee. You reach Königsallee and turn left before immediately turning right into Lassenstrasse, and then right again into Bismarckstrasse, which leads to a small square where you can marvel at the picturesque Neo-Gothic Grunewald-Kirche ⑥. From here go left into Furtwänglerstrasse, where it is worth looking at the villa at No. 15, a beautiful example of a southern German country house ⑦. Next turn right into Hubertusbader Strasse, where at No. 25 an interesting villa has survived with Neo-Classical motifs ⑧, which is the work of Arnold Hartmann dating from 1896. He is also responsible for the villa at No. 23

Rose window, Grunewald-Kirche

Seebergsteig, featuring fantastic elevations decorated with Secessionist motifs ⑨. From here continue along Hubertusbader Strasse to Hagenstrasse.

From Hagenstrasse to the Brücke-Museum

You cut through Hagenstrasse and continue further, straight into Wildpfad, where you turn left in Waldmeisterstrasse, which leads along the fence of the grounds of private clubs. Turn right into Eichhörnchensteig, which gradually becomes surrounded by forest and changes from being a

road into a forest path. Once past the grounds of the private clubs, follow a road which goes gently to the right, and down to the edge of the picturesque Grunewaldsee. Turn left and continue along its edge to Jagdschloss Grunewald ⑩. This is one of the oldest civic buildings to survive in Berlin. It was built for the Elector Joachim II in 1542, and around 1700 it was rebuilt in a Baroque style. Through the gate you enter a courtyard enclosed on three sides with household buildings. In the small palace is Berlin's only surviving Renaissance hall. It houses a collection of paintings, with canvases by Rubens and van Dyck among others. In the east wing is the small Waldmuseum, with illustrations that depict forest life. Following a recent fire, which destroyed the roof and other parts of the building, the Jagdschloss will reopen by 2005.

From the palace you proceed further along the edge to Forsthaus Paulsborn ⑪. This picturesque building was constructed in 1905, according to a design by Friedrich Wilhelm Göhre *(see p243)*. The entire building is maintained in the style of a hunting lodge with decorations that reflect hunting themes. During the summer the garden is filled with tables, where you can

The household buildings in the hunting lodge in Grunewald

enjoy a tasty meal and have a rest, following the walk.

From Paulsborn you return to Jagdschloss Grunewald; at the crossroads you should take the central avenue sign-posted "Wilmersdorf". This leads through the forest and emerges on Pücklerstrasse. Passing modern deluxe villas you continue straight on, and then turn right into Fohlenweg, then turn right again into Bussardsteig, at the end of which is the Brücke-Museum *(see p179)* ⑫. It is also worth looking at the exhibition of sculptures by Bernhard Heliger arranged in the garden surrounding the villa at Käuzchensteig No. 8. From here you continue to Clayallee where buses on the No. 115 route operate.

Detail from Toni-Lessler-Strasse No. 23

TIPS FOR WALKERS

Beginning of the walk: Grunewald S-Bahn station. *Distance:* 3 km (1.8 miles). *Duration:* 2.5–3 hours. *Getting there:* S-Bahn line 3 or 7; U-Bahn Oskar-Helene-Heim; Bus 115. **Museum:** Jagdschloss Grunewald. *Tel* 813 35 97. ▢ May 15–Oct 15: 10am–5pm Tue–Sun; Oct 16–May 14 (tours only) 11am, 1pm & 3pm. *Stops:* There are numerous cafés and restaurants in the Grunewald residential area. Near Jagdschloss Grunewald there is a very good restaurant, Forsthaus Paulsborn.

Restaurant in the Forsthaus Paulsborn near Jagdschloss Grunewald

0 metres 400

0 yards 400

KEY

····· Suggested route

Ⓢ S-Bahn

TRAVELLERS' NEEDS

WHERE TO STAY

Berlin has a good selection of hotels to suit any budget. Many of the expensive hotels belong to well-known international chains, but you can also find reasonably priced rooms in and around the centre. There are good-quality mid-range hotels in eastern Berlin, where many new hotels have been built recently. There is no lack of luxurious hotels in eastern Berlin, either, particularly around Unter den Linden. Many of the more affordable hotels in the western part of Berlin require urgent repairs. The area around Grunewald is an oasis of peace that will guarantee a good rest. From the numerous hotels in Berlin, this section highlights some of the best; these have been categorized according to location and price. Details about each of the hotels can be found on pages 220–29. Information about alternative ways of spending a night can be found on pages 218–19.

The elegant lobby of the Hotel Adlon (see p220)

WHERE TO LOOK

There are a few areas in Berlin with large concentrations of hotels. In each area there is usually at least one luxury hotel as well as several more affordable places. In Charlottenburg, around Kurfürstendamm and Tauentzienstrasse, are well-known hotels, such as the Kempinski, Savoy, Palace Berlin and the Steigenberger. Bear in mind that this part of Berlin was severely damaged during World War II and the majority of these hotels occupy modern buildings; hotels in old buildings, like the Brandenburger Hof, are a rarity. Inexpensive hotels and pensions can be found in the side streets off the main road, but ask to see the rooms before you decide. Good hotels are also situated in the east part of Charlottenburg, around Lützowufer.

There have been changes in recent years to hotels in the former East Berlin. These hotels have been privatized and the majority of them have been refurbished extensively. In addition, many new hotels have been built. The Adlon, Four Seasons and Ritz-Carlton, situated in the western part of Mitte around Unter den Linden, are the most luxurious. In the eastern part of this area, around Marx-Engels-Forum and Alexanderplatz, the hotels are more reasonably priced and offer good-quality rooms.

Grunewald is an oasis of peace far from the bustle of Berlin. There is the luxurious Schlosshotel Vier Jahreszeiten, as well as cosy pensions and little hotels, some of them in 19th-century villas and palaces.

If you want to be certain of finding a room and you don't mind staying outside the centre of Berlin, you should head for Neukölln. Here, close to Treptower Park, is the recently opened Estrel – the largest hotel in Germany.

HOTEL PRICES

The price of a hotel room in Berlin does not alter much with the season. However, major events and trade fairs do push up prices. Many more luxurious hotels offer weekend discounts and often, if you just turn up without a reservation, you can find yourself a good deal. If you intend to stay for an extended period of time, it is worth trying to negotiate a better rate.

HIDDEN EXTRAS

In Germany, taxes are included in hotel room rates, but like anywhere else, you are expected to tip for any additional services, such as bringing luggage to the room or booking a theatre ticket. Hotels from the Dorint chain are an exception: they provide a range of services (such as free bicycle hire) at no additional cost.

Swimming pool at the Grand Hotel Esplanade (see p222)

One of the artist-decorated rooms in the Kuenstlerheim Luise *(see p222)*

There is no hard and fast rule about breakfast: it is best to ask if it is included in the price when making a reservation.

The majority of Berlin hotels have their own parking spaces, but sometimes their rates are exorbitant. Ask about telephone charges before using the phone in your room and check the exchange rates and the commission for cashing travellers' cheques before using this service. Items from the minibar and paid-television channels can also turn out to be surprisingly costly.

FACILITIES

There is no standardized system of categorizing hotels by stars in Germany, although the price of a room usually reflects the quality. Small hotels usually include breakfast in the price of the room – they will probably not have a restaurant and their services are limited. Typically on offer for breakfast are rolls, jam, chocolate spread, cereal, cold meats, cheese and coffee. German cuisine offers a wide variety of bread and tea is usually served black. Larger hotels tend to also provide a full American buffet on top of the traditional German fare.

If you choose to stay for a longer period, an Aparthotel might be an option to consider. This type of accommodation is an apartment, complete with a fully equipped kitchen.

SAUNAS AND SPAS

Many of the more expensive hotels are equipped with spa and sauna facilities. These are usually unisex (though some spas have women's days) and it is very unusual for either sex to wear a swimsuit. Whilst a truly relaxing activity, guests should be prepared to only wear towels and for other sauna users to be in the nude.

HOW TO BOOK

You can book a room in Berlin by mail, telephone or fax, and some rooms can also be booked through the Internet. If you prefer, you can use the city's tourist service **Berlin Tourismus Marketing** *(see p219)*, which can be contacted via the internet or by telephone or fax. This company can make

Conference room in the Villa Kastania *(see p228)*

your booking in hotels throughout Berlin. When making a reservation, however, be prepared to give your credit card details.

If you are already in Berlin and would like to find a comfortable room, your best option is to go to one of the large tourist information bureaux. Some of the best of these are situated in the **Europa-Center**, at the **Brandenburg Gate**, and at **Alexanderplatz** *(see p219)*.

PRIVATE ROOMS

Bed & Breakfast-style accommodation is not particularly popular in Berlin, although this kind of service can be found in some of the residential districts far from the city centre. You can obtain information about them from tourist information bureaux and the other organizations whose numbers are listed in the Directory *(see p219)*.

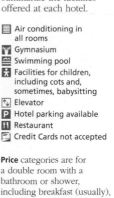

KEY TO SYMBOLS

The hotels listed on pages 220–29 are grouped according to area and price category. To help you make your choice, the following symbols summarize the facilities offered at each hotel.

▤ Air conditioning in all rooms
▼ Gymnasium
≋ Swimming pool
⚗ Facilities for children, including cots and, sometimes, babysitting
⇅ Elevator
ℙ Hotel parking available
▮▮ Restaurant
⬚ Credit Cards not accepted

Price categories are for a double room with a bathroom or shower, including breakfast (usually), service charges and 16 per cent VAT (in euros)

€ under €80
€€ €81–130
€€€ €131–€180
€€€€ €181–€230
€€€€€ over €230

The luxurious lounge at the Kempinski Hotel *(see p226)*

TRAVELLING WITH CHILDREN

Travelling with children in Berlin should not present a problem. A cot can be requested in most hotels, and there is usually no extra charge for having a small child in the room, although an extra bed for an older child may sometimes incur a cost. In better hotels, a reliable babysitter can be obtained at a few hours' notice. In hotel restaurants, high chairs for children are standard.

The elegant lobby area of the Marriott Hotel *(see p222)*

DISABLED TRAVELLERS

Nearly all top-quality and luxury hotels are able to accommodate disabled travellers – at least one entrance will have wheelchair access and some rooms will have specially-adapted bathrooms. Unfortunately, the situation in mid-range and lower standard hotels is not as promising; special equipment is a rarity

and in many cases these hotels are not situated on the ground floor. In very old buildings, there may not be an elevator. The **Hotel Mondial** *(see p226)*, located near Kurfürstendamm, is recommended for disabled travellers. It has many facilities for wheelchair users in all its public rooms and has as many as 22 bedrooms equipped for people with special needs.

DEPOSITS

In many Berlin hotels, a deposit may be requested either when reserving the room or upon checking in at the hotel. A credit card number is the most common way to secure a room over the telephone. If you do not have one, however, be prepared to use cash to pay about 20 to 40 per cent of the price for one night's stay. The amount you pay as a deposit should always be credited to the final bill. In some smaller hotels or pensions, don't be

surprised if you are asked to pay for your first night's accommodation in full when you arrive.

YOUTH HOSTELS

It is easy to find inexpensive accommodation in Berlin at a youth hostel. The **DJH (Landesverband Berlin-Brandenburg)**, an organization that belongs to the International Youth Hostels Association, gives discounts to all its members. Membership is usually inexpensive and if you are not a member, you will have to join to stay at a hostel. The DJH has hostels in different locations throughout Berlin. There are also several independent youth hostels as well as hotels for students in Berlin that do not belong to any organization.

The type of accommodation offered usually consists of dormitory-style rooms containing bunk beds. There is often a communal bathroom on each floor and a kitchen is usually also available for cooking your own meals. Most youth hostels have a dining room where breakfast and a hot evening meal are served. Some youth hostels are closed during the day, allowing no access to the rooms; confirm this in advance.

CAMPING

Camping is a popular pastime throughout Germany, and the **Deutscher Camping Club** has a lot of information about campsites in and around Berlin. This organization also

Illuminated façade of the Westin Grand *(see p220)*

provides information about other independently run campsites in Berlin.

Campsites are open usually from the beginning of April until the end of October. There are two exceptions: the Berlin-Kladow in Spandau and the Am Krossinsee in Köpenick, which are open year round. The majority of people that stay at campsites are young, particularly during the Oktoberfest *(see p50)* and in June, when the Christopher Street Day Parade takes place *(see p49)*. During these times some campsites can be very busy and noisy.

The spacious lobby of the Hotel Palace *(see p226)*

ORGANIZED YOUTH GROUPS

Berlin has a large base of accommodation for organized youth groups. Most of these consist of hostel-style accommodation, situated on the outskirts of the city, often in green belt areas. They were established not only for the purpose of school trips to Berlin but also for children from West Berlin; until the unification of Germany in 1990, it was difficult for youth groups to organize trips to the country-side so they had to opt for trips to the Grunewald instead. Information about availability and reservations is offered by **Berlin Tourismus Marketing** and by larger tourist information centres, such as the one in the Europa-Center.

DIRECTORY

INFORMATION AND BOOKING

Berlin Tourismus Marketing
Am Karlsbad 11, Berlin.
Map 12 D1.
Tel *25 00 25.*
www.berlin.de

Tourist Information
Europa-Center,
Budapester Strasse 45.
Map 10 E1.
◯ *8:30am–8:30pm Mon–Sat, 10am–6:30pm Sun.*

Alexanderplatz
Tourist Info Café at Fernsehturm. **Map** 7 C3.
◯ *10am–6pm daily.*
Also at: Europa-Center, Panoramastrasse 1a.
◯ *10am–6pm daily.*

Brandenburg Gate
Pariser Platz.
Map 6 E3, 15 A3.
◯ *9:30am–6pm daily.*

Infopoint KaDeWe
Kaufhaus des Westens, Tauentzienstrasse 21–24.
Map 10 F2.
◯ *Mon–Fri 9:30am–8pm, 9am–4pm Sat.*

Potsdam Tourismus Service
Friedrich-Ebert-Strasse 5.
Tel *(0331) 275 58 0.*
Fax *(0331) 275 58 99.*
www.potsdamtourismus.de

CAMPING

Deutscher Camping Club
Kladower Damm 207-13, 14089 Berlin.
Map 10 E3, 10 F3.
Tel *218 60 71.*
◯ *10:30am–6pm Mon, 8am–4pm Wed, 8am–1pm Fri.*

DCC-Campingplatz Berlin-Kladow (Spandau)
Krampnitzer Weg 111–117 14089 Berlin.
Tel *365 27 97.*
Fax *365 12 45.*

YOUTH HOSTELS

DJH (Landes-verband Berlin-Brandenburg)
Schulstrasse 9, 14482 Berlin.
Tel *264 95 20.*

Jugendgästehaus
Kluckstrasse 3
10785 Berlin.
Map 11 C1.
Tel *25 79 98 08.*
Fax *265 03 83.*

Jugendherberge Ernst Reuter
Hermsdorfer Damm 48–50
13467 Berlin.
Tel *404 16 10.*
Fax *404 59 72.*

Jugendherberge Berlin
Badeweg 1,
14129 Berlin.
Tel *803 20 34.*
Fax *803 59 08.*

DISABLED TRAVELLERS

Berliner Behinderten-verband
Jägerstrasse 63d
10117 Berlin-Mitte.
Tel *204 38 47.*

Behinderten-beauftragter des Landes Berlin
Oranienstrasse 106
10997 Berlin.
Tel *90 28 29 17.*

BED & BREAKFAST

Bed & Breakfast in Berlin
Tel *746 14 46.*
Fax *44 05 05 83.*

Coming Home
Tel *21 79 800.*
Fax *21 79 80 21*
www.coming-home.org

Erste Mitwohn-zentrale
Sybelstrasse 53.
10629 Berlin-Charlottenburg.
Map 9 A2.
Tel *324 30 31.*
Fax *324 99 77.*

Fine and mine
Neue Schönhauser Str. 20
10178 Berlin.
Map 7 C2.
Tel *23 55 120.*
Fax *23 55 12 12.*
@ office@fineandmine.de

Wohnwitz
Holsteinische Strasse 55.
10717 Berlin-Wilmersdorf.
Map 9 C4, 9 C5.
Tel *861 82 22.*
Fax *861 82 72.*

Choosing a Hotel

The choice of hotels selected in this guide is based on quality of accommodation and service as well as location. The list of hotels covers all the areas and price categories with additional information to help you choose a hotel that best meets your needs. Hotels within the same price category is listed alphabeticaly.

PRICE CATEGORIES
Listed below are the price ranges for a double room per night, including all taxes:

€ Under 80 euros
€€ 81–130 euros
€€€ 131–180 euros
€€€€ 181–230 euros
€€€€€ Over 230 euros

AROUND UNTER DEN LINDEN

Madison Friedrichstrasse   €€

Friedrichstrasse 185-190, 10117 **Tel** *202 920* **Fax** *202 929 20* **Rooms** *82*   **Map** *6 F4, 15 C4*

Offering suites for a price depending on the size and the duration of stay, the Madison provides services including car and bicycle rental, shopping, clothes repair and CD players in all rooms. Ideal for a week-long stay, though even on a per-night basis the prices are much lower than many other hotels. **www.madison-berlin.de**

NH Heinrich Heine   €€

Heinrich-Heinrich-Platz 11, 10179 **Tel** *278 040* **Fax** *278 047 80* **Rooms** *38*   **Map** *14 D1*

Despite its convenient location close to Unter den Linden and the historic Nikolaiviertel, the all-suite hotel is still a well-kept secret. The modern rooms all feature a kitchenette and a small office space, and even have VCR and CD players as well as wireless LAN. **www.nh-hotels.com**

Hotel Gendarm   €€€

Charlottenstrasse 61, 10117 **Tel** *206 06 60* **Fax** *206 066 66* **Rooms** *27*   **Map** *7 A4*

The Gendarm's reputation as one of the best and most popular smaller hotels in Berlin is more than justified. An excellent service, a great location off Gendarmenmarkt and historic, elegantly furnished rooms make this a serious competitor for the big five-star hotels nearby. **www.hotel-gendarm-berlin.de**

Berlin Hilton   €€€€

Mohrenstrasse 30, 10117 **Tel** *202 30* **Fax** *202 342 69* **Rooms** *589*   **Map** *7 A4, 16 D4*

This hotel is near the Gendarmenmarkt. There are spectacular views of the Konzerthaus and two churches from the rooms at the front of the building. The bedrooms are wonderfully furnished and spacious, and there are two splendid restaurants. **www.hilton.com**

Das Dorint Hotel am Gendarmenmarkt   €€€€

Charlottenstrasse 50-52, 10117 **Tel** *203 750* **Fax** *203 751 00* **Rooms** *92*   **Map** *7 A4, 16 D4*

This flagship establishment of the German hotel brand, Dorint, offers well-furnished rooms and an excellent service. Coveniently located near the Gendarmenmarkt, not far from Unter den Linden. The Aigner restaurant downstairs specializes in good Austrian food. **www.dorint.de**

Maritim ProArte Hotel Berlin   €€€€

Friedrichstrassse 151, 10117 **Tel** *203 35* **Fax** *203 342 09* **Rooms** *403*   **Map** *6 F3, 15 C2*

Although this hotel aims to attract mainly conference business, its central location and excellent facilities make it one of Berlin's most attractive hotels. An ultra-modern building with furnishings and art displays, it has lavish rooms in three categories with marble and granite bathrooms. **www.maritim.de**

Hotel Adlon   €€€€€

Unter den Linden 77, 10117 **Tel** *226 10* **Fax** *226 122 22* **Rooms** *401*   **Map** *6 E3, 15 A3*

This deluxe hotel located near the Brandenburg Gate opened in 1997 and continues the traditions of its illustrious predecessor, which was bombed during World War II. Marble, leather and exotic woods line the interior. The hotel has a good service. Special rooms for people with allergies. **www.hotel-adlon.com**

St. Regent Hotel   €€€€€

Charlottenstrasse 49, 10117 **Tel** *203 38* **Fax** *203 361 66* **Rooms** *204*   **Map** *7 A4, 16 D3*

Ranked as one of the best hotels in Berlin, St. Regent Hotel near the Gendarmenmarkt has an impressive façade and opulent Neo-Baroque interiors. It offers luxurious rooms in three categories and an impeccable service. The restaurant here serves excellent light cuisine. **www.fourseasons.com**

Westin Grand   €€€€€

Friedrichstrasse 158-164, 10117 **Tel** *202 70* **Fax** *202 733 62* **Rooms** *358*   **Map** *6 F3, 15 C3*

A lavish hotel built at the end of the 19th century in Empire and Secessionist styles. The main hall is particularly impressive, with a huge atrium and a breathtaking staircase. Close to most historic sites as well as various good restaurants and cafés. **www.westin-grand.de**

Key to Symbols *see back cover flap*

MUSEUM ISLAND

Derag Residenz Hotel Henriette
 €€

Neue Roßstrasse 13, 10179 **Tel** *246 009 00* **Fax** *246 009 40* **Rooms** *53* **Map** *8 C5*

The small and intimate Henriette is the nicest – and the most unknown – of the many Derag hotels in town. Though built recently, it exudes an incredibly elegant, historic flair, with oak furniture, precious carpets and beds. The hotel offers a great service. **www.deraghotels.de**

Art'otel Berlin Mitte
 €€€

Wallstrasse 70-73, 10179 **Tel** *240 622 22* **Fax** *240 622 22* **Rooms** *109* **Map** *7 C4*

Overlooking the Spree river, this upmarket hotel is well-priced and one of the most popular places in Mitte. Inside, it is modern with simple and elegant furniture. In summer there is a café on a riverboat tied to the bank of the Spree. The hotel is popular with young, culture-oriented guests. **www.artotel.de**

DeragHotel Grosser Kurfürst
 €€€

Neue Ross Strasse 11-12, 10179 **Tel** *246 000* **Fax** *246 003 00* **Rooms** *144* **Map** *7 C4*

A good middle-range hotel, with modern facilities and a convenient location close to the U-Bahn station Märkisches Museum. The breathtaking lobby has a statue of the Great Elector. The hotel's personal and impeccable services include free public transport or bicycle hire. **www.deraghotels.de**

Radisson SAS Hotel Berlin
 €€€€

Karl-Liebknecht-Strasse 3, 10178 **Tel** *238 280* **Fax** *238 28 10* **Rooms** *427* **Map** *16 F2, 7 B3*

The Radisson opened in 2004 and is one of the hotel group's stars. It is built around the AquaDom, a huge, cylindric aquarium in the lobby. Standard rooms face this atrium; superior rooms and suites overlook the neighbouring Berliner Dom and Alexanderplatz. All rooms are furnished with five-star amenities. **www.radissonsas.com**

EAST OF THE CENTRE

Alexander Plaza Berlin
 €€€

Rosenstrasse 1, 10178 **Tel** *240 010* **Fax** *240 017 77* **Rooms** *92* **Map** *7 B2, 16 F1*

This top-quality hotel, opened in 1997, is located near the S-Bahn station Hackescher Markt. Rooms in the late 19th-century building, an intriguing mixture of stucco ceilings, glass and steel, are large, comfortable and full of light, with soundproof windows. Nice lobby bar and café. **www.alexander-plaza.com**

Park Inn Berlin Alexanderplatz
 €€€

Alexanderplatz 8, 10178 **Tel** *238 90* **Fax** *238 943 05* **Rooms** *1005* **Map** *8 D2*

This 37-storey building was constructed under the GDR and, despite modernization, has an ugly exterior. Completely refurbished, it has standard rooms with very comfortable beds and great views of central Berlin. A rooftop casino and various restaurants offer entertainment. **www.parkinn.de**

NORTH OF THE CENTRE

Boardinghouse Berlin
 €

Mulackstrasse 1, 10119 **Tel** *283 884 88* **Fax** *283 884 89* **Rooms** *21* **Map** *7 C1*

The EKOS Boardinghouse consists of single and double, stylish, bright apartments with all the modern amenities of a good standard hotel room. These must be rented for a minimum of two nights. Breakfast is included in the tariff. There is also an attached kitchen. Ideal for a longer stay. **www.boarding-house-berlin.de**

Hotel am Scheunenviertel
 €

Oranienburgerstrasse 38, 10117 **Tel** *282 21 25* **Fax** *282 11 15* **Rooms** *18* **Map** *16 E1, 7 A1*

This small and privately-run hotel is right in the historic Jewish quarter near the renovated synagogue. An ideal starting point for exploring Mitte and Prenzlauer Berg, the hotel features small but clean standard rooms and mostly attracts international, art-oriented young guests. **www.hotelas.com**

MitArt Pension
 €

Linienstrasse 139, 10115 **Tel** *283 904 3 0* **Fax** *283 904 32* **Rooms** *30* **Map** *6 F1*

This trendy hotel near the alternative art centre, Tacheles, offers small, quiet rooms, all adorned by original paintings. It also has its own art gallery downstairs. Breakfast is a feast of natural-grown produce. The nightlife in Mitte is just around the corner. **www.mitart.de**

Artist Riverside Hotel & Spa
 €€

Friedrichstrasse 106, 10117 **Tel** *284 900* **Fax** *284 90 49* **Rooms** *18* **Map** *6 F3*

Proudly dubbing itself *tolles Hotel* (great hotel), this delightful place has late 19th-century, individual rooms stuffed with colourful Art-Nouveau antiques. When making a reservation, you might like to ask for the biggest and nicest room (Wedding), which even has a waterbed. **www.great-hotel.com**

Märkischer Hof
€€

Linienstrasse 133, 10115 **Tel** *282 71 55* **Fax** *282 43 31* **Rooms** *20* **Map** *6 F1*

A small, snug hotel with a family atmosphere. The building dates from the 19th century, but the rooms are recently redecorated. They are of a surprisingly high standard considering their low prices and all have a private bathroom and a TV set. Rooms with three beds are the best deal here. **www.maerkischer-hof-berlin.de**

Hackescher Markt
€€€

Grosse Präsidentenstrasse 8, 10178 **Tel** *280 030* **Fax** *280 031 11* **Rooms** *32* **Map** *7 B2, 16 F1*

Built in 1998, this charming hotel has an excellent location opposite Hackesche Höfe. The rooms are elegantly furnished and have stylish bathrooms with heated floors. Its restaurant, Mags, offers excellent French cuisine. The real highlight is a pretty courtyard where breakfast is served. **www.hackescher-markt.com**

Hotel Albrechtshof
€€€

Albrechtstrasse 8, 10117 **Tel** *308 860* **Fax** *308 861 00* **Rooms** *107* **Map** *6 F2, 15 B1*

This charming hotel is situated near the Spree river, in a modernized, early 19th-century building. It offers not only a bar, restaurant and banqueting hall, but a chapel as well. Weekend discounts are available. Internet access in all spacious rooms and a warm, personal service. **www.hotel-albrechtshof.de**

Hotel Künstlerheim Luise
€€€

Luisenstrasse 19, 10117 **Tel** *284 480* **Fax** *284 484 48* **Rooms** *47* **Map** *6 E2*

An authentic Berlin artist's hotel, the Küenstlerheim (literally "home for artists") welcomes the artsy crowd into individually designed rooms, created by various German artists. The early 19th-century house is steps away from the Scheunenviertel and has a great personal service. **www.kuenstlerheim-luise.de**

Jolly Hotel Vivaldi
€€€

Friedrichstrasse 96, 10117 **Tel** *206 26 60* **Fax** *206 266 999* **Rooms** *254* **Map** *6 F3*

This delightful designer hotel lies at the northern end of the Friedrichstrasse, just steps away from the hip Hackescher Markt and Unter den Linden. Its fairly large rooms feature extremely comfortable beds. It also has a wellbeing centre with a Turkish bath and an Italian restaurant. **www.jollyhotels.it**

TIERGARTEN

Hotel Berlin
€€

Lützowplatz 17, 10785 **Tel** *260 50* **Fax** *260 527 16* **Rooms** *701* **Map** *11 A1*

One of the city's biggest, the quiet Hotel Berlin is a favourite among US tour package groups. It is located near the Tiergarten Park and has large, modern rooms, a spa and sauna area and a great sports bar. The only disadvantage here is the lack of a decent restaurant. **www.hotel-berlin.de**

Berlin Marriott Hotel
€€€

Inge-Beisheim-Platz 1, 10785 **Tel** *220 000* **Fax** *220 001 000* **Rooms** *379* **Map** *6 D5*

The Marriott at the Beisheim-Center near Potsdamer Platz is an elegant four-star hotel with a towering entrance atrium. Its spacious rooms offer lovely views of the green Tiergarten and the government district. You get the same facilities for less than half the rate of the adjacent Ritz-Carlton. **www.marriott.de**

Dorint Schweizerhof Berlin
€€€€

Budapester Strasse 25, 10787 **Tel** *269 60* **Fax** *296 610 00* **Rooms** *384* **Map** *10 F1*

This luxurious hotel opened in 1999. It sports an elegant, sand-finished façade and offers beautifully furnished rooms, two restaurants, a ballroom and a conference centre. The rooftop indoor pool and fitness area is one of the most beautiful to be found in Berlin. **www.schweizerhof.com**

Grand Hotel Esplanade Berlin
€€€€

Lützowufer 15, 10785 **Tel** *254 780* **Fax** *254 788 222* **Rooms** *385* **Map** *11 A1*

A modern, lavish establishment overlooking the Landwehrkanal, the hotel has well-furnished rooms that attract prominent guests. Harry's New York Bar is famous and the Harlekin restaurant is one of the city's best. The hotel's boat offers trips along the rivers. **www.esplanade.de**

Inter-Continental Berlin
€€€€

Budapester Strasse 2, 10787 **Tel** *260 20* **Fax** *260 226 00* **Rooms** *584* **Map** *10 F1*

This newly-renovated hotel is situated on the outskirts of the Zoologischer Garten. The massive building is hard to miss, with a glass dome covering the lobby. The hotel offers large rooms in several categories. A swimming pool and a salon provide the chance to relax. **www.interconti.com**

Key to Price Guide *see p220* **Key to Symbols** *see back cover flap*

Madison Potsdamer Platz
€€€€

Potsdamer Strasse 3, 10785 **Tel** *590 050 000* **Fax** *590 052 000* **Rooms** *166* — **Map** *6 D5*

This all-suite four-star hotel, adjacent to the Sony Centre, has a perfect location for touring both the Eastern and Western downtown areas. Elegantly furnished with modern desks, hi-tech audio and big-screen TV equipment, as well as full kitchenettes. Impeccable service. **www.madison-berlin.de**

Grand Hyatt Berlin
€€€€€

Marlene-Dietrich-Platz 2, 10785 **Tel** *255 312 34* **Fax** *255 312 35* **Rooms** *342* — **Map** *6 D5*

One of Berlin's most modern and splendid hotels, the Hyatt is close to the Potsdamer Platz and Kulturforum. It has a sushi bar inside its stylish VOX restaurant and a bistro with cocktail bar. In February, it serves as the official host to the Berlinale film festival, attracting stars and fans alike. **www.hyatt.com**

The Ritz-Carlton Berlin
€€€€€

Potsdamer Platz 3, 10785 **Tel** *337 777* **Fax** *337 775 555* **Rooms** *302* — **Map** *6 E5*

The ultra-luxurious Ritz-Carlton Berlin's modern façade is reminscent of the Rockefeller Centre. The hotel lobby with its marble columns and gold leaf is as stunning as the bar, The Curtain Club, and the brasserie Desbrosses. Rooms with Prussian Neo-Classicist designs are comfortably furnished. **www.ritzcarlton.com**

KREUZBERG

Hotel am Anhalter Bahnhof
€

Stresemannstrasse 36, 10963 **Tel** *251 03 42* **Fax** *251 48 97* **Rooms** *33* — **Map** *12 E1*

This small and friendly hotel is situated in an old apartment block. Its low prices only apply to rooms without bathrooms; expect to pay more for en suite bathrooms. The more expensive rooms face on to a courtyard. **www.hotel-anhalter-bahnhof.de**

Hotel Transit
€

Hagelberger Strasse 53-54, 10965 **Tel** *789 04 70* **Fax** *789 047 77* **Rooms** *50* — **Map** *12 E4*

The Berlin namesake of its famous Paris counterpart is a small Kreuzberg "sleep-in" resembling a private youth hostel, located in two lofts. Every room comes with an attached modern bathroom, though the best deals are shared-bed rooms. The large, bright singles are particularly nice. **www.hotel-transit.de**

Jugendgästehaus der DSJ
€

Franz-Künstler-Strasse 10, 10969 **Tel** *615 10 07* **Fax** *614 011 50* **Rooms** *124* — **Map** *13 B2*

This pleasant youth hostel is well located in the central part of Kreuzberg. The rooms, accommodating three to five guests, do not have bathrooms, but there are shower-rooms on the corridors. A dormitory bed is the cheapest. The guest house is very popular among student groups. **www.schreberjugend-berlin.de**

Pension Kreuzberg
€

Grossbeerenstrasse 64, 10963 **Tel** *251 13 62* **Fax** *251 06 38* **Rooms** *13* — **Map** *12 F3*

This tiny hotel is one of the few upscale Kreuzberg *pensionen* offering a warm and personal service – and tourist information – by owner Angelika Dehner. Breakfast is appetizing and hearty. The location is great, while the district's nightlife is just a short walk away. **www.pension-kreuzber.de**

Hotel Antares
€€

Stresemannstrasse 97, 10963 **Tel** *254 160* **Fax** *261 50 27* **Rooms** *85* — **Map** *12 E1*

This modern hotel, close to Martin-Gropius-Bau and Potsdamer Platz, has a great location as both Kreuzberg and Mitte are just a couple of minutes away. It offers both economy- and business-class rooms with solid, but not outstanding furnishings. It is worth enquiring about special weekend rates. **www.hotel-antares.com**

Hotel Riehmers Hofgarten
€€€

Yorckstrasse 83, 10965 **Tel** *780 988 00* **Fax** *780 988 08* **Rooms** *22* — **Map** *12 F4*

Housed in a 19th-century Gothic red-brick complex, this is one of the most magnificent hotels in town. Though only sparsely furnished, its rooms are comfortable and elegant, and the best ones overlook the courtyard. Don't miss the German food served at its restaurant, E.T.A. Hoffman. **www.hotel-riehmers-hogarten.de**

Relexa Hotel Stuttgarter Hof
€€€

Anhalter Strasse 9, 10963 **Tel** *264 830* **Fax** *264 839 00* **Rooms** *207* — **Map** *12 F1*

This is a well-kept, top-quality hotel, dating back to 1907. Situated behind Potsdamer Platz, it has modern, good-sized rooms, a restaurant called Boulevard and a charming, green courtyard. The location is perfect for exploring both Kreuzberg and Mitte. **www.relexa-hotels.de**

Mövenpick Hotel Berlin
€€€

Schöneberger Strasse 3, 10963 **Tel** *230 060* **Fax** *230 061 99* **Rooms** *243* — **Map** *12 E1*

The brand-new Mövenpick is a surprisingly nice hotel in the rough, but fascinating, neighbourhood of Kreuzberg. The spacious designer rooms have all modern office and entertainment amenities. The deluxe rooms under the roof are particularly cosy. **www.moevenpick-berlin.com**

AROUND KURFÜRSTENDAMM

A & O Hostel am Zoo   🔲   ©
Joachimsthaler Strasse 1-3, 10623 **Tel** *297 78 10* **Fax** *297 781 20* **Rooms** *550*   **Map** *10 D1*

Located in a former Aldi budget grocery store, this hostel is a favourite among budget travellers looking for a cheap night's sleep. Conveniently located opposite the Zoo railway station, it offers packages such as combined hostel and dancing club weekends, which appeal to the younger guests. **www.aohostels.com**

Hotel Pension Korfu II   🔲 P   ©
Rankestrasse 35, 10789 **Tel** *212 47 90* **Fax** *212 479 60* **Rooms** *43*   **Map** *10 E1*

With a striking name matching its eye-catching bright-yellow façade, the Korfu is adjacent to the renowned Memorial Church. The comfortable, inexpensive rooms cater to young tourists from around the world. Double rooms are furnished with greater detail than the singles. **www.hp-korfu.de**

Hotel-Pension Elite   🔲   ©
Rankestrasse 9, 10789 **Tel** *881 53 08* **Fax** *882 54 22* **Rooms** *14*   **Map** *10 E1*

The small *Pension* on quiet Rankestrasse, not far away from bustling Breitscheidplatz, features late-Classicist, turn-of-the-19th-century rooms with an elegant ambience. Some rooms come with private bathrooms, while the cheaper rooms have shared ones. **www.hotel-pension-elite-berlin.de**

Hotel-Pension Funk   🔲 P 🚹   ©
Fasanenstrasse 69, 10719 **Tel** *882 71 93* **Fax** *883 33 29* **Rooms** *14*   **Map** *10 D2*

One of the last historic *Pensionen* in Berlin, the hotel reveals its legacy even in the decor and furnishings: heavy curtains and carpets, old furniture from all periods. Film buffs will be thrilled to sleep in an apartment once owned by movie legend Asta Nielsen. www.hotel-pensionfunk.de

Art Nouveau Hotel   🔲 P 🚹   ©©
Leibnizstrasse 59, 10629 **Tel** *327 74 40* **Fax** *327 744 40* **Rooms** *14*   **Map** *9 B1*

Tucked away in a 19th-century mansion, this typical Berlin *Hotelpension* has incredibly high, individually designed rooms with original stucco, featuring only a few modern pieces, such as futon-like beds. Many guests like the elegant "yellow room" best. **www.hotelartnouveau.de**

Best Western Hotel Boulevard   🔲   ©©
Kurfürstendamm 12, 10719 **Tel** *884 250* **Fax** *884 254 50* **Rooms** *57*   **Map** *10 D1*

Centrally located on Kurfürstendamm, this bland hotel is an insider's choice for travellers who want to be in the middle of a bustling big city. All western downtown sights are just steps away. Breakfast is served on a rooftop terrace with views of the famous boulevard. **www.boulevard.bestwestern.de**

Comfort Hotel Frühling am Zoo   🔲   ©©
Kurfürstendamm 17, 10719 **Tel** *889 110* **Fax** *889 111 50* **Rooms** *75*   **Map** *10 D1*

This hotel, centrally located at one of Berlin's busiest street corners on Kurfürstendamm, makes a great impression with its magnificent lobby, but somehow disappoints with the uninspired rooms. Nevertheless, this is a good alternative to the more expensive big hotels. **www.fruehling.com**

Hotel Askanischer Hof   🔲 🚹   ©©
Kurfürstendamm 53, 10707 **Tel** *881 80 33* **Fax** *881 72 06* **Rooms** *16*   **Map** *9 B2*

One of the few hotels that survived World War II. The interior is decorated in the style of 1920s and the rooms are cosy and comfortable, some have canopy beds and are surprisingly spacious. Authors Franz Kafka and Arthur Miller used to stay here. It also has an intimate little bar. **www.askanischer-hof.de**

Hotel Astoria   🔲 P 🚹   ©©
Fasanenstrasse 2, 10623 **Tel** *312 40 67* **Fax** *312 50 27* **Rooms** *32*   **Map** *4 D5*

Managed by the same family for three generations, this intimate hotel occupies a 19th-century building and is considered to be one of the best of its kind in town. The rooms are comfortable and the lack of a restaurant is made up for by the hotel's proximity to Savignyplatz. **www.hotelastoria.de**

Hotel Charlot   🔲   ©©
Giesebrechtstrasse 17, 10629 **Tel** *327 96 60* **Fax** *327 966 66* **Rooms** *42*   **Map** *9 A2*

The small hotel in a serene, upmarket side street off Kurfürstendamm, in one of Charlottenburg's most beautiful neighbourhoods, is a bargain for groups and younger travellers. Small but comfortable rooms and beds, great breakfast buffet in an old-style Berlin ambience. **www.hotel-charlot.de**

Hotel Garni Hardenberg Berlin   🔲   ©©
Joachimstaler Strasse 39-40, 10623 **Tel** *882 30 71* **Fax** *881 51 70* **Rooms** *43*   **Map** *10 D1*

This small family hotel is a good choice if you want to stay in the not-so-quiet western downtown area and don't mind somewhat time-worn but large rooms. The breakfast buffet and the obliging service make up for this, and the prices are unbeatable for this location. **www.hotel-hardenberg.de**

Key to Price Guide *see p220* **Key to Symbols** *see back cover flap*

Hotel Gates

Knesebeckstrasse 8-10, 10623 **Tel** *311 060* **Fax** *312 20 60* **Rooms** *100*　　　　　**Map** *3 C5*

Offering varying prices and standards, this art hotel presents original modern art, besides a stylish, private bathroom, minibar and TV in every room. The location in the most authentic Charlottenburg neighbourhood is a great plus, while the Ku'damm is just a few steps away. **www.hotel-gates.com**

Hotel Pension Augusta

€€

Fasanenstrasse 22, 10719 **Tel** *883 50 28* **Fax** *882 47 79* **Rooms** *42*　　　　　**Map** *10 D1*

This relatively inexpensive guesthouse is located in the very heart of Berlin. As it is based in a 19th-century building, the rooms are spacious and quiet. Some rooms lack en suite bathrooms and so are much cheaper. There is no hotel restaurant, but there are many good places to eat nearby. **www.hotel-augusta.de**

Hotel Pension Dittberner

€€

Wielandstrasse 26, 10707 **Tel** *881 64 85* **Fax** *885 40 45* **Rooms** *22*　　　　　**Map** *3 B5*

One of the charming old-style *Hotelpensionen*, once typical in Berlin, it promises a personal, if somewhat disorganized, service in a 19th-century setting. Rooms are large, with slightly moth-eaten furniture. The prime location off Kurfürstendamm and the flair of old Berlin more than make up for this. **www.hotel-dittberner.de**

Ku'Damm 101 Hotel

€€

Kurfürstendamm 101, 10711 **Tel** *520 05 50* **Fax** *520 055 555* **Rooms** *170*　　　**Map** *9 A2*

On the most elegant part of Kurfürstendamm, this designer hotel is striking in its use of clear forms, sparse furnishings, abstract paintings, a lot of glass, steel and beautiful wood. Every room has wireless LAN and spacious desks. Business lounge and a rooftop breakfast room with scenic views of Berlin. **www.kudamm101.com**

Propeller Island City Lodge

€€

Albrecht-Achilles Strasse 58, 10709 **Tel** *891 90 16* **Fax** *891 87 20* **Rooms** *31*

Situated in a 19th-century apartment block in one of the quiet streets off Kurfürstendamm, the Propeller is known as an art hotel. Each room is differently – and often outrageously – themed, with real works of art. An ideal place for those looking for a memorable stay. **www.propeller-island.de**

Remter

€€

Marburger Strasse 17, 10789 **Tel** *235 08 80* **Fax** *213 86 12* **Rooms** *31*　　　　　**Map** *10 E1*

This is a pleasant, quiet hotel, and is well located for tourists – close to the historic landmark Kaiser-Wilhelm-Gedächtniskirche. Although the prices for its rooms are not the cheapest in Berlin, the Remter is one of the best-value hotels in this central location. **www.hotel-remter-berlin.de**

Alsterhof

€€€

Augsburger Strasse 5, 10789 **Tel** *212 420* **Fax** *278 39 49* **Rooms** *200*　　　　　**Map** *10 E2*

This hotel is recommended for non-smokers, who can have special bedrooms and dine in a non-smoking breakfast room. During the summer, coffee is served under a pretty chestnut tree in an inner courtyard. A small wellness and fitness area and many other services are also offered. **www.alsterhof.com**

Bleibtreu Hotel

€€€

Bleibtreustrasse 31, 10707 **Tel** *884 740* **Fax** *884 744 44* **Rooms** *60*　　　　　**Map** *9 B2*

This hotel occupies a restored 19th-century building located on a quiet street. The sophisticated interiors are made of natural materials. The restaurant serves mainly organic food from farms outside Berlin. In summer, the inner garden in the pretty courtyard comes into its own. **www.bleibtreu.com**

Concept Hotel

€€€

Grolmannstrasse 41-43, 10623 **Tel** *884 260* **Fax** *884 265 00* **Rooms** *153*　　　**Map** *9 C1*

The building of this welcoming hotel is modern and some of its rooms have extra-long beds for taller guests. There is a roof terrace and during summer, dinner is served in the inner courtyard. Try to get a reservation for a calm front or a courtyard room. **www.concept-hotel.com**

Crowne Plaza Berlin City

€€€

Nürnberger Strasse 65, 10787 **Tel** *210 070* **Fax** *213 20 09* **Rooms** *423*　　　　**Map** *10 E2*

This luxurious hotel is located near Kaiser-Wilhelm-Gedächtnis-Kirche and Tauentzienstrasse. It has a swimming pool, a good restaurant, large rooms with all amenities and a pleasing amosphere. It offers special weekend rates combined with sightseeing tours. **www.cp-berlin.com**

Hecker's Hotel

€€€

Grolmannstrasse 35, 10623 **Tel** *889 000* **Fax** *889 02 60* **Rooms** *69*　　　　　**Map** *9 C1*

Situated in the very heart of town, this low-key, private hotel caters not only for its guests' needs but tries for a more individual approach. The plain façade hides a more sophisticated interior, with simple furniture in the style of Frank Lloyd Wright, and displays of contemporary art. **www.heckers-hotel.com**

Hotel am Zoo

€€€

Kurfürstendamm 25, 10719 **Tel** *884 370* **Fax** *884 377 14* **Rooms** *136*　　　　**Map** *10 D1*

The small but elegant Hotel Zoo is a charming, intimate combination of a modern, upmarket hotel with timeless furniture and large, very peaceful rooms, hidden in one of the few great old mansions left standing on Kurfürstendamm. Perfect for a stroll down the boulevard. **www.hotel-am-zoo.de**

Hotel Ambassador Berlin Patner of Sorat Hotels

Bayreuther Strasse 42-43, 10787 **Tel** *219 020* **Fax** *219 023 80* **Rooms** *198*   **Map** *10 F1*

This high-standard hotel is located near Wittenbergplatz. Its functional but large rooms are comfortable, traditionally furnished and have soundproofed windows. The restaurant, with its rustic interior, offers an *à la carte* menu or a Swedish-style buffet. **www.sorat-hotels.com**

Hotel Avantgarde

Kurfürstendamm 15, 10719 **Tel** *884 83 30* **Fax** *882 40 11* **Rooms** *27*   **Map** *10 D1*

Occupying the upper floors of a late 19th-century Neo-Baroque building, this hotel offers large rooms with soundproofed windows and decorative stucco ceilings. Although the hotel does not have a dining room, there is a Mövenpick restaurant on the ground floor. **www.hotel-avantgarde.com**

Hotel Mondial

Kurfürstendamm 47, 10707 **Tel** *884 110* **Fax** *884 111 50* **Rooms** *75*   **Map** *9 B2*

Wonderfully located near George-Grosz-Platz, close to several restaurants, this friendly hotel offers high-standard service. It is recommended for the disabled, as it is wheelchair-accessible and one quarter of the rooms have special facilities for disabled guests. **www.hotel-mondial.com**

Hotel Residenz Berlin

Meinekestrasse 9, 10719 **Tel** *884 430* **Fax** *882 47 26* **Rooms** *81*   **Map** *10 D2*

A recently restored 19th-century building, this appealing establishment is in a side street close to Kurfürstendamm. First-class suites are available as well as apartments with a kitchen. The price of the room includes a buffet breakfast. Special prices are available for long stays. **www.hotel-residenz.com**

Sorat Art'otel Berlin

Joachimstaler Strasse 29, 10719 **Tel** *884 470* **Fax** *884 477 00* **Rooms** *133*   **Map** *10 D2*

The Sorat Art'otel can be easily recognized from a distance by the figure of a discus-thrower on the façade. Its interiors are boldly designed in a colourful, ultra-modern style. The decor might evoke a mixed response from the guests, but they are nonetheless impressed by the service. **www.sorat.hotels.com**

Art'otel City Center West

Lietzenburger Strasse 85, 10719 **Tel** *887 77 70* **Fax** *887 777 777* **Rooms** *91*   **Map** *10 D2*

Just steps away from Kurfürstendamm is one of Germany's top art and designer hotels, filled with art reproductions of Andy Warhol's work. Rooms are individually designed and feature state-of-the-art furniture. This is a great place to stay if you like design, bright colours and a western city centre location. **www.artotels.com**

Hotel Brandenburger Hof

Eislebener Strasse 14, 10789 **Tel** *214 050* **Fax** *214 051 00* **Rooms** *82*   **Map** *10 E2*

An intimate family atmosphere, impeccable service and quiet, luxurious rooms make this one of the most desirable top-notch hotels in Berlin. The enchanting building has been restored and rooms feature Bauhaus furniture. The Michelin-awarded restaurant is a must. **www.brandenburger-hof.com**

Hotel Palace Berlin

Budapester Strasse 45, 10789 **Tel** *250 20* **Fax** *250 21 161* **Rooms** *282*   **Map** *10 E1*

The uninspiring shape of the building hides its charming interior, which is full of discreet elegance. The hotel is distinguished by the intimate atmosphere. Guests have included Julia Roberts and Isabella Rossellini. Rooms range from double to presidential suites. **www.palace.de**

Hotel Steigenberger Berlin

Los-Angeles-Platz, 10789 **Tel** *212 70* **Fax** *212 71 17* **Rooms** *397*   **Map** *10 E2*

With a very good location this hotel offers cosy, recently-refurbished rooms and several categories of apartments. The hotel's facilities include a swimming pool, sauna, massage, a bar and good Berlin cuisine in the hotel restaurant, Berliner Stube. **www.steigenberger.de**

Savoy Hotel

Fasanenstrasse 9-10, 10623 **Tel** *311 030* **Fax** *310 33 33* **Rooms** *125*   **Map** *10 D1*

Rated among the most beautiful hotels in Berlin, the Savoy's comfortable rooms and friendly atmosphere attract an exclusive clientele. The suites on the sixth floor offer good views. Facilities include babysitting, theatre ticket service and the city's first cigar bar. **www.hotel-savoy.com**

Swissôtel Berlin

Augsburgerstrasse 44, 10789 **Tel** *220 100* **Fax** *220 102 222* **Rooms** *316*   **Map** *10 D1*

One of the few first-class hotels on Ku'damm, the impressive building overlooks a busy cross section of the boulevard, making it perfect for sightseeing. The modern rooms are large, decorated in brown colours with comfortable lounge chairs, thick carpets and curtains. **www.berlin.swissotel.com**

Kempinski Hotel Bristol Berlin

Kurfürstendamm 27, 10719 **Tel** *884 340* **Fax** *883 60 75* **Rooms** *301*   **Map** *10 D1*

One of Berlin's most famous hotels, the Kempinski was redecorated in the 1990s and has a classic interior. Its luxurious rooms are very comfortable, and 18 rooms have wheelchair access. Its famous restaurant, Kempinski-Grill, serves international cuisine. **www.kempinskiberlin.de**

Key to Price Guide *see p220* **Key to Symbols** *see back cover flap*

AROUND SCHLOSS CHARLOTTENBURG

Pension Niebuhr   €

Niebuhrstrasse 74, 10629 **Tel** *324 95 95* **Fax** *324 80 21* **Rooms** *12*   **Map** *9 B1*

One of the smallest and most inexpensive *Pensionen* in all of Charlottenburg, the Niebuhr has only 12 tastefully, but not very elegantly furnished rooms. The location is perfect for exploring the district. Breakfast is served in your room. **www.pension-niebuhr.de**

Art Hotel Charlottenburger Hof   €€

Stuttgarter Platz 14, 10627 **Tel** *329 070* **Fax** *323 37 23* **Rooms** *46*   **Map** *9 A1*

A must for any individual traveller looking for a real Berlin experience, the Charlottenburger Hof is a successful version of a traditional *Hotelpensionen* for young tourists. The individually designed rooms are decorated with art by Mondrian. The staff here are very helpful. **www.charlottenburger-hof.de**

Hotel an der Oper   €€

Bismarckstrasse 100, 10625 **Tel** *315 830* **Fax** *315 831 09* **Rooms** *48*   **Map** *3 A4*

Located near the opera house in Charlottenburg. Although some rooms overlook the noisy Bismarckstrasse, windows have been soundproofed. The pastel-coloured rooms are fairly large and have basic furniture. There is a non-smoking breakfast room and an Italian restaurant serving Mediterranean food. **www.hotel-an-der-oper.de**

Hotel Econtel Berlin   €€€

Sömmeringstr. 24-26, 10589 **Tel** *346 810* **Fax** *346 811 63* **Rooms** *205*   **Map** *3 A2*

A large, family-oriented hotel that somehow lacks character but is the best deal for families in town. Provides many baby and toddler services, children-oriented rooms and large family apartments, all tastefully yet functionally decorated. The quiet location is yet another advantage. **www.econtel.de**

Schlossparkhotel   €€€

Heubnerweg 2a, 14059 **Tel** *326 90 30* **Fax** *326 903 600* **Rooms** *39*   **Map** *2 D2*

The modern Schlossparkhotel is part of a private clinic and is known as a very pleasant and small, but top-class, hotel near the beautiful gardens of Schlosspark Charlottenburg, making this the only downtown hotel in a green setting. The S-Bahn Westend is nearby. Request a room with a balcony overlooking the gardens. **www.schlossparkhotel.de**

FURTHER AFIELD

Die Fabrik   €

Schlesische Strasse 18, 10997 **Tel** *611 71 16* **Fax** *618 29 74* **Rooms** *45*

Set in an old factory building in the heart of alternative Kreuzberg, this youth-hostel type offers shared bathrooms and and simple furnishings, but its easy-going atmosphere appeals to all tastes. Very well-kept single, double and cheap dormitory rooms available. **www.diefabrik.com**

Hotel-Pension Kastanienhof   €

Kastanienallee 65, 10119 **Tel** *44 30 50* **Fax** *443 051 11* **Rooms** *35*   **Map** *1 B3*

The Kastanienhof is a budget *Pension* hidden in a fully restored, typical Berlin tenement house. Its location is perfect for exploring the clubbing scene in Prenzlauer Berg. Rooms are surprisingly nice, though, and come equipped with a hairdryer, minibar and safe. **www.hotel-kastanienhof-berlin.de**

Artemisia   €€

Brandenburgische Strasse 18, 10707 **Tel** *873 89 05* **Fax** *861 86 53* **Rooms** *12*

Artemisia caters exclusively for women and is often visited by business travellers. Men are allowed into the conference room. Some of the nice rooms, with many green plants, share modern bathrooms. The hotel has its own art gallery, while its breakfast room has a delightful terrace. **www.artemisia-berlin.com**

Best Western Kanthotel Berlin   €€

Kantstrasse 111, 10627 **Tel** *323 020* **Fax** *324 09 52* **Rooms** *70*   **Map** *9 A1*

This good-quality hotel is located near Charlottenburg railway station. There are special facilities for business travellers, and non-smoking rooms are available. The hotel also offers services such as babysitting and laundry. Close to many inexpensive ethnic places to eat. **www.kanthotel.com**

Dolce Berlin Müggelsee   €€

Am Grossen Müggelsee, 12559 **Tel** *658 820* **Fax** *658 822 63* **Rooms** *176*

This is an excellent hotel, far from the hustle and bustle of the city. Tucked away in the greenery on the Müggelsee in Köpenick, it is perfect for a relaxed stay. Rooms are fairly spacious, and all of the three guest floors are decorated differently in Italian, Asian and German styles. **www.dolceberlin.de**

East-Side Hotel
  €€

Mühlenstrasse 6, 10243   **Tel** *293 833*   **Fax** *293 835 55*   **Rooms** *36*   **Map** *8 F5*

The East-Side Hotel is located opposite the East-Side-Gallery, in a building that was formerly used to house workers. It opened in 1996, and has big, bright rooms with modern facilities and spacious bathrooms. The hotel has a comfortable family atmosphere. **www.eastsidecityhotel.de**

Forsthaus Paulsborn
€€

Am Grunewaldsee/Hüttenweg 90, 14193   **Tel** *818 19 10*   **Fax** *818 191 50*   **Rooms** *10*

Peaceful location, deep in the Grunewald, makes it better suited to visitors with cars. Stained-glass windows and a fireplace in the lobby add character to this stylish former hunting lodge that also has a nice restaurant serving char-broiled meat dishes. Rooms are nicely decorated in a country-style mix. **www.forsthaus-paulsborn.de**

Holiday Inn Berlin City Center East
€€

Prenzlauer Allee 169, 10409   **Tel** *446 610*   **Fax** *446 616 61*   **Rooms** *122*

The hotel calls itself an art hotel, and there is some original art to be found both in the public areas and rooms. Nonetheless, this Holiday Inn is primarily a standard business hotel with competitive prices. Rooms are quite clean and comfortable, though lacking in individuality. **www.hi-berlin.com**

Honigmond
  €€

Tieckstrasse 12, 10115   **Tel** *284 45 50*   **Fax** *284 455 11*   **Rooms** *40*   **Map** *6 F1*

The Honigmond is great for exploring the Mitte and Prenzlauer Berg arts scenes. Originally a traditional tenement house, it has individually designed rooms, some of which feature four-poster beds and parquet floors. Other rooms, in a 19th-century house with a courtyard, will entice you with their summerhouse look. **www.honigmond.de**

Hotel Pension Wittelsbach
  €€

Wittelsbacher Strasse 22, 10707   **Tel** *864 98 40*   **Fax** *862 15 32*   **Rooms** *31*

A pleasant, old-fashioned *Pension* in a 19th-century building. Ideal for families with small children, with one floor dedicated entirely to them. There are plenty of toys and nursery rooms are decorated in the style of "Wild West". Some rooms have a balcony or garden terrace. **www.hotel-pension-wittelsbach.de**

Hotel Schöneberg
€€

Hauptstrasse 135, 10827   **Tel** *780 96 60*   **Fax** *780 966 20*   **Rooms** *31*

This three-star hotel is away from many tourist sights, yet a good choice for its unbeatable prices and nice setting. Hotel Schöneberg is located in a beautiful Art Nouveau building. All the rooms of the three different categories are large, yet furnished with 1990s decor. Friendly service. **www.hotelschoeneberg.de**

Hotel Sylter Hof Berlin
  €€

Kurfürstenstrasse 114-116, 10787   **Tel** *212 00*   **Fax** *241 28 26*   **Rooms** *167*   **Map** *10 F1*

Once one of Berlin's leading first-class hotels, the Sylter Hof is still a good choice. Entering the hotel feels like stepping back into the late 1960s. Once inside the rooms, you will be pleasantly surprised by Classicist furniture, upscale bathrooms and modern amenities such as wireless LAN. **www.sylterhof-berlin.de**

Jurine
€€

Schwedter Strasse 15, 10119   **Tel** *443 29 90*   **Fax** *443 299 99*   **Rooms** *53*

This small hotel is located in a side street near Senefelderplatz, in the centre of Prenzlauer Berg. The nearby U-Bahn station gives easy access to the town centre. The recently-redecorated rooms are of a high standard and there is a surprisingly green hotel garden behind the house. **www.hotel-jurine.de**

Villa Kastania
€€

Kastanienallee 20, 14052   **Tel** *300 00 20*   **Fax** *300 002 10*   **Rooms** *43*   **Map** *1 A5*

A warm and intimate establishment with a high standard of service. It is located in a quiet street, a few minutes on foot from the complex of trade fair halls, Messegelände, and with excellent links to the centre. All rooms have balconies and standard rooms have kitchenettes. **www.villakastania.com**

Villa Toscana
€€

Bahnhofstrasse 19, 12207   **Tel** *768 92 70*   **Fax** *773 44 88*   **Rooms** *16*

This quiet hotel is situated in an Italian-style villa, dating from the late 19th century. It's more convenient for tourists who have their own transport as the hotel is far from the centre and from any S- and U-Bahn stations. The rooms are well furnished and the marble bathrooms are elegant. **www.villa-toscana.de**

Berlin Excelsior Hotel S.A.
€€€

Hardenbergstrasse 14, 10623   **Tel** *315 50*   **Fax** *315 510 02*   **Rooms** *330*   **Map** *3 C 5*

The Excelsior, once a first-class hotel, still exudes an elegant, international flair but lacks the service and amenities you would expect. Nevertheless, the large, stylishly decorated rooms with a view of quaint Steinplatz are appealing. Students' bars and cafés are footsteps away. **www.hotel-excelsior.de**

Estrel Hotel & Convention Center
 €€€

Sonnenallee 225, 12057   **Tel** *683 10*   **Fax** *683 123 45*   **Rooms** *1125*   **Map** *14 F5*

The biggest hotel in continental Europe, the Estrel opened in 1994 to house major conferences. It is also popular among tourists, being conveniently linked by S-Bahn to the town centre. In summer, you can enjoy a beer in the garden along the canal. The affordable rates and great service are add-ons. **www.estrel.com**

Key to Price Guide *see p220* **Key to Symbols** *see back cover flap*

Hotel Luisenhof

Köpenicker Strasse 92, 10179 **Tel** *241 59 06* **Fax** *279 29 83* **Rooms** *27* **Map** *8 D5*

Situated at the Märkisches Museum, this hotel occupies the oldest building (1882) in this part of Berlin. Extensive restoration has created a charming hotel with nice rooms and a delightful restaurant in the cellar. Given its size and decor, the Luisensuite is a great deal. **www.luisenhof.de**

Hotel Seehof Berlin

Lietzenseeufer 11, 14057 **Tel** *320 020* **Fax** *320 022 51* **Rooms** *75* **Map** *2 D5*

An amazing hotel, only ten minutes on foot from Messegelände, the complex of trade fair halls. Given the modern structure, the stylish interiors and large rooms come as something of a surprise. Its lovely restaurant, Au Lac, is one of the few places where you can dine with a view of a lake – the Lietzensee. **www.hotel-seehof-berlin.de**

Sorat Hotel Humboldt-Mühle Berlin

An der Mühle 5-9, 13507 **Tel** *439 040* **Fax** *439 044 44* **Rooms** *120*

Located near Tegel airport, Sorat occupies a former grain mill. The interior's modern style uses light-coloured woods and old architectural elements. Because of its history, dishes in the restaurant contain wholemeal grains. Rooms in the adjoining Verwaltervilla are more elegant and new. **www.sorat-hotels.com**

Sorat Hotel Spree-Bogen Berlin

Alt-Moabit 99, 10559 **Tel** *399 200* **Fax** *399 209 99* **Rooms** *220* **Map** *4 F1*

Beautifully located on the bank of the Spree river, the hotel is surrounded by modern tower blocks close to the Tiergarten. The building was an old dairy. Some stylishly-designed rooms have views of the river and the hotel has its own yacht for trips along the river. In summer, its restaurant has a great terrace. **www.sorat-hotels.com**

Schlosshotel im Grunewald

Brahmsstrasse 10, 14193 **Tel** *895 840* **Fax** *895 848 00* **Rooms** *54*

This exclusive hotel was formerly a palace, built in 1912 for Walter von Pannwitz, the Kaiser's personal lawyer. The contemporary interiors were created by Karl Lagerfeld. There is a breathtaking lobby with a magnificent coffered ceiling and decorative woodcarving. **www.schlosshotelberlin.com**

GREATER BERLIN

Clarion Collection Art'otel Potsdam

Zeppelinstrasse 136, 14471 **Tel** *0331 981 50* **Fax** *0331 981 55 55* **Rooms** *123*

Part of this luxurious hotel on the bank of Havel river occupies an old 19th-century granary, where rooms have beautiful ceilings with restored beams and designer furniture. The best features of rooms in the modern wing are the balconies overlooking the Havel. **www.artotel-potsdam.com**

Hotel am Luisenplatz

Luisenplatz 5, 14471 Potsdam **Tel** *0331 971 90* **Fax** *0331 971 919* **Rooms** *149*

Overlooking Potsdam's most charming square, this private four-star hotel is tastefully decorated in warm shades of brown and blue. Rooms are fairly large and equipped with all modern necessities. Suites, which come for 20 euros more, are even nicer. **www.hotel-luisenplatz.de**

NH Voltaire Potsdam

Friedrich-Ebert-Strasse 88, 14467 **Tel** *0331 231 70* **Fax** *0331 231 71 00* **Rooms** *143*

This is a top-quality hotel with a restaurant and bar in the centre of town, adjacent to the famous Dutch quarter. The comfortably furnished and surprisingly elegant rooms have individual colour schemes. The modern part of the building is joined to a converted Baroque palace. **www.nh-hotels.com**

Steigenberger MAXX Hotel Sanssouci

Allee nach Sanssouci, 14471 Potsdam **Tel** *0331 909 10* **Fax** *0331 909 19 09* **Rooms** *137*

This small-town hotel has all the business amenities you would expect from a Steigenberger hotel. The quieter rooms are decorated with non-kitschy Hollywood movie themes of the 1940s and 50s, combined with country-style furniture. The hotel has a restaurant and a bar. **www.potsdam.steigenberger.de**

Zur Bleiche Resort & Spa

Bleichestrasse 16, 03096 Burg im Spreewald **Tel** *035 603* **Fax** *035 603* **Rooms** *91*

Travellers looking for relaxation after an tiring day in the city will indulge in this exclusive, yet relaxed, spa resort set in a historic country house. Rooms range from rustic to elegant, there are extensive "wellness" packages and fitness services available. The restaurant is considered to be one of East Germany's best. **www.hotel-zur-bleiche.com**

Relexa Schlosshotel Cecilienhof

Neuer Garten, 14467 **Tel** *0331 370 50* **Fax** *0331 292 498* **Rooms** *41*

A treat for history-lovers, the hotel, furnished in an elegant British country style, occupies most of the Cecilienhof palace. In the evening, when the daytrippers have left, hotel guests can take a stroll in the gardens or a boat trip on the lake. The hotel restaurant serves fine regional fare. **www.relexa-hotel.de**

RESTAURANTS, CAFES AND BARS

Shield of the Forst-haus Paulsborn restaurant

Given that Berlin is so cosmopolitan, you will find a wider range of restaurants here than in any other city in Germany. This includes Indian, Greek, Chinese, Thai and Turkish as well as Alsatian and Cambodian. Recently, new places have been opened by famous chefs, which maintain high European standards of international-style cuisine. There are also plenty of restaurants specializing in local dishes: the food can be a little heavy, but it is usually very tasty and served in large portions. Wherever you are in Berlin, you won't have to travel far to find somewhere to eat – every area has its own cluster of restaurants, cafés and bars, covering a range of styles and prices. Some of the best places are listed on pages 236–43. These have been chosen for their delicious food and/or good value. The listings on pages 244–9 should help those who would like a bite to eat but want the more relaxed setting of a café or bar.

The elegant interior of Margaux (see p236)

WHERE TO GO

Although good restaurants and cafés can be found all over Berlin, some of the best gourmet restaurants tend to be located in exclusive hotels, including **Die Quadriga** in the Brandenburger Hof (see p241) or **First Floor** in the Hotel Palace Berlin (see p242). Alternatively, some good restaurants, such as the excellent **Margaux** (see p236), can also be found on quiet streets.

The largest concentrations of restaurants are in a number of well-known districts. In the former West Berlin, for example, the most famous restaurants are clustered around Savignyplatz. Good places to eat in the centre can be found in and around Oranienburger Strasse. One of the recent top spots in Berlin that is popular with young people is Prenzlauer Berg, near Kollwitzplatz.

Despite all the changes that have taken place in the eastern part of Berlin over the past few years, restaurants in Kreuzberg (particularly along Oranienstrasse) are among the busiest in the city. The places in these areas are all consistently good and offer a wide choice in style and price.

WHAT TO EAT

In the morning, nearly all eateries, including those in most hotels, will offer a substantial breakfast. This usually consists of eggs, ham or cold cuts and different kinds of cheese. On Sundays some places also serve a German buffet-style brunch (breakfast combined with lunch) until 2pm. At lunchtime, one can easily find an elaborate salad or a bowl of steaming soup almost anywhere. In addition many restaurants may also offer their standard menus with slightly reduced prices.

The options for an evening meal are practically unlimited. In a restaurant serving local food one can have, for example, a tasty pork knuckle or potato soup (see pp232–3). Lovers of Italian cuisine can easily find a good pizzeria or an Italian restaurant that serves sophisticated regional Italian dishes. Fans of Oriental food can choose between many Asian national cuisines, a great variety of which are situated along Prenzlauer Berg and around Savignyplatz. In addition, Berlin also has very good

Outside Oxymoron (see p237), in the Hackesche Höfe

Outside Dressler Unter den Linden
(see p236)

Mexican restaurants, particularly around Oranienburger Strasse and in Kreuzberg, and the food served at Greek restaurants is usually quite good and very inexpensive. Vegetarians can easily find something suitable at almost every restaurant; however places that offer a significant choice of meat-free dishes are specially marked in the restaurant listings *(see pp236–43)*.

PRICES AND TIPPING

Menus, showing meals and their prices, are usually on display outside restaurants and cafés. The price of meals can vary a great deal. It is possible to eat a three course meal, without alcohol, for €15, but in the centre of Berlin the price rises to €20–€25. In a top-notch establishment the cost of a meal can be over €80. The price of alcohol varies as well, but the most popular and cheapest drink is beer. Although prices include service and tax, many Germans will round up the bill. In more expensive restaurants a 10 per cent tip is customary.

EATING HOURS

In general, cafés open at 9am and restaurants at noon; the latter sometimes also close between 3 and 6pm. However, there are a lot of places that stay open very late, sometimes until 2 or 3am. Some of the most expensive and best restaurants are only open in the evening and are sometimes closed on one day during the week as well.

BOOKING

In the most up-market restaurants, reservations are almost certainly required – in popular places it is advisable to book well in advance. For the majority of good restaurants it is necessary to book only for Friday or Saturday evenings, when all restaurants are at their busiest. If you do not have a reservation, look for a street or square with a large concentration of restaurants – there is bound to be an empty table among these.

DISABLED DINERS

In order to avoid any problems in advance, you should discuss wheelchair access when booking. Bear in mind, however, that even if a dining room may be accessible on the ground floor, the toilets may be up or down stairs or through a narrow corridor.

CHILDREN

Casual restaurants usually welcome children, though this may not be the case in more upmarket establishments. Those that do cater for children may provide high chairs as well as light dishes, particularly during lunchtime. Some places will offer a separate children's menu with small portions. Children are also allowed in pubs and bars.

READING THE MENU

Menus are written out, in many places, in German and English, although some restaurants will provide menus in French as well. If you find yourself in a casual restaurant or bar, where the menu is perhaps hand-written, you can ask a waiter for help. Apart from the standard menu many restaurants will sometimes also offer a menu of the day containing seasonal dishes or the chef's specials, which are always worth considering.

The stylish Bocca di Bacco (see p236)

SMOKING

Smoking is allowed everywhere in Berlin – except in some fast-food places. There are special non-smoking rooms in some restaurants, but this is a rarity. To avoid a smoky meal, sit near a door or window, or look for a restaurant with high ceilings.

The elegant interior of Facil (see p239)

What to Eat in Berlin

To treat your senses in Berlin, you need do nothing more than stroll through the street markets, historic market halls and speciality food shops. Spicy, hot sausages such as *Currywurst* or *Thüringer* will lure you into the traditional German butcheries. The scent of freshly baked rolls and breads wafts from the corner bakeries. Fresh herbs, typical German garden vegetables such as red or green cabbage, and wild mushrooms are spectacularly displayed. Freshwater fish from the region's many lakes and rivers glisten on their beds of ice; particularly popular are pike-perch, eel, trout and even sweet river crabs.

Harzer Roller and Emmenthaler cheeses

Wild mushrooms, one of the region's most famous products

BERLIN'S HEARTY HERITAGE

Historically, Berlin has never been a gourmet capital, and neither has the surrounding, rural Brandenburg region. The Hohenzollern court focused more on its army than on culture and cuisine. But the Great Electors were formidable hunters, and game such as wild boar, rabbit, and duck, as well as goose and birds of prey were (and remain) an integral part of Berlin's cuisine. Later, in the 19th century, both the evolving Prussian well-to-do and the working class preferred hearty and simple food over fine dining – not only because Berlin was then a comparatively poor city, but also because of the long and hard winters and generally inclement weather.

BREAD AND POTATOES

There is an enormous variety of breads and rolls to be found on today's menus. Many are unique to Berlin, such as the wholewheat and rye, dark, crusty *Schuster-jungen* ("shoemaker's boy") or *schrippen*, the cheap roll eaten daily at every meal.

Potatoes were introduced by Frederick the Great. They appear at most German meals,

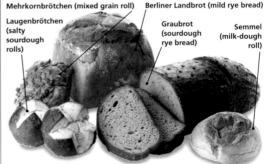

Mehrkornbrötchen (mixed grain roll)

Berliner Landbrot (mild rye bread)

Laugenbrötchen (salty sourdough rolls)

Graubrot (sourdough rye bread)

Semmel (milk-dough roll)

Selection of typical German loaves and bread rolls

LOCAL DISHES AND SPECIALITIES

Berliners have many ways of preparing pork, making it the most popular main dish. As *Kasseler*, created by Berlin butcher Cassel in the late 19th century, the meat is salted and then dried before being served with sauerkraut, mashed potatoes and very spicy mustard. Berlin's traditional pork knuckle, also accompanied by sauerkraut and potatoes, isn't complete without a portion of split pea purée (called *Erbspuree* in Berlin). Pork sausages include *Currywurst* – a post-World War II invention by Berlin Imbiss (food stall) owner Hedwig Mueller – which are served with a spicy sauce of curry, tomatoes and chili along with a roll or French fries. You can find this filling snack at Imbisse throughout the city.

Zanderfilet, *or Havel-Zander, is pan-fried pike-perch with a vegetable sauce and onions, served with mashed potatoes.*

Display of traditional German sausages in a Berlin butcher's shop

BERLIN'S FINE DINING REVOLUTION

With the city's reunification came a new international influence, which gave birth to many Michelin-starred and other gourmet restaurants. Restaurants often prepare Berlin signature dishes with a more healthy or an exotic twist, giving traditional dishes a modern flavour. One of the Mark Brandenberg's most important products, fresh wild mushrooms, such as *Pfifferlinge* or *Steinpilze*, figure prominently, and classic ingredients like sauerkraut, cabbage and beet may be paired with Mediterranean fish or Asian spices.

alongside fish or meat or cooked in a broth for dishes such as *Kartoffelsuppe*.

THE BRANDENBURG INFLUENCE

Berlin's restaurants only rediscovered the region's true heritage after the fall of the Wall, absorbing culinary traditions from the Mark Brandenburg, the suddenly re-accessible rural countryside surrounding Berlin with its thick forests, rivers and lakes. Today, the fresh produce provided by the region's farms are an integral part of Berlin's cuisine. Old recipes have returned to modern kitchens. Freshwater fish like pike-perch, or game such as wild boar or duck, are flavoured with fresh herbs such as dill and parsley, and the famous

Brandenburger Landente (Brandenburg country duck), stuffed with apples, onions and herbs, slowly roasted and coated with a honey-oil to make it perfectly crusty, is once again a favourite on Berlin menus.

Fresh vegetables from the Mark Brandenberg region

BEST LOCAL FOOD

Restaurants: Altes Zollhaus (*p240*); Leibniz-Klause (*p241*); Reinhard's (*p238*); Lorenz- Adlon-Gourmet (*p236*); Zur letzten Instanz (*p238*); Mutter (*p242*); Dressler (*p236*).

Shops and markets: Marheineke-Markthalle; Turkish Market, Maybachufer; KaDeWe gourmet food floor (*p258*); Rogacki Gourmet Centre (*p259*); Butter Lindner delicatessen chain.

Imbisse (food stalls): Konnopke (below train tracks, Eberswalder Strasse subway, Prenzlauer Berg); Ku'damm 195 Imbiss, Kurfürstendamm; Currywurstbude, Amtsgerichtsplatz, Charlottenburg.

Kasseler Nacken *is salted and dried pork served with sauerkraut or green cabbage and mashed potatoes.*

Berliner Leber *is veal or pork liver on a bed of mashed potatoes, with fried onions and pan-fried apple slices.*

Brandenburger Landente *is stuffed duck served with red cabbage and potato dumplings or mashed potatoes.*

What to Drink in Berlin

In Berlin, as throughout the rest of Germany, beer is the most widely drunk alcoholic beverage. There are no productive vineyards around Berlin, but wines from the Rhine and Mosel regions are always popular. As an *aperitif*, or with pork dishes, Berliners often enjoy a shot of rye vodka *(Korn)*, sometimes flavoured with herbs. With dessert, a glass of herbal liqueur often fits the bill.

Engelhardt brewery logo

LAGER *(PILSNER)*

Berliners drink beer on every occasion, and Germany's many beers are some of the best and purest in the world. Some of the best-known Berlin breweries are Schultheiss, Berliner Kindl, Berliner Pils and Engelhardt, but beers brewed in other parts of Germany are just as popular. Although beer is available in all sorts of venues and *"Ein Bier bitte"* can be heard in pubs, cafés and restaurants, it is worth experiencing the atmosphere of an old-fashioned beerhouse, or *Kneipe*. The most highly esteemed beer is draught beer, drawn from the cask *(vom Fass)* and poured slowly into tall glasses. Pouring in a thin trickle is essential to achieve a thick head of foam, and a good barman will take a few minutes to fill your glass. Berliners drink mostly lager *(Pils)*, but other beers are also popular.

Pilsner beers from Berlin breweries

Strong, dark
Bock beer

OTHER BEERS

A *Brezel* makes a good
snack with beer

In addition to the usual light, Pilsner-type beers, Berlin's breweries, many of them small and independent, also make a number of more adventurous brews. Dark, sweetish beer, known as *Schwarzbier* or black beer, is becoming more and more popular and has rather more than the standard four per cent alcohol. *Weizenbier* is made from wheat rather than barley, and is usually served in half-litre (one pint) glasses with a slice of lemon. Another unusual drink is *Bock*, an especially strong beer made with barley. *Maibock* is a special version, available only in May.

BERLINER WEISSE MIT SCHUSS

A Berlin speciality, called *Berliner Weisse mit Schuss*, is a light, newly-fermented wheat beer that continues fermenting in the bottle. On its own, it is not very palatable as it is rather watery and sour, but when mixed with raspberry cordial it becomes fruity and delicious. Mixing with sweet woodruff syrup gives it a vivid green colour and a slightly medicinal flavour. *Berliner Weisse mit Schuss* is served in large wine glasses with a straw, and makes a very refreshing drink, particularly popular during the hot summer months.

Berliner Weisse,
a light malted-
wheat beer

Berliner Weisse
with raspberry and
woodruff cordials

WINE

No wine is produced around Berlin as the climate here is too cold for vines, but a variety of wines from Germany's southern and western regions are available in Berlin. The most famous are the white wines, particularly those made from Riesling grapes. Most expensive are those from the Rheingau region. The northern climate dictates that most German wines are white, but lovers of red wine can try the Rhine Assmanshausen Spät-burgunder, made from Pinot Noir grapes. Although there is no regional system of classification like the French *Appellation d'Origine Contrôlée,* a national quality control system divides German wines into three categories: *Tafelwein* or table wine is the most basic; next comes *Qualitätswein,* and the highest is *Qualitätswein mit Prädikat,* which includes wines made from specially selected grapes. *Trocken* means dry, *halbtrocken* means medium dry and *süss* means sweet. You can also find some very good sparkling wines known as *Sekts.*

A prize-winning bottle of German red wine

Riesling from Schloss Vollrads

OTHER ALCOHOLIC BEVERAGES

Vodka is often drunk with more substantial meals, particularly those based on pork. Especially recommended is one of the rye vodkas, such as *Weizendoppelkorn,* that are popular in Berlin. Many establishments also serve brandies, known gene-rically as *Weinbrand.* In addition, various digestive liqueurs and vodkas flavoured with plant extracts are quite popular, particularly *Kümmerling, Jägermeister* and, a Berlin favourite, *Kaulzzdorferkräuter Likör.* In many restaurants you will come across a speciality honey liqueur from east Prussia known as *Bärenfang.* More of an acquired taste is *Goldwasser* from Danzig, a traditional herbal liqueur containing flakes of gold leaf. It is made according to a secret 16th-century German recipe.

Weizendoppel-korn rye vodka   **Herbal digestive liqueur**   **Bitter-sweet Jägermeister liqueur**

NON-ALCOHOLIC COLD DRINKS

Although berlin tap water is safe to drink, it is not usually served with restaurant meals. If you want water you should order a bottle of mineral water *(Mineralwasser)* adding *"ohne Kohlen-Säure"* if you prefer still water. A wide variety of canned sparkling soft drinks, ubiquitous across Europe and the US, are popular in Berlin. Fruit juices are also widely drunk and a wide selection is available in every restaurant and café. Another popular soft drink is *Apfelschorle,* apple juice mixed in equal proportions with sparkling mineral water.

Apfelschorle

COFFEE AND TEA

Coffee is very popular in Berlin and is served in a variety of ways. The most usual is filter coffee, served by the cup or the pot, generally with condensed milk and sugar. If you prefer something stronger and more aromatic you should go for an espresso. It is also easy to enjoy a good cup of tea in Berlin, herbal or otherwise. Germans drink a lot of herbal teas, two of the most common being peppermint *(Pfefferminz-tee)* and camomile *(Kamillentee).* If you want a cup of non-herbal tea, you can make a point of ordering *Schwarzen Tee.* If you want milk with your tea, then ask for *Tee mit Milch.*

Peppermint and camomile, two widely available herbal teas

Choosing a Restaurant

The restaurants in this guide have been selected because of their good value, good food and attractive interiors. The chart below lists restaurants in Berlin area by area, and the entries are alphabetical within each price category. Some of the specialities served at the restaurants have been mentioned in the listings.

PRICE CATEGORIES
For a three-course meal per person, including tax and service but not alcohol:

€ Under 25 euros
€€ 26–35 euros
€€€ 36–45 euros
€€€€ 46–55 euros
€€€€€ Over 56 euros

AROUND UNTER DEN LINDEN

XII Apostel   ♿🎵   €
*Georgenstrasse 2 (S-Bahnbögen 177-180), 10117 **Tel** 201 02 22*   **Map** 7 A2, 16 D2

Picturesquely situated in the old arcade of an S-Bahn railway bridge near Museum Island, this restaurant offers popular Italian cuisine. The thin, crispy pizza creations fresh from a stone oven are a speciality here, named after the twelve apostles. Ironically, Judas is the most sumptuous.

Borchadt   €€€
*Französische Strasse 47, 10117 **Tel** 818 862 62*   **Map** 6 F4, 15 C3

One of the few restaurants in Berlin with an original interior, including marble columns, mosaics and patterned floors in the Wilhelmine style. Good food, such as the French *steak et frites*, comes reasonably priced. Weekends are crowded so don't forget to make a reservation.

Dressler   €€€
*Unter den Linden 39, 10117 **Tel** 204 44 22*   **Map** 6 E4, 15 A3

Dressler is the perfect setting for a quick dinner before or after a theatre visit. Serves traditional German and French cuisine in an Art Deco-designed dining hall. In season, it has some of the city's best seafood. In winter, try their hearty German fare, such as oven-roasted duck with red cabbage and dumplings.

Fridericus im Opernpalais   €€€
*Unter den Linden 5, 10117 **Tel** 202 684 50*   **Map** 7 A3, 16 E3

Situated in the basement of the historic Kronprinzenpalais, this is a good place to dine before or after going to the opera next door. It offers a high standard of German and international dishes. A special emphasis is put on fresh local fish, such as perch with a mustard sauce and fried potatoes.

Lutter & Wegner   🪑♿   €€€
*Charlottenstr. 56, 10117 **Tel** 202 954 17*   **Map** 7 A4

The first restaurant to start the revitalization of the gourmet scene in the historic centre of Eastern Berlin. A fine German champagne brand until today, it now serves delicious German-Austrian food. The huge *Wiener Schnitzel* with potato salad, best served luke-warm, is a delight as are the duck and goose specialities in winter.

Bocca Di Bacco   🪑♿   €€€€
*Friedrichstrasse 167/168, 10117 **Tel** 206 728 28*   **Map** 7 A4, 16 D3

One of Western Berlin's oldest and most traditional upmarket Italian restaurants, the elegant Bocca attracts the rich and the famous. Tom Hanks and Spielberg are among its fans. Chef Lorenzo Pizetti has earned 14 Gault Millau points, and delights his patrons with probably the best pasta and fresh fish dishes outside Italy.

Lorenz-Adlon-Gourmet   €€€€€
*Unter den Linden 77, 10117 **Tel** 226 119 60*   **Map** 6 E4, 15 A3

This establishment is worthy of the hotel in which it is located, the Adlon. From the day it opened, this restaurant has been rated among Berlin's best. Under the guidance of its new chef, Thomas Neeser, Lorenz-Adlon has managed to maintain its top reputation. It now serves light nouvelle cuisine.

Margaux   €€€€€
*Unter den Linden 78, 10117 **Tel** 226 526 11*   **Map** 6 E4, 15 A3

The stylish and urban Margaux represents the new Berlin better than any other gourmet restaurant, even though it has lost some of its class after being taken over by new management. Classic yet creative French dishes are served. The restaurant also offers an extensive wine list and affordable lunch specials.

Vau   €€€€€
*Jägerstrasse 54-55, 10117 **Tel** 202 97 30*   **Map** 6 F4, 15 C4

This restaurant stands out with its elegant and unpretentious interiors. The excellent and imaginative Austrian- and French-based dishes are created by Berlin's star chef, Kolja Kleeberg. The service is welcoming and there is a selection of good wines. The small courtyard is used during lunch.

Key to Symbols *see back cover flap*

MUSEUM ISLAND

Brauhaus Georgbräu
Spreeufer 4, 10178 **Tel** *242 42 44*

€€
Map *7 C3*

At first sight, this restaurant looks like a typical tourist trap – large tables, big dining halls and masses of people. If you are not a fan of sausages, try *Brauhausknüller*, a Berlin dish with pork knuckle, mashed split peas, *Sauerkraut* and potatoes with cold beer.

Heat
Karl-Liebknecht-Strasse 3, 10178 **Tel** *238 283 472*

€€
Map *7 B2, 16 F2*

Heat is Berlin's latest fusion-cuisine restaurant, serving an eclectic mixture of Asian, Indian and Mediterranean dishes. A lunch restaurant, its light cuisine consists mainly of fresh fish and salads. In summer, a table on the terrace, just above the Spreekanal, is one of the nicest restaurant spots in Mitte.

Raabe Diele
Märkisches Ufer 10, 10179 **Tel** *275 829 99*

€€
Map *7 C4*

A pleasant restaurant that specializes in Berlin cuisine and is based in the cellar of Ermeler-Haus. The portions are huge. Pork knuckle with puréed peas and *Sauerkraut (Eisbein mit Erbsenpuree und Sauerkraut)* is the speciality. Everything served is drowned in the heavy but tasty sauces typical of the region.

Ermeler-Haus Factory & Bar
Märkisches Ufer 10, 10179 **Tel** *240 620*

€€€€
Map *7 C4*

Good regional cuisine in a modern style, with a Mediterranean flair. The restaurant is part of the gastronomic complex of Art'otel and is situated in a stylishly decorated basement. After a good fill of beef filet with fried potatoes and green beans, or green salad with filled rabbit neck, enjoy a cocktail at the bar counter.

EAST OF THE CENTRE

Blaues Band
Alte Schönhauser Strasse 7/8, 10119 **Tel** *283 850 99*

€
Map *7 C1*

Despite its location in the trendy Mitte district, the Blaues Band is a secret to many Berliners. The ambience is friendly and relaxed, and the food delicious. It offers specialities from a specific country or region. German cuisine is particularly recommended. The menu has fresh asparagus in early summer and duck and goose in winter.

Monsieur Vuong
Alte Schönhauser Strasse 46, 10119 **Tel** *308 726 43*

€
Map *7 C1*

This tiny Vietnamese restaurant is one of the new most popular eateries among the young, stylish Mitte crowd. It offers inexpensive yet delicious Asian and Vietnamese dishes, primarily excellent soups and snacks. Monsieur Vuong, whose black-and-white photograph is in the restaurant, is the father of current owner, chef Doug Vuong.

Historische Weinstuben
Poststrasse 23, 10178 **Tel** *242 41 07*

€€
Map *7 C3*

This popular wine bar is housed in one of the most decorative buldings of the Nicolaiviertel. Traditional dishes from Berlin, such as *Kohl* or *Rinderrouladen*, rolled and roasted stuffed beef, can be accompanied by a drink from a small but exquisite wine list with 50 mostly-German vintages.

Oxymoron
Rosenthaler Str. 40-41, 10178 **Tel** *283 918 86*

€€
Map *7 B2*

This fashionable restaurant, with its distinctive red-and-gold interior reminiscent of a 19th-century salon, has mainly Mediterranean and light German dishes on the menu. For lunch, dine at a table in the courtyard, the most beautiful inside historic Hackesche Höfe, and enjoy a small fare at a reasonable price.

Zoe
Rochstrasse 1, 10178 **Tel** *240 456 35*

€€
Map *7 C 2*

Zoe is a highly successful combination of German nouvelle cuisine and Asian dishes. The menu changes daily, but there is always a roasted, pan- or deep-fried meat, fish and vegetable creation, served with noodles, mushrooms and salads, in delicious Asian sauces. German recipes are more creative.

Zum Nussbaum
Am Nussbaum 3, 10178 **Tel** *242 30 95*

€€
Map *7 C3*

Situated in an alley in the Nicolaiviertel, this is a reconstruction of a 16th-century country inn, serving traditional Berlin cuisine, with tender pork knuckle, rollmops or *Berliner Boulette*, a spicy hamburger pattie without a bun. In summer, dine in its garden and enjoy the various brands of local beer.

Zur letzten Instanz
€€

Waisenstrasse 16, 10179 **Tel** *242 55 28* **Map** *8 D3*

Berlin's oldest restaurant dating back to 1621, this used to be a meeting place for lawyers. Today, almost every visiting head of state pays homage to this pub. It specializes in traditional German food, such as pork knuckle *(Eisbein)* and beef olive *(Rinderroulade)* and big mugs of German beer.

La Riva
€€€

Spreeufer 2, 10178 **Tel** *242 51 83* **Map** *7 C4*

This restaurant, serving good-quality Italian food, stands on the bank of the Spree river. Different types of pasta are served in apparently endless variations, and good Italian wines appear on the menu. Equally tasty is the huge mixed fish dish. In summer, diners can enjoy views of the river from the terrace.

Reinhard's
€€€

Poststrasse 28, 10178 **Tel** *238 42 95* **Map** *7 C3*

The interior of this enchanting place is decorated in style of the Roaring Twenties. The food is excellent. The speciality is *Das Geheimnis aus dem Kaiserhof* (the secret of the Kaiser's court), a succulent steak served with a sauce that was apparently created for Max Liebermann.

NORTH OF THE CENTRE

Yosoy
€

Rosenthaler Strasse 37, 10787 **Tel** *283 912 13* **Map** *7 B2*

A pleasant and inexpensive restaurant with a large selection of Spanish wines and dishes. The tapas are excellent, you can choose from 20 different creations presented *comme il faut* behind glass. A good deal is the *Yosoy-Tapasplatte*, a sampler of the best tapas for just 7.50.

Hackescher Hof
€€

Rosenthaler Strasse 40/41, 10178 **Tel** *283 52 93* **Map** *7 B2*

A very popular spot, this café-restaurant, divided into a bar and pub and a dining hall, serves breakfast from early morning, followed by inexpensive fixed-price lunches and Italian fare in the evenings. The food is excellent and the dishes are creative. In summer, the best tables are outside. Book ahead.

Kamala
€€

Oranienburger Strasse 69, 10117 **Tel** *283 27 97* **Map** *7 A1*

Though this small restaurant has simple furnishings, the service is prompt and the quality of food is high. The menu features standard Thai dishes, prepared with a very careful use of spices, as well as excellent soups flavoured with delicate Thai flowers. The Kamala is part of the Mao Thai chain, a group of Berlin's four best Thai restaurants.

Kellerrestaurant im Brecht-Haus
€€

Chausseestrasse 125, 10115 **Tel** *282 38 43* **Map** *6 E1*

This restaurant is located in the cellar of the house where Bertolt Brecht used to live. The mostly hearty dishes served here are prepared according to the recipes of Helene Weigel, the wife of the famous writer. A very good creation is *Tafelspitz*, a boiled and marinated rump steak.

Nolle
€€

Georgenstrasse, S-Bahnbogen Nr. 203, 10117 **Tel** *208 26 55* **Map** *7 A3*

The Nolle is a pleasantly decorated, 1920s-style Berlin restaurant tucked away under the S-Bahn tracks. The lush greenery around the place, the elegantly appointed tables, and candlelights make a perfect setting for international and German dishes. The *schnitzel* selection is impressive.

Orange
€€

Oranienburger Strasse 23, 10117 **Tel** *283 852 42* **Map** *7 A1*

Diners sit in a pleasing interior in the style of a café-restaurant, offering Italian and international dishes. Try a leisurely three-course meal or a snack. The Orange, a good location for starting a tour through Scheunenviertel, is also recommendable for its great breakfast selection.

Ganymed
€€€

Schiffbauerdamm 5, 10117 **Tel** *285 990 46* **Map** *6 F2, 15 C1*

A good-quality brasserie restaurant in charming surroundings with a small garden and views of the Spree river. The chef favours fish dishes, including Berlin fish specialities, but also offers traditional French fare such as *Steak Tartare*, fresh scallops sautéed in white wine, and a good cheese selection.

Schwarzenraben
€€€

Neue Schönhauser Strasse 13, 10178 **Tel** *283 916 98* **Map** *7 B2*

A fashionable venue with a bistro and a restaurant – the latter being only open in the evening. A very hip crowd enjoys classy Italian cuisine with creative pasta and meat dishes. It also serves good Italian cheeses and wines as well as a rare and exquisite selection of Italian sausages – all freshly cut at your table.

Key to Price Guide *see p236* **Key to Symbols** *see back cover flap*

TIERGARTEN

Desbrosses
P ☂ ♿ ♫   €€€

Potsdamer Platz 3, 10785 **Tel** *337 776 400*   **Map** 6 D5

Desbrosses has the most authentic French brasserie interior in all of Berlin. Dark wood-panelled walls, comfortable, plush leather banks, bistro chairs, an open show kitchen and music by Piaf, all make for a real French experience. A must here is the seafood platter.

Käfer im Bundestag
€€€

Reichstag, Platz der Republik, 10557 **Tel** *226 299 33*   **Map** 6 D3

A favourite dining place of the Mitte district, thanks to its unique location on the rooftop of the Reichstag, right next to Sir Norman Foster's cupola. The German cooking is creative and true to the owner, German catering star Käfer. Service is impeccable. Book ahead for lunch.

Midtown Grill
P ☂ ♿   €€€

Eberstrasse 3, 10785 **Tel** *220 006 410*   **Map** 6 E5

Steak and fresh seafood are the order of the day at this restaurant. While waiting for your dinner, you can watch the chefs in the open show kitchen, enjoy vintages from one of Berlin's best overseas wine menu and listen to jazz. Service is very friendly, though somewhat slow when the restaurant is full.

Oktogon Fusion Restaurant
☂ ♿   €€€

Leipziger Platz 10, 10117 **Tel** *206 428 64*   **Map** 6 E5

The cuisine and service here are on level with top, first-class restaurants, though the prices are still affordable. The menu reads like a trip around the world in just five courses: dim sum from China, *falafel* rolls from Turkey, exotic French quail with lentils from India, Scottish salmon filet in a Thai marinade.

Facil
P ☂ ♿   €€€€€

Potsdamer Strasse 3, 10785 **Tel** *590 051 234*   **Map** 6 D5

Germany's finest (and most affordable) Michelin-starred restaurant, Facil delights both food and interior design connoisseurs. A seven-course dinner with French and German dishes is a feast for the eye. The food is served in a sleek, elegant rooftop dining hall. In summer the restaurant front opens onto a small garden.

Hugo's
€€€€€

Budapesterstrasse 2, 10787 **Tel** *260 212 63*   **Map** 10 F1

This newly opened restaurant, in the Inter-Continental hotel, is one of the best in Berlin. Unusual French and international dishes are prepared with a German influence. The fish and seafood dishes are proof of the chef's real mastery. An attraction is the restaurant's rooftop location with great views. Reservations necessary.

Vox
P ☂ ♿ ♫   €€€€€

Marlene Dietrich Platz 2, 10785 **Tel** *255 312 34*   **Map** 6 D5

The Grand Hyatt's leading hotel-restaurant is undoubtedly one of the town's finest. The exquisite food is a sleek, modern fusion of Asian and international dishes, with an emphasis on Japanese (sushi) recipies and French-Italian creations. The show kitchen was one of the first in Berlin and is a major attraction. Reservations necessary.

KREUZBERG

Defne
☂ ♿   €

Planufer 92c, 10967 **Tel** *817 971 11*   **Map** 14 D3

This intimate place has been voted as Berlin's best Turkish restaurant, probably because it is different from the area's other Turkish eateries. It serves fresh, slightly modernized versions of traditional meat and fish dishes. The emphasis is on top-quality produce. In summer, the garden terrace with a view of the canal is very inviting.

Hasir
P ☂ ♿   €

Adalbertstrasse 10, 10999 **Tel** *614 23 73*   **Map** 14 E2

One of the city's oldest and most traditional Turkish restaurants, now part of a chain by the same name, this is where it all started.The Hasir offers one the most extensive Turkish-Arabian menus to be found in town. Apart from the various traditional *kebab* dishes, the soups are exceptionally good.

E.T.A. Hoffmann
☂ ♿   €€

Yorckstrasse 83, 10965 **Tel** *780 988 09*   **Map** 12 F4

Once a leading newcomer on Berlin's gourmet scene, this restaurant has re-opened with a new chef. Young Thomas Kurt reinvents German cuisine with fresh produce and international touches. Light fish dishes accented with carefully composed sauces and veggies, are signature dishes in summer; more hearty German fare can be enjoyed in winter.

Osteria No. 1
€€

Kreuzbergstraße 71, 10965 **Tel** *786 91 62*
Map *12 E4*

This Osteria was one of the first in Berlin and thus quickly gained its reputation as the hippest Italian restaurant in town. Those days are gone, but patrons can still enjoy the well-prepared, brick-oven pizzas. Main dishes such as rabbit or lamb are particularly good as are the fresh salads and exquisite pasta creations.

Parlamento
€€

Bergmannstrasse 3, 10961 **Tel** *694 77 45*
Map *12 F4*

Delicious Mediterranean dishes that taste home-made and an informal atmosphere enable this place to compete easily with other restaurants in this area. Typical dishes include *Stroh und Heu*, a combination of pasta with poultry in tomato sauce, or rolled veal, filled with ricotta cheese and spinach in a sage sauce.

Sale E Tabacchi
🅿 🔆
€€€

Kochstrasse 18, 10969 **Tel** *252 11 55*
Map *13 A1*

The Sale E Tabacchi offers reliable Italian food (but almost never pizza) in a dark, cosy Kreuzberg interior. In summer, the courtyard is the preferred dining area, mostly frequented by politicians and journalists from the neighbouring newspaper companies. For lunch, try one of the inexpensive three-course meals.

Altes Zollhaus
€€€€

Carl-Herz-Ufer 30, 10961 **Tel** *692 33 00*
Map *13 B3*

This restaurant is situated on the picturesque bank of the Landwehrkanal in what used to be a border control point. Excellent gourmet-style German food is served here without the usual heavy sauces. Dishes based on wild mushrooms, when in season, are delicious.

AROUND KURFÜRSTENDAMM

Ali Baba
🔆 ♿
€

Bleibtreustrasse 45, 10623 **Tel** *881 13 50*
Map *9 B1*

A long-time favourite among Berlin's students, the small, budget Italian pizzeria is open until the wee hours of the morning, mostly serving two different kinds of pizza by the slice – cheese or salami. These and all other freshly-baked stone-oven pizzas are simply delicious and affordable. No reservations.

Marché
€

Kurfürstendamm 14, 10719 **Tel** *882 75 78*
Map *10 D1*

A self-service restaurant under the Mövenpick umbrella, Marché caters for the many tourists visiting Kaiser-Wilhelm-Gedächtniskirche. Choose from meat, poultry and fish dishes, plenty of desserts, beer and wine. All food is freshly prepared at market-like stalls. The nicer tables are upstairs.

XII Apostel
€

Bleibtreustrasse 49, 10623 **Tel** *312 14 33*
Map *9 B1*

The Italian food served is available nearly 24 hours, but this place is always busy. The menu includes all types of pastas and pizza creations fresh from a stone oven. Choose between a cosy dining room and dining tent or, in summer, outside in a picturesque alley. Reservations for dinner strongly advised.

Borriquito
🔆 ♿ 🎵
€€

Wielandstrasse 6, 10625 **Tel** *312 99 29*
Map *9 B1*

A small dining room stuffed with Iberian memorabilia and an authentic staff make this a charming place. Seafood and meat dishes are very good here; the best is probably the lamb, served with a home-made sauce. Almost every night, a guitar player gives a soulful recital. In summer, tables are put out on the street.

Café Einstein
🔆
€€

Kurfürstenstrasse 58, 10785 **Tel** *261 50 96*
Map *11 A1*

This Berlin landmark is located in an elegant villa once owned by a German movie star. The old-fashioned waiters are dressed in black suits and bow-ties, while the fine Viennese food has fin-de-siècle Austrian charm. All the traditional dishes are good, but *Wiener Schnitzel* and *Gulasch* are exceptional.

Good Friends
🔆
€€

Kantstrasse 153, 10623 **Tel** *313 26 59*
Map *9 B1*

Packed for dinner each night, a mixed crowd of tourists, students and other locals relish the authentic Cantonese and other Oriental delicacies at Good Friends. The interior is somewhat tacky, the service not particularly friendly, and the noise is too loud. But the food is worth it.

Hamlet
€€

Uhlandstrasse 47, 10719 **Tel** *882 13 61*
Map *9 C3*

Don't be misled by the name – the menu offers mainly French and a few Oriental dishes, but nothing English or Danish. Specialities include couscous dishes, fresh salads, lamb curry and rump steak. The stylish Hamlet, mostly frequented by locals from the neighbourhood, always welcomes its guests with a cheerful, friendly atmosphere.

Key to Price Guide *see p236* **Key to Symbols** *see back cover flap*

Leibniz-Klause

Leibnizstrasse 46, 10629 **Tel** *323 70 68*

Map 6 D5

One of the few good restaurants that exclusively serve Berlin dishes, this is a traditional German neighbourhood restaurant where you still get large portions for your money. *Eisbein, Berliner Leber, Havelzander, Wurst,* and *Sauerbraten,* served along with red or green cabbage or *Sauerkraut,* are always on the menu.

Lubitsch

Bleibtreustrasse 47, 10623 **Tel** *882 37 56*

Map 9 B1

This popular restaurant is in one of the liveliest streets around Savignyplatz. A wide variety of German and international dishes is on the menu, with very reasonable prices at lunchtime. For dinner, try one of their two- or three-course meals – one of the best deals in town.

Moon Thai

Knesebeckstrasse 15, 10625 **Tel** *312 90 42*

Map 3 C5

Many tourists walk by this small but friendly Thai restaurant, leaving the tables to the local mix of students, artists and other typical Charlottenburg bohemians. They all indulge in the fabulous, hot Thai red or green curries, spicy appetizers and cherish the attentive, quiet service.

Bovril

Kurfürstendamm 184, 10719 **Tel** *881 84 61*

Map 9 B2

A popular bistro, although a bit elitist. During lunchtime, it's usually visited by people working around the Ku'damm. Good, light food influenced by German cuisine. On summer nights, the four tables on the tiny terrace are one of the most pleasant "people-watching" spots.

Cassambalis Taverna

Grolmanstrasse 35, 10623 **Tel** *885 47 47*

Map 9 C1

The Cassambalis exudes the flair of an upscale Greek tavern with a big, open buffet table dominating the dining room. Apart from Greek and Turkish delicacies, it also serves Italian fare, such as freshly-made pasta, various kinds of fish and all kinds of salads and beef dishes.

Florian

Grolmannstrasse 52, 10623 **Tel** *313 91 84*

Map 3 C5

The daily specials in this restaurant, frequented by filmmakers and actors, vary with the seasons. The best dishes are created during the asparagus and wild mushroom seasons. Also on offer is a wide selection of wines. Reservations required.

Kashmir Palace

Marburger Strasse 14, 10789 **Tel** *214 28 40*

Map 10 E1

This superb Indian restaurant prepares authentic, but not overly spicy, dishes based on ancient royal recipes. The chef only uses fresh produce and rare spices, often imported directly from India. Among the top-rated dishes are tandoori creations fresh from from the earthenware oven.

Kuchi

Kantstrasse 30, 10623 **Tel** *315 078 15*

Map 9 B1

Kuchi, one of the best-value Japanese restaurants in Berlin, offers excellent sushi and regional dishes. A simple, unpretentious Asian interior and a welcoming service make it the ideal venue for a dinner for two. The dim sum rotation and the sampler are particularly tasty. Reservations advised.

Ottenthal

Kantstrasse 153, 10623 **Tel** *313 31 62*

Map 10 D1

The simple interior is adorned by a clock from the Ottenthal Church in Austria and the background music is mainly Mozart. Fine Austrian cuisine and heavenly desserts are served with a fantastic wine list with more than 150 vintages from the Alps. Reservations required.

Paris Bar

Kantstrasse 152, 10623 **Tel** *313 80 52*

Map 9 C1

This is an exclusive bistro frequented by artists and politicians. Fairly expensive, and the food is good – particularly meat dishes such as blood sausage with potatoes *(Blutwurst mit Kartoffeln)* are recommended. Book ahead. If don't get your table on time, have a drink at the neighbouring Le bar du Paris Bar.

Bacco

Marburger Strasse 5, 10789 **Tel** *211 86 87*

Map 10 E1

An intimate restaurant, with a modern interior and marvellous food from Tuscany. This a more quiet and relaxed version of the now famous, upscale Bocca di Bacco in Mitte. Prices are fairly high and the portions are small, but the quality makes it worthwhile.

Die Quadriga

Eislebener Strasse 14, 10789 **Tel** *214 050*

Map 10 E1

Hotel Brandenburger Hof's most obvious attraction is this gourmet restaurant, one of Berlin's best. This cosy establishment serves unusual French dishes accompanied by perfect service. Chef Bobby Bräuer loves fresh produce from France and carefully re-invents traditional and international dishes. Book ahead.

First Floor €€€€€
Budapester Strasse 45, 10787 **Tel** *250 210 20*   ***Map** 10 E1*

An elegant restaurant of the highest-quality German cuisine, run by Berlin star chef Matthias Buchholz. The Michelin-starred restaurant offers traditional food as well as unrivalled creations with fish, crayfish and truffles. The menu changes according to season, and at times the dishes can be quite heavy. Book in advance.

AROUND SCHLOSS CHARLOTTENBURG

Angkor €€
Seelingstrasse 34-36, 14059 **Tel** *325 59 94*   ***Map** 2 E4*

A striking restaurant with a gaudy interior that used to be an insider's secret. The menu offers aromatic dishes that often include an array of delicate spices and coconut milk, typical of Cambodian cuisine. It integrates recipes from Vietnam, Thailand and other Asian countries. The service is friendly and forthcoming.

Hitit €€
Knobelsdorffstrasse 35, 14059 **Tel** *322 45 57*   ***Map** 2 D4*

The extravagant, but minimalist dining room is adorned with modern sculptures inspired by Turkish art. For lovers of *kofta* and *kebab*, the Hitit is a true paradise. In fact, all of the 90-plus dishes on the menu, particularly the barbecue fare with various sauces, are delicious. A good selection of Turkish wines available.

Le Piaf 🚶♿🎵 €€
Schlossstrasse 60, 14059 **Tel** *342 20 40*   ***Map** 2 E3*

A small French restaurant-cum-bistro, typical for this kind of well-to-do neighbourhood. The down-to-earth cooking is a fine mixture of Alsatian and traditional French recipes, presented by the very personal and friendly staff or owner, Mr. Claude Trendel. In summer, there is a nice, leafy beer garden right in front of the restaurant.

Ana e Bruno €€€€€
Sophie-Charlotten-Strasse 101, 14059 **Tel** *325 71 10*   ***Map** 2 D3*

One of the best Italian restaurants in Berlin. An elegant interior creates the perfect atmosphere to sample the magnificent creations prepared by the chef. Everything is delicious, including the roasted sturgeon in Mediterranean sauce. Menus given to women omit prices, but provide a calorie count for each dish.

GREATER BERLIN

Schöneberg: Mutter 🚶♿ €
Hohenstaufenstrasse 4, 10781 **Tel** *216 49 90*   ***Map** 11 A3*

True to its name, Mutter (German for "mother") serves generous portions to its patrons, mostly students. A fixture of the bustling Winterfeldplatz nightlife scene, it offers cool Caribbean drinks and an eclectic mix of some traditional German, Italian and Asian dishes, with an emphasis on sushi and Thai food.

Zehlendorf: Blockhaus Nikolskoe €€
Nikolskoer Weg 15, 14109 **Tel** *805 29 14*

This restaurant is an old *dacha* (Russian-style log cabin) built by Prussian king Friedrich Wilhelm III for his daughter who married Tsar Nicholas I. The terrace has views on the lake. Fresh game and fish dishes are particularly recommended. The menu also offers German dishes and tasty cakes.

Prenzlauerberg: Mao Thai €€
Wörtherstrasse 30, 10405 **Tel** *441 92 61*

This is one of Berlin's best Thai restaurants, with an interior filled with beautiful antiques. The menu offers a full range of aromatic dishes, toned down to suit European tastes. Fresh and top-quality vegetables, carved into creative forms, are a speciality here. Reservations for dinner strongly advised.

Grunewald: Merhaba 🎵 €€
Wissmannstrasse 32, 12049 **Tel** *692 17 13*

People from all over Berlin come to this charming restaurant to join the local Turks and Germans who enjoy the food served here. Even if you are not particularly hungry, you will not be able to resist the various appetizers. There is outdoor dining in summer and belly dancing on Fridays and Saturdays.

Schöneberg: Pranza e Cena €€
Goltzstraße 32, 10781 **Tel** *217 35 14*   ***Map** 11 A3*

This neighbourhood Italian pizzeria, set in a simple but cosy old-style Berlin pub, is a trendy hangout for the Schöneberg scene. The selection of freshly-made pasta is impressive. Try *Tris di Pasta*, a combination of three pasta dishes. There is a standard wine selection of German and Italian vintages. Reservations are a must.

Prenzlauerberg: Restauration 1900

Husemannstrasse 1, 10435 **Tel** *442 24 94*

One of the oldest and most traditional in this part of Berlin, this restaurant welcomes its guests into a simple dining room with a outstanding historic bar counter and other antiques. It offers light cuisine with some dishes of German origin and a large selection for vegetarians. The terrace looks over to Husemannstrasse.

Zehlendorf: Waldhaus

Onkel-Tom-Strasse 50, 14169 **Tel** *813 75 75*

Set in leafy surroundings, the Waldhaus is a lovely place to spend an evening enjoying the barbecue, a speciality it is famous for. Pork, beef and fish are grilled on charcoal to order. In winter, the menu offers mostly German dishes, such as duck, goose and venison. The meat comes fresh from Berlin's state forests.

Zehlendorf: Wirtshaus Moorlake

Moorlakeweg 1, 14109 **Tel** *805 58 09*

Situated on the secluded bank of the Havel river, this historic restaurant serves German dishes. Though it is worth trying all the game dishes on its menu, the most highly recommended are game ragout with cranberries and buttered *spaetzle*, and the barbecue sampler, *Moorlake* with pork filets and sauce Bearnaise.

Wilmersdorf: Bieberbau

Durlacherstrasse 15, 10715 **Tel** *853 23 90*

Partner chefs Max Stoll and Stephan Garkisch turned this legendary nightspot into a brilliant gourmet newcomer. Lovers of Berlin food will find a typical dish like *Eisbein* or *Berliner Leber*, creatively served with a salad and Pommery potatoes (instead of *Sauerkraut* and mashed split peas). Reservations advised.

Grunewald: Diekmann im Chalet Suisse

Clayallee 99, 14195 **Tel** *832 63 62*

Occupying a picturesque wooden building, this is a perfect place for a rest after walking in the Grunewald forest. Now run by the Diekmann restaurant chain, it offers an impeccable service. The menu has become more imaginative. There is a large selection of Swiss and German dishes. Serves a *Crème brulée* to die for.

Grunewald: Forsthaus Paulsborn

Hüttenweg 90, 14195 **Tel** *818 19 10*

This excellent restaurant is on the ground floor of a former hunting palace – now used as a lodge – located deep in the forest. In summer, the Forsthaus extends into the garden. The food is magnificent. On weekends, it also has a great brunch buffet. Home-made cakes and pastries are served every afternoon.

Grunewald: Grunewaldturm

Havelchaussee 61, 14193 **Tel** *300 07 30*

Combining a meal in this restaurant with a trip to Grunewald forest is a fine way to spend an afternoon. The menu mostly offers game or hearty meat dishes but also serves some local fish such as perch. Lunch or supper with wonderful views is an ideal end for this kind of outing.

Wedding: Maxwell

Bergstrasse 22, 10115 **Tel** *280 71 21*

This highly regarded, upmarket, but very well-known, restaurant offers exquisite Berlin and German food with Mediterranean influences. The Maxwell always guarantees a laid-back and unpretentious atmosphere with a friendly, helpful service. There is a cheaper menu for lunch but only a few affordable wines.

Prenzlauerberg: Pasternak

Knaackstrasse 22-24, 10405 **Tel** *441 33 99*

Comfortable armchairs, sofas, and food from St. Petersburg can be found here. A mixed clientele of Russian expats and German students and artists come here for the joyous atmosphere and tasty but heavy food. Specialities include: beetroot soup *(borscht)*, *blinis* and *beef stroganov*. Vodka and caviar are available for brunch.

Johannisthal: Spree-Athen

Leibnizstrasse 60, 10629 **Tel** *324 17 33*   **Map** *9 B1*

This is an excellent place to try typical Berlin dishes as the old-fashioned interior, service and food make this the quintessential Berlin restaurant and pub. The menu changes daily but always includes traditional fare, such as pork knuckles with *Sauerkraut* and mashed split peas.

Zehlendorf: Remise im Schloss Klein-Glienicke

Königstrasse 36 (Klein-Glienicke), 14109 **Tel** *805 40 00*

This is an ideal place for an elegant meal on the outskirts of Berlin. Now run by Franz Raneburger, one of Berlin's most prominent chefs, the restaurant offers excellent German cuisine, with perch, crayfish and game, all prepared with a dose of imagination. The restaurant is also a good choice for lunch.

Grunewald: Vivaldi

Brahmsstrasse 10, 14193 **Tel** *895 845 20*

A luxurious restaurant in the expensive Schlosshotel. The interior, designed by Karl Lagerfeld, features panelled walls, gold leaf and chandeliers. Due to the many changes in hotel management, the restaurant has lost its gourmet standard, but still makes for a pleasant evening with exquisite French food. Book ahead.

Light Meals and Snacks

There are many popular fast-food bars and restaurants in Berlin that serve the all-pervading burgers, French fries and pizzas, some of them run by well-known international chains. By way of contrast, many of the self-service places specialize in local foods. The city's cafés are ideal stopping places for a quick meal and always offer something on the menu that will fill you up. Even more convenient are the many bars on wheels or small kiosks – *Imbissbuden* – that serve the traditional Berlin *Currywurst (see p233)*.

IMBISSBUDEN AND SNACK BARS

The classic *Imbissbude* is a simple little kiosk selling drinks and a few light snacks, such as *Currywurst* or French fries *(Pommes)* served with mayonnaise or ketchup (or both). The former is a genuine Berlin speciality consisting of grilled, sliced sausage *(Bratwurst)*, topped with a spicy sauce, and served on a paper plate with a plastic fork. These kiosks are usually located in convenient sites near the S-Bahn or U-Bahn stations, or on busy streets and junctions. **Ku'damm 195**, **Amtsgerichtsplatz** and **Konnopke** are considered the best places to experience traditional *Currywurst*, which is served with home-made spicy sauce instead of the now standard tomato ketchup sprinkled with curry powder and fiery paprika.

Other popular snacks sold on the streets include various grilled sausages, collectively referred to as *Bratwurst*. The most common types are frankfurters *(Wienerwurst)* and a thicker kind of sausage known as *Bockwurst*. These are heated in hot water. The German variation on the hamburger theme is called *Boulette*. Unfortunately there are few places similar to the *Imbissbude* that offer visitors the chance to try food from other regions of Germany. One of the exceptions is **Weizmann**, which can be found in an arcade under the S-Bahn railway bridge near Bellevue station. Short, thick noodles called *Spätzle* feature in many dishes on its typically southern German menu.

SPECIALITIES FROM AROUND THE WORLD

Traditional Berlin specialities are facing stiff competition from further afield. Turkish restaurants serving excellent *Döner Kebab* are on every corner. Typically a kebab is a piece of warmed flat *pitta* bread stuffed with hot sliced meat, lettuce, cucumber, and tomatoes, and covered with a thick, aromatic, yogurt-based sauce. Obviously the best kebabs are made by the Turks living around Kreuzberg, but you can also have an excellent version of this dish in most of the other Berlin districts. The restaurants worth trying are **Kebab** or indeed any of the places around Kottbuser Tor or Oranienstrasse.

Although Turkish cuisine does have a reputation for not catering for vegetarians, **Kulinarische Delikatessen** goes some way to disprove this by offering many delicious kinds of vegetarian kebabs.

Also suitable for vegetarians are *falafel*, a Middle Eastern speciality widely available in Berlin. Balls of chickpeas and coriander or parsley are rolled in breadcrumbs and deep fried, then served stuffed inside flat bread with salad and yogurt sauce. The best places to try this excellent snack are around Winterfeldt-platz, for example, **Habibi**, **Dada Falafel** and **Baharat Falafel**, or **Hasir** in the eastern part of the city.

Fragrant Thai dishes are offered by **Fish & Vegetables** in Goltzstrasse, while those with a passion for Chinese food should eat at **Pagode** in Kreuzberg on Bergmann-strasse. If you wish to try

Korean cuisine, then go to **Kwang-Ju-Grill**, where the variety of dishes is quite over-whelming, or to **Korea-Haus**. A visit to **Vietnam Imbiss** is a good opportunity to try out some Vietnamese specialities, and if you fancy genuine Mexican tacos and burritos, visit **Viva Mexico!** which is managed by a Mexican family. There are also many restaurants offering Indian food, mainly along Grolmanstrasse. Nearby, in Wielandstrasse, the Italian **Briganti** deserves a special recommendation.

Berlin's Japanese restaurants tend to be of the more exclusive type but still offer excellent soups and sushi. The best are **Sushi Bar Ishin**, **Cat Food sushi bar**, **Sushi-Bar**, **FUKU Sushi** and **Musashi**.

LIGHT SNACKS

Those with an appetite for more traditional snacks are easily catered for in the establishments around S- and U-Bahn stations and along the main streets offering fresh baguettes filled with ham or cheese.

For an instant solution to hunger pangs, try one of the bakeries that offer delicious freshly baked croissants or excellent *Brezeln* (pretzels) covered with coarse salt. During lunchtime, the popular **Nordsee** chain of restaurants offers fish sandwiches to take away, as does the stylish **Syltgosch**. Some sandwich bars offer mouth-watering quiches and tarts alongside baguettes and rolls. If this is what you are looking for, it is worth visiting the snackbar **Fressco** in Kreuzberg.

If a traditional American-Jewish bagel bar is what you fancy, then **Bagels & Bialys** in Rosenthaler Strasse or **Salomon Luna Bagels** in Joachimstaler Strasse are the places to go, where the variety of fillings is quite staggering.

Some places also specialize in one particular kind of dish or food. For example **Soup-Kultur** serves only soup, but in a multitude of varieties – hot, cold, exotic, spicy or mild. Garlic lovers should visit **Knofel** in Prenzlauer Berg. **Diekmann im Weinhaus Huth** is an upscale bistro tucked away in the Weinhaus Huth, the only historic building still standing in the ultra-modern Potsdamer Platz. Also worth mentioning are **Deli 31** and **Deli Street**.

Another way to ensure a quick and inexpensive fill-up is to visit one of the self-service pizzerias such as **Piccola Italia**.

EATING IN SHOPPING CENTRES

One of the problems for the dedicated shopper is that eating can seriously cut down on shopping time. Fortunately, many snack bars in shopping centres have put the emphasis on fast service. Some, however, such as **KaDeWe** manage this in stylish surroundings. A visit to this enormous shop features on most tourists' list of things to do, and its self-service café is therefore very popular. Lunch at one of the tables with a view of Wittenbergplatz is a very pleasant adjunct to a Berlin shopping trip.

Another equally busy venue is the self-service café situated in the basement of the chic **Galeries Lafayette** in Friedrichstrasse. If you are visiting the boutiques of Quartier 205, it is also worth taking a refreshing break from the shopping for a quality cup of coffee or tea in **E33**.

For those reluctant shoppers who put more emphasis on the food, a new oasis of bars and cafés has opened near to Potsdamer Platz, in the **Arkaden** shopping centre. As well as a branch of Salomon Bagels, this centre provides a taste of the Orient in Asia Pavillon, while fans of potatoes should pay a visit to Pomme de Terre. Here, the humble potato becomes the star of the meal and is served in a myriad of guises and with just as many different fillings.

For short stops, both the dedicated and the reluctant shopper should visit the classic **Wiener Café** for coffee and cakes and the **Caffé e Gelato** for delicious ice cream.

CAFES

Berlin is well served by cafés that provide a wide range of light snacks or cakes to suit everyone's budget and tastes. They are normally open from 9 or 10 in the morning until late at night. In the mornings they serve breakfast, either à la carte or as a buffet. After that the regular café menu comes into force, although breakfast items are often still available. Main meals on the menu might include several salads, several hearty soup-type stews *(Eintöpfe)* and a few simple hot dishes. Prices are quite reasonable, not greater than ten euros. Invariably, every café has a great choice of desserts, ice creams and cakes, as well as a range of alcoholic drinks.

Café Kranzler, a familiar landmark for many decades, has recently closed. Around the Technical University, **Café Hardenberg** is popular with students, and near Kantstrasse you can visit **Schwarzes Café**, which is open 24 hours a day. If you are on Savignyplatz you might want to try **Café Aedes**, which has two good branches, one by the architecture gallery and the other in the second courtyard of Hackesche Höfe in Mitte. **Café am Neuen See** is situated near the lake in the Tiergarten Park. **Patisserie Buchwald**, in Hansaviertel, offers a wide range of *Baumkuchen* (so-called "tree cakes" that resemble tree stumps).

Other renowned cafés include the charming **Café Wintergarten**, located in the Literaturhaus on Fasanenstrasse, and the Viennese-style **Café Einstein**. Here you can enjoy coffee made with beans fresh from their own roasting room. The original café, in Kurfürstenstrasse, has been joined by another branch in Mitte, on Unter den Linden, whose delicious cakes are in welcome competition with those of the nearby **Opernpalais** *(see p259)*.

If you prefer Hungarian cakes and desserts then you should pay a visit to **Café Zsolnay**. While taking a walk around Checkpoint Charlie, you could drop in to **Sale e Tabacchi**, where, along with an excellent Italian restaurant, you will find the equally admirable **Café Adler**.

There are many places that offer light lunches and coffee around Oranienburger Strasse and Alte and Neue Schönhauser Allees. In the evening they attract livelier crowds in search of decent music and good beer. You can stop by **Die Eins**, an atmospheric café, and the **Café Cinema**, which is decorated with film ephemera. If that is not to your taste, **Café Zucca** serves Italian cuisine.

An interesting evening can be spent investigating the options in Prenzlauer Berg. You can join the in-crowd at **Anita Wronski** then move on to **Tantalus**, which serves excellent pancakes. If you prefer a cosier environment, then **Chagall** is the place to visit, with its welcoming open fire and Russian ballads. During hot days a good spot to enjoy the sun is on the terrace in **November** or at **Seeblick**, which is a good place to eat.

Other reliable cafés that are well worth looking out for inlcude **Atlantic**, **Café Berio**, **Keyser Soze**, **Rathauscafé**, **Telecafé**, **Voltaire** and **Café Savigny**, where the menu changes daily.

COFFEE BARS AND TEA ROOMS

There are not many coffee bars in Berlin, but they are easily spotted as they tend to be run by well-known coffee producers such as Eduscho or Tschibo. **Barcomi's** is a real treat, an American-style coffee bar with its own roasting room and a large selection of coffees. If you need more sustenance than coffee and muffins, try **Barcomi's Deli** where you can build your own sandwiches.

If you want a good cup of tea, then you should go to **Tadschikische Teestube**, or **TTT (Tee, Tea, Thé)**, where the choice is quite amazing – but smokers beware, it has a no-smoking policy. **Mittendrin** also has a wide choice of teas.

DIRECTORY

IMBISSBUDEN AND SNACK BARS

Amtsgerichtsplatz
Kantstrasse/Suarezstrasse.
Map 2 E5. ☐ *11:30am–11pm Mon–Fri, 1pm–11pm Sat & Sun.* ◐ *Tue.*

Konnopke
Schönhauser Allee 44a
(U-Bahnhof Eberswalder Str).
Tel *442 77 65.*
☐ *6am–8pm Mon–Fri.*

Ku'damm 195
Kurfürstendamm 195.
Map 9 B2.
☐ *6pm–1am Mon–Fri, 5pm–7am Sat & Sun.*

Weizmann
Lüneburger Strasse 390.
Map 5 A3. **Tel** *394 20 57.*
☐ *11:30am–midnight Mon–Fri, 6am–midnight Sat.*

SPECIALITIES FROM AROUND THE WORLD

Baharat Falafel
Winterfeldstrasse 37.
Map 11 B3.
Tel *216 83 01.*
☐ *11am–2pm daily.*

Briganti
Wielandstrasse 15.
Map 9 B1. **Tel** *323 53 62.*
☐ *11am–8pm Tue–Fri, 10am–2pm Sat.*

Cat Food sushi bar
Körterstrasse 8.
Map 13 C4. **Tel** *693 02 27.*
☐ *6pm–midnight daily.*

Dada Falafel
Linienstrasse 132. **Map** 6 F1. **Tel** *27 59 69 27*
☐ *10am–2am Sun–Wed, 10am–4am Thu–Sat.*

Fish & Vegetables
Goltzstrasse 32. **Map** 11 A3. **Tel** *215 74 55.* ☐ *noon–midnight daily.*

FUKU Sushi
Rosenthaler Strasse 61.
Map 7 B1. **Tel** *28 38 77 83.* ☐ *noon–11pm Mon–Fri, 4–11pm Sat, Sun.*

Habibi
Goltzstrasse 24.
Map 11 A3. **Tel** *215 33 32.* ☐ *11am–3am Mon–Fri, 11am–5am Sat & Sun.*

Hasir
Oranienburger Strasse 4.
Map 7 B2. **Tel** *28 04 16 16.* ☐ *11:30am–1am daily.*

Kebab
Goltzstrasse 37a.
Map 11 A3, 11 A4.
☐ *10am–11pm daily.*

Korea-Haus
Danziger Strasse 195.
Tel *423 34 41.*
☐ *noon–11pm daily.*

Kulinarische Delikatessen
Oppelner Strasse 4.
Tel *618 67 58.*
☐ *11am–11pm daily.*

Kwang-Ju-Grill
Emser Strasse 24.
Map 9 B3. **Tel** *883 97 94.*
☐ *noon–midnight daily.*

Musashi
Kottbusser Damm 102.
Map 14 E3. **Tel** *693 20 42.* ☐ *noon–10:30pm Mon–Sat, 2–10pm Sun.*

Pagode
Bergmannstrasse 88.
Map 13 A4. **Tel** *691 26 40.*
☐ *noon–midnight daily.*

Sushi-Bar
Friedrichstrasse 115.
Map 6 F1. **Tel** *281 51 88.*
☐ *11am–11pm daily.*

Sushi Bar Ishin
Schlossstrasse 101.
Map 2 E4. **Tel** *797 10 49.*
☐ *11am–8pm Mon–Fri, 11am–6pm Sat.*

Sushi Imbiss
Pariser Strasse 44.
Map 9 B2. **Tel** *881 27 90.*
☐ *noon–midnight Mon–Sat, 4pm–midnight Sun.*

Vietnam Imbiss
Damaschkestrasse 30.
Tel *324 93 44.*
☐ *noon–9pm Mon–Fri, 9am–9pm Sat.*

Viva Mexico!
Chausseestrasse 36.
Map 6 F1. **Tel** *280 78 65.*
☐ *noon–11pm Mon–Fri, 5pm–midnight Sat, 5–11pm Sun.*

LIGHT SNACKS

Bagels & Bialys
Rosenthaler Strasse 46–48. **Map** 7 B2.
Tel *283 65 46.*
☐ *24 hours daily.*

Diekmann im Haus Huth
Alte Potsdamer Str. 5.
Map 6 D5. **Tel** *25 29 75 24.* ☐ *noon–1am daily.*

Deli 31
Bleibtreustrasse 31. **Map** 9 B2. **Tel** *88 47 46 02.*
☐ *8am–9pm Mon–Sat, 8am–8pm Sun.*

Deli Street
Chausseestrasse 4.
Map 6 F1. **Tel** *28 09 28 33.* ☐ *8:30am–5:30pm Mon–Fri.*

Fresco
Zossener Strasse 24.
Map 13 A4.
Tel *69 40 16 13.*
☐ *5:30pm–1am Tue–Sun.*

Knofel
Wichertstrasse 33.
Tel *447 67 17.*
☐ *6pm–late Mon–Thu, 2pm–late Fri, 1pm–late Sat–Sun.*

Nordsee
Spandauer Strasse 4.
Map 7 C3, 16 F2.
Tel *24 26 881.*
☐ *10am–8pm daily.*

Piccola Italia
Oranienburger Strasse 6.
Map 7 B2. **Tel** *283 58 43.*
☐ *11am–1am Mon–Thu, 11am–3am Fri–Sun.*

Salomon Luna Bagels
Joachimstaler Strasse 13.
Map 10 D2. **Tel** *8870 26 17.* ☐ *8:30am–8pm Mon–Fri, 10am–6pm Sat.*

Soup-Kultur
Kurfürstendamm 224.
Map 10 D1. **Tel** *88 62 92 82.* ☐ *noon–7pm Mon–Fri, noon–6pm Sat.*

EATING IN SHOPPING CENTRES

E33
Friedrichstadtpassage,
Friedrichstrasse 67.
Map 6 F4, 15 C4.
Tel *20 94 50 20.*
☐ *8am–8pm daily.*

Galeries Lafayette
Französische Strasse 23.
Map 6 F4, 15 C3.
Tel *20 94 80.*
☐ *9:30am–8pm Mon–Fri, 9am–4pm Sat.*

KaDeWe
Tauentzienstrasse 21–24.
Map 10 E1. ☐ *9am–8pm Mon–Fri, 9am–4pm Sat.*

Potsdamer Platz Arkaden
Alte Potsdamer Strasse 7.
Map 6 D5.
☐ *9:30am–8pm Mon–Fri, 9am–4pm Sat.*

Wertheim
Kurfürstendamm 231.
Map 10 D1. **Tel** *880 030.*
☐ *9:30am–8pm Mon–Fri, 9am–8pm Sat.*

CAFES

Anita Wronski
Knaackstrasse 26–28.
Tel *442 84 83.*
☐ *9am–2am Mon–Sat, 10am–2am Sun.*

Atlantic
Bergmannstrasse 100.
Map 12 F4. **Tel** *691 92 92.* ☐ *9am–2am daily.*

Buchwald
Bartningallee 29.
Map 4 F2. **Tel** *391 59 31.*
☐ *9am–6pm Mon–Sat, 10am–6pm Sun.*

Café Adler
Friedrichstrasse 206.
Tel *251 89 65.*
☐ *10am–midnight Mon–Sat, 10am–7pm Sun.*

Café Aedes
Savignyplatz (arcade under the S-Bahn bridge).
Map 9 C1.
Tel 31 50 95 35.
☐ *8am–10pm Mon–Fri, 9am–10pm Sat & Sun.*

Rosenthaler Strasse 40–41 (Hackesche Höfe, second courtyard).
Map 7 B2.
Tel 28 58 275.
☐ *11am–midnight daily.*

Café am Neuen See
Lichtensteinallee 1.
Map 4 F5. *Tel 254 49 30.*
☐ *May–Sep: 10am–midnight daily; Oct–Apr: 10am–11pm Mon–Fri, 10am–8pm Sat–Sun.*

Café Ständige Vertretung
Schiffbauerdamm 8.
Tel 282 39 65.
☐ *10am–1am daily.*

Café Berio
Maassenstrasse 7.
Map 11 A2. *Tel 216 19 46.* ☐ *8am–1am daily.*

Café Cinema
Rosenthaler Strasse 39.
Map 7 B2. *Tel 280 64 15.*
☐ *noon–2am daily.*

Café Einstein
Kurfürstenstrasse 58.
Map 11 A2.
Tel 261 50 96.
☐ *9am–2am daily.*

Unter den Linden 42.
Map 6 F3, 15 C3.
Tel 204 36 32.
☐ *7am–1am daily.*

Café Ephraim's
Spreeufer 1. **Map** 7 C4.
Tel 24 72 59 47.
☐ *noon–10pm daily.*

Café Hardenberg
Hardenbergstrasse 10.
Map 3 C5.
Tel 312 26 44.
☐ *9am–1am daily.*

Café Lebensart
Unter den Linden 69–73.
Map 6 E3, 15 B3.
Tel 229 00 18.
☐ *8am–9pm Mon–Fri, 10am–midnight Sat & Sun.*

Café Möhring
Charlottenstrasse 55.
Map 7 A4.
Tel 20 30 92 240.
☐ *8am–midnight daily.*

Café Savigny
Grolmanstrasse 51.
Map 3 C5, 9 C1.
Tel 312 81 95.
☐ *9am–1am daily.*

Café Tomasa
Motzstrasse 60.
Map 10 F3. *Tel 21 32 345.* ☐ *8am–1am Mon–Thu, 8am–2am Fri & Sat, 9am–1am Sun.*

Café Wintergarten im Literaturhaus
Fasanenstrasse 23.
Map 10 D1.
Tel 882 54 14.
☐ *9:30am–1am daily.*

Café Zsolnay
Karl-Liebknecht-Strasse 9.
Map 7 C2. *Tel 241 57 15.*
☐ *2–10pm daily.*

Café Zucca
Am Zwirngraben 11–12 (in the S-Bahn arcade).
Tel 24 72 12 12.
☐ *9am–3am daily.*

Catherine's
Im Dussmann-Haus, Friedrichstrasse 90.
Map 6 F3.
Tel 20 25 15 55.
☐ *11am–10pm Mon–Sat.*

Chagall
Kollwitzstrasse 2.
Tel 441 58 81.
☐ *11am–late daily.*

Die Eins
Wilhelmstrasse 67A (eingang Reichstagsufer).
Map 6 E3.
Tel 22 48 98 88.
☐ *9am–midnight Mon–Sat, 10am–midnight Sun.*

Eckstein
Pappelallee 73.
Tel 441 99 60.
☐ *9am–1am daily.*

Filmbühne am Steinplatz
Hardenbergstrasse 12.
Map 4 D5.
Tel 312 65 89.
☐ *9am–1am daily.*

Kaffeestube am Nikolaiplatz
Poststrasse 19.
Map 7 C3.
Tel 242 71 20.
☐ *9am–midnight daily.*

Keyser Soze
Tucholskystrasse 33.
Map 7 A1.
Tel 28 59 94 89.
☐ *8am–3am daily.*

Kleine Orangerie
Spandauer Damm 20.
Map 2 E3.
Tel 322 20 21.
☐ *9am–9pm daily (10am–8pm in winter).*

November
Husemannstrasse 15.
Tel 442 84 25.
☐ *10am–2am Mon–Fri, 9am–2am Sat & Sun.*

Operncafé
Unter den Linden 5.
Map 7 A3, 16 E3.
Tel 20 26 83.
☐ *8am–midnight daily.*

Sale e Tabacchi
Kochstrasse 18.
Tel 252 11 55.
☐ *9am–2am Mon–Fri, 10am–2am Sat & Sun.*

Schwarzes Café
Kantstrasse 148.
Map 9 C1.
Tel 313 80 38.
☐ *24 hours daily.*

Seeblick
Rykestrasse 14.
Tel 442 92 26.
☐ *8am–2am daily.*

Syltgosch
Kurfürstendamm 212.
Map 9 C2.
Tel 88 68 28 00.
☐ *11am–midnight Mon–Sat.*

Telecafé
Alexanderplatz (TV Tower).
Map 8 D2.
Tel 242 33 33.
☐ *10am–midnight daily.*

Voltaire
Stuttgarter Platz 14.
Tel 324 50 28.
☐ *24 hours daily.*

COFFEE BARS AND TEA ROOMS

Balzac Coffee
Hardenbergstrasse 4–5
Map 3 C5. Friedrichstrasse 194. **Map** 15 C4 & 6 F4.
☐ *7:30am–8pm Mon–Fri, 7:30am–6pm Sun.*

Barcomi's
Bergmannstrasse 21.
Map 13 A5.
Tel 694 81 38.
☐ *8am–9pm Mon– Thu, 8am–10pm Fri, 9am–10pm Sat, 10am–9pm Sun.*

Barcomi's Deli
Sophienstrasse 21 (second courtyard).
Map 7 B1. **Tel** *28 59 83 63.* ☐ *9am–10pm Mon–Sat, 10am–10pm Sun.*

Cafezeit
Kurfürstendamm 200
Map 9 C2. **Tel** *88 25 814.*
☐ *8am–midnight Mon–Sat, 9am–10pm Sun.*

Einstein Coffeeshop
Friedrichstrasse 190 & 168. **Map** 15 C4 & 6 F4. Savignyplatz 5. **Map** 9 C1.
☐ *10am–late daily.*

Mittendrin
Sophienstrasse 19.
Map 7 B1. **Tel** *28 49 77 40.* ☐ *noon–11pm Mon–Thu, noon–1am Fri & Sat, 2–8pm Sun.*

Tadschikische Teestube
Am Festungsgraben 1.
Map 7 A3, 16 E2.
Tel 204 11 12.
☐ *5pm–midnight Mon–Fri, 2pm–midnight Sat & Sun.*

TTT – Tee, Tea, Thé
Goltzstrasse 2. **Map** 11 A4. *Tel 21 75 22 40.*
☐ *9am–midnight Mon–Sat, 10am–midnight Sun.*

Bars and Wine Bars

Trying to make a clear distinction between wine bars, bars, pubs and *Bierstuben* or giving a precise definition for the word *Kneipe* is practically impossible. However, regardless of the nuances behind all these names, they do share some basic characteristics: they are places where drinking is the primary activity, although eating is sometimes possible; they are usually open from late afternoon or early evening but do not close till late at night or even till morning, if the atmosphere is lively.

KNEIPEN

In general terms, a *Kneipe* means a cosy sort of place which serves beer (although other drinks are available, too) and where you can have something to eat. The typical *Alberliner Kneipe* is a dark room with panelled oak walls, a big bar and buffet with snacks such as *Buletten* (made from pork), *Soleier* (pickled eggs), *Rollmöpse* (marinated herring) and a selection of cold meats, black pudding (blood sausage) and patés. This kind of traditional pub can still be found in the less affluent districts of Berlin – in Moabit, Kreuz-berg and in Prenzlauer Berg, for example, but they are not as common in the city centre. Among the most popular are **Zur Kneipe** and **Ranke 2**, as well as several *Kneipen* in Mitte around the Nikolaiviertel, including **Zum Nussbaum**.

Each *Kneipe* has its own character. More and more of them are choosing modern and inventive interiors, often specializing in less traditional kinds of food: Italian, French or Oriental. Whatever the blend, however, a relaxed atmosphere and a big choice of alcoholic beverages seem to be common features. Many *Kneipen* are evolving into a fashionable mix of *Kneipe*, bar, lounge and beer garden. One such is **Reingold** in Mitte. In Savignyplatz, you might want to visit **Dicke Wirtin**, where you can try a hearty *Eintopf* (a rich soup-type stew). The majority of these fashion-able places are situated in Kreuzberg and in Prenzlauer Berg – especially around Kollwitzplatz, which is dotted with all sorts of bars and pubs. At **Ankerklause** students and political activists come together to drink, dance and put the world to rights.

BIERGARTEN

A *Biergarten* is an outdoor venue only open during the summer months, and usually located somewhere scenic, maybe in a park or by a lake. In addition to the usual food and drinks, it completes the outdoor experience with a barbecue. **Golgatha** and **Schleusenkrug** provide a much welcome breath of fresh air in the centre of Berlin; or if you are exploring Prenzlauer Berg, try the **Prater**. After enjoying the views or, for the more active, the water sports at Wannsee, the **Loretta am Wannsee** is a pleasant place to end the day.

A new Berlin trend is the open-air beach bar situated on one of the city's waterways, the most popular of these being **Bundespressestrand**.

WINE BARS

Berlin wine bars tend to have a Mediterranean feel to them. Interiors are often quite rustic in style, but there are exceptions. They open from early evening and stay open late. As for food, menus feature predominantly Italian, Spanish and French cuisine, while the bar serves a huge selection of wines by the glass, bottle or carafe. **Le Bar du Paris Bar** – a wine bar with an established reputation, features French food and wine, as does **Il Calice**. If you are visiting Prenzlauer Berg you might want to try **Weinstein** which offers French and Spanish food and wine. By way of contrast, at **Lutter & Wegener** in Mitte you can match German-Austrian food with appropriate, native wines, or sample a selection of American snacks and cocktails at **Billy Wilder's**.

BARS

A Berlin bar is a good place to finish your evening, and the dedicated barfly is spoiled for choice. You should not count on food but you can drink till late, as most bars do not open until 8pm or later. Although there is no strict dress code, scruffy clothes are not really appropriate. The **Riva Bar**, one of the city's most elegant and hip bars, is tucked away under the S-Bahn viaduct, and serves some of the best cocktails in town. A Latin American atmosphere is created at **Roter Salon** by tango, salsa and all the fantastic dancers. You might step in to **Vox Bar** to try one of its huge range of cocktails in a pre-war movie setting. Don't forget to visit some of the hotel bars which are among the best late-night venues in the city. Two worthy of mention are **Harry's New York Bar** (the later the better), in the Hotel Esplanade and the **Newton Bar**.

GAY AND LESBIAN BARS

Berlin has a unique tradition of nightlife for homosexuals, dating back to the 1920s, when its cabarets and bars, especially around Nollendorfplatz, were the most outrageous in Europe. Today that hardcore legacy remains, but there are also bars to suit every taste. Some, like **Café Seidenfaden**, are for women only, while **Roses** is exclusively for men. Many, like **Die Busche**, are frequented by both gays and lesbians. For a more mixed ambiance, the friendly attitude of bars such as **Lenz** or **So 36** means they are popular with both gay and straight visitors alike.

DIRECTORY

KNEIPEN

Ankerklause
Maybachufer 1.
Map 14 E3.
Tel 693 56 49.

Dicke Wirtin
Carmerstrasse 9.
Map 3 C5.
Tel 312 49 52.

Diener Tattersall
Grolmanstrasse 47.
Map 9 C1.
Tel 881 53 29.

Gerichtslaube mit Bierschenke und Ratsherren-Stube
Poststrasse 28.
Map 7 C3.
Tel 241 56 97.

Meilenstein
Oranienburger Strasse 7.
Map 7 B2, 16 F1.
Tel 282 89 95.

Mutter
Hohenstaufenstrasse 4.
Map 11 A3.
Tel 216 49 90.

Oberwasser
Zionskirchstrasse 6.
Tel 448 37 19.

Ranke 2
Rankestrasse 2.
Map 10 E1.
Tel 883 88 82.

Reingold
Novalisstrasse 11.
Map 6 F1.
Tel 21 75 16 45.

Slumberland
Goltzstrasse 24.
Map 11 A3.
Tel 216 53 49.

Titanic
Winsstrasse 30.
Tel 442 03 40.

Zum Nussbaum
Am Nussbaum 3.
Map 7 C3.
Tel 242 30 95.

Zum Patzenhofer
Meinekestrasse 26.
Map 10 D1.
Tel 882 11 35.

Zur Kneipe
Rankestrasse 9.
Map 10 D2.
Tel 883 82 55.

BIERGARTEN

Bundespressestrand
Reichstagsufer, corner of Otto-von-Bismarck-Allee.
Map 6 E2. *Tel 28 09 91 19.*

Golgatha
Dudenstrasse 48–64, in Viktoriapark.
Map 12 E5.
Tel 78 52 453.

Loretta am Wannsee
Kronprinzessinnenweg 260.
Tel 803 51 56.

Prater
Kastanienallee 7–9.
Map 1 A5, 1 B3.
Tel 448 56 88.

Schleusenkrug
Müller-Breslau-Strasse/at Tiergartenschleuse.
Map 4 E4.
Tel 313 99 09.

WINE BARS

Billy Wilder's
Potsdamer Strasse 2.
Map 6 D5.
Tel 26 55 48 60.

Le Bar du Paris Bar
Kantstrasse 152.
Map 10 D1.
Tel 31 01 50 94.

Lutter & Wegener
Gendarmenmarkt 56.
Map 7 A4, 16 D4.
Tel 202 95 40.

Vox Bar at the Grand Hyatt
Marlene-Dietrich-PLatz 2.
Map 6 D5.
Tel 030 2553 1234.

Weinstein
Lychener Strasse 33.
Tel 441 18 42.

BARS

Ballhaus Berlin
Chausseestrasse 102
Map 6 F1.
Tel 282 75 75.

Bar am Lützowplatz
Lützowplatz 7.
Map 11 A1.
Tel 262 68 07.

b-flat
Rosenthaler Strasse 13.
Map 7 B1.
Tel 28 38 68 35.

Blue Note Bar
Courbièrestrasse 13.
Map 11 A2.
Tel 69 50 50 17.

Green Door
Winterfeldtstrasse 50.
Tel 215 25 15.

Haifischbar
Arndtstrasse 25.
Map 13 A5.
Tel 691 13 52.

Harry's New York Bar
Lützowufer 15 (in Hotel Esplanade). **Map** 11 A1.
Tel 25 47 88 21.

Kumpelnest 3000
Lützowstrasse 23.
Map 11 B1.
Tel 26 16 918.

Newton Bar
Charlottenstrasse 57.
Map 16 D4.
Tel 20 29 54 21.

Riva Bar
Dircksenstrasse, S-Bahnbogen 142.
Map 7 C2.
Tel 24 72 26 88.

Roter Salon
Rosa-Luxemburg-Platz.
Map 7 C1.
Tel 24 06 58 06.

Times Bar (cigar bar)
Fasanenstrasse 9–10.
Map 10 D1.
Tel 31 10 30.

Trompete
Lützowplatz 9.
Map 11 A1.
Tel 23 00 47 94.

Zur weissen Maus
Ludwigkirchplatz 12.
Map 9 C3.
Tel 886 792 88.

GAY AND LESBIAN BARS

Blu Cocktail Lounge
Neue Schönhauser Strasse 20.
Map 7 C2.

Café Seidenfaden
Dircksenstrasse 47.
Map 7 C3.
Tel 283 27 83.

Die Busche
Mühlenstrasse 11–12.
Tel 296 08 00.

Hafenbar
Motzstrasse 19.
Map 11 A2.
Tel 211 41 18.

Lenz
Eisenacher Strasse 3.
Map 11 A2.
Tel 217 78 20.

Roses
Oranienstrasse 187.
Map 14 E2.
Tel 615 65 70.

So 36
Oranienstrasse 190.
Map 13 B1, 14 D1.
Tel 61 40 13 06.

SHOPPING IN BERLIN

With a shopping centre in every district, each selling a wide variety of merchandise, Berlin is a place where almost anything can be bought, so long as you know where to look. The most popular places are Kurfürstendamm and Friedrichstrasse, but the smaller shops in Wedding, Friedrichshain, Schöneberg and the Tiergarten are also worth a visit. Small boutiques selling flamboyant Berlin-style clothes crop up in unexpected courtyards, while the top fashion houses offer the latest in European elegance. Early on Saturday morning is often the best time to visit the city's various markets, the most popular of which – with their colourful stalls full of hats, bags and belts – can be found on Museum Island and at the Tiergarten. The Galeries Lafayette, KaDeWe and any of the city's numerous bookshops all make ideal venues for a pleasant afternoon's window shopping.

Inside the modern, multi-level Europa-Center *(see p150)*

OPENING HOURS

The majority of shops are open Monday to Friday from 10am to 8pm (10am to 4pm on Saturday), but some department stores open as early as 9am, and some smaller shops open in the afternoons only. Generally, there are no lunch-breaks unless the shop is a one-person business. During the six weeks before Christmas, shops stay open until 8pm on Saturdays and the local transport authority, the Berliner Verkehrs-Betriebe, or BVG *(see pp294–5),* runs a useful service for shoppers. You can leave your bags in a special Weihnachtsgeschenke-Bus (Christmas-gift bus) and shop without dragging all your purchases around with you.

DEPARTMENT STORES

Kaufhaus Des Westens, better known as **KaDeWe** at Wittenbergplatz *(see p155),* is undoubtedly the biggest and the best department store in Berlin. Only products of the highest quality are sold in these luxurious halls, where virtually everything you need is on sale – from unusual perfumes and elegant under-wear to *haute couture,* all sold in a system of shops-within-shops. The food hall on the sixth floor is legendary for its restaurant overlooking Tauentzienstrasse.

Galeries Lafayette on Friedrichstrasse is nothing less than a slice of Paris placed in the heart of Berlin. Perfumes, domestic accessories and clothing attract an enormous clientele, many of whom also visit the food counter which offers a wide range of French specialities. An extraordinary glass cone rises through the middle of the store, reflecting the interiors of the shops.

Another very popular store is **Wertheim** on the Ku'damm.

A typical street-side stall, brimming with souvenirs for visitors

Although its range of goods is not as broad as the range at Galeries Lafayette, there is still an enormous choice and the top-floor restaurant offers excellent views over the city.

SHOPPING CENTRES

In addition to the two biggest shopping districts in town – Ku'damm and Friedrichstrasse – new shopping

The spacious interior of the Hugendubel department store

Milano tie shop on Kurfürstendamm

DIRECTORY

DEPARTMENT STORES

Wertheim
Kurfürstendamm 231.
Map 10 D1.
Tel 88 00 30.

KaDeWe
Tauentzienstrasse 21.
Map 10 F2.
Tel 21 21 00.

Galeries Lafayette
Französische Strasse 23.
Map 7 A4.
Tel 20 94 80.

SHOPPING CENTRES

Galleria
Schlossstrasse 101.
Map 2 E3.

Gesundbrunnencenter
Gesundbrunnen S-Bahn.

Potsdamer Platz Arkaden
Debis Gelände.
Map 6 E5.

Shopping Guide
Claudia Barthel
Tel 28 59 86 22.

SHOPPING GUIDE

If you are planning to do some serious shopping in Berlin, and are worried about getting lost among the many possibilities, you may want to use the services of a "shopping guide". These are specialists who will tell you what is currently on offer in both the big department stores and in the smaller boutiques.

centres are constantly being built, usually conveniently situated close to S-Bahn stations. These massive three-level structures, resembling huge arcaded passageways, contain an enormous number of shops, ranging from supermarkets and chemists to bars, high-street fashion and bookshops. Like most of the shops in Berlin they stay open until 8pm during the week. They also do business on Sundays. One of the newest shopping centres is the **Potsdamer Platz Arkaden**. Built in October 1998 it is very popular both as a shopping mall and a meeting place. It is visited by thousands of tourists and Berliners every day.

Of a similar character, although built on a slightly smaller scale, is **Galleria** on Schlossstrasse in Steglitz. Here, under one roof, you can browse through an extraordinary selection of goods. **Gesundbrunnencenter** is the biggest shopping passage in Berlin, and has countless stalls and tables offering every kind of bargain. A large number of bars also makes this a popular place to meet friends for a beer or a coffee.

SEASONAL SALES

All shops in Berlin empty their racks and shelves in the sale, or *Schlussverkauf,* which takes place twice a year. At the end of January, before the new year's collections are displayed in shop windows, you can buy winter clothes for as little as 50 per cent of their original price. During the summer sales *(Sommerschlussverkauf),* which take place at the end of July, you can find similarly-reduced summer outfits. Goods bought in a sale are officially non-returnable, but if you are really keen to take an item back, there is no harm in at least trying to negotiate with the shop assistant.

A number of shops sell a variety of articles marketed as "second season" items. These are always new articles, albeit stocked for the previous season, and they are offered at often generously-reduced prices. You will also find that various shops specialize in top-brand jeans, selling them at much-reduced rates owing to what are often very minor defects. These represent excellent value for money.

HOW TO PAY

When it comes to paying for goods you may find that some small shops still insist on cash. In the centre of Berlin there should be a suitable cash machine not too far away *(see p284).* Larger shops and department stores will also accept most major credit cards.

A shop-floor display in the lobby of KaDeWe *(see p155)*

Clothes and Accessories

There are many shopping centres in Berlin, and nearly every district has its own high street where residents do their shopping. If it's luxury, elegance and a wide variety of goods you are after, however, then head for the shops on Kurfürstendamm, Friedrichstrasse and Potsdamer Platz. This is where all the major fashion houses and perfume makers have their shops, right in the heart of the city. Alternatively, if you want to explore the smaller boutiques of some lesser-known designers, make your way to Hackescher Markt in the Mitte district, or to Prenzlauer Berg.

WOMEN'S FASHIONS

The most famous fashion houses are on the Ku'damm (Kurfürstendamm) and its side streets, particularly in the area around the quietly elegant Fasanenstrasse. Among the many famous names doing business here are **Yves Saint Laurent**, **Max Mara**, **Sonia Rykiel**, **Gianni Versace**, **Bogner**, **Louis Vuitton**, **Chanel**, **Donna Boutique** and **Gucci**. Simplicity is the order of the day in the **Designer Depot** shop, making it the ideal place to buy a straight-forward dress with exquisite accessories. Gucci has two shops in the area, one in Fasanenstrasse and another in the fashionable Quartier 206 on Friedrichstrasse. The latter shares the street with many other fashion houses that specialize in women's clothes: **Evelin Brandt**, **Department Store 206**, **Strenesse**, **Strenesse Blue** and **ETRO**, to name a few.

MEN'S FASHIONS

For the full range of the latest in fashion for men, on or near Kurfürstendamm is the place to go shopping, for this is where various retailers sell clothing straight from Europe's best-known fashion houses. **Patrick Hellmann** is certainly worth a visit with its wide choice of the best designer labels around. Clothes by Giorgio Armani, Helmut Lang, Christian Dior and Dolce E Gabbana can all be found here. Also very popular are **Anson's** and the more upmarket **Mientus**, which has a second outlet on Wilmersdorfer Strasse. **Peek & Cloppenburg**, Germany's second largest speciality store, sells its own budget labels as well as designer clothes by Boss, Armani and Joop.

CHILDREN'S CLOTHING

Shops selling children's clothes can generally satisfy any taste, depending on how much you are willing to spend. **Anastasia** has a wide range of clothes for children up to 14, while **I Pinco Pallino** offers *haute couture* for all ages. Alternatively, the Prenzlauer Berg district, which has the highest birth rate in the whole of Germany, is dotted with small children's boutiques offering both brand names and handmade clothes. The needs of children whose parents have a more restricted budget can be met in **H&M Kinder**, which sells fashionable items at relatively moderate prices.

YOUNG DESIGNERS

A number of galleries, studios and boutiques specialize in the so-called Berlin style, the collections on sale usually consisting of short-series items that are produced in strictly limited numbers. At one time it was possible to find shops like this across the whole of the city, but now they are concentrated mainly in the northern part of the Mitte area, where a unique fashion centre is firmly established. **NIX** offers timeless clothes made from heavy, dark fabrics and cut in classical fashion. A great selection of clothing by 19 very different designers is on offer in **Tagebau** in Rosenthaler Strasse 19, where just about every kind of item can be bought, from evening dresses and luxury wedding gowns to elegant hats and other fashion accessories.

Among the other shops in Mitte, **Fishbelly** on Sophienstrasse is noted for its unique range of erotic underwear, designed by Jutta Teschner. At **Molotow**, in Kreuzberg, the choice is more classical than the trendy name might suggest. Another very popular place to buy clothes is **Chapeaux**, in Charlottenburg, while **Lisa D.** offers classic and elegant dresses by one of Berlin's top female designers.

SHOES AND ACCESSORIES

One of the largest shoe shops in Berlin is **Schuhtick**, which has three branches in the city, though the highest quality can be found in the **Budapester Schuhe** chain. A good selection can also be found at the **Görtz** outlets around Kufürstendamm. The latest Italian designs are available at **Riccardo Cartillone**.

Penthesileia on Tucholskystrasse offers an amusing range of handbags, which come in all kinds of shapes and sizes. If it's a hat you are after, then you need go no further than **Hut Up**, in the Heckmannhöfen. All kinds are headgear are available here, from typical Russian *shlapas* to party hats with Rastafarian dreadlocks.

PERFUMES

All of the large department stores, including **KaDeWe** and **Galeries Lafayette**, offer a sizeable selection of the best-known perfumes, but there are also a number of specialist shops dotted around the city. The **Douglas** chain, which has numerous outlets, has a wide range of perfumes at very reasonable prices. **Quartier 206** has a good selection of the better-known perfumes, but if you are looking for something unusual, then **Harry Lehmann** is the place to visit. This unique store is a perfume-lover's paradise, where Mr Lehmann himself continues an 80-year-long family tradition of mixing your very own perfume from a variety of 50 scents. He also stocks long-forgotten brands. The **Body Shop** group is popular in Berlin. Natural perfumes of all kinds can be bought here, and its policy of no animal testing is popular with customers. It also encourages the return of its containers for recycling.

DIRECTORY

WOMEN'S FASHION

Bogner
Kurfürstendamm 42.
Map 9 C2.
Tel 88 71 77 80.

Chanel
Fasanenstrasse 30.
Map 9 C3.
Tel 885 13 24.

Department Store 206
Friedrichstrasse 23.
Map 6 F4.
Tel 20 94 80.

Designer Depot
Rochstrasse 2.
Map 7 C2.
Tel 28 04 67 00.

Donna Boutique
Uhlandstrasse 145.
Map 9 C3.
Tel 881 73 60.

ETRO
Friedrichstrasse 71.
Map 6 F3.
Tel 20 94 61 20.

Evelin Brandt
Savignyplatz 6.
Map 9 C1.
Tel 313 80 80.

Gianni Versace
Kurfürstendamm 185.
Map 10 D1.
Tel 885 74 60.

Gucci
Fasanenstrasse 73.
Map 9 C2.
Tel 885 63 00.

Friedrichstrasse 71.
Map 6 F3.
Tel 201 70 20.

Louis Vuitton
Friedrichstrasse 71.
Map 6 F4.
Tel 20 94 68 68.

Max Mara
Kurfürstendamm 178.
Map 10 D1.
Tel 885 25 45.

Sonia Rykiel
Kurfürstendamm 186.
Map 9 A2.
Tel 882 17 74.

Strenesse & Strenesse Blue
Friedrichstrasse 71.
Map 6 F3.
Tel 20 94 60 35.

Yves Saint Laurent
Kurfürstendamm 52.
Map 9 A2.
Tel 883 39 18.

MEN'S FASHIONS

Anson's
Schlossstrasse 122.
Tel 79 09 60.

Mientus
Wilmersdorfer Strasse 73.
Map 2 F3, 3 A5, 9 A1.
Kurfürstendamm 52.
Map 9 A2.
Tel 323 90 77.

Patrick Hellmann
Fasanenstrasse 26.
Map 10 D2.
Tel 882 42 01.

Peek & Cloppenburg
Tauentzienstrasse 19.
Map 10 E1.
Tel 21 29 00.

CHILDREN'S CLOTHING

Anastasia
Uhlandstrasse 170.
Map 9 C1.
Tel 883 72 12.

H&M Kinder
Schlossstrasse 1 (Steglitz).
Map 2 E3, E4.

I Pinco Pallino
Kurfürstendamm 46.
Map 10 D1.
Tel 881 28 63.

YOUNG DESIGNERS

Chapeaux
Bleibtreustrasse 51.
Map 9 B1.
Tel 20 38 81 10.

Fishbelly
Sophienstrasse 7a.
Tel 28 04 51 80.

Lisa D.
Hackesche Höfe,
Rosenthaler Strasse 40–41.
Map 7 B2.
Tel 28 29 061.

Molotow
Gneisenaustrasse 112.
Map 13 A4.
Tel 693 08 18.

NIX
Oranienburger Strasse 32.
Map 7 A2.
Tel 281 80 44.

Tagebau
Rosenthaler Strasse 19.
Map 7 B1.
Tel 28 39 08 90.

SHOES AND ACCESSORIES

Budapester Schuhe
Kurfürstendamm 199.
Map 10 D1.
Tel 88 11 707.

Bleibtreustrasse 24.
Map 9 B1.
Tel 88 17 001.

Friedrichstrasse 81.
Map 6 F3.
Tel 20 38 81 10.

Görtz
Kurfürstendamm 13-14.
Map 10 D1.
Tel 88 68 37 52.

Hut Up
Oranienburger Strasse 32.
Map 7 A2.
Tel 28 38 61 05.

Penthesileia
Tucholskystrasse 31.
Map 7 A2, 16 D1.
Tel 282 11 52.

Riccardo Cartillone
Savignyplatz 4.
Map 9 C1.
Tel 31 50 33 27.

Schuhtick
Savignyplatz 11.
Map 9 C1.
Tel 315 93 80.

Tauentzienstrasse 5.
Map 10 E1.
Tel 214 09 80.

PERFUMES

Body Shop
(in the main hall of Zoologischer Garten railway station).
Map 10 D1.
Tel 31 21 391.

Douglas
Kurfürstendamm 216.
Map 10 D1.
Tel 881 25 34.

Galeries Lafayette Parfümerie
Franzözische Strasse 23.
Map 6 F4.
Tel 20 94 80.

Harry Lehmann
Kantstrasse 106.
Map 9 A1.
Tel 324 35 82.

KaDeWe Parfümerie
Tauentzienstrasse 21–24.
Map 10 E1.
Tel 21 21 00.

Quartier 206
Friedrichstrasse 71.
Map 6 F3.
Tel 20 94 68 00

Gifts and Souvenirs

Unlike London, Paris or Rome, where whole industries are devoted to providing mementos for travellers and tourists, Berlin doesn't have a great variety of typical souvenirs. But this doesn't mean you won't be able to find an interesting gift – a browse through any of the major markets or a trip along one of the main shopping thoroughfares should be sufficient for you to buy whatever you need. Posters and CDs are easy to find, but if you're looking for something elegant, then a piece of china made by Königliche Porzellan-Manufaktur Berlin (see p133) might be a good idea. For a child, a teddy bear is always an option, particularly in this city, where it is part of the official insignia. For hand-made jewellery or contemporary art, head for Strasse des 17 Juni during one of its Sunday markets (see p256).

BOOKS AND MUSIC

The best places to buy books on art are the shops at major museums, where you will also find a good selection of cards, posters and general souvenirs. The best of these are in **Hamburger Bahnhof** (see pp110–11), **Gemälde-galerie** (see pp122–25), **Sammlung Berggruen** (see p164), **Schloss Charlottenburg** (see pp160–61) and **Altes Museum** (see p75).

The **Bücherbogen** chain offers a huge choice of books and has several outlets in the city; the one under the S-Bahn bridge near Savigny-platz has the largest stock. Other good stores include **Autorenbuchhandlung** or, if you want to combine shopping for books and art appreciation, **Artificium** has a gallery attached. The biggest stores also have sections on Berlin art such as the huge **Hugendubel**, which sells CDs as well as books, and **Kulturkaufhaus Dussmann**.

For English-language books or papers, **Books** and **English Books** are the places to go with their wide choice of both English and American literature. **Prinz Eisenherz** also has a good selection of gay literature. In all of these shops the staff are usually very helpful.

Music lovers should head for **Artificium** in Schloss-strasse, **Cover Music** near the Ku'damm or, if it is classical music you are after, then **L & P Classics** has one of the finest selections. For something avant-garde don't miss **Gelbe Musik** on Schaper-strasse. If you happen to be short of funds there is always the option of flicking through the second-hand CDs on offer at the Sunday antique market on Strasse des 17 Juni (see p256). The market is always crammed with souvenirs and is a great hunting-ground for collectors of old vinyl records.

TOYS

You won't have to travel far to buy a typical Berlin teddy bear – you can find them in stores all over the city, especially the gift shops in the Nikolaiviertel. If you're after a wider variety of toys, then **KaDeWe** (see p155) is the place to go. Like all the major department stores, KaDeWe (see p155) offers a whole range of toys for children of all ages, but its teddy bear section is second to none in Berlin. From the highly portable half-inch bear to the life-size 2-metre model, every kind of bear you can imagine is on sale here, so you shouldn't be disappointed. Also, the store can arrange a delivery to your home, so if your child has always dreamed of having an enormous teddy bear, this is a perfect opportunity to fulfil the dream.

Small manufacturers still make old-style wooden toys, from doll's house furniture to traditional jigsaw puzzles, and these make excellent gifts to take home. **Heidi's Spielzeug-laden** on Kantstrasse, **Johanna Petzoldt** on Sophienstrasse and **Spielen** on Hufelandstrasse are the best places to go for souvenirs of this kind. Train lovers hoping to extend their tracks and build more depots and stations should visit **Michas Bahnhof** on Nürnberger Strasse, the city's top provider of model train set accessories. An amazing range of goods is available here.

As an old Prussian capital, Berlin is also a good place to find Germanic lead soldiers; the best place to look is **Berliner Zinnfiguren Kabinett**. While most of the soldiers available are designed for children, collecting them is a popular hobby among adults, and the rarities often fetch very high prices on the market.

FLOWERS

It is very easy to find a nice bouquet in Berlin. Flower shops stand on nearly every street corner and the majority of them are open for business on Sundays. **Blumen-Koch** in Wilmersdorf offers an amazing selection of beautiful and colourful plants and is famous for its bouquets of exotic flowers which are always arranged and wrapped with real artistry. However, if you want to arrange a surprise delivery then a good place to go is **Fleurop** on Kurfürstendamm, which will send a bouquet of flowers to a given address.

CHINA AND CERAMICS

The history of European china started in Germany in 1708. The alchemist Böttger, while searching for the secret of making gold, discovered instead how to make Chinese-style porcelain. Berlin soon became a major producer. **KPM (Königliche Porzellan-Manufaktur Berlin)** (see p133) is still in operation, and its products will satisfy even the most choosy of porcelain collectors. Plenty of newly made china is available, but if you are looking for something older, then an afternoon could be spent in some of the city's antique shops *(see pp256–7)*. Currently manufactured pieces can be bought in the KPM factory shop or in the elegant salon on the ground floor of the Kempinski hotel *(see p226)*. Those who prefer Meissen porcelain will be able to find it in several shops along the Ku'damm.

While porcelain is expensive, an equally precious gift can be made of a ceramic dish or breakfast set, traditionally manufactured in Thuringia.

With their characteristic blue and white patterns, a wide choice of exquisite Thuringian ceramics can be found in **Bürgel-Haus** on Friedrichstrasse.

SPECIALIST SHOPS

If you are determined to find something unique, or even quirky, you may want to visit some of the interesting specialist shops – like **Knopf Paul**, which specializes in extraordinary buttons, or **Bären-Luftballons**, which

offers a delightful variety of colourful and amusing balloons. There are also a number of shops which specialize in teas and tea-time accessories. **King's Teagarden** and **TeeHaus** offer the best selection in this field.

Smart letter paper and good pens can be bought in **Papeterie**, but if you're still stuck for ideas, there's no harm in browsing through the specialist departments in **KaDeWe** *(see Toys)* where there's always something guaranteed to catch the eye.

DIRECTORY

BOOKS AND MUSIC

Artificium
Rosenthalerstrasse 40/41.
Map 7 B1.
Tel 30 87 22 80.

Autorenbuchhandlung
Carmerstrasse 10.
Map 3 C5.
Tel 313 01 51.

Books
Goethestrasse 69.
Map 3 B5.
Tel 31 31 233.

Bücherbogen
Savignyplatz.
Map 9 C1.
Tel 31 86 95 11.

Cover Music
Kurfürstendamm 11.
Map 10 D1.
Tel 88 55 01 30.

English Books
Unter den Eichen 97.
Tel 831 40 04.

Gelbe Musik
Schaperstrasse 11.
Map 10 D2.
Tel 211 39 62.

Gemäldegalerie
Matthäikirchplatz 8.
Map 5 C5.
Tel 20 90 55 60.

Grober Unfug
Zossener Strasse 32–33.
Map 13 A3.
Tel 69 40 14 90.

Hamburger Bahnhof
Invalidenstrasse 50/51.
Map 6 D1.
Tel 397 83 40.

Hugendubel
Tauentzienstrasse 13.
Map 10 E1.
Tel (01801) 48 44 84.

Lehmann's
Hardenbergstrasse 5.
Map 3 C4.
Tel 61 79 11 73.

Kulturkaufhaus Dussmann
Friedrichstrasse 90.
Map 15 C2.
Tel 202 50.

L & P Classics
Knesebeckstrasse 33-34.
Map 9 C1.
Tel 88 04 30 43.

Prinz Eisenherz
Lietzenburger Strasse 9a.
Map 9 B2.
Tel 313 99 36.

Sammlung Berggruen
Schlossstrasse 1.
Map 2 E3.
Tel 20 90 55 66.

TOYS

Berliner Zinnfiguren Kabinett
Knesebeckstrasse 88.
Map 3 C5.
Tel 313 08 02.

Heidi's Spielzeugladen
Kantstrasse 61.
Map 2 F5.
Tel 323 75 56.

Johanna Petzoldt
Sophienstrasse 9.
Map 7 B1.
Tel 282 67 54.

KaDeWe
Tauentzienstrasse 21.
Map 10 E1.
Tel 21 21 00.

Michas Bahnhof
Nürnberger Strasse 24.
Map 10 E2, 10 F2.
Tel 218 66 11.

Quisebel
Niebuhrstrasse 12.
Map 9 B1.
Tel 88 91 28 00.

FLOWERS

Blumen Damerius
Potsdamer Platz Arkaden.
Tel 45 38 005.

Blumen-Koch
Westfälische Strasse 38.
Map 9 A4.
Tel 896 69 00.

Fleurop Blankenberg
Kurfürstendamm 69.
Map 9 A2.
Tel 881 91 23.

CHINA AND CERAMICS

Bürgel-Haus
Friedrichstrasse 154.
Map 6 F3, 15 C3.
Tel 204 45 19.

KPM
Strasse des 17 Juni 100.
Tel 39 00 92 15.

Fasanenstrasse 27.
Map 10 D1.
Tel 886 72 10.

SPECIALIST SHOPS

Bären-Luftballons
Kurfürstenstrasse 31/32.
Map 9 C1.
Tel 261 92 99.

Kings Teagarden
Kurfürstendamm 217.
Map 10 D1.
Tel 883 70 59.

Knopf Paul
Zossener Strasse 10.
Map 13 A4.
Tel 692 12 12.

Papeterie
Uhlandstrasse 28.
Map 9 C2.
Tel 881 63 63.

TeeHaus
Krumme Strasse 35.
Map 3 A5.
Tel 31 50 98 82.

Antiques and Objets d'Art

The antique and art markets in Berlin are booming. New galleries are opening all the time, particularly in the eastern areas of town. Spandauer Vorstadt is full of antique shops and contemporary art galleries, but the northern part of Mitte (the area around East of the Centre) is the focus of the Berlin art market. Constantly raising their standards, the galleries attract numerous art dealers and collectors, while non-commercial exhibitions organized by art societies like NGbK, NBK and Kunst-Werke add to the creative atmosphere. As for the antique trade, a walk through any of the city's main thoroughfares should show that it is active in just about every district.

AUCTION HOUSES

Berlin's oldest and most prestigious auction houses are **Gerda Bassenge** and **Villa Grisebach**, both of which organize sales at the start of the year and in the autumn. Bassenge specializes in graphic art, and a month before each sale an auction of books and autographs is held. A photographic auction takes place a few days after the main sale of graphic art. The prices are usually higher at Grisebach which deals mainly in 19th-century paintings. Expressionists and modern classics often go under the hammer here. Another good auctioneer is **Kunst-Auktionen Leon Spik** on Ku'damm; top London auction house **Christie's** has facilities on Fasanenstrasse.

GALLERIES

If you are pressed for time, Spandauer Vorstadt in the northern part of Mitte might be the place to go. Since the fall of the Berlin Wall, some 30 galleries have been set up in the Linienstrasse, August-strasse, Sophienstrasse and Gipsstrasse areas. Among these are **Arndt & Partner** and **Eigen & Art**, both on August-strasse, **Contemporary Fine Arts**, **Gebauer**, **Max Hetzler**, **Mehdi Chouakri** and **Wohn-maschine**. **Wiens Laden & Verlag** and **Neugerriemensch-neider** are both on Linien-strasse. So-called "open days" take place three or four times a year when all the galleries open at the same time to exhibit the new collections. One is always in early

October, when the Art Forum Berlin fair is held, providing a chance to spot the changing trends in contemporary art.

The galleries near Kurfürsten-damm, such as **Brusberg**, offer high-quality art in a quieter atmosphere. Other galleries include **Hartmann & Noé** and **Galerie Rafael Vostell**, both on Knesebeck-strasse, as well as **Anselm Dreher**, **Barbara Weiss**, **Franck & Schulte** and **Poll**.

ANTIQUE SHOPS

Antique shops can be found in every district of Berlin. Near Kurfürstendamm and around Ludwigkirchplatz there are a number of high-class shops offering expensive *objets d'art*, from Chinese furniture in **Alte Asiatische Kunst** to Secession trinkets in **ART 1900** and glass from different periods in the **Galeries Splinter**.

Furniture specialists can be found in Suarezstrasse in Charlottenburg, where orig-inal Thonets can be bought as well as modern steel items by well-known designers. For a slightly lower grade of antique, the best place to go is Berg-mannstrasse in Kreuzberg. In its mildly Oriental atmosphere you can often find valuable pieces among masses of junk. **Das Zweite Büro** in Zossener Strasse specializes in trading old desks, cupboards and filing cabinets, which don't come cheap, but the quality of the merchandise is excellent. Standing opposite Das Zweite Büro is **Radio Art** with its extensive collection of old radios and record

players. Some other interesting shops to try are **Antiklampen**, **Bleibtreu Antik** and **Art Déco**.

There's a real market atmosphere in the arcades of the S-Bahn railway bridge near Friedrichstrasse where a host of street traders sell all kinds of knick-knacks, from clothes and books to cutlery and domestic accessories.

FLEA MARKETS

Many Berliners spend their Saturday and Sunday mornings at flea markets, and after a coffee go for a walk in the Tiergarten or take a stroll to a museum. Trödel- und Kunstmarkt, on Strasse des 17 Juni near Tiergarten S-Bahn station, is the most popular market in town. It is divided into two parts, and the antique section deals with books and magazines as well as pricey rarities. If you have the time and patience to sift through the enormous amount on offer, you are likely to find some great bargains. Arts and crafts trading takes place on the other side of Charlotten-burger Brücke, and the goods on offer range from leather items and ceramics to colour-ful silk clothes and jewellery. Shops from all over Berlin are usually represented here.

From **Berliner Kunst-und Nostalgiemarkt an der Museumsinsel**, it is only a few steps to the museums. The stalls along Kupfergraben stand opposite the Pergamon- and Altes Museum, and art objects, books, records and other antiques are always on display around the Zeughaus.

The flea market operating in the car park near the Fehr--belliner Platz U-Bahn station opens at the weekends at 8am. If you are interested in going, you would do well to get there as early as possible as it is full of experienced collectors who only need a few minutes to spot something valuable. Another flea market can be found on Arkonaplatz, in the centre of a residential district in the eastern part of the town. If you are after memorabilia from the former GDR, you should try the stalls around Potsdamer Platz and Leipziger Platz. However the quality and authenticity of what is on sale is often questionable.

Another great market is the **Treptower Hallentrödel** on Eichenstrasse, which offers everything under one roof. Old telephones and army boots can be found beside bathroom accessories and piles of very cheap books (5 for 2 euros). The hall itself, a former bus depot, is worth visiting for its interesting architecture alone.

Other flea markets to visit include **Antik & Trödelmarkt am Ostbahnhof**, **Kunstmarkt Mulackstrasse** and **Kiezmarkt am Moritzplatz**.

Berliner Stadtreinigungsbetriebe is an organization responsible for disposing of rubbish, and a number of "BSR" shops sell old furniture which is still in good condition. They are ideal places to pick up a bargain, although you are often in competition with small traders.

DIRECTORY

AUCTION HOUSES

Christie's
Giesebrechtstrasse 10.
Map 9 A2.
Tel 885 69 50.

Gerda Bassenge
Erdener Strasse 5a.
Tel 89 38 02 90.
◯ 9am–6pm Mon–Fri.

Kunst-Auktionen Leo Spik
Kurfürstendamm 66.
Map 10 D1.
Tel 883 61 70.

Villa Grisebach
Fasanenstrasse 25.
Map 10 D2.
Tel 885 91 50.

GALLERIES

Anselm Dreher
Pfalzburger Strasse 80.
Map 9 C2.
Tel 883 52 49.
◯ 2–6:30pm Tue–Fri, 11am–2pm Sat.

Arndt & Partner
Zimmerstrasse 90–91.
Map 7 B1.
Tel 280 81 23.
◯ 11am–6pm Tue–Sat.

Barbara Weiss
Zimmerstrasse 88–91.
Map 7 A5.
Tel 262 42 84.
◯ 11am–6pm Tue–Sat.

Brusberg
Kurfürstendamm 213.
Map 9 C1.
Tel 882 76 82.
◯ 10am–6:30 pm Tue–Fri, 10am–2pm Sat.

Contemporary Fine Arts
Sophienstrasse 21.
Map 7 B1.
Tel 28 87 870.
◯ 11am–1pm 2–6pm Tue–Fri, 11am–5pm Sat.

Eigen & Art
Auguststrasse 26.
Map 7 B1.
Tel 280 66 05.
◯ 11am–6pm Tue–Sat.

Eva Poll
Lützowplatz 7.
Map 11 A1.
Tel 261 70 91.
◯ 11am–1pm Mon, 11am–6:30pm Tue–Fri, 11am–3 pm Sat.

Galerie Rafael Vostell
Schönhauser Allee 175.
Tel 885 22 80.
◯ noon–6pm Tue–Sat.

Gebauer
Holzmarktstrasse 15–19, S-Bahn-Bogen 51–52.
Map 6 F1.
Tel 280 81 10.
◯ 11am–6pm Tue–Sat.

Max Hetzler
Zimmerstrasse 90–91.
Map 6 F5.
Tel 229 24 37.
◯ 11am–6pm Tue–Sat.

Mehdi Chouakri
Gipsstrasse 11.
Map 7 B1.
Tel 28 39 11 53.
◯ 11am–6pm Tue–Sat.

Michael Schultz
Mommsenstrasse 34.
Tel 32 41 591.
◯ 10am–7pm Tue–Fri, 10am–2pm Sat.

Neugerriemschneider
Linienstrasse 155.
Map 7 A1.
Tel 30 87 28 10.
◯ 11am–6pm Tue–Sat.

Thomas Schulte
Mommsenstrasse 56.
Map 7 A1.
Tel 324 00 44.
◯ 11am–6pm Mon–Fri, 11am–3pm Sat.

Wiens Laden & Verlag
Linienstrasse 158.
Map 7 C1.
Tel 28 38 53 52.
◯ 2–7pm Tue–Fri, noon–6pm Sat.

Wohnmaschine
Tucholskystrasse 35.
Map 7 A2, 16 D1.
Tel 30 87 20 15.
◯ 11am–6pm Tue–Sat.

ANTIQUE SHOPS

Alte Asiatische Kunst
Fasanenstrasse 71.
Map 10 D1.
Tel 883 61 17.

Antiklampen
Motzstrasse 32.
Map 10 F3.
Tel 213 72 27.

Art Déco
Grolmanstrasse 51.
Map 3 C5.
Tel 31 50 62 05.

ART 1900
Kurfürstendamm 53.
Map 9 B2.
Tel 881 56 27.

Bleibtreu Antik
Schlüterstrasse 54.
Map 9 B1.
Tel 883 52 12.

Das Zweite Büro
Zossener Strasse 6.
Map 13 A3. **Tel** 693 07 59. ● Mon.

Galerie Splinter
Sophienstrasse 20–21.
Map 7 B1. **Tel** 28 59 87 37. ● Mon.

Lakeside Antiques
Neue Kantstrasse 14.
Map 2 E5.
Tel 25 45 99 30.

Radio Art
Zossener Strasse 2.
Map 13 A3.
Tel 693 94 35.
◯ noon–6pm Thu & Fri, 10am–1pm Sat.

FLEA MARKETS

Antik & Trödelmarkt am Ostbahnhof
Erich-Steinfurth-Strasse.
◯ 9am–3pm Sat, 10am–5pm Sun.

Berliner Kunst- und Nostalgiemarkt an der Museumsinsel
Museumsinsel & Kupfergraben.
Map 7 A2, 16 D1.
◯ 11am–5pm Sat & Sun.

Kunstmarkt Mulackstrasse
Mulackstrasse 12.
◯ 2pm–9pm Sat & Sun.

Kiezmarkt am Moritzplatz
Moritzplatz.
◯ 8am–4pm Sat & Sun.

Treptower Hallentrödel
Puschkinallee.
◯ 10am–6pm Sat & Sun.

Food Products

Food specialities from all over the world can be found in Berlin, a fact which is due partly to the city's own lack of traditional cuisine. Gone are the days when local fare was restricted to pork knuckle with cabbage, cutlets, *Currywurst* and potatoes. Today the side-streets and thoroughfares are teeming with the shops and restaurants of many nationalities – Italian, Greek, Turkish, Spanish and French as well as Mexican, American, Japanese, Chinese and Thai. As befits any major European capital, the food is of the highest quality, and there are more and more shops providing organic products, from vegetables and wholemeal bread to various wines and beers.

PATISSERIES AND SWEET SHOPS

Berliners certainly have a sweet tooth for there are plenty of patisseries and sweet shops all over the city, and a wide range of cakes is available. A typical speciality is a doughnut known simply as a *Berliner*, but the majority of places offer a whole range of cakes along with French pastries and fruits. **Buchwald** is renowned for producing some of the best cakes in town, mainly to take away, but there are also a number of patisseries, or *Konditoreien*. Among the best of these is **Opernpalais**.

Delicacies from Vienna can be bought in **Wiener Konditorei Caffeehaus**, while **Leysieffer** shops, with their exquisite chocolates and pralines, are a serious temptation for chocoholics. Visitors with a sweet tooth should also try the large stores: **KaDeWe's Feinschmecker Etage** and **Galeries Lafayette's Gourmet** departments both have a wonderful range of confectioneries.

CHEESES

The largest selection of cheeses in Berlin can be found at Galeries Lafayette which has a particularly broad choice from France. KaDeWe's cheese department also offers a wide variety, while Maître Philipe sells only select cheeses from small producers. You won't find any fridges here but the whole shop is air-conditioned and the aroma whets the appetite. Italian cheese can be bought in Südwind on Akazienstrasse, together with Italian wines and oils, and **Einhorn** specializes in international products, mainly sandwiches, pasta, meats and a wide variety of cheeses. **Lindner** and **Salumeria** are also a must for cheese lovers.

WINES

Between them, **KaDeWe** and **Galeries Lafayette** have the biggest wine cellars, while smaller businesses usually specialize in wines from a particular region. **Der Rioja-Weinspezialist**, for example, sells only wines originating from northern Spain, while **Vendemmia** specializes in Tuscan wines. A wide selection of German wines is available at **Viniculture**.

MEATS, COLD CUTS AND FISH

Berliners eat quite a lot of meat and meat products – the latter in particular are real German specialities. So if you are not vegetarian you should try something from the bewildering range of sausages and meat rolls. As well as the well-stocked departments in the big stores **KaDeWe** and **Galeries Lafayette**, small shops offer excellent quality products. **Fleischerei Bachhuber** is good, and **Alternative Fleischerei** specializes in chemical- and hormone-free meats, while a broad selection of fish (both fresh- and salt-water) and game is offered in **KaDeWe's** delicatessen. **Rogacki** is another good fishmonger and in **Schlemmermeyer** you can find good quality cold meats.

FOOD HALLS

The old 19th-century food halls are not as important today as they were before World War II, when they were the chief source of produce. The biggest of them all was on Alexanderplatz. The place used to teem with people 24 hours a day, but the hall wasn't rebuilt after sustaining damage during World War II. The GDR authorities had no use for such a large food hall, and with the advent of supermarkets, there was no need for it.

Today there are only three food halls in operation; **Arminiushalle** in Moabit, the **Markthalle am Marheinekeplatz** and **Eisenbahnhalle**, both in Kreuzberg. All of these are usually open all day six days per week – Monday to Saturday. Typically, Berliners use the food halls to pick up the one or two speciality items they can't find in the supermarkets. Shopping in these halls is a good opportunity to try traditional German *Currywurst*: the outlets in these food halls are regarded as the best in town.

MARKETS

Markets offer an additional way of shopping for food. They take place twice a week, and one of the best is the **Winterfeldtmarkt** which takes place on Wednesdays and Saturdays from 7am till 2pm. On Saturdays the opening hours are extended if the crowd is big, which it often is. You can buy everything from high quality fruits, through vegetables and cheeses from all over the world to clothing and domestic accessories. Fast-food outlets offer *falafel* or grilled sausages, and the place is surrounded by bars and cafés full of clients and traders relaxing with a glass of beer. The atmosphere and range of goods on offer is truly international.

Türken Markt am Maybachufer is a big Turkish market which opens on Tuesdays and Fridays until 6:30pm. It is popular with Turks living in Kreuzberg and Neukölln. The stalls offer all kinds of Turkish specialities. There are also markets in the city centre on Wittenbergplatz – **Wochenmarkt Wittenbergplatz** on Tuesdays and Fridays, Winterfeldtmarkt on Wednesdays and Saturdays and the **Bauernmarkt Wittenbergplatz** on Thursdays. In fact, Thursday is the day when Wittenbergplatz is invaded by farmers from all over the region offering a variety of products. You won't find any exotic fruits at these, but if you have had enough of tasteless supermarket tomatoes and apples then they should provide a good alternative. Depending on the season, you can buy pickled gherkins *(Salzgurken)* from the Spreewald, asparagus from the Beelitz region and delicious, sweet aromatic strawberries.

DIRECTORY

DEPARTMENT STORES WITH FOOD HALLS

Feinschmecker Etage at KaDeWe
Tauentzienstrasse 21.
Map 10 E2.
Tel 21 21 00.

Gourmet in Galeries Lafayette
Friedrichstrasse 23.
Map 6 F4.
Tel 20 94 80.

PATISSERIES AND SWEET SHOPS

Buchwald
Bartningallee 29.
Map 4 F3.
Tel 391 59 31.

Fassbender & Rausch
Charlottenstrasse 60.
Map 7 A4.
Tel 20 45 84 40.

Kolbe & Stecher Bonbonmacherei
Heckmann Höfe,
Oranienburger
Strasse 32.
Map 7 A1.
Tel 4405 52 43.

Konditorei Am Hagenplatz
Hagenplatz 3.
Tel 826 16 38.

Leysieffer
Kurfürstendamm 218.
Map 10 D1.
Tel 885 74 80.

Leysieffer
at Hotel Adlon
Unter den
Linden 77.
Map 6 E3, 15 A3.
Tel 22 67 98 65.

Opernpalais
Unter den
Linden 5.
Map 7 A3, 16 E3.
Tel 20 26 83.

Wiener Konditorei Caffeehaus
Hohenzollerndamm 92.
Tel 89 59 69 22.

Wiener Konditorei Caffeehaus
Reichsstrasse 81.
Tel 364 10 612.

CHEESES

Einhorn
Wittenbergplatz 5–6.
Map 10 F2.
Tel 218 63 47.

Lindner
Olivaer Platz 17
(near Kurfürstendamm).
Map 9 B2.
Tel 881 35 53.

Maître Philipe
Emser Strasse 42.
Map 9 B3, 9 C3.
Tel 88 68 36 10.

Salumeria
Windscheidstrasse 20.
Map 2 E5.
Tel 324 33 18.

Südwind
Akazienstrasse 7.
Map 11 A5.
Tel 782 04 39.

WINES

Der Rioja-Weinspezialist
Akazienstrasse 13.
Tel 782 25 78.

Vendemmia
Akazienstrasse 20.
Tel 784 27 28.

Viniculture
Grolmanstrasse 44–45.
Tel 883 81 74.

MEATS, COLD CUTS AND FISH

Alternative Fleischerei
Körtestrasse 20.
Map 13 C4.
Tel 691 64 86.

Fleischerei Bachhuber
Güntzelstrasse 47.
Map 9 C4.
Tel 873 21 15.

Rogacki
Wilmersdorfer Strasse
145–146.
Map 2 F4.
Tel 343 82 50.

Schlemmermeyer
Tauentzienstrasse 16
Map 10 E1.
Tel 217 72 09.

FOOD HALLS

Arminiushalle
Arminiusstrasse.
Map 4 E1. ◻ 8am–6pm
Mon–Thu, 8am–7pm Fri,
8am–2pm Sat.

Eisenbahnhalle
Pücklerstrasse. **Map** 14
E2. ◻ 8am–7pm Mon–
Fri, 8am–2pm Sat.

Markthalle am Marheinekeplatz
Marheinekeplatz. **Map** 13
A5. ◻ 8am–7pm Mon–
Fri, 8am–2pm Sat.

Markthalle Tegel-Center
Gorkistrasse 13–17.
Tel 43 43 849.
◻ 8am–7pm Mon–Fri,
8am–3pm Sat.

MARKETS

Bauernmarkt Wittenbergplatz
Wittenbergplatz.
Map 10 F1.
◻ 10am–7:30pm Thu.

Winterfeldtmarkt
Wittenbergplatz.
Map 11 A3.
◻ 8am–noon Wed & Sat.

Türken Markt am Maybachufer
Maybachufer. **Map** 14 E3,
F4. ◻ noon–6:30pm
Tue & Fri.

Wochenmarkt Wittenbergplatz
Wittenbergplatz.
Map 10 F2.
◻ 8am–2pm Tue & Fri.

ENTERTAINMENT IN BERLIN

With so much on offer, from classical drama and cabaret to variety theatre and an eclectic nightclub scene, it is possible to indulge just about any taste in Berlin. During the summer months many bars and restaurants set up outdoor tables, and the area around Unter den Linden, the Kurfürstendamm, Kreuzberg and Prenzlauer Berg in particular, seems to turn into one large social arena. The city really comes into its own at night, when its clubs, all-night cafés and cocktail bars give you

Flute player in costume

the chance to dance till dawn. The city has many night-life centres, each with a slightly different character. Prenzlauer Berg is best for mainstream bars, cafés and clubs, while Friedrichshain is more exclusive, and Kreuzberg has a vibrant gay scene. The Mitte district *(see* East of the Centre*)* offers a true mixture, its opera house and classical theatre surrounded by lively and inexpensive bars. On a Sunday, a quiet trip down the river or along the canals offers a pleasant way to unwind.

The Berlin Philharmonic Orchestra

PRACTICAL INFORMATION

There are so many things going on in Berlin that it can be difficult to find what you're looking for. The Information Centre offers basic information *(see p279)*, but for greater detail you can buy a copy of the listings magazines *Tip* or *Zitty* which offer the widest range of suggestions. Information on festivals, sports events, cinema programmes, theatre schedules, cabarets and concerts can be found on the following websites: berlinonline.de and berlin.de

But if you've only just arrived in town and haven't made it yet to an internet café or a kiosk, the chances are the bar you're sitting in, or your hotel foyer, has leaflets on the wall to point you in the right direction. And there is no end of posters around town telling you what's on offer.

GUIDES

You won't be short of cultural guides in Berlin. The fortnightly listings magazines *Tip* and *Zitty*, which cover the widest choice of events, are issued on Wednesdays, while the daily newspaper *Berliner Morgenpost* has a supplement, *"bm Live"*, which is available each Thursday. The Thursday supplement to *Tagesspiegel* is

called *Ticket*, and *Taz* publishes cinema programmes every other Thursday in *Cinemataz*. All of these can be bought at news kiosks.

Berlin Programm provides details of the month ahead and *Berlin Magazin*, issued by Berlin Tourismus Marketing GmbH, contains quarterly information. The free magazine *Flyer* is full of news about nightclubs and discos, and it should be available in restaurants.

If you want general information about the whole range of cultural events on offer, including current exhibitions in galleries and museums, then turn to the monthly *Kunstkalender* which is available in most bookshops, museums and galleries.

TICKETS

Tickets can usually be bought two weeks before an event, and you can buy them directly at theatre box offices

Prokofiev's *The Love of Three Oranges* staged at the Komische Oper

Berlin's Jazzfest features traditional jazz music *(see p268)*

or make a telephone booking. Reserved tickets have to be picked up and paid for at least half an hour before a show. Students, pensioners and the disabled are entitled to a 50 per cent discount, but you will need to present appropriate documentation. You can also pre-book tickets at special outlets all over Berlin but they charge a 20 per cent commission. All the major theatres and concert halls have special wheelchair access, but the number of places for the disabled is limited; make it clear when buying a ticket that you need an appropriate place. Tickets to some theatres include a pass for public transport.

If a performance has sold out, you can always try to find tickets just before the show, for some of the pre-booked tickets may not have been collected. One agency which specializes in these last-minute purchases is called **Hektiket Theaterkassen**. You can buy tickets on the day, even an hour before a performance. If someone has already returned their ticket, you might be able to buy it at a 50 per cent discount.

Other agencies to contact for tickets are **Fullhouse Service**, on Budapester Strasse, and **Showtime Konzert- und Theaterkassen**.

INFORMATION FOR THE DISABLED

In all the guides to theatres and concert halls the availability of wheelchair access is noted by a distinctive blue sign. The majority of the bigger theatres, halls and opera houses have special places for wheelchairs and seats reserved for people with walking difficulties. When buying a ticket you must specify your need as the number of places is limited.

If you are disabled you should be able to commute without restriction on public transport, as the majority of U- and S-Bahn stations have lifts, and they are clearly marked on maps of the underground. Many buses now have special ramps and facilities for wheelchairs, but if you experience any difficulty members of the BVG staff will always help.

PUBLIC TRANSPORT AT NIGHT

The last U-Bahn trains run at around 1am, but buses and trams continue running every half an hour, making Berlin's

Elephant Gate at the Zoologischer Garten *(see p150)*

night-time transport one of the most efficient in Germany. Bus and tram timetables are linked, and there are two major interchange points: one on Hardenbergplatz, near the Zoo railway station, and the other on Hackescher Markt. On Friday and Saturday nights you can also use lines 1 and 9 of the U-Bahn which operate every 15 minutes. Some S-Bahn lines also work at night over the weekend. Every ticket office and information point in town has brochures with all the relevant details about night-time public transport.

Afternoon with the children in the Museumsdorf Düppel *(see p180)*

DIRECTORY

TICKET AGENTS

Fullhouse Service
Hannoversche Strasse 19.
Map 6 F1. *Tel* 308 78 56 85.

Hekticket Theaterkassen
Hardenbergstrasse 29d.
Map 10 D1.
Tel 230 99 30.

Karl-Liebknecht-Strasse 12.
Map 7 C2. *Tel* 24 31 24 31.

**Showtime Konzert-
und Theaterkassen**
KaDeWe department store
(6th floor), Tauentzienstrasse 21.
Map 10 F2.
Tel 217 77 54.

Wertheim department store
(ground floor), Kurfürstendamm
181. **Map** 10 D1. *Tel* 882 25 00.

Theatres

Thanks to Reinhardt and Brecht, Berlin became a landmark in the European theatre scene in the 1920s, and its success continues to this day. During the years of Nazi rule, many people working in the business were killed or forced to emigrate as the stage became a propaganda machine, but after World War II a revival spread through Berlin's theatres. At the heart of this revival were Bertolt Brecht and his Berliner Ensemble, and Peter Stein who ran the Schaubühne.

MODERN HISTORY

Following the construction of the Berlin Wall, the number of venues doubled as each part of the divided city worked to build its own theatres. The Volksbühne in the East had its equivalent in the West called the Freie Volksbühne, and the eastern acting school, the Academy, was matched by a second Academy in the west.

The economic difficulties caused by the reunification of Germany forced a number of places to shut down, but the theatres of East Berlin managed to survive. In the west, the Freie Volksbühne and the Schiller-Theater (the largest stage in Germany) had to close, but the Volksbühne, under Frank Castorf, and the Deutsches Theater, led by Thomas Langhoff, continued to do well. Independent theatres have fared equally well in both parts of the city.

The theatre season runs from September to July, with its peak in May during Berliner Theatertreffen (Berlin Theatre Forum), when many other German theatre groups are invited to stage their plays. There are also a number of youth theatres which produce the work of young writers, and these follow the seasons of the major venues.

Repertoires are published in the listings magazines *Tip* and *Zitty*, and also displayed on yellow posters in U-Bahn stations and throughout Berlin. Leaflets are available in many restaurants around the city.

MAJOR STAGES

The **Deutsches Theater** and its small hall **Kammerspiele** on Schumannstrasse is a top-class theatre and offers a varied repertoire of productions with very professional modern stagings. From the Greek classics to the modern classics and contemporary plays, the Deutches Theater has successfully staged them all. Tickets for these plays can be difficult to obtain, but it is worth persevering.

At **Volksbühne** you can see interesting performances of classical plays in modern settings, as well as adaptations of books or films or pieces written by young writers. Concerts, lectures and dance evenings are organized in the Red and Green Salon of the theatre, and with so much going on the Volksbühne now seems more of a cultural centre with a multimedia character than just a stage.

Although it was particularly important for German theatre in the 1970s and 80s, **Schaubühne am Lehniner Platz** is no longer as popular as it was, which is a shame, for production values don't get any higher than this. The close attention to detail – on everything from the sets and scenery to the choice of music and the editing of the printed programme – is extraordinary, and distinguishes it from the other theatres in town; every performance is an event.

The **Berliner Ensemble** (or BE for short) has been managed by such influential dramatists as Bertolt Brecht from 1949 and then Heiner Müller in 1970. The spectacles created by these two are still performed today. The whole theatre is magnificent, and it has some superb architecture including the stage; after each performance you can meet the actors in the canteen in the courtyard, behind the building. Another venue well worth visiting is the **Hebbel-Theater** – an ambitious place with a programme that includes contemporary plays from all over the world and works of modern dance.

Other major venues include the **Maxim Gorki Theater**, the **Renaissance-Theater** and the **Schlosspark Theater**.

SMALL STAGES AND ALTERNATIVE THEATRE

There are a number of alternative theatres in Berlin, each enthusiastically playing the works of what are generally lesser known authors. **Theater am Halleschen Ufer** is devoted to avant-garde theatre and dance and is considered to be the city's best alternative stage. The smaller boulevard theatres, like **Theater am Kurfürstendamm**, **Komödie am Kurfürstendamm** or **Berlins Volkstheater Hansa**, offer different, lighter programmes.

Among other small theatres are **Bat-Studiotheater** and **Kleines Theater**. There are many other notable venues, including **Theater zum Westlichen Stadthirschen**, **Hackesches-Hoftheater**, **Theater 89**, **Theater Zerbrochene Fenster**, **Theater Kreatur**, and the **Vagantenbühne**.

MUSICALS, REVIEWS AND CABARETS

There are three main musical theatres in Berlin, in addition to the many small venues which fit musicals into their more general repertoire. **Friedrichstadtpalast**, in the eastern part of the city, stages many of the new major shows as well as classical musicals, and a smaller stage is reserved for cabaret. The **Theater des Westens** in Charlottenburg is more traditional, while the **Musical Theater Berlin am Potsdamer Platz** is a modern theatre established in the newly built city on Potsdamer Platz in 1999.

As for cabaret, there are probably as many acts in Berlin today as there were in the 1920s. They are usually performed by small itinerant groups which rely on the hospitality of theatres for a venue.

Distel, in Friedrichstrasse, continues its success from GDR times, and **Stachelschweine** celebrates its popularity in western Berlin.

There are many more venues for musicals, reviews and cabarets. Among these are **Bar jeder Vernunft**, **Chamäleon Variété**, **Dr Selt-sam Kabarett**, **Musical-Zelt**, **Scheinbar**, **Wintergarten Variété** and **Wühlmäuse**.

TICKETS

It is usually possible to pre-book tickets two weeks before a performance. You can buy them directly from the box office of the theatre or by telephone booking. There are also ticket vendors all over town, but they usually charge a 15–22 per cent commission. Even if the theatre or concert has been sold out,

there is still a chance of buying something just before the performance, provided that not all pre-booked tickets have been collected.

Hekticket Theaterkassen specializes in this kind of last-minute ticket. If you are lucky enough to pick up a ticket on the day of performance, you may find it has been returned and reduced to half its former price.

DIRECTORY

MAJOR STAGES

Berliner Ensemble
Bertold-Brecht-Platz 1.
Map 6 F2, 15 C1.
Tel 28 408 155.

Deutsches Theater
Schumannstrasse 13.
Map 6 E2, 15 A1.
Tel 28 44 12 25.

Hebbel-Theater
Stresemannstrasse 29.
Map 12 F2.
Tel 25 90 04 27.

Kammerspiele
Schumannstrasse 13a.
Map 6 E2, 15 A1.
Tel 28 44 12 22.

Maxim Gorki Theater
Am Festungsgraben 2.
Map 7 A3, 16 E2.
Tel 20 22 11 29.

Renaissance-Theater
Hardenbergstrasse 6.
Map 3 C5.
Tel 312 42 02.

Schaubühne am Lehniner Platz
Kurfürstendamm 153.
Tel 89 00 20.

Schlosspark Theater
Schlossstrasse 48.
Map 2 E4.
Tel 700 96 90.

Volksbühne
Rosa-Luxemburg-Platz.
Map 8 D1.
Tel 247 67 72.

SMALL STAGES AND ALTERNATIVE THEATRE

Bat-Studiotheater
Belforter Strasse 15.
Tel 44 01 89 12.

Berlins Volkstheater Hansa
Alt-Moabit 48.
Tel 39 90 99 09.

Hackesches Hoftheater
Rosenthaler Strasse 40.
Map 7 B2.
Tel 283 25 87.

Kleines Theater
Südwestkorso 64.
Tel 821 20 21.

Komödie am Kurfürstendamm
Kurfürstendamm 206.
Map 9 C2.
Tel 88 59 11 88.

Sophiensaele
Sophienstrasse 18.
Map 7 B1.
Tel 283 52 66.

Theater 89
Torstrasse 216.
Map 6 F1.
Tel 282 46 56.

Theater am Halleschen Ufer
Hallesches Ufer 32.
Map 12 F2.
Tel 251 09 41.

Theater am Kurfürstendamm
Kurfürstendamm 206.
Map 9 C2.
Tel 88 59 11 88.

Theater am Ufer
Tempelhofer Ufer 10.
Map 12 F2.
Tel 251 31 16.

Theater Zerbrochene Fenster
Schwiebusser Strasse 16.
Map 12 F5.
Tel 694 24 00.

Theater zum Westlichen Stadthirschen
Kreuzbergstrasse 37.
Map 12 D4.
Tel 785 70 33.

Vagantenbühne
Kantstrasse 12a.
Map 10 D1.
Tel 312 45 29.

MUSICALS, REVIEWS & CABARETS

Bar jeder Vernunft
Schaperstrasse 24.
Map 10 D2.
Tel 883 15 82.

Chamäleon Variété
Rosenthaler Strasse 40–41.
Map 7 B2.
Tel 282 71 18.

Distel
Friedrichstrasse 101.
Map 6 F2, 15 C1.
Tel 204 47 04.

Friedrichstadtpalast
Friedrichstrasse 107.
Map 6 F2, 15 C1.
Tel 23 26 23 26.

Kalkscheune
Johannisstrasse 2 (behind Friedrichstadtpalast).
Map 6 F2.
Tel 28 39 00 65.

Musical Theater Berlin am Potsdamer Platz
Marlene-Dietrich-Platz 1.
Tel (0180) 544 44.

Scheinbar
Monumentenstrasse 9.
Map 11 C5.
Tel 784 55 39.

Stachelschweine
Europa-Center.
Map 10 E1.
Tel 261 47 95.

Theater des Westens
Kantstrasse 12.
Map 2 E5, 9 A1, 10 D1.
Tel (0180) 882 28 88.

Wintergarten Variété
Potsdamer Strasse 96.
Map 11 C2.
Tel 25 00 88 88.

Wühlmäuse am Theo
Pommernallee 2–4.
Map 1 B5.
Tel 213 70 47.

TICKETS

Hekticket Theaterkassen
Hardenbergstrasse 29d.
Map 10 D1.
Tel 23 09 930.

Karl-Liebknecht-Strasse 12.
Map 7 C2.
Tel 24 31 24 31.

Cinema

Berlin has always been the capital of German cinema, and it is likely to remain so. In November 1895, exactly two months after the Lumière Brothers presented their first moving pictures in France, brothers Emil and Max Skladanowsky showed a series of short films to a spellbound German public. Wintergarten Varieté-theater was the place where you could go to see those famous pioneering films of kangaroos fighting, acrobats tumbling and children performing folk dances. By 1918 there were already some 251 cinemas with 82,796 seats available in Berlin, and by 1925 the number of people involved in the film industry had reached 47,600. The history of UFA (Universal Film AG), established in 1917, is intimately linked to that of Berlin, for the company has its two studios here.

BIG SCREENS AND BIG FILMS

The majority of cinemas can be found in the western part of town, around Breitscheidplatz, near the Ku'damm and Tauentzienstrasse, and this is where the big American and German blockbusters are shown. After the fall of the Berlin Wall, many new multiplex cinemas were built, the biggest being the **CinemaxX Potsdamer Platz** and the **Cinestar Sony Center**. Mainstream Anglo-American movies are dubbed, rather than subtitled, but you can also see films in their original language here.

Next door to CinemaxX is the **IMAX** cinema – the biggest screen in Germany. It can only show films that are shot with an Imax camera, but the spectacle is always breathtaking. Its huge curved screen is 27 m (89 ft) across and covers approximately 1000 sq m (10,750 sq ft). It shows a range of films including natural history, travel and underwater features, as well as a selection of 3D films that require special viewing glasses. There are three other areas of Berlin that are known as cinema centres: East of the City, in Friedrichshain and in Prenzlauer Berg.

The **International** on Karl-Marx-Allee is typical of cinemas built in the communist era. It was built in 1963 and may be of interest to anyone curious about the days of the GDR, but it's pretty austere and only

has 551 seats. Another venue on Karl-Marx-Allee is the **UFA-Palast Kosmos**. It is is now a modern multiplex with ten screens, but it was originally very small; only the exterior of the building provides hints of its GDR-era origins.

STUDIO CINEMAS

There are plenty of small studio cinemas scattered across town, and it is in these that new independent films and retrospectives of particular actors and directors are shown. Cinemas like **Hackesche Höfe Kino** or **Central**, situated near Hackescher Markt, offer a pleasant break from the bustle of modern city life, and most have bars of their own. The café at Hackesche Höfe Kino is noteworthy as it offers light snacks as well as a wonderful 5th-floor view over the neighbourhood.

The **Arsenal**, on Potsdamer Platz, belongs to the Freunde der Deutschen Kinemathek (Friends of German Cinema), and is ideal for lovers of German film for this is where you can see all the national classics. The venue has a detailed monthly programme which includes four screenings per day, many of which come with a small introductory lecture. Copies of the programme are distributed in bars all over town.

If you're interested in original language movies, **Cinéma Paris** in Charlottenburg is the place to go for French films,

while the **Odeon** in Schöneberg specializes in English and American films.

OPEN-AIR CINEMA

Open-air cinemas start operating as soon as the weather allows. The biggest is **Waldbühne** – a concert hall with seating for an audience of 20,000. Others can be found in Hasenheide, Künstler Haus Bethanien garden, in Friedrichshain or in UFA-Fabrik. All of these outdoor venues show a selection of current first-run films as well as the established classics. Screenings start at around 9pm, which is when it starts to grow dark during summer.

NON-COMMERCIAL FILMS

Although most people tend to go to the cinema nowadays to see the latest blockbuster movie from Hollywood, it is still possible to track down some of the venues which show less popular films including documentaries and other non-commercial films.

The **Zeughauskino**, which has recently reopened its doors, specializes in non-commercial films. It coordinates its interesting and informative repertoire with exhibitions in the Deutsches Historisches Museum (the German Historical Museum), as well as showing its own series of documentaries.

What used to be known as the Museum für Völkerkunde (the Museum of Mankind) in Dahlem (see p170), but now goes under the new name of the **Ethnologisches Museum**, also organizes various film showings, usually in conjunction with exhibitions of non-European culture. As at Zeughauskino, a ticket is very reasonably priced.

PRICES

Cinema tickets usually cost between €5–8 and students and senior citizens don't always receive a discount. Many cinemas declare Tuesday or Wednesday as Cinema

Day, when tickets are €1–2 cheaper. Some cinemas also organize so-called "Blue Mondays" when tickets are reduced to as little as €4.

In most cinemas there are usually three shows per evening, the first starting at 6pm, the last at around 10pm. All cinemas accept telephone bookings, but you have to turn up to pay for your ticket at least half an hour before a show, otherwise it may go to somebody else. Most ticket offices don't take credit cards, so have cash in hand.

Twenty minutes of commercials tend to precede the screenings of most films, although some venues use this time to show short films by up-and-coming directors.

THE FILM BUSINESS

If you're interested in the business of film production then you will want to visit Studio UFA in Babelsberg, Potsdam. A must for all cinema fans, the **Studiotour Babelsberg** allows you to see a live film crew working on a current production *(see p205)*. You will also get a chance to see some classic film sets – some going back to the days of Marlene Dietrich – as well as samples of the latest technical wizardry.

A wide variety of books, in many different languages, about cinema and film can be found in **Bücherbogen** under the arcade of the S-Bahn railway bridge at Savignyplatz. Alternatively you can try **Bücherstube Marga Schoeller** at 33 Knesebeckstrasse, near Kurfüstendamm.

DIRECTORY

BIG SCREENS AND BIG FILMS

CinemaxX
Potsdamer Platz
Potsdamer Strasse 1–19.
Map 6 D5.
Tel (0180) 524 63 62 99.

Cinestar
Sony Center
Potsdamer Strasse 4.
Map 6 D5.
Tel 26 06 62 60.

IMAX
Potsdamer Strasse 4.
Tel 26 06 64 00.

International
Karl-Marx-Allee 33
(corner of Schillingstrasse).
Map 8 E3.
Tel 24 75 60 11.

UFA-Palast
Kosmos
Karl-Marx-Allee 131a.
Map 8 E3.
Tel 42 20 160.

STUDIO CINEMAS

Arsenal 1–2
Potsdamer Strasse 2/Sony Center.
Map 10 F2.
Tel 26 95 51 00.

Central
Rosenthaler Strasse 39.
Map 7 B1.
Tel 28 59 99 73.

Cinéma
Paris
Kurfürstendamm 211.
Map 9 A2, 10 D1.
Tel 881 31 19.

Hackesche
Höfe Kino
Rosenthaler Strasse 4041.
Map 9 C2.
Tel 283 46 03.

Odeon
Hauptstrasse 116.
Map 11 B5.
Tel 78 70 40 19.

OPEN-AIR CINEMA

Waldbühne
Glockenturmstrasse 1.
Tel (01805) 33 24 33.

NON-COMMERCIAL FILMS

Ethnologisches
Museum
Filmbuehne Museum,
Lansstrasse 8.
Tel 830 14 38.
◻ *during festivals.*

THE FILM BUSINESS

Bücherbogen
am Savignyplatz
Stadtbahnbogen 593.
Tel 31 86 95 11.

Studiotour
Babelsberg
August-Bebel-Str. 26–53,
Potsdam (entrance
Grossbeerenstrasse).
Tel (0331) 721 27 55.

FAMOUS FILMS ABOUT BERLIN

Berlin Alexanderplatz
Germany 1931, directed by Phillip Jutzi, based on Alexander Döblin's book.

Berlin Alexanderplatz
GDR 1980, directed by Rainer Werner Fassbinder.

Berlin, Chamissoplatz
GDR 1980, directed by Rudolf Thome.

Berlin – Ecke
Schönhauser
GDR 1957, directed by Gerhard Klein.

Berliner Ballade
(Berlin Ballad)
American Occupied Zone 1948, directed by Robert Stemmle.

Berlin, die Symphonie einer Grosstadt
(Berlin, Symphony of a Great City)
Germany 1927, directed by Walter Ruttmann.

Coming Out
GDR 1988/1989, directed by Heiner Carow.

Der Himmel über Berlin
(The Sky Above Berlin)
GDR/France 1987, directed by Wim Wenders.

Die Legende von
Paul und Paula
(The Legend of
Paul and Paula)
GDR 1973, directed by Heiner Carow.

Eins, zwei, drei
(One, two, three)
USA 1961, directed by Billy Wilder.

Kuhle Wampe
Germany 1932, directed by Slatan Dudow, script by Bertolt Brecht.

Menschen am Sonntag
(Men on Sunday)
Germany 1930, directed by Robert Siodmak and Edgar G Ulmer.

Lola rennt
(Run, Lola, Run)
Germany 1998, directed by Tom Tykwer.

Sonnenallee
Germany 1998, directed by Leander Haußmann.

Classical Music

Berlin has one of the world's finest orchestras (the Berlin Philharmonic Orchestra) as well as one of the most beautiful concert halls (the Philharmonie). The Berlin Philharmonic has long been pre-eminent among the city's three symphonic orchestras, all of which perform regularly in Berlin. There are three major opera houses to choose from and a smaller one for lovers of the avant-garde. Apart from regular concerts the city offers many festivals, two of the most popular being the Musik-Biennale and the Open Air Festival on Gendarmenmarkt. Smaller concerts are organized year-round in the city's many churches, halls and palaces.

CONCERT HALLS

The **Philharmonie** is one of Europe's grandest concert halls, with excellent acoustics. The Berlin Philharmonic Orchestra itself was founded in 1882 by a group of 54 ambitious musicians, and it achieved great popularity under the conductor Herbert von Karajan, who stayed at the helm from 1954 through to 1989. The orchestra was taken over by Claudio Abbado, a worthy successor, and since 2002 it has been directed by Sir Simon Rattle, an acclaimed British conductor. Tickets for popular programmes quickly sell out, but the more obscure concerts will usually have some seats available. It is easier to obtain tickets when other orchestras such as the Berlin Symphony Orchestra and the Berlin Radio Symphony Orchestra are playing in the Philharmonie.

Chamber orchestras perform special chamber pieces in the smaller **Kammermusiksaal** attached to the bigger hall. **Konzerthaus Berlin**, formally known as the Schauspielhaus *(see p65)*, is another important venue for classical music. The building was restored after World War II and now contains a large concert hall and a smaller room for chamber music. It is one of the best places to hear classical music in elegant surroundings. Two unusual places that also sometimes put on musical concerts are the **Universität der Künste** on Hardenbergerstrasse and the **Staatsbibliothek** (State Library) on Potsdamer Strasse.

Many churches in Berlin also open their doors for concerts throughout the year. For a guide to all these events, look up the listings magazines *Tip* or *Zitty (see p260)*.

OPERA

Among Berlin's three major opera houses, the **Staatsoper Unter den Linden** *(see p63)*, under the leadership of Daniel Barenboim, is a gem. In this beautiful building, painstakingly restored according to Knobelsdorff's original design, performances take place in the Grosser Saal and the Apollo-Saal. The repertoire includes the traditional German classics, Italian opera and to a lesser extent, contemporary pieces.

Komische Oper *(see p68)*, managed by Harry Kupfer, is known for its broad range of lighter opera. Its operas usually have a long run, so you can nearly always find tickets. The ballet produced here is particularly innovative.

Deutsche Oper Berlin on Bismarckstrasse is the only one of the three main opera houses to be a modern building. The interior is a rather plain 1960s style, but the repertoire includes all kinds of music from different periods ranging from major Italian operas and Mozart to Wagner and Saint Saëns. There is often an exhibition organized in the foyer so the waiting time passes quickly.

A fourth opera house is the **Neuköllner Oper** in the Neukölln district. Less famous than the others, it is known for its unconventional approach.

CONTEMPORARY MUSIC

The Berlin organization **Initiative Neue Music Berlin e.V.** publishes a bulletin every two months containing information about current performances of contemporary music. It always includes **BKA** near Mehringdamm with its **Unerhörte Music** series. The **Akademie der Künste** and **Rundfunk Berlin-Brandenburg (RBB)** initiated a project to promote contemporary music; it is called *Insel Music* and one of its achievements is a series of concerts organized each November in the Haus des Rundfunks.

FESTIVALS

The **Berliner Festwochen** takes place throughout the month of September, and every year there is a different theme. Each festival promises a range of exhibitions, theatrical events and concerts, and the most famous orchestras and soloists from around the world come to take part each year.

Every other year in March you can also experience the **Musik-Biennale Berlin**, where contemporary music dominates. At this international festival numerous world premieres are made, both of music by new names and that of established composers.

A real treat for opera lovers is the summer festival of opera – Classic Open Air – which is organized on an open stage on Gendarmenmarkt, specially built for the occasion. Another musical feast well worth volunteering for is the Bach-Tage festival, a charming showcase of Baroque music, which takes place every year in July.

OPEN AIR CONCERTS

There are two open stages in Berlin and during the summer months a number of classical concerts are staged. **Waldbühne**, located near the Olympia Stadion, has seating for 20,000, and is the venue for concerts by European youth orchestras. The atmosphere is relaxed and informal, very often with children running around while their parents eat and drink during the shows. After sunset, when the crowds light the candles they have brought for the occasion, the atmosphere becomes quite magical.

Although the concerts organized the **Parkbühne Wuhlheide** are every bit as good as the ones held in Waldbühne, the audiences tend to be smaller.

MUSIC IN PALACES AND NOTABLE BUILDINGS

During music festivals, recitals are often held in Berlin's beautiful historic buildings, and a concert in the Berliner Dom *(see p77)*, the Eichengallerie in Schloss Charlottenburg *(see pp160–61)* or Schloss Friedrichsfelde *(see p174)* can be an unforgettable

experience. The **Universität der Künste** *(see Concert Halls)* has very good acoustics, but if you prefer a more modern environment, try one of the rooms in **Staatsbibliothek** *(see Concert Halls)* or the concert hall in the **Akademie der Künste** *(see Contemporary Music)*. Occasionally classical concerts are also held in venues that are normally reserved for popular music.

VARIOUS

The **Musikinstrumenten-Museum** offers concerts on selected Sunday mornings, and as a part of the Alte Musik Live scheme you can listen to the music of old masters played on their original instruments. A special booklet covering all the museum's events is published

twice a year and is available from all theatres, concert halls and music shops.

The **Kulturkaufhaus Dussmann** shop offers the widest range of music in Berlin, with a stock of over 50,000 titles, and competent staff always ready to help you find what you are after. They also stage literary readings, lectures, and other special cultural events at the store. **Gelbe Musik** on Schaperstrasse is also more than a shop; it has a gallery specializing in contemporary music and co-ordinates many concerts and recitals. **Schöne Künste Exkursionen** organizes walks around the city under the theme of Musikstadt Berlin; these take place on Saturday and set off from Bebelplatz, at the back of the opera building on Unter den Linden *(see p57)*.

DIRECTORY

CONCERT HALLS

Konzerthaus Berlin
(Schauspielhaus)
Gendarmenmarkt 2.
Map 7 A4, 16 D4.
Tel 203 09 21 01/02.
www.konzerthaus.de

Philharmonie Kammermusiksaal
Herbert-von-Karajan-Strasse 1. **Map** 6 D5.
Tel 25 48 81 32.

Staatsbibliothek
Potsdamer Strasse 33.
Tel 2660.

Universität der Künste
Hardenbergstrasse 33.
Map 4 E3.
Tel 31 85 23 74.

OPERA

Deutsche Oper Berlin
Bismarckstrasse 34–37.
Map 3 A4.
Tel 34 10 249.

Komische Oper
Behrenstrasse 55–57.
Map 6 F4, 15 C3.
Tel 47 99 74 00.

Neuköllner Oper
Karl-Marx-Str. 131–133,
Neukölln.
Map 14 F5.
Tel 688 90 777.

Staatsoper Unter den Linden
Unter den Linden 7.
Map 7 A3, 16 D3.
Tel 20 35 45 55.

CONTEMPORARY MUSIC

Akademie der Künste
Hanseatenweg 10.
Map 4 F3.
Tel 390 76 0.

Initiative Neue Musik Berlin e.V.
Klosterstrasse 68–70.
Map 8 D3.
Tel 242 45 34.

Rundfunk Berlin-Brandenburg (RBB)
Masurenallee 8–14.
Haus des Rundfunks.
Map 1 B5.
Tel 30 31 0.

Unerhörte Musik (BKA)
Mehringdamm 34.
Map 12 F3, 12 F4.
Tel 202 20 44.

FESTIVALS

Berliner Festwochen
Berliner Festspiele GmbH
Schaperstrasse 4. **Map** 10
D2. **Tel** 25 48 91 00.

Musik-Biennale Berlin
Berliner Festspiele GmbH
Schaperstrasse 4.
Map 10 D2. **Tel** 25 48 90.

OUTDOOR CONCERTS

Parkbühne Wuhlheide
An der Wuhlheide.
www.wuhlheide.de

Waldbühne
Glockenturmstrasse 1.
Tel (01805) 33 24 33.

VARIOUS

Gelbe Musik
Schaperstrasse 11. **Map**
10 D2. **Tel** 211 39 62.

Kulturkaufhaus Dussmann
Friedrichstrasse 90.
Tel 202 50.

Musikinstrumenten-Museum
Tiergartenstrasse 1.
Map 6 D5.
Tel 20 90 55 55.

Schöne Künste Exkursionen
Tel 782 12 02.

TICKETS

Fullhouse Service
Unter den Linden 36–38.
Map 15 B3.
Tel 308 78 56 85.

Showtime Konzert-und Theaterkassen
KaDeWe department store
(6th floor)
Tauentzienstrasse 21.
Map 10 F2.
Tel 217 77 54.

Wertheim department store (ground floor)
Kurfürstendamm 181.
Map 10 D1.
Tel 882 25 00.

Rock, Jazz and World Music

To music lovers Berlin can mean anything from techno to the Berlin Philharmonic Orchestra, for the city has a thriving and multi-faceted music industry. Between its classical and ultra-modern extremes the full spectrum of musical taste is catered for, from bar-room blues to rock'n'roll and international pop. Whether it's a major event by a world-famous band or a small-scale evening of jazz improvization, you needn't look far to find what you want. The biggest events take place in sports halls and stadiums, but most of the action can be found in discos, bars and the city's various clubs *(see pp270–71)*. There are also a number of cultural centres where you can stop by to listen to modern music. The best way to find something for yourself is to get hold of a copy of the listings magazines *Zitty* or *Tip*, and look out for flyers and leaflets in bars.

BIG CONCERTS

Berlin is always high up on the list when major pop, rock or jazz bands go on tour. While people flock from all over the country to attend these events, there are a number of smaller events which attract an equally devoted audience. Since the closure of the huge Deutsch-landhalle, the big events take place in **Max-Schmeling-Hall** and the Velodrom *(see p273)*. For the really big crowds, events are usually held at the **Olympia Stadion** *(see p184)* which has seating for 100,000. The **Waldbühne** next door has a capacity of 20,000 and hosts both classical orchestras and rock bands. **Parkbühne Wuhlheide** is another equally flexible venue. For detailed information about what's on and where, consult the websites berlinonline.de and berlin.de or the listings magazines *Zitty* and *Tip*.

OTHER MUSICAL EVENTS

There are plenty of smaller venues in Berlin where concerts are held. Among them are the **Loft** in Metropol on Nollendorfplatz, nearby **Café Swing**, and the famous **SO 36** in Kreuzberg. Schöne-berg was notorious in the 1980s for its punk rock scene, but while those days are now over, there are still plenty of exciting things on offer here today. One of the most popular places in town is

Tempodrom (check listings magazines for details).

Columbia Halle, which is located near Columbiadamm, is a well-known location for medium-size events, and so is the **Knaack Club**, a multi-sited venue on Greifswalder Strasse. If you are looking for particularly atmospheric concerts, try the **Passions-kirche**, a church in Kreuzberg. For a whole range of cultural events the **Palais Podewils** *(see p97)* is the place to go. Everything is on offer here from theatrical performances to dance and evenings of jazz improvization – and all in a truly modern style.

Concerts and plays are also organized at the popular **Arena** in Treptow – a very large music hall, dating from the 1920s, which used to be a local bus depot.

JAZZ

Jazz lovers from all over the world descend on Berlin for the **Jazzfest Berlin**, and its accompanying **Total Music Meeting**, both of which are held each year. The former is more traditional, but the latter is devoted to modern experi-mental work. "Jazz across the Border" takes place in July; it is a festival at which all kinds of borders are crossed, not least those of musical inhibition.

As far as regular clubs are concerned, jazz is still very popular in Berlin, in spite of

the pull of its perhaps better known electronic and techno discotheques. The **A Trane** and **b-flat** are classical jazz bars where you can listen to small bands just about every night of the week, and **Flöz**, on the ground floor and basement of a place in Nassauische Strasse, is famous for its excellent acoustics.

Another great venue is **Quasimodo** on Kantstrasse, but its concerts only start after 10pm when perfor-mances at Theater des Westens have finished; the vibrations would otherwise disturb the neighbouring audience. The acoustics at Quasimodo are also excellent, which is perhaps just as well as little can be seen through the clouds of cigarette smoke. Two other venues which fit evenings of jazz into their otherwise varied programmes are **Kalkscheune** on Johannisstrasse and **Palais Podewil** on Klostestrasse. Another good venue for enjoying jazz is **Bilderbuch**, on Akazienstrasse.

Apart from the typical, classical jazz clubs, jazz can also be heard in many of the city's smaller bars, like **Schlot** on Kastanienallee or **Harlem** in Prenzlauer Berg. If it's a mixture of soul, rap and jazz you want to listen to then head for the **Junction Bar** in Kreuzberg. The **pipapo**, near Nollendorfplatz, is a worthy choice on Sunday. The **Badenscher Hof Jazzclub** on Badensche Strasse is another great place for jazz.

WORLD MUSIC

As a broadly cosmopolitan city with an increasingly multi-national population, Berlin is home to a wide variety of music. The SFB4 MultiKulti radio station and Weltmusikfestival Heimak-länge were established here in 1988, and the presence of music from all parts of the world is never that far away.

The **Haus der Kulturen der Welt** on John-Foster-Dulles-Allee is an institution set up by the Berlin Upper Chamber to support this cosmopolitanism, and its main aim is to make non-European cultures more accessible to Germany. As music is one of the best ways of bridging cross-cultural differences, the Haus der Kulturen der Welt organizes all kinds of concerts at its own **Café Global** – one of the best Saturday evening venues for listening to and dancing to music from all over the world. Details of the bands on offer can be found in a booklet which should be available in bookshops and restaurants around town.

A similar organization is the **Werkstatt der Kulturen** on Wissmannstrasse which has been staging all kinds of cultural events for some years now. These include regular concerts and music festivals. Between them, the Haus der

Kulturen der Welt and the Werkstatt are the most reliable providers of world music in town, but you can also find a number of bars and clubs that specialize in the music of one particular nation. Details of these can be found in the listings magazines *Zitty* and *Tip*, and on flyers all over town.

Latin American discos are becoming ever more popular throughout Berlin – **Havanna** in Schöneberg is one of the city's most popular and largest.

Irish music is also well represented in the city, and all you have to do is visit a few pubs. Live music is played in **Wild at Heart** on almost every night of the week. However, if it's Russian ballads you want then head for the ever popular **Chagall**.

TICKETS

The price of tickets for major pop concerts can be astronomical, particularly if you want to secure a good seat. At the other extreme, you should be able to get into smaller clubs for €5–12, but again, if a famous person or band is playing you will have to pay a good deal more. Often you will find the ticket price includes a drink at the bar.

Tickets for major events are likely to sell out quickly and should be booked well in advance; there are numerous ticket offices in the busier parts of town (*see p261*).

If you just want to spend the night at a club you should have no trouble buying a ticket at the door.

DIRECTORY

BIG CONCERTS

Parkbühne Wuhlheide
An der Wuhlheide.
www.wuhlheide.de

Tränenpalast
Friedrichstrasse 17.
Map 6 F2.
Tel 20 61 00 11.

Waldbühne
Glockenturmstrasse 1.
Tel (01805) 33 24 33.

OTHER MUSIC EVENTS

Arena
Eichenstrasse 4.
Tel 533 73 33.

Columbia Halle and Columbia Club
Columbiadamm 13–21.
Tel 69 80 980.

Knaack Club
Greifswalder Strasse 224.
Tel 442 70 60.

Loft (Metropol)
Nollendorfplatz 5.
Map 11 A2.
Tel 217 36 80.

Palais Podewils
Klosterstrasse 68–70.
Map 8 D3.
Tel 24 74 97 77.

Passionskirche
Marheineckeplatz.
Map 13 A5.
Tel 69 40 12 41.

SO 36
Oranienstrasse 190.
Map 14 E2.
Tel 61 40 13 06.

Tempodrom
Am Anhalter Bahnhof, Möckernstrasse 10. **Map** 12 E1. *Tel 69 53 38 85.*

tipi-das Zelt
Grosse Querallee, Tiergarten. **Map** 5 C3.
Tel (0180) 327 93 58.

JAZZ

A Trane
Pestalozzistrasse 105.
Map 3 C5.
Tel 313 25 50.

Badenscher Hof Jazzclub
Badensche Strasse 29.
Map 10 D5.
Tel 861 00 80.

b-flat
Rosenthaler Strasse 13.
Map 7 B1.
Tel 28 38 68 35.

Bilderbuch
Akazienstrasse 28.
Map 11 A5.
Tel 78 70 60 57.

Flöz
Nassauische Strasse 37.
Map 9 C5.
Tel 861 10 00.

Musik-Café Harlem
Rodebergstrasse 37.
Tel 444 56 54.

Jazzfest Berlin
Schaperstrasse 24.
Map 10 D2.
Tel 25 48 90 .

Junction Bar
Gneisenaustrasse 18.
Tel 694 66 02.

Kalkscheune
Johannisstrasse 2.
Map 6 F2.
Tel 28 39 00 65.

Palais Podewils
Klosterstrasse 68–70.
Map 8 D3.
Tel 24 74 97 77.

pipapo
Grossgörschenstrasse 40.
Map 11 C4.
Tel 216 15 43.

Quasimodo
Kantstrasse 12a.
Tel 312 80 86.

Schlot
Chausseestrasse 18.
Map 1 A4. *Tel 448 21 60.*

Soultrane
Kantstrasse 17 (at Stilwerk).
Map 9 C1.
Tel 315 18 60.

WORLD MUSIC

Chagall
Kollwitzstrasse 2.
Tel 441 58 81.

Haus der Kulturen der Welt & Café Global
John-Foster-Dulles-Allee 10. **Map** 5 C3.
Tel 39 78 71 75.

Havanna
Hauptstrasse 30.
Map 11 A5.
Tel 784 85 65.

Werkstatt der Kulturen
Wissmannstrasse 32.
Map 14 E5.
Tel 609 77 00.

Wild at Heart
Wiener Strasse 20 (Kreuzberg).
Tel 611 92 31.

Classical and Modern Dance

With so much on offer in the arts, Berlin is a place where you can spend the early evening watching a ballet or musical, and later go out dancing yourself. The three opera houses have interesting ballet programmes built into their repertoires, and these are performed largely by resident dance companies. The city also attracts international ballet groups, not only during the May and August festivals but throughout the year. These productions are usually held in the Hebbel-Theater on Stresemannstrasse, although in recent years the Tanzfabrik in Kreuzberg has become a centre of contemporary dance. Berlin also has a thriving techno scene, which spills out on to the streets for the annual Love Parade *(see p49)*, and a plethora of dance clubs.

CLASSICAL BALLET

All three ballet groups working within Berlin's opera houses regularly stage new performances which appeal to a wide variety of audiences. To provide a balance, ballet evenings are often arranged to combine elements of classical and ballet with modern choreography. The Komische Oper *(see p68)* has a more modern repertoire, while the Staatsoper Unter den Linden *(see p63)* has a programme that focuses on classical work, such as *Swan Lake* with its traditional choreography.

MODERN DANCE

The **Hebbel-Theater** is the customary venue that welcomes foreign avant-garde dance companies. In return for its hospitality, its own productions are staged in co-operation with other dance groups all over the world. Together with **Theater am Halleschen Ufer**, it organizes the dance festival called "Tanz", which takes place every August. As the seating capacity for both theatres is limited, buying a ticket can be difficult; it is worth booking well in advance.

The **Sophiensaele**, a theatre now mainly used for drama, also features contemporary and avant-garde dance companies from time to time. **Tanzfabrik**, based on Möckernstrasse in Kreuzberg, is an excellent stage for all kinds of modern dance, and it also organizes dance workshops as well as popular body-work courses.

The International Choreographic Theatre of Johann Kresnik, in the Volksbühne on Rosa-Luxemburg-Platz *(see p263)*, has earned a great reputation, with many outstanding performances of their productions of *Frida Kablo*, *Hotel Lux* and *Malinche*.

TANGO

You can dance the tango in Berlin every day of the week. A full schedule could incorporate the **Checkpoint** on Monday, **Kalkscheune** on Tuesday, the Red Salon on Wednesday and the Grüner Salon on Thursday (both at Volksbühne) and Friday at the **Walzerlinksgestrickt**. For the grand finale on Saturday you can always improve your dance moves at one of the many dance schools. But if that still hasn't satisfied your appetite, Saturday lessons can even be extended to Sunday to fully prepare yourself for the week ahead.

TECHNO

Among its many artistic claims, Berlin is also the techno capital of Europe, with over a million devotees celebrating the genre at the annual Love Parade. The festival is held at the beginning of July and most of the action takes place around the Tiergarten, but even over the following weekend, after the event has ended, streets all over Berlin are still packed with people dancing. Parties and discos are organized throughout Berlin, and the areas around clubs turn into meeting areas where people exchange news about what's going on elsewhere in the city.

The Love Parade lasts only one weekend, but techno fans can spoil themselves all year round at any of countless clubs, most of which stay open through the night until noon the following day. **Tresor** is at the very heart of it all, situated in the old vault of a defunct department store (Wertheim on Leipziger Platz). This is where the best DJs in town can be heard.

Few clubs specialize in a particular kind of music, but most reserve certain days of the week for different styles. Find out where the latest techno outfits can be heard – a good way to start is to get hold of a copy of the free publications *Flyer* or *Partysan*, both of which are distributed widely in bars.

The clubs **Matrix** and **Columbia Club** are guaranteed to provide what you're after, and so too is the special techno-room known as Subground, which is located in the subways of **Pfefferbank**. Techno dominates the menu here, but Subground also caters for music lovers of all kinds.

DISCOS AND OTHER CLUBS

If it's a good old-fashioned disco you're looking for, with happy tunes and a little less of the techno, then **Far Out** and **Metropol** are the places to go. It was famous before the fall of the Wall and attracts a teenage crowd every weekend. Tuesdays are devoted to thirtysomethings, who come here to dance to classic funk, soul and pop. For a crowded house with 2000 Watts for 2000 people, head for the **Loft** *(see p268)* which is always packed, but, if you're no longer a teenager and fancy a bit of retro, then a night at the **Tränenpalast** could be the choice; it's based in the pavilion that served as the former passport control between East and West Berlin *(see p41)*. The **Privat Club** is known for arranging a good disco or two, aside from its customary repertoire of jazz.

During the summer, you can dance to pop music in the open air at **Golgatha** in Kreuzberg's Viktoriapark, or in **Die Insel**, a café built on an island in Treptow.

Delicious Doughnuts is one of the best places in town for ambient, house and acid-jazz. If it's Latin-American rhythms you are looking for, then **Salsa** *(see p269)*, **Havanna** and **Cueva Buena Vista** are the best places to go. The **Akba-Lounge** is another good choice of venue. Many smaller bars have a space for itchy feet. Lovers of soul and reggae should head for **Fat Cat** or **Lumumba Tanzcafé**, while pop music can be heard in the **Mitte Bar**. For something a little more intimate, the romantic atmosphere of **Sophienclub** might be worth investigating.

There are also a few places where you can waltz and step back in time to experience the ambience of the old dance halls. Among the oldest is **Clärchens Ballhaus**.

GAY AND LESBIAN CLUBS

Berlin generally maintains a very tolerant attitude to people with different sexual orientations. A big day for the gay community is the gigantic parade on Christopher Street Day, which takes place annually at the end of June. On a daily basis, homosexual men and women meet in their own clubs and discos, or during special evenings organized by places normally frequented by heterosexuals.

The city's most popular gay discos are **SchwuZ**, on Mehringdamm, **Connection**, on Fuggerstrasse and **Ostgut**. Gay-only discos are also held regularly in Stellwerk *(see Techno)* and other clubs around town.

For lesbians the best clubs in Berlin are **Ackerkeller** and **So 36**. The latter also admits gay men.

DIRECTORY

MODERN DANCE

Hebbel-Theater
Stresemannstrasse 29.
Map 12 F2.
Tel 25 90 04 27.

Sophiensaele
Sophienstrasse 18.
Map 7 B1.
Tel 283 52 66.

Tanzfabrik
Möckernstrasse 68.
Map 12 E4.
Tel 786 58 61.

Theater am Halleschen Ufer
Hallesches Ufer 32.
Map 12 E2, 12 F2.
Tel 251 09 41.

TANGO

Checkpoint
Leipziger Strasse 55.
Map 16 F5.
Tel 208 25 96.

Kalkscheune
Johannisstrasse 2.
Map 6 F2.
Tel 28 39 00 65.

Walzerlinks-gestrickt
Am Tempelhofer Berg 7e.
Map 12 F5.
Tel 69 50 50 00.

TECHNO

Columbia Club
Columbiadamm 9–11
(Kreuzberg).

Matrix
Warschauer Platz 18.

Pfefferbank
Schönhauser Allee 176.
Tel 20 91 49 90.

Tresor
Leipziger Strasse 126a.
Map 6 F5.

DISCOS AND OTHER CLUBS

90 Grad
Dennewitzstrasse 37.
Map 12 D2.
Tel 27 59 62 31.

Akba-Lounge
Sredzkistrasse 64.
Tel 441 14 63.

Clärchens Ballhaus
Auguststrasse 24. **Map** 7
A1, 7 B1. *Tel 282 92 95.*

Cox Orange
Dircksenstrasse 40.
Map 7 C2.
Tel 281 05 08.

Cueva Buena Vista
Andreasstrasse 66.
Tel 24 08 59 51.

Delicious Doughnuts
Rosenthaler Strasse 9.
Map 7 B1.
Tel 28 09 92 74.

Die Insel
Alt Treptow 6.
Tel 53 60 80 20.

Far Out
Kurfürstendamm 156.
Map 9 A2.
Tel 32 00 07 23.

Golgatha
Dudenstrasse 48–64.
Map 12 D5, 12 E5.
Tel 785 24 53.

Havanna
Hauptstrasse 30. **Map** 11
A5. *Tel 784 85 65.*

Lumumba Tanzcafé
Steinstrasse 12. **Map** 7
C1. *Tel 28 38 54 65*

Metropol
Nollendorfplatz 5.
Map 11 A2.
Tel 217 36 80.

Mitte Bar
Oranienburger Strasse 46.
Map 6 F1. *Tel 283 38 37.*

Privat Club
Markthalle Pücklerstrasse
34. **Map** 14 F2.
Tel 617 55 02.

Sage-Club
Köpenicker Strasse 76–78.
Map 8 D5.
Tel 278 98 30.

Sophienclub
Sophienstrasse 6.
Map 7 B1.
Tel 282 45 52.

Tränenpalast
Reichstagufer 17.
Map 6 D2, 6 F3.
Tel 20 62 00 11.

GAY & LESBIAN DISCOS

Ackerkeller
Ackerstrasse 12 (Mitte).

Connection
Fuggerstrasse 33.
Map 10 F2.
Tel 218 14 32.

Ostgut
Mühlenstrasse 26–30
(Friedrichshain).

SchwuZ
Mehringdamm 61.
Map 12 F4.
Tel 693 70 25.

So 36
Oranienstrasse 190.
Map 14 E2.
Tel 61 40 13 06.

Sport and Recreation

Berlin is a sports-loving town, and every year the major sports events attract a growing number of fans and competitors. The Berlin Marathon, run in September, is now the third largest in the world, its 42-km (26-mile) distance tackled by runners and roller-skaters – able-bodied and disabled alike. The Bundesliga (German football league) cup final takes place in May in the Olympia Stadion. Crowds of each team's supporters converge on the city a few days before the game, and after the match they all join a huge party for the winners along the Ku'damm. The world tennis élite battle it out during the German Open championship every April.

CYCLING

The flat terrain, numerous parks and countless special routes for cyclists – which reach a total of 850 km (530 miles) – make Berlin a cycle-friendly city. Outside rush hour you can take your bike on S- or U-Bahn trains, which provide easy access to the three most popular routes – along the Havel river, around the Grunewald forest, and around the Müggelsee.

There are many places all over Berlin where you can rent a bike for € 5–12 per day (see p293), provided you leave a deposit, either as cash or a cheque. The best hotels in town also hire out their own bikes for guests. The route from the historic centre of Mitte to the Ku'damm via Tiergarten can be an unforgettable experience.

In January those lovers of two wheels meet during Berliner Sechs-Tage-Rennen in the newly built **Velodrom** on Paul-Heyse-Strasse. You might have some problems buying a ticket as the event is very popular, so give them a call beforehand. For information concerning routes, events, tours, or anything else you may need to know about cycling in Berlin, contact the **ADFC (Allgemeiner Deutscher Fahrrad-Club)**.

GOLF

Just about every sporting discipline is catered for in Berlin, and golfing is no exception. The Driving Range golf club is situated in the centre of the town on Chausseestrasse, and during spring and summer it is open from noon until sunset. Entrance to the course is free, but you have to leave a deposit on hiring golf clubs. A bucket of 30 balls costs only €1.50. Golf coaching is available either for individuals or in a group.

There are two golf courses within Berlin: the **Golf und Landclub Berlin-Wannsee**, which has a large 18-hole course and a smaller one with 9 holes, and **Berliner Golfclub-Gatow** which only has a 9-hole course. There are a total of 15 golf clubs around Berlin, most of which have excellent restaurants and are situated close to hotels.

SWIMMING POOLS

Public swimming facilities in Berlin are extremely clean and you can always swim there safely. Some of the best places to try are on the Havel river and the city's lakes. Swimming on natural beaches is free, but there are no changing rooms or toilet facilities. Berlin also has a number of artificial beaches which are all manned by lifeguards. The best known is the **Strandbad Wannsee**, which was built in the 1920s and remains very popular today. Another excellent spot is the **Strandbad Müggelsee**, which also has an area for nude bathing. The entrance fee to these beaches is similar to that of swimming pools – usually around €3.

One of the most beautiful swimming pool complexes is **Olympia Stadion** (see p184) which was a venue for the 1936 Berlin Olympic Games. A special pool for diving has a 10-m (33-ft) tower with a lift. Alternatively, you can simply sunbathe on the steps and admire the view.

The three most beautiful swimming pools are situated in Mitte, Neukölln and Wilmersdorf. **Stadtbad Mitte**, on Gartenstrasse, is a painstakingly restored building which dates from the 1930s. It has a 50-m (164-ft) pool designed for sporting events as well as recreational swimming. **Stadtbad Charlottenburg**, on the other hand, offers a smaller pool which is more appropriate for relaxation than serious swimming; it is also beautifully decorated with Secessionist paintings. But if it's a swim in luxurious surroundings you want, then take a dive at the **Stadtbad Neukölln**; the extraordinary decorative mosaics, frescos, and marble-and-bronze ornamentation is enough to make you forget why you came here in the first place.

A good day out for the whole family can be had at **"blub" Badeparadies**, situated on Buschkrugallee in the southern part of town. More than simply a pool, this is an aquapark with a 120-m (394-ft) long slide, a wave-pool and diving boards, as well as several saunas.

BADMINTON, SQUASH AND TENNIS

You won't have to travel far in Berlin to find facilities to play badminton, squash or tennis as numerous courts are scattered all over town, from local parks to sophisticated sports centres. It is customary to bring your own sports shoes, but rackets are almost always available to rent.

The entrance fee in most cases includes the use of a sauna. **Fit-Fun Squash und Fitness Center** has 14 courts for squash, and at **Sportoase** there are 18 badminton courts in addition to 8 squash courts. **Tennis & Squash City** offers an opportunity to play tennis on any of its five courts. Other addresses can be found in the telephone directory.

OTHER SPORTS

Every weekend in August, John-Foster-Dulles-Allee in Tiergarten is closed to traffic to become a genuine paradise for rollerblade and in-line skaters. If you fancy trying this yourself, there are plenty of shops in the area offering skates and safety equipment at reasonable rates.

If you fancy a boat trip, rowing boats are available for hire at many places along the banks of the lakes. In the Tiergarten you can rent them near Café am Neuen See and around Schlachtensee; the price is usually somewhere around €7–€10 per hour.

FITNESS

There are always new gyms opening and others closing down in Berlin, so your best bet is to check the telephone directory for the most up-to-date listings. At many gyms you can buy a daily card, rather than becoming a member. But if your visit to Berlin is a long one, it may be worth joining. **Ars Vitalis** is the best independent fitness club and spa for men and women. **Jopp-Frauen-Fitness-Berlin** is one of the best options for women; it has five studios across the city and they are all large and well equipped. The main one is on Tauentzienstrasse and has a pleasant terrace overlooking town. A one-day ticket costs €25.

SPECTATOR SPORTS

As a rule, Berlin's sports teams tend to be among the country's best, and rank highly in each of their respective leagues. Football matches of Hertha BSC take place in the Olympia Stadion and tickets are usually available at approximately €6–€18.

Alba Berlin is among the top basketball teams in Germany, and its matches in **Max-Schmeling-Halle** can be attended by up to 8,500 fans. For international events it's best to pre-book tickets well in advance, and these can vary between €10 and €52, depending on the match. Berlin has two very good hockey teams: Berlin-Capitals and Eisbären Berlin – both of whose matches always sell out of tickets very quickly.

HORSE RACING

Lovers of horse racing have two tracks to choose from in Berlin. **Trabrennbahn** in Mariendorf is open all year and the races held here are strictly commercial. **Galopprennbahn Hoppegarten**, on the other hand, has a more approachable feel.

MARATHON

Marathon running isn't everyone's cup of tea, but when you see the enormous crowds gathered to run the **Berlin-Marathon** in August, you may well wish you were one of the pack.

The route is one of the fastest in the world, attracting top sponsors and athletes alike; the world record was broken here in 1998. Thousands of viewers gather en route to cheer the runners, rollers and disabled athletes – the latter having their own group which starts before the others.

DIRECTORY

CYCLING

ADFC
Brunnenstrasse 28.
Tel 448 47 24.

Velodrom
Paul-Heyse-Strasse.
Tel 44 30 44 30.

GOLF

Berliner Golfclub-Gatow
Kladower Damm 182–288, Gatow.
Tel 365 77 25.

Golf und Landclub Berlin-Wannsee
Golfweg 22.
Tel 806 70 60.

SWIMMING

"blub" Badeparadies
Buschkrugallee 64.
Tel 609 06 0.

Stadtbad Charlottenburg
Krumme Strasse 9–10.
Tel 34 38 38 65.

Stadtbad Mitte
Gartenstrasse 5.
Plan 7 A1.
Tel 30 88 09 10.

Stadtbad Neukölln
Ganghoferstrasse 3.
Tel 68 24 98 12.

Strandbad Müggelsee
Fürstenwalder Damm 838.
Tel 64 87 777.

Strandbad Wannsee
Wannseebadweg 25.
Tel 80 40 45 55.

BADMINTON, SQUASH, TENNIS

FitFun Squash und Fitness Center
Uhlandstrasse 194.
Tel 312 50 82.

Sportoase
Stromstrasse 11–17.
Plan 4 F1, 4 F2.
Tel 394 50 94.

Tennis & Squash City
Brandenburgische Strasse 53.
Map 9 A3, 9 B5.
Tel 873 90 97.

MARATHON

Berlin-Marathon
Informations Bureau
Waldschulallee 34.
Tel 30 12 88 10.

SPECTATOR SPORTS

Max-Schmeling-Halle
Am Falkplatz.
Tel 44 30 44 30.

FITNESS

Ars Vitalis
Hauptstrasse 19.
Map 11 A5.
Tel 788 35 63.

Jopp-Frauen-Fitness-Berlin
Tauentzienstrasse 13.
Map 10 E1.
Tel 21 01 11
(central switchboard).

HORSE RACING

Galopprennbahn Hoppegarten
Goetheallee 1.
Tel (03342) 389 30.
🕐 4–10pm Sat & Sun.

Trabrennbahn Mariendorf
Mariendorfer Damm 222, Tempelhof.
Tel 740 12 12.
🕐 1pm Sun.

CHILDREN IN BERLIN

When it comes to entertainment, people of all ages are catered for in Berlin, and children are no exception. There are numerous shops, theatres and cinemas to keep them occupied, not to mention circuses and zoological gardens. Additionally, there is the Deutsches Technikmuseum

One of Berlin's young roller skaters

(German Museum of Technology), the Museumsdorf Düppel, or the Kinder- und Jugendmuseum, all of which encourage children to take part in the displays. Tickets for children under 14 are almost always reduced, and very young children are often admitted for free. Restaurants often have special areas for toddlers.

The Potsdam train, always a favourite among children

INFORMATION

Berlin is very welcoming to its younger visitors. Families with children are entitled to public transport discounts, and children can travel free or at a reduced rate, depending on their age. For detailed information on the discounts and opportunities for children, contact **Berlin Tourismus Marketing GmbH**. From this organization you can obtain the so-called Ferienpass, valid for the whole summer, which entitles the holder to all kinds of reductions around town. For girls there is a special pocket diary on offer, called Berta, which has much information and advice about current events.

ZOOLOGICAL GARDENS

One of Berlin's zoological gardens can be visited the moment you arrive in town, as it is located opposite the Zoo railway station. The **Zoologischer Garten** offers extensive parkland and many animal enclosures, as well as an excellent aquarium with the biggest collection of aquatic fauna in the world.

The second zoo, **Tierpark Berlin** in Friedrichsfelde, isn't quite so convenient but it is much bigger and can still be reached by U-Bahn. Covering a wide area around Schloss Friedrichsfelde, the Tierpark is the largest park in Europe.

Apart from these zoological gardens, a lot of the parks in Berlin contain mini-zoos where many different kinds of animals can be seen. In a garden behind the Märkisches Museum, for example, you can see a family of bears.

As well as the more exotic animals, however, it is also possible to see the familiar favourites. Small children will love the **Kinderbauernhof Görlitzer Bauernhof**, which has a collection of domestic animals. Here geese, pigs and rabbits run happily around the Görlitzer Park.

MUSEUMS

Generally speaking, Berlin's museums are well set up for children. Perhaps the most entertaining is the **Deutsches Technikmuseum** *(see p144)* where children can take part in all kinds of experiments. The **Ethnologisches Museum** *(see p178)* also prepares

special exhibitions for children. On some days you can take part in a game with Mexican papier-mâché dolls, on others you can participate in a Japanese ceremonial bath. A visit to the **Museumsdorf Düppel** is an excellent way to show a child the workings of a medieval village. The Museum für Naturkunde *(see p109)* is another fun place for children, particularly the dinosaur sections and the dioramas of animals in their natural habitats. The **Kindermuseum Labyrinth** is another favourite.

Another great place to visit is the **Puppentheatermuseum**, which is always lively, and offers a chance for children to take part in minor performances. For more information about museum events try to get hold of the brochure *Museumpädagogischer Dienst*. Exhibitions and events change regularly, but you are bound to find something of interest. The website **Kinder-Berlin** also offers information about children's activities and events.

Children admiring Neptune's Fountain by the Town Hall

A visit to the medieval village at Museumsdorf Düppel

OTHER ENTERTAINMENT

An ascent of the Fernsehturm (television tower) at Alexanderplatz *(see p93)* is a great way to treat a child, perhaps for afternoon tea. You will also be able to buy cake and juice in the tower's rotating café. A lift in the Funkturm (radio tower) in the Messegelände *(see p183)* offers an excellent view of the city, from a slightly lower height.

The Story of Berlin is a fun way for both parents and children to experience the history of Berlin in a thrilling multimedia exhibit. And the **Berliner Gruselkabinett** (Room of Fear) is enough to frighten anybody.

For an out-of-the-ordinary experience, you can't go wrong at either the **Zeiss-Planetarium** or the **Planetarium am Insulaner**. A fascinating programme of wonderful shows allows you to explore the known universe and to have a good look at the stars.

THEATRES

Established in 1969, **Grips Theater** is probably the most interesting theatre for children and teenagers. Its independent and ambitious programme attracts many spectators and one of its performances, *Linie 1*, was made into a film. Other venues worth trying are the **carrousel-Theater an der Parkaue**, **Theater o.N.**, **Zaubertheater Igor Jedlin** and the **Puppentheater Berlin**. Another option is to go to one of the city's many circuses, all of which prepare their programmes with children in mind.

SPORTS

Ice-skating in winter and roller-skating in summer are popular in Berlin, and football and swimming are popular year-round. You can swim in rivers, lakes and swimming pools (Hotline **Berliner Bäderbetriebe** offers useful information) but "blub" Badeparadies *(see p273)* is the best place for children. Each district has its own ice-skating rink, but the **Eisstadion Berlin Wilmersdorf** is outstanding with its 400-m (1,312-ft) run and large ice-hockey rink. **FEZ Wuhlheide** offers a special daily programme for kids.

DIRECTORY

INFORMATION

Berlin Tourismus Marketing GmbH
Am Karlsbad 11.
Tel 25 00 25.
www.btm.de

Kinder-Berlin
www.kinder-berlin.de

ZOOLOGICAL GARDENS

Kinderbauernhof a Görlitzer Park
Wiener Strasse 59
Tel 611 74 24.

Tierpark Berlin
Am Tierpark 125,
Lichtenberg.
Tel 51 53 10.

Zoologischer Garten
Hardenbergplatz 9,
Charlottenburg.
Tel 25 40 10.

MUSEUMS

Kindermuseum Labyrinth
Osloer Strasse 12.
Tel 49 30 89 01.
☐ 1pm–6pm Tue–Sat,
11am–6pm Sun.

Museumsdorf Düppel
Clauertstrasse 11.
Tel 802 66 71.
☐ Apr–Oct: 3–7pm Thu,
10am–5pm Sun and
holidays.

Puppentheater-Museum Berlin
Karl-Marx-Strasse 135.
Tel 687 81 32.
☐ 9am–4pm Mon–Fri,
11am–5pm Sun.

THEATRES

carrousel-Theater an der Parkaue
Parkaue 29.
Tel 55 77 52 52.

Grips Theater
Altonaer Strasse 22.
Tel 39 74 74 77.

Puppentheater Berlin
Haubachstrasse 26.
Tel 342 19 50.

Theater o.N.
Kollwitzstrasse 53.
Tel 440 92 14.

Zaubertheater Igor Jedlin
Roscherstrasse 7.
Tel 323 37 77.

SPORTS

Berliner Bäderbetriebe
Tel (01803) 10 20 20.

Eisstadion Berlin Wilmersdorf
Fritz-Wildung-Strasse 9.
Tel 824 10 12.

FEZ Wuhlheide
An der Wuhlheide,
Köpenick.
Tel 53 07 15 04.

OTHER ENTERTAINMENT

Berliner Gruselkabinett
Schöneberger Strasse 23a.
Map 12 E1.
Tel 26 55 55 46.

Planetarium am Insulaner
Munsterdamm 90.
Tel 790 09 30.

The Story of Berlin
Kurfürstendamm 207–208.
Map 9 A2.
Tel 88 72 01 00.

Zeiss-Großplanetarium
Prenzlauer Allee 80.
Tel 42 18 45 12.

SURVIVAL GUIDE

PRACTICAL INFORMATION

erlin is a tourist-friendly city, so you shouldn't have too much difficulty getting around. Many Germans speak English and Berliners as a rule are welcoming to newcomers. Cash machines, telephones and parking meters all have clear instructions, and public transport is of the highest standard *(see pp292–3)*. For reduced fares on public transport, buy

Berlin tourist information sign

yourself a daily or weekly travel card, or a Welcome Card which also gives you reduced access to many museums. There are plenty of information centres in the busiest areas of town, and a number of different listings magazines and brochures are available for tourists. If you have access to the Internet, BerlinOnline will point you in the right direction.

Entrance tickets for some of Berlin's historic buildings

MUSEUMS AND HISTORIC BUILDINGS

There are over 150 museums and galleries in Berlin, but exhibitions change and collections move continually. This guide covers the most important places, but plenty of information is also available on lesser-known museums and galleries. A tourist information office could be your first port of call, but better still is the museum information centre itself, run by **Museum-pädagogischer Dienst Berlin**. Details of current and forthcoming exhibitions can be picked up here, including

information on seasonal events, like the bi-annual Lange Nacht der Museen, when museums stay open until midnight. A good information line is the **Info-Telefon der Staatlichen Museen zu Berlin** and there are also information centres devoted to the Pergamonmuseum and the Sanssouci complex in Potsdam. Contact the **Besucherbetreuung der Schlösser und Gärten Potsdam-Sanssouci** for more details.

Museums and historic buildings are usually open Tuesday to Sunday, from 10am to 5pm (sometimes 6pm). Some museums, however, close on another day instead of Mondays. For reduced entrance prices, you may want to get hold of the Museums-Pass, which allows three days' unlimited access to the major museums. This pass is sold in the **Europa-Center** and **Brandenburg Gate** information centres. It can be used at all the national museums, including the whole Museum

Island complex, the Kulturforum, Museumszentrum Dahlem and four additional institutions in Charlottenburg (Ägyptisches Museum, Galerie der Romantik, Sammlung Berggruen, Museum für Vor- und Frühgeschichte). In this case, the Museums-Pass is like a one-day ticket, allowing you to visit all the sites in the same complex.

Another option is the Welcome Card. This entitles you to free public transport for three days within Berlin and Potsdam, and a discount on many museums. Each Welcome Card is valid for one adult and up to three children.

OPENING HOURS

Offices in Berlin usually open from 9am until 6pm, with an hour's lunch break, but many people in the east of the city still work to the old timetable of 8am till 4 or 5pm. Smaller shops open from 9:30 or 10am until 8pm, and on Saturdays most shops close at 4pm. The majority of shops are also open on Sundays in the period leading up to Christmas, and opening hours are extended during the week. Bank hours are 9am until 3pm (Monday and Wednesday), 6pm (Tuesday and Thursday) and 1pm (Friday).

TOURIST INFORMATION

There are many excellent tourist information centres in Berlin. The two biggest are at the **Europa-Center** and the **Brandenburg Gate**, but others can be found at **Tegel Airport**, in the KaDeWe department store

A modern rickshaw providing alternative transport on Berlin's streets

(see p155) and in a new information café on the ground floor of the TV tower in Alexanderplatz. The **Potsdam Tourismus Service** office is in the centre of Potsdam, on Friedrich-Ebert-Strasse.

For up-to-the-minute news, turn to the Internet; **Berlin-Online**, which is managed by **Berlin Tourismus Marketing** is a very reliable source of information for tourists.

ENTERTAINMENT

The three best magazines devoted to cultural events are *Zitty*, *Tip* and *Berlin-Programm*, all of which cover the major (as well as minor) concerts, exhibitions and lectures held throughout Berlin. The very latest news can also be obtained from tourist information centres and the Internet, the most popular site being Berlin-Online. There are many ticket offices all over town where you can pre-book tickets (see p261), some of them offering excellent bargain deals. On-the-day tickets can often be bought at half price.

Popular listings magazines

Guided bus tour offering an overview of Berlin and its environs

GUIDED TOURS

There are many bus tours available in Berlin, each of which, in 3 or 4 hours, introduces you to the city's chief historic buildings. A single ticket usually allows you to get off at any stage and rejoin the tour at different stops. However, if you want to save some money, the public transport bus No. 100 follows a similar route (see p295). If you would rather go on foot, walking tours are also possible – these provide a more intimate tour of the city, stopping at all the major landmarks and museums. Organized trips to buildings just nearing completion can also be arranged. For information on these and other tours, visit the red Info-Box, currently on the corner of Leipziger and Postdamer Platz. If you are in Potsdam you can ride a train around town, starting outside the Kutscherhaus Inn in Sanssouci.

DISABLED VISITORS

Not all of Berlin's streets and shops have been altered to cater for the disabled, but the majority of theatres and galleries do have the required facilities. Detailed information can be obtained from the **Informations-und Beratungsgruppe für Behinderte** on Landesamt für Zentrale Soziale Aufgaben. Two other organizations to turn to are the **Berliner Behindertenverband** and **Deutscher Service-Ring**. Give them a call if you want to hire a wheelchair, a special bus, or someone to help you for the day.

DIRECTORY

MUSEUM INFORMATION

Besucherbetreuung der Schlösser und Gärten Potsdam-Sanssouci
Tel (0331) 969 42 02.

Info-Telefon der Staatlichen Museen zu Berlin
Tel 20 90 55 55.

Museumpädagogischer Dienst Berlin
Tel 902 69 94 44.

TOURIST INFORMATION

Berlin Tourismus Marketing
Am Karlsbad 11.
Tel (0190) 01 63 16 (24-hour).
Fax 25 00 24 24.
www.berlin.de and
www.btm.de

BerlinOnline
www.berlinonline.de

Brandenburg Gate
Pariser Platz. Map 6 E3, 15 A3.
◯ 9:30am–6pm.

Europa-Center
Entrance from Budapester Strasse.
Map 10 E1. ◯ 8:30am–8:30pm
Mon–Sat, 10am–6:30pm Sun.

Info Café at Fernsehturm
Alexanderplatz.
Map 7 C2. ◯ 10am–6pm daily.

Potsdam Tourismus Service
Friedrich-Ebert-Strasse 5.
Tel (0331) 27 55 80.
Fax (0331) 275 58 29.

Tegel Airport
Main hall. ◯ 5am–10:30pm.

DISABLED VISITORS

Berliner Behindertenverband
Jägerstrasse 63d. *Tel 204 38 47.*

Behinderten-beauftragter des Landes Berlin
Oranienstrasse 106.
Tel 90 28 29 17.

Deutscher Service-Ring e.V
Tel 859 40 10.

Additional Information

A typical kiosk selling newspapers, drinks and cigarettes

VISAS AND CUSTOMS

A valid passport is necessary for all visitors to Germany. Visas are not required for citizens of EU countries. A list, available from all German embassies, specifies other countries whose nationals do not need a visa for visits of less than 90 days. Non-EU citizens wishing to stay in Germany for longer than three months will need a special visa, available from German consulates. These need to be obtained in advance. All visitors should however check requirements before travelling.

On arrival in Germany, you will not be charged duty on personal articles. As in other European countries, no drugs or weapons may be brought across the border. The amount of cigarettes and alcohol allowed in or out of the country is restric-ted. Adults resident outside the EU can bring up to 200 cigarettes (50 cigars, or 250g of tobacco), and one litre of spirits (or two litres of wine).

VAT REFUND

If you buy non-edible goods in Berlin you are entitled to a VAT refund *(Mehrwertsteuer)*, unless you are a citizen of another EU country. Individual shops differ on the minimum taxable amount, but it is usually somewhere around 50. If you enter a shop with a Tax-Free sign outside, ask for a special form or Tax-Free cheque (you will need to present your passport). This form must be stamped when you go through Customs – but do be prepared to show your goods, which must still be in their original packing (you won't be able to claim a refund on any-thing that has been opened or which has been used). The tax is refunded either at the border or sent to the address on the envelope containing the cheque. Make sure you leave the right details with Customs staff – chasing old claims is a time-consuming and often fruitless task.

Antique pump

A Welcome Card with a small information brochure

INFORMATION FOR YOUNG PEOPLE

Before you arrive in Berlin it is worth getting hold of an ISIC card (or International Student Identity Card). This entitles you to a 50 per cent reduction in some museums, and to occasional discounts on theatre, plane and rail tickets. For similar reasons you might want to have a GO25 or EURO<26 card, both of which entitle you to a variety of reductions. These cards are only valid in Europe, but can earn you up to 300,000 different discounts.

A selection of Berlin's most popular daily newspapers

NEWSPAPERS

Newspapers can be bought in shops all over Berlin, but mostly they are sold by the city's numerous street vendors. In the evenings you will also find them on sale in bars and cafés. The most popular titles are the *Berliner Zeitung*, *Der Tagesspiegel*, the *Berliner Morgenpost* and *BZ*. Foreign language papers can be found all over the city, especially at airport and rail-way kiosks. Some of the major department stores also sell newspapers and maga-zines. A whole range of English-language books and newspapers is available at the British Bookshop at Mauer-strasse No. 83–4 in Mitte.

Theatre ticket office outside Friedrichstadtpalast *(see p105)*

TELEVISION AND RADIO

You may find yourself spoiled for choice when it comes to television channels in Germany. Apart from the national ARD and ZDF there are many regional and private channels (Berlin has its own, alongside RTL, RTL2, SAT1 and PRO7). You can also pick up special interest channels, like DSF for sport and VIVA or MTV for music. In addition to these there is even an option for Turkish programmes in Berlin, and thanks to cable and satellite television you can easily tune into foreign programmes in English, American, French and many other languages. In hotels the channels mainly cover the news, music and sport. For radio news in English, you can tune into Info-Radio (93.1 MHz), the BBC World Service (90.2 MHz), or the very popular SFB4 Multi-Kulti (106.8 MHz), which transmits in a number of different languages.

TIME

Germany is in the Central-European time zone, which means that Berlin is one hour ahead of Greenwich Mean Time; six hours ahead of US Eastern Standard Time, and 11 hours behind Australian Eastern Standard Time.

ELECTRICAL EQUIPMENT

Most electrical sockets carry 220V, although in bathrooms the voltage may be slightly lower for safety reasons. Plugs are all of the standard continental type, with two round pins. A European travel adaptor (buy it before you leave home), will allow you to use electric appliances.

EMBASSIES AND CONSULATES

Until the unification of Germany, many countries had an Embassy in Eastern Berlin and a Consulate in the West. Currently, because of the government's move from Bonn to Berlin, many countries have employed top architects to build luxurious embassies in the central part of the town; as a result, the addresses listed here are liable to change. If you are in any doubt, check at a tourist information point or in the telephone directory.

PUBLIC CONVENIENCES

There are plenty of public toilets in Berlin, but you can also use the facilities in museums, stores and cafés. In some places the convenience comes with a charge, usually around 25 cents. Men's toilets are marked by the word *"Herren"* or a triangle with the vertex pointing downwards; ladies', by the word *"Damen"* or *"Frauen"*, or a triangle with its vertex pointing upwards.

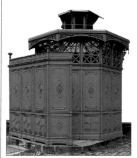

A refurbished antique public convenience in Kreuzberg

DIRECTORY

EMBASSIES

Australian Embassy
Friedrichstrasse 200.
Map 6 F4.
Tel 880 08 80.

British Embassy
Wilhelmstrasse 70.
Map 6 A4, 15 A3.
Tel 20 45 70.

Canadian Embassy
Friedrichstrasse 95.
Map 6 F2, 15 C1.
Tel 20 31 20.

New Zealand Embassy
Friedrichstrasse 60.
Map 6 F2, 15 C1.
Tel 20 62 10.

South African Embassy
Tiergartenstrasse 18.
Tel 22 07 30.

US Embassy
Neustädtische Kirchstrasse 4.
Map 6 F3, 15 B2.
Tel 830 50.

RELIGIOUS SERVICES

American Church
Alte Dorfkirche, Zehlendorf
Clayallee 355.
🕇 *10am Sun (in English).*
Tel 813 20 21.

Anglican Church
St Georg, Preussenallee 17–19. 🕇 *10am daily.*
Tel 304 12 80.

Huguenot
Französischer Dom, Friedrichstadtkirche, Gendarmenmarkt.
Map 7 A4.
🕇 *10am Sun.*

Jewish
Joachimstaler Strasse 13.
Map 10 D2.
✡ *9:30am Sat.*

Muslim
Islamische Moschee, Brienner Strasse 7–8.
Map 9 A5.
☾ *12:30pm Fri.*

Protestant
Berliner Dom, Lustgarten,
Map 7 B3.
🕇 *10am & 6pm Sun.*

Kaiser-Wilhelm-Gedächtnis-kirche, Breitscheidplatz.
Map 10 E1. 🕇 *10am & 6pm Sun; service in English: 9am Sun Jun–Aug.*

Marienkirche, Karl-Liebknecht-Strasse.
Map 7 C3.
🕇 *10:30am Sun.*

Roman Catholic
St-Hedwigs-Kathedrale, Bebelplatz.
Map 7 A3, 16 D3.
🕇 *8am, 10am, noon & 6pm Sun.*

Security and Health

Berlin police insignia

Gone are the days when demonstrations were held against the influx of foreign nationals, for Berlin is now a broadly cosmopolitan city. Nevertheless, as with all major European destinations, you should always be careful with your wallet, particularly on public transport during rush hours. If you do run into trouble, or simply need advice, you can always get help from the police. For minor health problems, which don't require a doctor, advice from a competent pharmacist is often sufficient.

Policeman   **Policewoman**

PERSONAL PROPERTY

Unfortunately, tourists are more frequently targeted by thieves than any other group, which is why all valuables should be kept in a hotel safe. Major robberies are rare in Berlin, but pickpockets are active, particularly on the U-Bahn. If you are travelling by car, don't leave photographic equipment or luggage in open view, and try to use a parking lot or hotel garage when possible. Zoo railway station is notorious for its drug pushers, so be careful there late at night. Like most big cities, few of the S- and U-Bahn stations are pleasant after dark, but these are often patrolled by guards – if you need assistance, don't hesitate to turn to them. There are also panic buttons installed on each platform, to be used in the event of emergency.

Before you set off for Berlin, it is advisable to buy insurance, and, if you are unlucky enough to be the victim of street crime, you must report it to the police straight away. Remember to obtain a statement confirming what was stolen – you will need this when it comes to making your insurance claim.

If you spot a fire, phone the **Fire Brigade**, or *Feuerwehr*, or use one of the bright-red public fire alarms placed strategically around Berlin.

LOST PROPERTY

There is one central bureau for lost property in Berlin (the **Zentrales Fundbüro**), and this is where anything left in public is deposited. It is worth noting, however, that the BVG (Berliner Verkehrs-Betriebe) has its own office (the **Fundbüro der BVG**) for items left on buses or trams or in the U-Bahn. Some items left on S-Bahn trains may also be sent to the new **Zentrales Fundbüro der Deutschen Bahn AG** in Wuppertal.

WOMEN TRAVELLING ON THEIR OWN

In Berlin it is quite normal for women to go to theatres, bars and restaurants on their own. You won't find yourself in danger during the day, but some basic precautions should be taken late at night, when it is preferable to avoid empty platforms or S-Bahn and U-Bahn trains. Night buses are a much safer option, and if something should go wrong the driver can always call the **police** with his radio. The safest, and

A public fire alarm

Police boats patrolling the water 24-hours a day

An independent chemist in Berlin's city centre

most expensive, way to travel is by taxi. If you are determined to walk alone in a park or in one of the quieter districts, is is best to do so during daylight hours only. For all kinds of advice there is a **Confidential Help-Line for Women**.

MEDICAL CARE AND INSURANCE

Citizens of the EU do not have to buy special insurance to cover emergency treatment, but non-EU visitors should do so. In case of sudden illness you can call an

Symbol for *Apotheke* (pharmacy)

ambulance, but if the state of the patient allows, then drive them to the nearest Emergency Room. If the complaint is minor, a chemist should be able to help. Chemists, such as **Bären-Apotheke**, usually keep the same hours as other shops, but there are always a few places open overnight. There is a special telephone line offering **Information about Chemists**. Other telephone helplines include a **Narcotics Emergencies** service and a **Confidential**

Help-Line for Spiritual and Religious Support. There is also the English-speaking **Helpline International**. Another option is to contact your embassy which should be able to inform you which doctors are able to speak your language.

DIRECTORY

EMERGENCY SERVICES

Fire Brigade and Ambulance
Tel 112.

Police
Tel 110.

DRK-Rettungsdienst (German Red Cross)
Tel 85 00 55.

Ambulance
Tel 31 00 32 22.

Narcotics Emergencies
Tel 192 37.

Confidential Help-Line for Women
Tel 615 42 43.

Confidential Help-Line for Religious Support (Telefon-Seelsorge)
Tel (0800) 111 02 22 (Catholic) or (0800) 111 0 111 (Protestant).

Helpline International
Tel 44 01 06 07.
⬛ 6pm–midnight daily.

CHEMISTS

Information about Chemists
Tel 11 880.

Bären-Apotheke
Tel 40 91 11 12.

LOST PROPERTY

Zentrales Fundbüro
Platz der Luftbrücke 6.
Tel 75 60 31 02.

Fundbüro der BVG
Potsdamer Strasse 180–82.
Tel 194 49.

Zentrales Fundbüro der Deutschen Bahn AG
Döppersberg 37, 42103 Wuppertal. *Tel* (0180) 599 05 99.

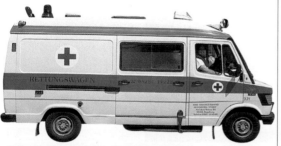
Rettungswagen or ambulance bearing the red cross

German police van, a common sight around the city

Banking and Local Currency

Logo of ReiseBank

Only a few years ago, some credit cards, like VISA, were far less popular in Germany than they were in other countries, but recently things have started to change. Now, on the whole, tourists have few problems using credit cards. There are plenty of cash machines available, as well as numerous banks and Bureaux de Change for exchanging foreign currencies.

CHANGING MONEY

There are no restrictions on the amount of cash you can bring into Germany, but most visitors use travellers' cheques or debit cards for safety.

Cash can be exchanged at banks and Bureaux de Change *(Wechselstuben)*. The major banks, such as **Berliner Bank** and **ReiseBank**, usually have similar rates of exchange, but some charge a commission; be sure to ask how much before commencing your transaction. Banks have limited office hours, so try to get to one immediately on arrival at the airport or station.

Bureaux de Change are often located close to railway stations and other places frequented by tourists. **Travelex** and **American Express** are among the best known places for exchanging travellers' cheques. Other Bureaux de Change can be found near the Bahnhof Zoo railway station on Joachimstaler Strasse, between Hardenbergstrasse and Kurfürstendamm.

You can also exchange cash at hotel reception desks, but this should be a last resort as their rates tend to be poor.

A typical cash machine

TRAVELLERS' CHEQUES

Travellers' cheques are a secure method of carrying money, with the advantage that you can change as much or as little as you need. Keep your receipts separate from the cheques themselves for added security. It may be convenient to carry cheques denominated in euros.

At many of the larger hotels you can pay for your room with travellers' cheques. For most other purchases, however, it is easier to use cash.

DEBIT AND CREDIT CARDS

Credit cards can be used in most larger hotels, shops and restaurants. A sign on the door should tell you which are accepted - **American Express**, **VISA**, **MasterCard** and **Diners Club** are most frequently used. Some cafés and restaurants require a minimum purchase to use a credit card. If you are only ordering a snack, check that you have some cash in case your card is not accepted.

DIRECTORY

BANKS AND BUREAUX DE CHANGE

American Express
Bayreuther Strasse 37.
Tel 214 98 30.

American Express
Friedrichstrasse 172.
Tel 23 84 10 25.

Berliner Bank
Kurt-Schuhmacher-Platz.
Tel 31 05 31 05.
▢ 9am–5pm Mon, Wed, Fri, 9am–6pm Tue–Thu.

ReiseBank
Bahnhof Zoo.
Tel 881 71 17.
▢ 7:30am–10pm daily.

ReiseBank
Ostbahnhof, Friedrichshain
Tel 296 43 93 or 426 70 29.
▢ 7am–10pm Mon–Fri, 8am–8pm Sat & Sun.

Travelex
Friedrichstrasse 56.
Tel 20 16 59 16.

LOST CARDS AND CHEQUES

American Express
Tel (069) 97 97 10 00.

Diners Club
Tel (01805) 33 66 95.

MasterCard
Tel (069) 74 09 87.

VISA
Tel (01803) 61 76 170.

One of the city's many Bureaux de Change

THE EURO

The Deutschmark (German mark) was the sole German currency until the end of 2001. But on 1 January 2002 the euro (the common currency of the European Union) was introduced into general circulation. Before this, it was already quoted in non-cash transactions. A transition period allowed the euro and the Deutschmark to be used simultaneously, but the Deutschmark (both notes and coins) was finally phased out by mid-2002. Now only the euro is accepted in Germany.

The euro was issued in 11 European Union countries in addition to Germany: Austria, Belgium, Finland, France, Greece, Holland, Ireland, Italy, Luxembourg, Portugal and Spain.

Bank Notes
Euro bank notes have seven denominations. The 5-euro note (grey in colour) is the smallest, followed by the 10-euro note (pink), 20-euro note (blue), 50-euro note (orange), 100-euro note (green), 200-euro note (yellow) and 500-euro note (purple). All notes show the 12 stars of the European Union.

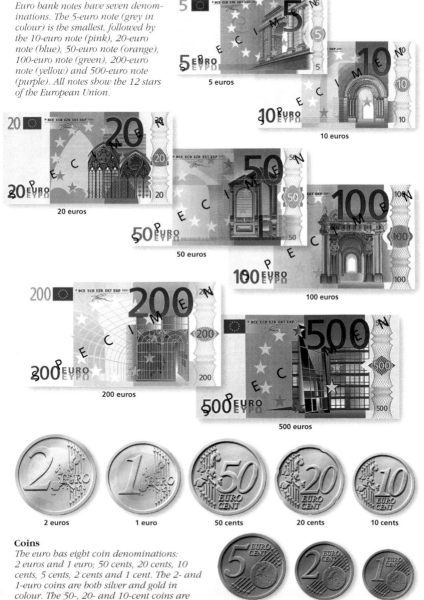

5 euros

10 euros

20 euros

50 euros

100 euros

200 euros

500 euros

2 euros

1 euro

50 cents

20 cents

10 cents

Coins
The euro has eight coin denominations: 2 euros and 1 euro; 50 cents, 20 cents, 10 cents, 5 cents, 2 cents and 1 cent. The 2- and 1-euro coins are both silver and gold in colour. The 50-, 20- and 10-cent coins are gold. The 5-, 2- and 1-cent coins are bronze.

5 cents

2 cents

1 cent

Communications

Logo for Deutsche Telekom

The postal and telecommunications services in Germany are both very efficient. You may have to wait a minute or two at the post office, but letters addressed within the country are usually delivered within 24 hours. Making a telephone call certainly shouldn't be difficult: public telephones stand on just about every street corner, and many restaurants and cafés have phone booths of their own. U-Bahn and S-Bahn stations always have a telephone or two, and often a mailbox to post your letters.

A typical Deutsche Telekom public telephone booth in Berlin

USING THE TELEPHONE

There are various types of public phone booths in Berlin, all of which are owned by Deutsche Telekom. The oldest is the coin-operated telephone. If you make a call that costs less than the amount of coins inserted, then the telephone will retain only those coins required to cover the cost of the call and will return the rest.

Telephone cards are far more convenient to use, and these are sold at all post offices. When using a card-operated telephone, your credits are displayed on a panel beside the receiver, so you should have plenty of warning before your card runs out and you need to buy a new one.

There are also some public phones which accept credit cards. Most of these are in the busy centre of town. As with a phone card, all you have to do is place your credit card in the phone, which will then ask you for your PIN (personal identification number).

Many public phones have their own numbers and accept incoming calls, so you can be called back if your card or money runs out. Every public phone should also have a set of phone directories.

Charges depend on the type of call (local or international) and the time of day. Early mornings, evenings and week-ends have the cheapest rates.

If you are staying in a hotel, making telephone calls from your room is usually the least economical option.

USING A COIN TELEPHONE

1 Lift the receiver and wait for the dial tone.

2 Insert coins into the slot.

3 Dial number and wait to be connected.

4 Add another coin when requested to do so.

5 When you have finished your call, replace the receiver and press the button above the slot to collect any unused coins.

USING A CARD TELEPHONE

1 Lift the receiver and wait for the dial tone.

2 Choose an appropriate language.

3 Insert your card and the display will show your balance.

4 Dial number and wait to be connected.

5 When you have finished, replace the receiver, press the green button and remove your card.

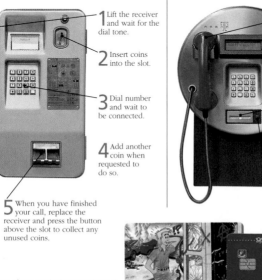

One of many telephone cards available, complete with instructions

Rear entrance to the post office (Deutsche Post) on Joachimstaler Strasse

MAIN POST OFFICES

Joachimstaler Strasse 7
8am–midnight Mon–Sat,
10am–10pm Sun.

Flughafen Tegel
8am–6pm Mon–Fri,
8am–1pm Sat.

Bahnhof Friedrichstrasse
6am–10pm Mon–Fri,
8am–10pm Sat & Sun.

THE INTERNET AND E-MAIL

The internet and e-mail have become increasingly popular and are especially useful for people who are abroad on holiday or business. As a result, many hotels now offer guests access to these facilities. Internet cafés can be found in most towns and cities, while computers can often be hired by the hour in commercial centres.

POSTAL SERVICES

German post offices are difficult to miss with their distinctive yellow Deutsche Post signs. Mailboxes, too, are an eye-catching yellow.

As in other European countries, you can send registered letters, parcels, telegrams and money orders from the post office. In addition to stamps, a number of products are sold here, too, including telephone cards and the usual variety of postal stationery. Local postcards are also available, as are limited-edition German stamps.

SENDING A LETTER

Stamps for letters and cards can be bought at the post office, but sometimes they are sold together with cards, and there are also special stamp machines around town. When posting a letter, always check the signs on the mailbox. Some boxes are divided, with one side accepting only mail for within Berlin, and the other accepting everything else.

POST OFFICES

Post offices in Berlin usually open from 8am until 6pm weekdays, and until noon on Saturdays. Those with extended hours, including Sundays, are at the airports

and major railway stations, such as **Flughafen Tegel** and **Bahnhof Friedrichstrasse**. Poste restante letters can be collected from **Joachimstaler Strasse** post office, which is open daily until midnight.

A rare antique mailbox, predating the contemporary yellow boxes

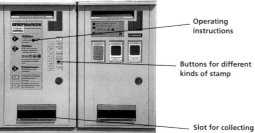

Operating instructions

Buttons for different kinds of stamp

Slot for collecting stamps

Street vending machine for buying postage stamps as well as telephone cards

Information about collection times

Slot for non-local letters

Slot for local letters

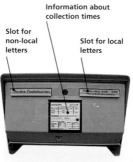

Typical Berlin-style mailbox found on street corners

IMPORTANT NUMBERS

- Germany country code 49.
- Berlin area code 030.
- Potsdam area code 0331.
- National directory inquiries 11 8 33.
- International directory inquiries 11 8 34.
- Operator 1 11 41.
- Police 110.

- To make an international call, dial 00 followed by the country code, area code and number, omitting the initial 0. Country codes: UK 44; Eire 353; Canada and US 1; Australia 61; South Africa 27; New Zealand 64.

GETTING TO BERLIN

Berlin lies at the heart of Europe and has excellent rail and air links with the rest of the continent. Its three airports receive regular flights from major European cities as well as North America, the Middle East and southeast Asia. Likewise Lufthansa, the German national carrier, offers flights to destinations around the world. The railway network is as good as

A Lufthansa aeroplane

anywhere in Europe, and takes you right to the centre of Berlin. One of the cheapest ways to travel to the city is by international coach, although this is usually the slowest form of transport. If you are travelling by car, the *Autobahn* (motorway) leads to the Berliner Ring (Berlin Circular Road), from where a number of exits are signposted to the city centre.

Airport information signs, directing passengers to various services

ARRIVING BY AIR

Although Berlin receives numerous flights from destinations in Europe, Asia and North America, Frankfurt is still Germany's chief intercontinental airport. However, expansion at Schönefeld, formerly East Berlin's airport, may change this, and low-cost carrier **Ryanair** has started a service three times daily to Schönefeld from London Stansted. For the time being, however, Tegel Airport is still Berlin's busiest terminal. The most frequent flights are by **Lufthansa** and **British Airways**, but the airport is also used by many other carriers, offering flight connections from all over Europe and beyond. From North America, Lufthansa flies

non-stop to Tegel from Washington DC. **Air Berlin** flies twice daily from London Stansted to Tegel, and Lufthansa also has flights from London's City Airport to Tempelhof, Berlin's third, and most central, airport.

TICKETS AND FARES

When planning your trip to Berlin, it is always worth shopping around for a ticket as prices can vary enormously. Some of the best deals are offered by inclusive tour operators; see your local press or travel agent for details. Air fares are usually cheaper when booked well in advance, and discounts are available for children and students. Low-cost airlines, such as Ryanair, can only be booked via the Internet. It is also worth checking other airlines' websites; a useful source of up-to-date information on schedules and fares to Berlin can be found at www.opodo.com which is a site operated by a consortium of European airlines including Lufthansa.

Destinations listings on the departures board

If you are willing to travel at short notice, you can occasionally find a last-minute bargain.

TEGEL AIRPORT

Tegel Airport is located conveniently within Berlin, only 5 miles (8 km) from the city centre. It has one terminal, designed for maximum convenience. In the main hall you can find an information point, a bank with Bureau de Change and a post office, as well as a number of shops for gifts, souvenirs and newspapers.

The city centre can be reached easily by bus or taxi, both of which stop in front of the main hall. Bus No. 109 stops at Bahnhof Zoologischer

Tegel Airport, the main international airport serving Berlin

The busy main hall at Tegel Airport

Garten and several other places in the centre before terminating at Budapester Strasse. Bus No. 128 links the airport with U-Bahn Kurt-Schumacher-Platz, while No. X9 takes you to Kurfürstendamm. TXL buses are a little more expensive, but they take you quickly to Unter den Linden. A journey by bus from the airport to the centre of Berlin usually takes between 25 and 30 minutes.

Taxi ranks are located in front of the lower exit leading from the arrivals hall and on the inner square at the back of the main hall. A taxi from the airport to the city centre is not very expensive; the journey to Bahnhof Zoologischer Garten costs around €12–15 and takes about 15 minutes.

SCHONEFELD AIRPORT

Located about 12 miles (20 km) south of the city centre, Schönefeld Airport

used to be the main airport of East Berlin. Bus No. 171 can take you from the airport to Flughafen Berlin Schönefeld railway station, from where you can catch the S-Bahn 9 or S-Bahn 45 train (or any of the long-distance trains which stop here) straight to the city centre. Another option is to take bus No. 171 to Rudow U-Bahn station. A taxi ride from Schönefeld to the centre of Berlin is quite expensive.

TEMPELHOF AIRPORT

The oldest airport in Berlin, Tempelhof is also the least busy of the three. It is located close to the city centre, at the border of Kreuzberg and Tempelhof. The easiest way to get from Tempelhof Airport to the centre of Berlin is by U-Bahn train from Platz der Luftbrücke station. Otherwise, bus No. 119 will take you to Kurfürstendamm.

DIRECTORY

AIRPORTS

Tegel Airport
Tel (01805) 00 01 86.

Schönefeld Airport
Tel (01805) 00 01 86.

AIRLINES

Air Berlin
Saatwinkler Damm 42. *Tel* (01805) 73 78 00. **www**.airberlin.com

British Airways
Budapesterstrasse 18b. *Tel* (01805) 26 65 22. **www**.ba.com

Lufthansa
Kurfürstendamm 21. *Tel* (01803) 80 38 03. **www**.lufthansa.com

Ryanair
www.ryanair.com

Airport check-in counter for First-Class passengers

TEGEL AIRPORT

Tegel Airport is relatively small and easy to use. A series of circular corridors leads to the departure gates. Shops and other services are situated in the main hall on two levels.

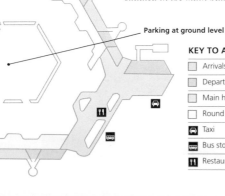

Parking at ground level

KEY TO AIRPORT

☐	Arrivals
☐	Departures
☐	Main hall
☐	Round corridor
🚕	Taxi
🚌	Bus stop
🍴	Restaurant

Leaflets offering special deals on international train travel

TRAVELLING BY TRAIN

The standards of European public transport are generally very high, particularly in central Europe, so whichever rail link you take to Berlin your journey is bound to be comfortable. The city has excellent connections with most major German and European cities. There are direct services between Berlin and Zürich, Brussels, Prague, Amsterdam, Paris, and Warsaw. Besides these lines, there are many convenient international routes to choose from, via other German cities.

If you are thinking of staying in Germany for quite a while, and are keen to travel around a lot by train, one of the cheapest options is an InterRail card. This can be bought by persons of any

Logo of Deutsche Bahn
(German Railways)

age, from any European country, Morocco or Turkey, and gives the traveller unlimited access to rail transport in a selection of European countries. North American visitors can enquire into Eurail cards, available through travel agents. The prices differ depending on your age and the number of countries you want to visit; the younger the visitor, and the more limited number of countries you wish to visit, the cheaper the card.

At various times of the year, but especially in summer, there are often special deals offering discounted travel. Among these are weekend tickets and family tickets. It pays to visit the information desk and ask about the different fares currently on offer.

What promises to be the biggest railway station in Berlin is currently under construction near the Lehrter Bahnhof S-Bahn station, but for the time being the majority of Germany's long-distance trains arrive at **Bahnhof Zoo** (Zoo station) – a small-scale station in which it is impossible to get lost. The trains stop at platforms from which you descend to reach the main hall. This hall contains a small shopping precinct with a restaurant, a left-luggage office, a bank (see p284), a hotel reservation point and a car rental kiosk.

Deutsche Bahn railway workers wearing the distinctive uniform

One downside to the station is the number of drug pushers, pickpockets and other strange characters who tend to hang around. Police patrols make sure that the area is safe for travellers, but be careful here, particularly late at night.

Bahnhof Zoo is situated in the centre of old West Berlin and has excellent connections with the other districts via five U-Bahn and three S-Bahn lines. There is also a taxi rank located outside the station and a number of bus stops, for both day and night buses.

The best place to obtain information about public transport is the BVG pavilion on Hardenbergplatz (see p295). You can also buy tickets from the pavilion.

Some trains coming from destinations in the south or east arrive in **Ostbahnhof** (the former Hauptbahnhof), a convenient station where you can easily exchange money, send mail and use the tourist information office. Ostbahnhof is linked to other districts in Berlin via S-Bahn.

Some international trains arriving in Berlin from the east terminate at **Bahnhof Berlin Lichtenberg**, but from there you can get to the Alexanderplatz or Bahnhof Zoo by S-Bahn lines S5, S7 or S75 or U-Bahn line U5.

Always remember that the ticket for your journey to Berlin is also valid on all S-Bahn connections to other stations, providing you use it immediately on arrival. For details of train times and destinations telephone the **Railway Information** line.

Main hall of Zoo railway station (Bahnhof Zoo)

COACH TRAVEL

One of the many express coaches available in Berlin

Wherever you can travel by train, the chances are you can also travel by coach, and Germany is no exception. On international routes, the fast network of *Autobahnen* (motorways) enables coaches to nearly match the speed of the trains. Some try to raise the level of comfort by showing videos and serving light refreshments; but coaches generally are less roomy and less comfortable than trains. It often a question of cost. Coach (bus) travel is nearly always cheaper than rail travel.

After you have visited Berlin, you may decide to take a coach trip to another German city or further afield. If so, the place to go is the **Zentral-Omnibus-Bahnhof**, situated near the Funkturm between Masurenallee and Messedamm. This is the city's largest long-distance bus station, and you will find connections to towns all over Germany, as well as links to other major European cities. Some coach companies, on overnight journeys, offer more comfortable sleeper seats for a small extra charge.

Information signs for passengers at a railway station

TRAVELLING BY CAR

Berlin is surrounded by a circular *Autobahn* or motorway (the Berliner Ring), which is linked to *Autobahnen* leading to Dresden, Nürnberg, Munich, Hannover, Hamburg and beyond. Numerous exits from the ring road are sign-posted into the city centre, but the road is so long that it is sometimes quicker to cut through town to get to wherever you're going (although not during rush hour).

While driving around the city, keep an eye on your speed; the police are extremely vigilant at doing speed checks. Less experienced drivers may feel a little uneasy on the *Autobahn* (motorway) as German drivers tend to zoom along at speeds reaching 125 mph (200 km/h). Keep to the right, unless you are overtaking. Always remember to check your side- and rear-view mirrors before switching to a left-hand lane. If you want to overtake, make sure there's nobody coming up behind. The speed at which fast cars come up behind you can be surprising. On some stretches of the *Autobahn* speed limits are imposed depending on weather and road conditions.

Driving licences from all European countries are valid in Germany. Visitors from other countries need an international licence. You must also carry your passport and the standard documentation (including insurance certificate or "green card") if driving your own car. To rent a car you will need a credit card. There are several places to rent vehicles around the city, including the major train stations and airports *(see p293)*.

As in most countries, German law is tough on drinking and driving. In the event of an accident, or being pulled over by the police, you may find yourself in serious trouble if alcohol is found in your blood-stream. It is better not to take the risk in the first place, and abstain from drinking.

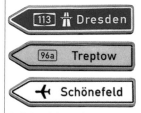

Typical road signs indicating the *Autobahn* and sights within Berlin

DIRECTORY

USEFUL NUMBERS

Bahnhof Zoo
Hardenbergplatz.
Map 4 E5. *Tel* 29 70.

Ostbahnhof
Strasse der Pariser Kommune.
Tel 29 70.

Bahnhof Berlin Lichtenberg
Travel Office, Weitlingstrasse 22.
Tel 29 70.

Railway Information
Tel 11 8 61.
Tel 0190 50 70 90 (24 hours).
Tel 0800 150 70 90 (automated).

Zentral-Omnibus-Bahnhof
Am Funkturm,
Masurenallee 4–6. **Map** 1 C5.
Tel 301 03 80.

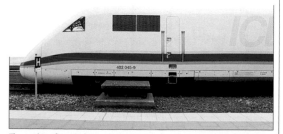

The engine of an ICE (Inter-City Express) train

GETTING AROUND BERLIN

Taxi rank sign

Berlin isn't the easiest of cities to move around in, largely because of the endless work being done to the roads. Building sites are scattered all over the city, and the number of parking spaces is still inadequate, so congestion is bad and driving should be avoided if possible. The centre of town (Mitte) can easily be seen on foot, but more peripheral areas should be reached by public transport. The U- and S-Bahn are by far the quickest way to travel, but the buses are very reliable – and if you happen to get a double-decker, they are excellent for sightseeing. Cyclists are exremely well catered for, so you may well want to hire a bike; there are many cycling routes around the city and further afield.

Lights at a pedestrian crossing

BERLIN ON FOOT

German drivers are generally careful and watch out for pedestrians, but it always pays to be vigilant. Cyclists travelling at speed can be dangerous as many cycle routes run along the pavements (sidewalks), only marked by a line

Various old-fashioned local street signs in Berlin

or by a different colour. You may not be aware of a cyclist coming up behind you, so be warned; you can easily be hit, or at least scolded for being in the wrong lane.

When walking in Berlin one thing worth remembering is that street numbers sometimes increase along one side of the street and then "turn round" at the end and continue on the other side. Usually, for example along Unter den Linden, the numbers increase equally on both sides, with odd and even numbers separated. If you are looking for a particular address, always make a note of where the street ends – although finding the right house is also made much easier by the street signs on every corner. These include the name of the street, as well as the numbers within that particular block.

Disabled tourists should get in contact with **Telebus-Zentrale** for transport details.

DRIVING

Although congestion is often quite bad in the centre of town, driving around Berlin is not as difficult as it is in some European capitals, for the town doesn't have a typical old centre with narrow, winding streets. You can drive to Unter den Linden and Museum Island along the wide boulevards with few delays.

Local drivers are usually very careful and don't break speed limits or enter junctions on yellow lights; you are legally allowed to turn right on a red light if there is also a green arrow showing.

You won't have a problem hiring a car in Berlin, as long as you show your passport and a valid driving licence; a credit card is the preferred method of payment. There are many international hire companies with offices at the airports, railway stations and

Stopping and parking prohibited from Monday to Friday

Parking permitted during working hours and Saturday mornings only with a ticket

Parking Meter
Parking meters are used on most streets. You have to pay for parking between 9am and 7pm on weekdays and 9am and 2pm on Saturdays.

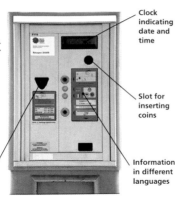

Clock indicating date and time

Slot for inserting coins

Information in different languages

Ticket is dispensed here

Some of the best known and most reliable car hire companies

in the city centre, some of which require the driver to be over 21 years of age. **Hertz, Sixt** and **AVIS** are three of the most reliable – and if you experience any trouble on the road, you should telephone **ADAC Auto Assistance**.

Taxis are also a very reliable and convenient method of transport around Berlin, three of the best companies being **Funk Taxi Berlin**, **Würfelfunk** and **Spree Funk**.

German road sign indicating various locations

PARKING

Finding a parking place won't always be easy, especially during lunchtime, but with a bit of luck you should be able to leave your car, free of charge, in the middle lane of the Ku'damm or in Alexanderplatz. There are also parking meters situated on just about every street, and many multi-storey car parks around West Berlin. Parking your car illegally certainly is not worth the risk; Berlin traffic wardens are constantly on the prowl, and apart from giving you a ticket, they can arrange to have your vehicle towed away. Retrieving an impounded car from the police is expensive and can be very inconvenient as these places are usually located out of town.

When using a parking meter, always check its time limit. These vary from area to area, so you may have to return after an hour or two to feed more money into the meter.

CYCLING

Cycling is very popular in Berlin, so most of the main roads have separate cycling lanes and even special traffic lights at intersections. Many offices, schools and banks have bicycle racks outside, but make sure your bike is securely locked and don't leave it there for too long.

You can also take your bike on S-Bahn trains, but you must enter the carriage by a marked door and leave your bike in a designated place. There are various places around town where you can hire a bike; one of the most reliable is **Fahrradstation**, with several outlets in the city.

A cycling lane between the pavement and the main road

DIRECTORY

CAR RENTAL

AVIS
Tel 23 09 370.
Tel (0180) 55 577.
(International booking).
www.avis.com

Europcar
Tel (01805) 22 11 22.
www.europcar.com

Hertz
Tel 26 11 053.
www.hertz.com

Sixt
www.sixt.com

BICYCLE RENTAL

Fahrradstation
Hackesche Höfe/Rosenthaler Strasse 40–41.
🕐 10am–7pm Mon–Fri, 10am–4pm Sat. *Tel* 28 38 48 48.

ROAD ASSISTANCE

ADAC Auto Assistance
Tel (01802) 22 22 22.

DISABLED VISITORS

Telebus-Zentrale (Special bus)
Esplanade 17 🕐 9am–6pm Mon–Fri. *Tel* 41 02 00.

TAXI

Funk Taxi Berlin
Tel 261 026.

Würfelfunk
Tel 210 101.

Taxi Funk Berlin
Tel 44 33 22.

Buses, Trams and Taxis

Travelling by bus in Berlin can be something of a trial during rush hour, but at other times of the day it is highly recommended. Most of the major roads have special bus lanes so buses are punctual even when the main roads are getting congested. A double-decker bus is worth taking if you're new in town and want to have a good look round. Trams are another option in the eastern part of the centre; like the buses and S-Bahn lines they are part of BVG and accept the same tickets.

BVG pavilion on Hardenbergplatz provides transport information

TICKETS

The whole of Berlin is divided into three travel zones: A, B and C. Zone A covers the city centre, Zone B the outskirts of town, while Zone C includes Potsdam and its environs. Travel between the zones is very simple, with tickets for each combination of zones. The most expensive option is to travel by buying single tickets, which come in two kinds, the normal ticket *(Normal-tarif)* and the cheaper ticket *(Kurzstrecke)*.

Three-day Welcome Card

The former is valid for two hours and gives you access to all methods of public transport, including S- and U-Bahn trains, with as many changes as you need, while the latter can only be used for three stops on trains and

six stops on buses. Single tickets can be bought from ticket offices at U- or S-Bahn stations, or from the bus driver. You must validate your ticket before you start your journey by inserting it in a red machine *(Entwerter)* found on the train platforms or in the bus, where it will be punched with the date and time. Children under 14 years old are entitled to a discount *(Ermässigungstarif)* and those under 6 can travel for free. No fee is charged for bringing a pram or a dog on board.

At most stations there are machines selling tickets and cards. The One-Day Ticket *(Tageskarte)* is valid from the moment it is punched until 3 o'clock the following morning. Weekly cards *(7-Tage-Karte)* are valid for seven days until midnight and are transferable. The three-day Welcome Card is another good option, giving unlimited travel in Berlin and Potsdam. Cheap tickets are also made available on special occasions. During the Love Parade *(see p49)*, for example, people are allowed to use all kinds of transport at a cheaper rate for two days.

Tram Stop

Every tram stop displays the appropriate tram numbers, timetables and maps. Buses sometimes also use the stops and are listed accordingly.

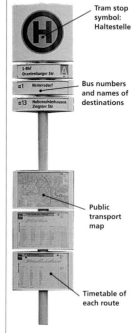

Tram stop symbol: Haltestelle

Bus numbers and names of destinations

Public transport map

Timetable of each route

For information about tickets and public transport in general, telephone **BVG Information (BVG-Kundendienst)** or the **Ticket Information** line – or the **U-Bahnhof Turmstrasse** for information about trains. If you think you may have mislaid something on a bus or a tram, give the **BVG Lost Property** number a call.

TRAVELLING BY BUS

All bus routes have a detailed timetable on display at each stop. Apart from its number, a bus will also have its destination on show, and it is important to pay attention to this as many buses shorten their routes outside rush hour. In the more modern buses you have to press a button to open the door. Until 8pm you can use all the doors to enter the bus, but after 8pm you should

A typical double decker bus

only use the front door near the driver; you will have to show him or her your ticket. The driver usually calls out the next stop, which may also be displayed electronically. Outside the city centre, however, the electronic display is something of a rarity. When travelling in the suburbs (and in the city centre outside rush hour) you need to press the *"Halt"* ("Stop") button as necessary, since most stops are made "on request" only.

TYPES OF BUS SERVICE

There are several different bus services operating in Berlin. Buses run frequently throughout the week, but somewhat less often on Saturdays and Sundays. Apart from the regular buses, marked by three-digit numbers, there are also some slightly more expensive "express" buses. These carry a two digit number preceded by an X, amd stop less frequently than other services. The regular daytime bus services start to wind down at around 11pm, but their place is taken by a very reliable network of night buses. These are marked by the letter N and require special tickets which can be bought from the driver.

ROUTES 100 AND 200

These special routes are served by double-deckers and include the most attractive parts of town. The buses operate between Bahnhof Zoo and Prenzlauer Berg, passing most of the city's interesting historic sites. Using a one-day ticket you can get off at any bus stop and visit Museum Island, Unter den Linden, the Brandenburg Gate, the Reichstag, the Tiergarten or Kaiser-Wilhelm-Gedächtniskirche. An extremely useful map and leaflet with descriptions (in German and English) of the route can be obtained from the **BVG Pavillon** on Hardenbergplatz.

TRAMS

Trams operate mainly within the area of former East Berlin; only one route was extended to Wedding. They can be relied upon to depart on time as they never have traffic jams to deal with. A tram ticket can also be used on buses, S- and U-Bahn trains.

TAXIS

Taxis are a comfortable but expensive way of getting around Berlin. Regardless of the make of car, all taxis are of the same cream colour and have a big TAXI sign on the roof. You can easily hail one on the street or arrange a cab by phone *(see p293)*. You can also get a taxi at a taxi rank, though these are quite rare. If the taxi rank is empty, you can use the rank telephone to

Modern tram operating in the former East Berlin quarter

call a cab directly, as each car has its own phone. The fare is calculated by a meter on the driver's dashboard. The cheapest fares are charged on weekdays in the centre of town (night-time and weekend rates are higher). There is also a special rate called *Kurzstreckentarif*: if you flag down a taxi and the journey is less than 2 km (1¼ miles), you pay a fixed rate of €3. It is generally a good idea to find out the name and telephone number of the taxi company nearest to your hotel.

DIRECTORY

USEFUL NUMBERS

BVG Information
(BVG-Kundendienst)
Tel 194 49.

Ticket Information
S-Bahn Berlin
Bahnhof Alexanderplatz.
Tel 29 72 06 48. ◷ 8am–9pm Mon–Fri, 9am–6pm Sat, Sun.

U-Bahnhof Turmstrasse
Service Centre
◷ 5:30am–8:30pm Mon–Fri, 8:45am–4pm Sat.

BVG Pavillon
Hardenbergplatz.
◷ 5:30am–10pm daily.

BVG Lost Property
U-bahn station Kleistpark.
Tel 194 49.
www.bvg.de

A typical Berlin bus stop during rush hour

U-Bahn and S-Bahn

U-Bahn information sign

While in theory Berlin has two separate train networks – the U-Bahn and S-Bahn systems – in practical terms there is not much difference between them, and commuters use the same tickets for both. Strictly speaking, the U-Bahn operates as a metro system, with trains running underground, while the S-Bahn is a longer-distance commuter service. In practice however, there is a great deal of overlap between the two systems, and many stations have both S- and U-Bahn platforms. The U-Bahn is owned by BVG and the S-Bahn by the independent S-Bahn GmbH.

U-Bahn display board with U-Bahn platform (Gleis), and destination

only valid for three stops. Vending machines stand at the entrance to each station, selling single tickets, returns, and one- and seven-day travel cards. The red machines that punch your ticket are usually behind the vending machines at the entrance to each platform. You may notice that there are no gates to stop free-riders trying their luck on the trains, but attempting to travel free of charge is a rather risky business in Berlin. Trains are patrolled by ticket inspectors who always work in plain clothes. They go on their rounds as soon as the train starts moving, and tend not to accept any excuses; fines for not having a ticket are high.

Trains arriving and departing at a station on U-Bahn line 6

U-BAHN

The U-Bahn network is very dense, with numerous stations very close together, many of them on lines which do not connect. During rush hours trains are very frequent, usually arriving every minute or two. There are ten U-Bahn lines in all, although one of them (number 15) has no branches, while number 12 uses partly the same rails as U1 and U2. Most of the service closes down between midnight and 5am. There are two exceptions to this: U1 and U9, which run an overnight service during the weekends.

S-BAHN

Train routes are usually a bit longer on the S-Bahn, which doesn't have as dense a network as the U-Bahn. As many as five lines go along the same route between Ost- and Westkreuz, but the stations are spaced much further apart than U-Bahn

stops, and trains run every ten or 20 minutes. There are a total of 17 S-Bahn lines, all running well beyond the confines of the city.

TICKETS

Tickets for S- and U-Bahn trains are the same as the tickets used on local buses and trams. The *Kurzstrecke* (short stretch) single ticket is also acceptable, although it is

SIGNS

There's no mistaking a U-Bahn station with its large rectangular sign and trademark white U on a blue background; similarly for S-Bahn stations, which have a round sign with a large white S on a green background. On metro maps each line is marked by a different colour. The direction of the train is noted by the displays which always give the final destination of the train. White ovals or circles on the map indicate where you can change to another line. All stations have maps of the local area as well as maps of the entire metro

Buying an S-Bahn ticket from a machine on the platform

An S-Bahn line 5 train heading out to Pichelsberg

system. Maps of the network are also on view in the train carriages. When embarking, always check both the line number and the final destination of the train as it is very easy to confuse your direction.

Older-style carriages have manually-opened doors which will close behind you automatically. Newer ones are fully automatic. A station attendant on each platform is responsible for co-ordinating departures. When you hear *"Zurück bleiben!"* you must not enter the train as this means it is ready to depart. During the journey the next station is often announced inside the carriage – on more modern trains information about your journey is given on an electronic screen.

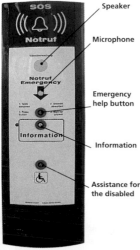

Speaker

Microphone

Emergency help button

Information

Assistance for the disabled

Information and emergency help point for the S-Bahn and U-Bahn

JOURNEY BY U- AND S-BAHN

1 Find the station you want on a map and see which line runs there. Do not forget to make a note of the final destination of the line so you can be sure of travelling in the right direction.

Map of U- and S-Bahn lines
(see inside back cover)

2 Find the button showing the type of ticket you require. After making your selection, the price is displayed and you can insert your coins in the slot.

Map of the U- and S-Bahn system

Coins

Bank notes

Tickets and change

Ticket types

3 A ticket from the machine looks different from one bought at the counter, but it will always contain information about its type and price.

Weekly travel card and one-day travel card

4 After entering the station you must validate your ticket in one of the red stamping machines located on the platform.

Ticket

Colour-coded sign of various S-Bahn stations

5 Follow the signs to the appropriate platform and choose the correct side by checking the destinations of departing trains.

An information board indicating the destinations of departing trains

S 3	Westkreuz
S 5	Pichelsberg
S 7	Potsdam Stadt
S 9	Westkreuz
S 75	Pichelsberg

U U2 U5 U8

Sign indicating where to wait for these U-Bahn lines

6 After leaving a train, proceed to the exit marked by the *Ausgang* sign. If there are several exits from the station additional signs will tell you the names of the streets outside.

Ausgang ↑ Am Weidendamm Reichstagufer

A typical exit sign

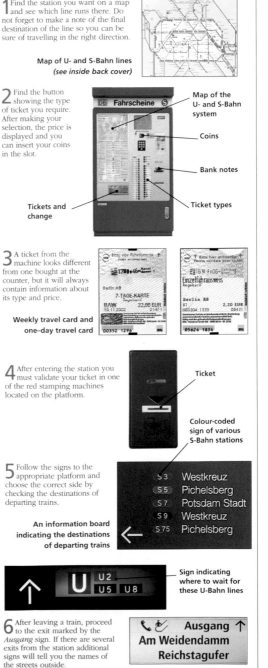

Getting Around by Boat

The river routes of Berlin may not be as dense as those of Amsterdam or Venice, but the Spree and the Havel offer more than just a pleasure cruise in the sun. An extensive system of canals and lakes links the city centre with Potsdam, Spandau, Charlottenburg and the area of Müggelsee. All kinds of transport are available, from rowing boats to catamarans and barges.

A ship's bell

One of many tourist boats on the Spree river

Timetable and routes of various boats near the Nikolaiviertel

GETTING AROUND BERLIN ON THE WATER

One of the most relaxing ways to spend the afternoon in Berlin is to take a leisurely three- or four-hour journey by boat along the Spree river and the Landwehrkanal. There is no shortage of companies offering this kind of trip. Four of the most reliable are **Reederei Bruno Winkler**, **Stern und Kreis**, **Reederei Hartmut Triebler** and **Reederei Riedel**. Each has its own dock, but the routes they follow are similar. You can admire the historic buildings of Mitte as the boat passes by the Berliner Dom along Museum Island, before heading off to the new government district and the Reichstag. You should have a good view of the Haus der Kulturen der Welt and the new city in Moabit shortly before entering the Landwehr-kanal. This runs alongside the Zoological Garden and new city buildings on Potsdamer Platz, and passes through Kreuzberg on its way to the junction with the Spree at Oberbaumbrücke. Most of the boats available along this

route have closed lower decks and open upper decks, with a bar serving snacks and drinks. All the sights are ex-plained by a guide along the way; the commentary is usually in German, but some companies can arrange for an English speaker.

TRIPS ALONG THE SPREE AND HAVEL RIVERS

If you want to try something a little more adventurous there are longer trips to choose from, some of which cover the

western lakes as well as the city centre. A particularly nice route takes you along the Spree, past the Mitte district, to Treptow, Charlottenburg and Spandau. From here you can carry on along the Havel river to the Grunewald and the Wannsee, then take a trip past Pfaueninsel to Potsdam. To do this, enquire at Stern und Kreis. Companies Reederei Bruno Winkler and Reederei Hartmut Triebler offer similar trips starting at Spandau and Charlottenburg.

Other options include a trip from Tegel port to Spandau and Wannsee, or a journey from Treptow to Köpenick. If you really want to, you can cover the whole of Berlin by boat, starting from Tegel in the north and finishing at Köpenick in the southeast, all within five or six hours.

Boat moored along the river in the summer

One of the larger boats available on the Spree

LONGER JOURNEYS AROUND BERLIN

For even longer tours, you may decide to take a whole day exploring the rivers, canals and lakes of Berlin. From Treptow you can take a boat to Woltersdorf which takes you through the charming lakeland area of Müggelsee. This region really is one of Berlin's greatest

A sight-seeing boat negotiating a lock on a canal

treasures, and is ideal for anyone searching for a quiet place to relax. There are many man-made beaches to choose from, as well as summer gardens and cafés - and a large white fleet of ships to show you around the area. Müggelsee is best visited on a warm summer's day when you can easily spend a few hours on one of its beaches.

Another adventurous idea is to take a voyage along the Teltowkanal from Treptow to Potsdam, from where **Weisse Flotte Potsdam** can take you not only to Wannsee and the other familiar routes around town, but also to Caputh, Werder and to many other sights to the south and west of Potsdam. For the absolute die-hards of the waterways, there is still one other option, which is to

Reederei Riedel company logo

take a boat all the way to Szczecin in Poland. You will need to allow a whole day to reach Szczecin, so be prepared to stay the night there as well. Perhaps the best idea is to leave your boat at the docks, spend a restful day exploring the city, and return by coach to Berlin.

DIRECTORY

TOUR BOAT COMPANIES

Reederei Bruno Winkler
Mierendorffstrasse 16.
Tel 349 95 95.
www.ReedereiWinkler.de

Reederei Hartmut Triebler
Bratringweg 29. **Tel** 371 16 71.

Reederei Riedel
Planufer 78.
Tel 691 37 82, 693 46 46,
Fax 694 21 91.
www.reederei-riedel.de

Stern und Kreis
Schiffahrt GmbH Berlin
Puschkinallee 16/17.
Tel 53 63 60 0.
Fax 53 63 60 99.
www.STERNundKREIS.de

Weisse Flotte Potsdam
Lange Brücke.
Tel (0331) 275 92 10.

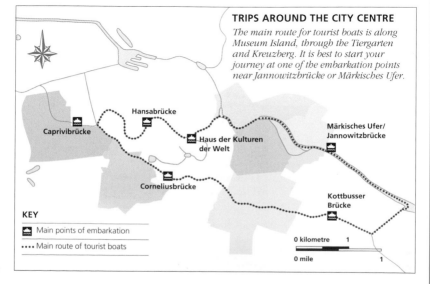

TRIPS AROUND THE CITY CENTRE

The main route for tourist boats is along Museum Island, through the Tiergarten and Kreuzberg. It is best to start your journey at one of the embarkation points near Jannowitzbrücke or Märkisches Ufer.

Hansabrücke

Caprivibrücke

Märkisches Ufer/ Jannowitzbrücke

Haus der Kulturen der Welt

Corneliusbrücke

Kottbusser Brücke

KEY

⛴ Main points of embarkation

•••• Main route of tourist boats

0 kilometre 1

0 mile 1

STREET FINDER

Map references given for historic buildings, hotels, restaurants, bars, shops and entertainment venues refer to the maps included in this section of the guidebook. A complete index of street names and all places of interest can be found on the following pages. The key map below shows the area of Berlin covered by the *Street Finder*. The maps include all the major sightseeing areas, historic attractions, railway stations, bus stations and the suburban stations of the U-Bahn and S-Bahn, as well as the ferry embarkation points. The names of the streets and squares in the index and maps are given in German. The word Strasse (Str.) indicates a street, Platz a square, Brücke a bridge and Bahnhof a railway station.

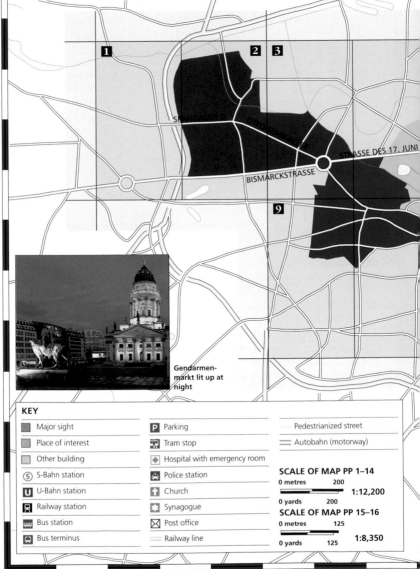

Gendarmen-markt lit up at night

KEY

■ Major sight	P Parking	Pedestrianized street
□ Place of interest	Tram stop	Autobahn (motorway)
□ Other building	✚ Hospital with emergency room	
Ⓢ S-Bahn station	Police station	**SCALE OF MAP PP 1–14**
U U-Bahn station	Church	0 metres 200
Railway station	Synagogue	0 yards 200 **1:12,200**
Bus station	Post office	**SCALE OF MAP PP 15–16**
Bus terminus	Railway line	0 metres 125
		0 yards 125 **1:8,350**

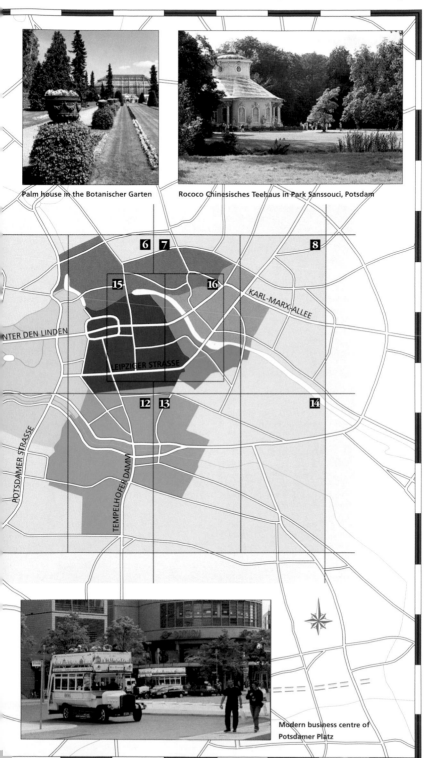

Palm house in the Botanischer Garten

Rococo Chinesisches Teehaus in Park Sanssouci, Potsdam

Modern business centre of Potsdamer Platz

Street Finder Index

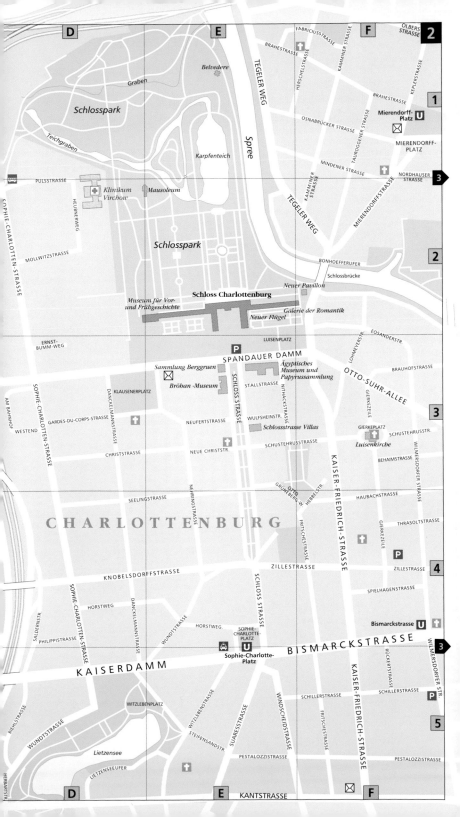

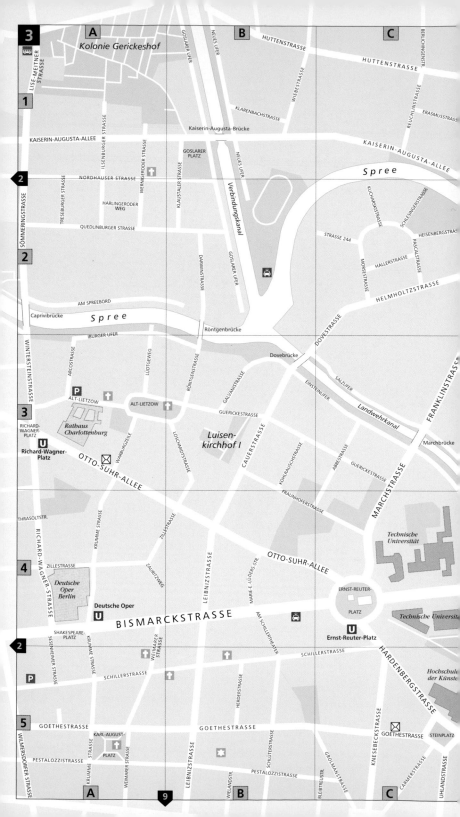

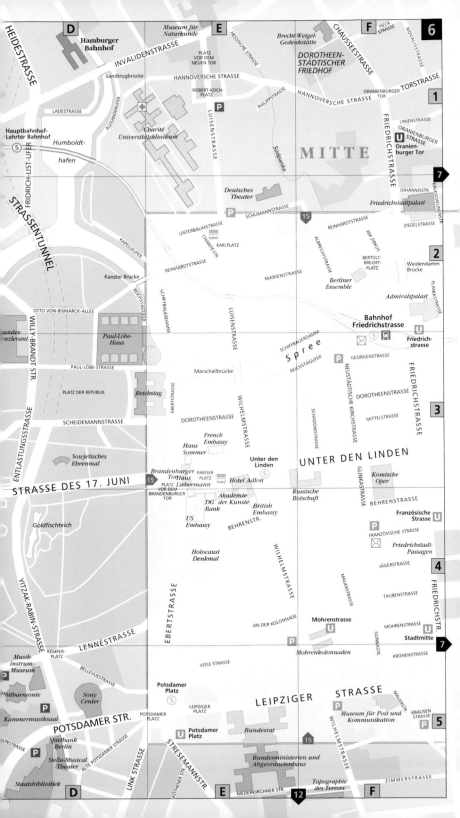

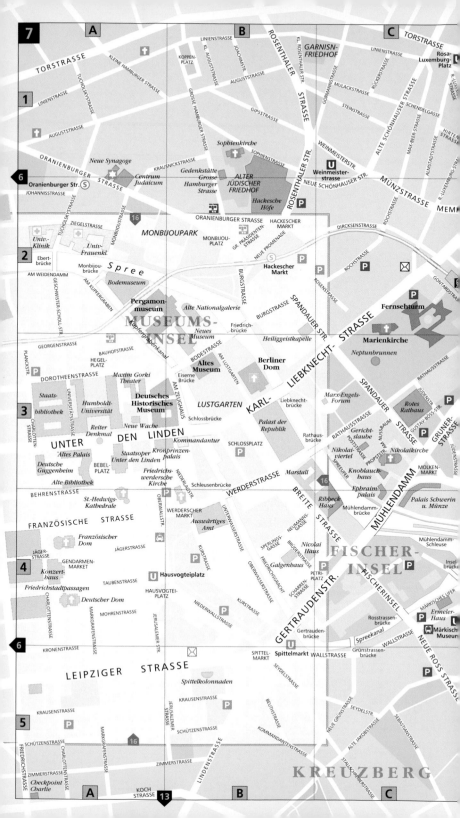

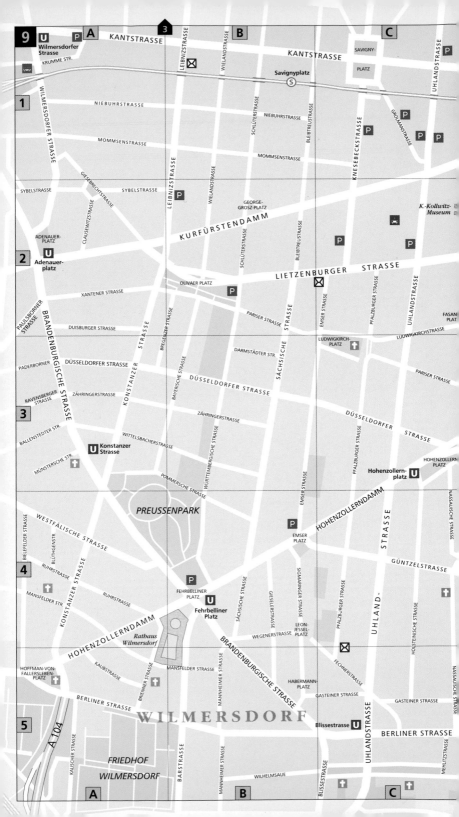

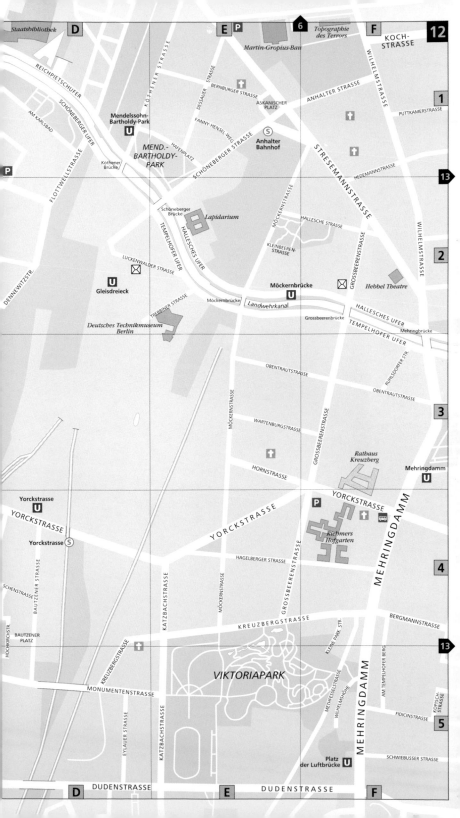

A

7

B

C

U Kochstrasse

WALDECKPARK

ORANIENSTRASSE

KOMMANDANTENSTR.

ALEXANDRINENSTRASSE

SEBASTIANSTRASSE

1

CHARLOTTENSTRASSE

MARKGRAFENSTRASSE

LINDENSTRASSE

FEILNERSTRASSE

RITTERSTRASSE

OTTO-SUHR-
SIED'UNG

STALLSCHREIBERSTRASSE

BESSELSTRASSE

ENCKESTR.

Berlinische
Galerie

ALTE JAKOBSTRASSE

ALEXANDRINENSTRASSE

RITTERSTRASSE

JAKOBIKIRCHSTR.

LOBECKSTRASSE

MORITZ-
PLATZ

FRIEDRICHSTRASSE

AM BERLIN-MUSEUM

U Moritzplatz

12

Berlin-
Museum

HOLLMANNSTRASSE

FRANZ-KÜNSTLER-STRASSE

PRINZENSTRASSE

Jüdisches
Museum

2

FRANZ-KLÜHS-STRASSE

LINDENSTRASSE

ALTE JAKOBSTRASSE

NEUENBURGER STRASSE

ALEXANDRINENSTRASSE

LOBECKSTRASSE

MORITZSTRASSE

WASSERTORSTRASSE

PRINZENSTRASSE

BERGFRIED-
STRASSE

MEHRINGPLATZ

BRANDESSTR.

U Prinzenstrasse

U Hallesches Tor

GITSCHINER STRASSE

GITSCHINER STRASSE

Halplansche-Tor-Brücke

Zossener Brücke

BÖCKLERSTRASSE

WATERLOO-UFER

BRACHVOGELSTR.

Waterloobrücke

Sommerbad
Kreuzberg

PRINZENSTRASSE

BÖCKLERPARK

BLÜCHERPLATZ

ZOSSENER STRASSE

JOHANNITERSTRASSE

Landwehrkanal

Baerwaldbrücke

3

BLÜCHER STRASSE

KIRCHHOF JERUSALEM
U. NEUE KIRCHE I, II, III

BRACHVOGELSTR.

BRACH AM JOHANNISTISCH

CARL-HERZ-UFER

TEMPELHERRENSTRASSE

WILMSSTRASSE

BAERWALDSTRASSE

CARL-HERZ-UFER

Urbanhafen

GEIBELSTRASSE

BARUTHER STR.

BARUTHER
STRASSE

MITTENWALDER STRASSE

URBANSTRASSE

SOLMSSTRASSE

ZOSSENER STRASSE

FÜRBRINGERSTRASSE

SCHLEIERMACHERSTR.

4

STRASSE

NOSTITZ

GNEISENAUSTRASSE

U Gneisenaustrasse

KREUZBERG

BAERWALDSTRASSE

BLÜCHERSTRASSE

FONTANEPROMENADE

FREILIGRATHSTRASSE

KÖRTESTRASSE

RIEMANNSTRASSE

ZOSSENER STRASSE

MITTENWALDER STRASSE

SCHLEIERMACHERSTRASSE

GNEISENAUSTRASSE

SÜDSTERN

U Südstern

SOLMSSTRASSE

BERGMANNSTRASSE

MARHEINEKEPLATZ

HASENHEIDE

12

ARNDTSTRASSE

FRIESENSTRASSE

HEIMSTRASSE

BERGMANNSTRASSE

DREIFALTIGKEITS-
KIRCHHOF II

FRIEDRICHS-
WERDERSCHER
KIRCHHOF

KIRCHHOF
JERUSALEM U.

N.D. KIRCHHOF

STANDORTFRIEDHOF
LILIENTHALSTR.

CHAMISSO-
PLATZ

WILLIBALD-ALEXIS-STRASSE

ARNDTSTRASSE

NEUE KIRCHE IV

LILIENTHALSTRASSE

5

FIDICIN-
STRASSE

KLOEDENSTR.

JÜTERBOGER STRASSE

GÖSSENER STRASSE

KIRCHHOF
LUISENSTADT I

ZÜLLICHAUER STRASSE

SCHWIEBUSSER STRASSE

A

B

C

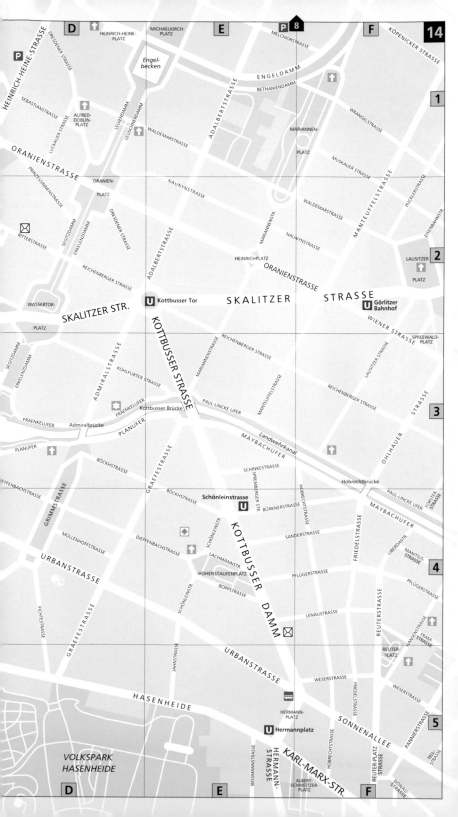

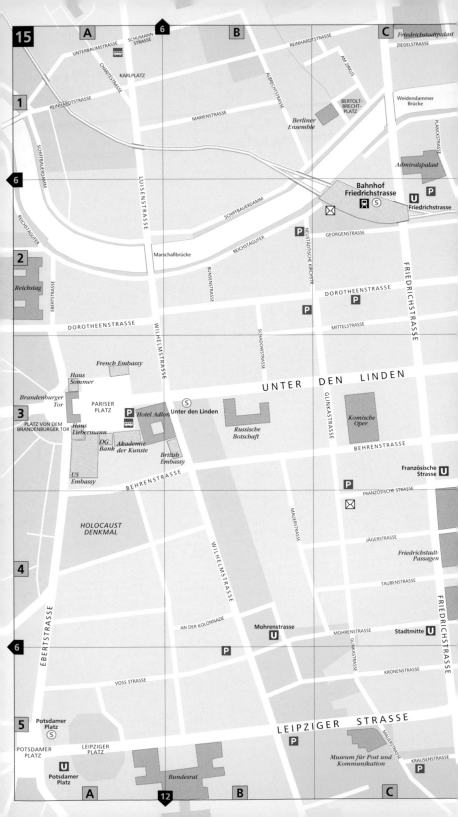

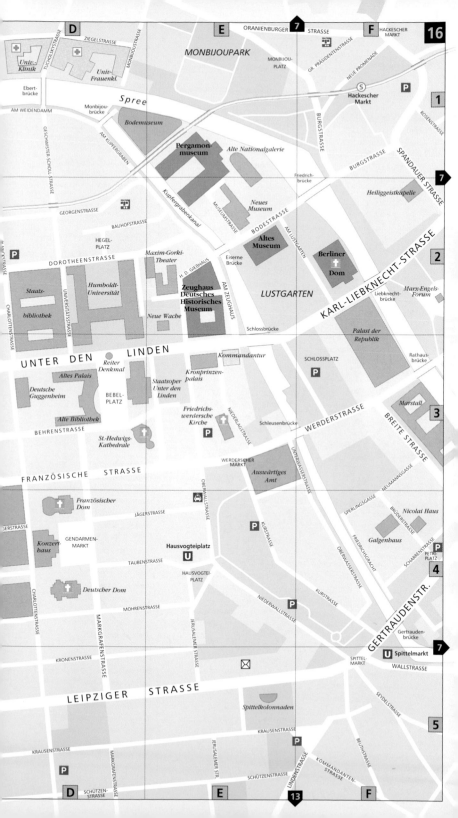

Index   <small>Page numbers in bold type refer to main entries</small>

Acknowledgements

DORLING KINDERSLEY would like to thank the following people whose contributions and assistance have made the preparation of this book possible.

Managing Art Editor
Kate Poole
Editorial Director
Vivien Crump
Art Director
Gillian Allan
Consultant
Gordon McLachlan
Fact Checker
Jürgen Scheunemann
Translators
Magda Hannay, Anna Johnson, Ian Wisniewski
Proofreader
Stewart Wild
Indexer
Hilary Bird

Design and Editorial Assistance
Gillian Andrews, Brigitte Arora, Tessa Bindloss, Arwen Burnett, Lucinda Cooke, Jessica Hughes, Franziska Marking, Ellen Root, Simon Ryder, Sands Publishing Solutions, Sadie Smith, Andrew Szudek, Leah Tether, Conrad van Dyk

DTP
Samantha Borland, Lee Redmond

Additional Illustrations
Paweł Pasternak

Additional Photography
Amir Akhtar, Francesca Bondy, Catherine Marshall, Ian O'Leary, Jürgen Scheunemann

Additional Text
Jürgen Scheunemann

Special Assistance
DORLING KINDERSLEY would like to thank the staff at the featured museums, shops, hotels, restaurants and other organizations in Berlin for their invaluable help. Special thanks go to the following for providing photographs and pictures: Heidrun Klein of the Bildarchiv Preussischer Kulturbesitz; Frau Betzker and Ingrid Jager of the Bröhan Museum; Margit Billeb of the Centrum Judaicum; Brucke-Museum; Deutsche Press Agency (DPA); Renate Forster of the Deutsches Technikmuseum Berlin; Andrei Holland-Moritz of Forschung- und Gedenkstätte Normannenstrasse (Stasi-Museum); Matthias Richter of Konzerthaus Berlin and the Berlin Symphony Orchestra; Georg Kolbe Museum; Carl Kamarz of Stiftung Preussische Schlösser und Gärten Berlin and the Berlin and Potsdam Palaces; Thomas Wellmann of the Museum of the City of Berlin; Hamburger Bahnhof; Annette Jäckel of DeragHotels for providing photographs of the interiors of DeragHotel Grosser Kurfürst; Reinhard Friedrich; Hans-Jürgen Dyck of Haus am Checkpoint Charlie; Gaby Hofmann of Komische Oper Berlin; Gesine Steiner of Museum für Naturkunde; Ute Grallert of Deutsches Historisches Museum; Elke Pfeil of the Brecht-Weigel-Museum; Ingrid Flindell of the Käthe-Kollwitz-Museum; Sylvia U Moller of Villa Kastania; Manuel Volsk of the Savoy Hotel; Sabine Rogge of the Grand Hotel Esplanade Berlin; Claude Borrmann of the Hotel Palace Berlin; Gerald Uhligow of the Einstein Café; Hotel Adlon; Hotel Brandenburger Hof and Restaurant Die Quadriga; Hotel Kempinski; Rockendorf's Restaurant; The Westin Grand Hotel.

Photography Permissions
DORLING KINDERSLEY would like to thank the following for their kind permission to photograph at their establishments: Margaret Hilmer of the Berliner Dom; Kaiser-Wilhelm-Gedächtniskirche; Galeries Lafayette; KaDeWe; Frau Schneider of BVG (Berlin Underground system); Deutsche Bundesbahn for allowing photography of the Zoo railway station; Dorotheenstädtischer Friedhof for allowing photographs of the tombs; Flughafen Schönefeld for allowing photography of the airfield; Annie Silbert of the Zoologischer Garten Berlin for allowing photography of the animals and attractions; Hilton Hotel; Carlos Beck of the Sorat Art'otel, Berlin; Manuel Volsk of the Savoy Hotel, Berlin; Sabine Rogge of the Grand Hotel Esplanade; Claude Borrmann of the Hotel Palace Berlin; Gerald Uhligow of the Einstein Café; the Olive restaurant; the Bamberger Reiter restaurant; Sklepo for allowing photography of its interiors and porcelain. Count Lehmann of Senatsverwaltung für Bauen, Wohnen und Verkehr for providing cartographic information as well as copyright for the use of maps; Ms Grazyna Kukowska of ZAIKS for her help in securing permission to reproduce works of art.

Picture Credits
t=top; tl= top left; tc=top centre; tr= top right; cla=centre left above; ca= centre above; cra= centre right above; cl=centre left; c=centre; cr=centre right; clb=centre left below; cb= centre below; crb=centre right below; bl=bottom left; bc=bottom centre; br=bottom right; b=bottom.

Every effort has been made to trace the copyright holders and we apologize in advance for any unintentional omissions. We would be pleased to insert the appropriate acknowledgements in subsequent editions of this publication.

The publisher is grateful to the following individuals, companies and picture libraries for their permission to reproduce their photographs. The works of art have been reproduced with the consent of the copyright owners.

John Cage *Not Wanting to Say Anything About Marcel* (1969) 111c; Sandro Chia *Genova* (1980) 110cl; Keith Haring *Untitled* (1983) © The Estate of Keith Haring 110bl; Bernhard Heligerd, sculpture near Brücke-Museum © Bild-Kunst 179tr; Oskar Kokoschka *Pariser Platz in Berlin* (1925–26) 67bl; Pablo Picasso *Head of the Faun* (1937) 34tr, *Woman in a Hat* (1939) 159tl, all © Succession Picasso 2000; Robert Rauschenberg *First Time Painting* (1961) © Robert Rauschenberg 111bl; Karl Schmidt-Rottluff *Farm in Danger* (1910) © Bild-Kunst 126tl; Andy Warhol *Mao* (1973) © 2000 Andy Warhol Foundation for the Visual Arts/ARS, New York 111br. ALAMY IMAGES: CroMagnon 10tc; europhotos front endpaper tl, 112; Leslie Garland Picture Library 134br; Joern Sackerman 11b; ALLSTAR: cinetext 141t; AMJ HOLDING GMBH & CO. KG: Steffen Janicke 65br; ANA E BRUNO 231cr; AKG LONDON: Dieter E Hoppe front cover cl and 166, Lothar Peter front cover cbr; ANTHONY BLAKE PHOTO LIBRARY front cover ccr; BERGER + PARKKINEN ARCHITEKTEN ZIVILTECHNIK GMBH: 42br; BILDARCHIV PREUSSISCHER KULTURBESITZ 9c, 22–23c, 31tr, 32tr, 32br, 34tr, 34br, 35t, 35b, 54cb, 67b, 73ca, 80ca, 82tl, 82b, 83tl, 85b, 115cra, 118tl, 118tr, 122cb, 123clb, 126t, 158cra, 162t, 163cl, 165tl, 178tr, 178b; Jorg P Anders 20tc, 20cl, 21t, 29cl, 30cl, 73ca, 114c, 114b, 117t, 122tl, 122tr, 122ca, 122b, 123t, 123cr, 123b, 124t, 124ca, 124b, 125t, 125cb, 125cb, 187b; Hans-Joachim Bartsch 118cla, 118c, 120tl, 121cr; Margarete Busing 34c; Ingrid Geske-Heiden 32tl, 75tr, 121b; Klaus Goken 60t, 33crb, 78t, 80b, 81b; Dietmar Katz 43crb; Johannes Laurentius 75b; Erich Lessing 72t, 80t, 81cb; Jürgen Liepe 33cra, 75cla, 80cb, 82t, 83b, 118b, 164b; Saturia Linke 34tl; Georg Niedermeiser 80t, 81ca; Arne Psille 118c, 119t, 119b, 120c, 121t, 120b; Steinkopf 114tr; G Stenzel 83tr; Jens Ziehe 110t, 111c; Jürgen Zimmermann 29tl; BRIDGEMAN ART LIBRARY 47c, 175b; BERLINER FESTSPIELE: Bianka Göbel 261t; BERLINISCHE GALERIE: *Stadtwandelverlag* (2004) © Florian Bulk and *Dreiheit* (1993) © Brigitte and Martin Matschinsky-Denninghoff 139b; BRECHT-WEIGEL- GEDENKSTÄTTE 46t, 109b; BRÖHAN-MUSEUM 165cb; CENTRUM JUDAICUM 102t; CORBIS: Sygma/Aneebicque Bernard 233t; Adam Woolfitt 232cl; Michael S. Yamashita 233c; DEUTSCHES HISTORISCHES MUSEUM (Zeughaus) 8–9, 24cb, 24bl, 25tr, 25b, 25clb, 26–27b, 27tr, 28tl, 28cr, 28cb, 28dp, 29tr, 29bl, 46br,

47cra, 58tl, 58tr, 58ca, 58cb, 58br, 59t, 59ca, 59cb, 59b; DEUTSCHES TECHNIKMUSEUM BERLIN 33bl, 136; DEUTSCHE PRESS AGENCY (DPA) 10bl, 46ca, 46cb, 46bl, 47t, 47crb, 47b, 48tc, 48cla, 48b, 50t, 50b, 67t, 151br, 199b; EUROPEAN COMMISSION 285; FILMPARK BABELSBERG: 205 cla/crb/bl; FIT TO PRINT, BERLIN: 283tl; GEDENKSTÄTTE UND MUSEUM SACHSENHAUSEN 169b; GEORG KOLBE MUSEUM 183tr; GRAND HOTEL ESPLANADE 216b; HAMBURGER BAHNHOF 110ca, 110cb, 110b, 111t, 111cra, 111b; HAUS AM CHECKPOINT CHARLIE 39br; HOTEL ADLON 68t; HOTEL PALACE BERLIN 219tr; HAYDER ADAM 233br; IMAGEWORKSHOP BERLIN: Vincent Mosch 131br; JEWISH MUSEUM BERLIN: 143 br; Deutsches Technikmuseum Berlin 143cl; Jens Ziehe, Berlin 142cl; Leo Baeck Institute, New York 142tr; KÄTHE-KOLLWITZ -MUSEUM 148b; KaDeWe: 51b; KOMISCHE OPER MONIKA RITTERSHAUS 49b, 68b; KONZERTHAUS BERLIN 65t; MEYER NILS 29crb, 40tr; MUSEUM FÜR NATURKUNDE 109t; PRESS ASSOCIATION PICTURE LIBRARY 261tl; PRESSEFOTOSPETERS: 10c; PRESSE- UND INFORMATIONSAMT DES LANDES BERLIN: BTM 294c; BTM/Drewes 45bl; BTM/ Koch 45tl, 129 tl; G. Schneider 51c; Landesarchiv Berlin 129br; Meldepress/Ebner 126b; Partner fuer Berlin: FTB-Werbefotografie 128cl, 143cr, 143br; RAINER KIEDROWSKI: Nils Koshofer 30, 112; ROBERT HARDING PICTURE LIBRARY 52–53, 274tc, Walter Rawlings 208cl; SCHNEIDER, GUENTER: 41tr, 52–53; SCHIRMER, KARSTEN: 260cl; JÜRGEN SCHEUNEMANN: 49cr, 138tr, 139tl; STAATLICHE MUSEEN ZU BERLIN-PREUSSISCHE KULTURBESITZ/KUNSTGEWERBEMUSEUM: Hans-Joachim Bartsh 119cl; Irmgard Mues-Funke 121tl; STADTMUSEUM BERLIN 23tr, 24t, 26cla, 133tr; Hans-Joachim Bartsch 18, 19b, 20c, 21tl, 21br, 27br, 85t; Christel Lehmann 18tl, 18cb; Peter Straube 88b, 90tr; STASI-MUSEUM 174cr; STIFTUNG PREUSSISCHE SCHLÖSSER UND GÄRTEN BERLIN 16t, 21c, 160t, 160c, 161ca, 161c, 161b, 188clb, 194tl, 194cla, 194clb, 194br, 195cra, 195br, 195bl, 198t, 200cla, 200b, 201cra, 201crb, 201bl, 201br; TELEGRAPH COLOUR LIBRARY: Bavaria-Bildagentur front cover cbc, Messerschmidt front cover t; TONY STONE IMAGES: Doug Armand 214; VIEW PICTURES: William Fife 43bl; VILLA KASTANIA 217b; THE WESTIN GRAND 218b; WÓJCIK PAWEŁ 235bl, STUART N.R. WOLFE (STUART@SNR-WOLFE.COM): 181tr.

JACKET Front - GETTY IMAGES: Hans Wolf bl; LONELY PLANET IMAGES: David Peevers main image. Back – BILDARCHIV PREUßISCHER KULTURBESITZ, Berlin: Dietmar Katz cla; DK IMAGES: Dorota and Mariusz Jarymowicz tl, cbl, bl. Spine – DK IMAGES: Dorota and Mariusz Jarymowicz b; LONELY PLANET IMAGES: David Peevers t. All other images © Dorling Kindersley. For further information see: www.dkimages.com

SPECIAL EDITIONS OF DK TRAVEL GUIDES

Phrasebook

In an Emergency

English	German	Pronunciation
Where is the telephone?	Wo ist das Telefon?	voh ist duss tel-e-fone?
Help!	Hilfe!	hilf-uh
Please call a doctor	Bitte rufen Sie einen Arzt	bitt-uh roof'n zee ine-en artst
Please call the police	Bitte rufen Sie die Polizei	bitt-uh roof'n zee dee poli-tsy
Please call the fire brigade	Bitte rufen Sie die Feuerwehr	bitt-uh roof'n zee dee foyer-vayr
Stop!	Halt!	hult

Communication Essentials

English	German	Pronunciation
Yes	Ja	yah
No	Nein	nine
Please	Bitte	bitt-uh
Thank you	Danke	dunk-uh
Excuse me	Verzeihung	fair-tsy-hoong
Hello (good day)	Guten Tag	goot-en tahk
Goodbye	Auf Wiedersehen	owf-veed-er-zay-ern
Good evening	Guten Abend	goot'n ahb'nt
Good night	Gute Nacht	goot-uh nukht
Until tomorrow	Bis morgen	biss morg'n
See you	Tschüss	chooss
What is that?	Was ist das?	voss ist duss
Why?	Warum?	var-room
Where?	Wo?	voh
When?	Wann?	vunn
today	heute	hoyt-uh
tomorrow	morgen	morg'n
month	Monat	mohn-aht
night	Nacht	nukht
afternoon	Nachmittag	nahkh-mit-tahk
morning	Morgen	morg'n
year	Jahr	yar
there	dort	dort
here	hier	hear
week	Woche	vokh-uh
yesterday	gestern	gest'n
evening	Abend	ahb'nt

Useful Phrases

English	German	Pronunciation
How are you? (informal)	Wie geht's?	vee gayts
Fine, thanks	Danke, es geht mir gut	dunk-uh, es gayt meer goot
Until later	Bis später	biss shpay-ter
Where is/are?	Wo ist/sind...?	voh ist/sind
How far is it to...?	Wie weit ist es...?	vee vite ist ess
Do you speak English?	Sprechen Sie Englisch?	shpresh'n zee eng-glish
I don't understand	Ich verstehe nicht	ish fair-shtay-uh nisht
Could you speak more slowly?	Könnten Sie langsamer sprechen?	kurnt-en zee lung-zam-er shpresh'n

Useful Words

English	German	Pronunciation
large	gross	grohss
small	klein	kline
hot	heiss	hyce
cold	kalt	kult
good	gut	goot
bad	böse/schlecht	burss-uh/shlesht
open	geöffnet	g'urff-nett
closed	geschlossen	g'shloss'n
left	links	links
right	rechts	reshts
straight ahead	geradeaus	g'rah-der-owss

Making a Telephone Call

English	German	Pronunciation
I would like to make a phone call	Ich möchte telefonieren	ish mer-shtuh tel-e-fon-eer'n
I'll try again later	Ich versuche es später noch einmal	ish fair-zookh-uh es shpay-ter nokh ine-mull
Can I leave a message?	Kann ich eine Nachricht hinterlassen?	kan ish ine-uh nakh-risht hint-er-lahss-en
answer phone	Anrufbeantworter	an-roof-be-ahnt-vort-er
telephone card	Telefonkarte	tel-e-fohn-kart-uh
receiver	Hörer	hur-er
mobile	Handy	han-dee
engaged (busy)	besetzt	b'zetst
wrong number	Falsche Verbindung	falsh-uh fair-bin-doong

Sightseeing

English	German	Pronunciation
library	Bibliothek	bib-leo-tek
entrance ticket	Eintrittskarte	ine-tritz-kart-uh
cemetery	Friedhof	freed-hofe
train station	Bahnhof	barn-hofe
gallery	Galerie	gall-er-ree
information	Auskunft	owss-koonft
church	Kirche	keersh-uh
garden	Garten	gart'n
palace/castle	Palast/Schloss	pallast/shloss
place (square)	Platz	plats
bus stop	Haltestelle	hal-te-shtel-uh
national holiday	Nationalfeiertag	nats-yon-ahl-fire-tahk
theatre	Theater	tay-aht-er
free admission	Eintritt frei	ine-tritt fry

Shopping

English	German	Pronunciation
Do you have/ Is there...?	Gibt es...?	geept ess
How much does it cost?	Was kostet das?	voss kost't duss
When do you open/ close?	Wann öffnen Sie? schliessen Sie?	vunn off'n zee shlees'n zee
this	das	duss
expensive	teuer	toy-er
cheap	preiswert	price-vurt
size	Grösse	gruhs-uh
number	Nummer	noom-er
colour	Farbe	farb-uh
brown	braun	brown
black	schwarz	shvarts
red	rot	roht
blue	blau	blau
green	grün	groon
yellow	gelb	gelp

Types of Shop

English	German	Pronunciation
antique shop	Antiquariat	antik-var-yat
chemist (pharmacy)	Apotheke	appo-tay-kuh
bank	Bank	bunk
market	Markt	markt
travel agency	Reisebüro	rye-zer-boo-roe
department store	Warenhaus	vahr'n-hows
chemist's, drugstore	Drogerie	droog-er-ree
hairdresser	Friseur	freezz-er
newspaper kiosk	Zeitungskiosk	tsytoongs-kee-osk
bookshop	Buchhandlung	bookh-hant-loong

bakery	Bäckerei	beck-er-**eye**
post office	Post	posst
shop/store	Geschäft/Laden	gush-**eft/lard**'n
film processing shop	Photogeschäft	fo-to-gush-**eft**
self-service shop	Selbstbedienungs-laden	selpst-bed-**ee**-nungs-lard'n
shoe shop	Schuhladen	shoo-lard'n
clothes shop	Kleiderladen, Boutique	klyder-lard'n boo-**teek**-uh
food shop	Lebensmittel-geschäft	**lay**-bens-mittel-gush-eft
glass, porcelain	Glas, Porzellan	**glars, Port-sellahn**

Staying in a Hotel

Do you have any vacancies?	Haben Sie noch Zimmer frei?	harb'n zee nokh **tsimm**-er-fry
with twin beds?	mit zwei Betten?	mitt tsvy bett'n
with a double bed?	mit einem Doppelbett?	mitt ine'm **dopp**'l-bet
with a bath?	mit Bad?	mitt **bart**
with a shower?	mit Dusche?	mitt **doosh**-uh
I have a reservation	Ich habe eine Reservierung	ish **harb**-uh ine-uh rez-er-**veer**-oong
key	Schlüssel	shlooss'l
porter	Pförtner	**pfert**-ner

Eating Out

Do you have a table for...?	Haben Sie einen Tisch für...?	harb'n zee tish foor
I would like to reserve a table	Ich möchte eine Reservierung machen	ish **mer**-shtuh ine-uh rezer-**veer**-oong makh'n
I'm a vegetarian	Ich bin Vegetarier	ish bin vegg-er-**tah**-ree-er
Waiter!	Herr Ober!	hair oh-**bare**!
The bill (check), please	Die Rechnung, bitte	dee **resh**-noong bitt-uh
breakfast	Frühstück	**froo**-shtock
lunch	Mittagessen	**mitt**-targ-ess'n
dinner	Abendessen	**arb**'nt-ess'n
bottle	Flasche	**flush**-uh
dish of the day	Tagesgericht	**tahg**-es-gur-isht
main dish	Hauptgericht	**howpt**-gur-isht
dessert	Nachtisch	**nahkh**-tish
cup	Tasse	**tass**-uh
wine list	Weinkarte	vine-kart-uh
tankard	Krug	khroog
glass	Glas	**glars**
spoon	Löffel	**lerff**'l
teaspoon	Teelöffel	tay-lerff'l
tip	Trinkgeld	**trink**-gelt
knife	Messer	**mess**-er
starter (appetizer)	Vorspeise	**for**-shpize-uh
the bill	Rechnung	**resh**-noong
plate	Teller	**tell**-er
fork	Gabel	**gahb**'l

Menu Decoder

Aal	**arl**	eel
Apfel	**upf**'l	apple
Apfelschorle	**upf**'l-shoorl-uh	apple juice with sparkling mineral water
Apfelsine	**upf**'l-seen-uh	orange
Aprikose	upri-**kawz**-uh	apricot
Artischocke	arti-**shokh**-uh	artichoke
Aubergine (eggplant)	or-ber-jeen-uh	aubergine
Banane	bar-**narn**-uh	banana
Beefsteak	**beef**-stayk	steak
Bier	beer	beer

Bockwurst	**bokh**-voorst	a type of sausage
Bohnensuppe	burn-en-zoop-uh	bean soup
Branntwein	brant-vine	spirits
Bratkartoffeln	brat-kar-toff'ln	fried potatoes
Bratwurst	brat-voorst	fried sausage
Brötchen	bret-tchen	bread roll
Brot	brot	bread
Brühe	bruh-uh	broth
Butter	**boot**-ter	butter
Champignon	shum-pin-yong	mushroom
Currywurst	**kha**-ree-voorst	sausage with curry sauce
Dill	**dill**	dill
Ei	**eye**	egg
Eis	**ice**	ice/ ice cream
Ente	**ent**-uh	duck
Erdbeeren	ayrt-**beer**'n	strawberries
Fisch	**fish**	fish
Forelle	for-**ell**-uh	trout
Frikadelle	Frika-dayl-uh	rissole/hamburger
Gans	ganns	goose
Garnele	**gar**-nayl-uh	prawn/shrimp
gebraten	g'**braat**'n	fried
gegrillt	g'**grilt**	grilled
gekocht	g'**kokht**	boiled
geräuchert	g'**rowk**-ert	smoked
Geflügel	g'**floog**'l	poultry
Gemüse	g'**mooz**-uh	vegetables
Grütze	**grurt**-ser	groats, gruel
Gulasch	**goo**-lush	goulash
Gurke	**goork**-uh	gherkin
Hammelbraten	hamm'l-**braat**'n	roast mutton
Hähnchen	haynsh'n	chicken
Hering	**hair**-ing	herring
Himbeeren	him-beer'n	raspberries
Honig	**hoe**-nikh	honey
Kaffee	kaf-**fay**	coffee
Kalbfleisch	kalp-flysh	veal
Kaninchen	ka-**neensh**'n	rabbit
Karpfen	**karpf**'n	carp
Kartoffelpüree	kar-toff'l-poor-ay	mashed potatoes
Käse	**kayz**-uh	cheese
Kaviar	**kar**-vee-ar	caviar
Knoblauch	k'**nob**-lowkh	garlic
Knödel	k'**nerd**'l	noodle
Kohl	**koal**	cabbage
Kopfsalat	**kopf**-zal-aat	lettuce
Krebs	**krayps**	crab
Kuchen	**kookh**'n	cake
Lachs	**lahkhs**	salmon
Leber	**lay**-ber	liver
mariniert	mari-neert	marinated
Marmelade	marmer-**lard**-uh	marmalade, jam
Meerrettich	may-re-tish	horseradish
Milch	**milsh**	milk
Mineralwasser	minn-er-**arl**-vuss-er	mineral water
Möhre	**mer**-uh	carrot
Nuss	**nooss**	nut
Öl	**erl**	oil
Olive	o-**leev**-uh	olive
Petersilie	payt-er-**zee**-li-uh	parsley
Pfeffer	**pfeff**-er	pepper
Pfirsich	**pfir**-zish	peach
Pflaumen	**pflow**-men	plum
Pommes frites	pomm-**fritt**	chips/ French fries
Quark	kvark	soft cheese
Radieschen	ra-**deesh**'n	radish
Rinderbraten	**rind**-er-brat'n	joint of beef
Rinderroulade	**rind**-er-roo-lard-uh	beef olive
Rindfleisch	**rint**-flysh	beef
Rippchen	**rip**-sh'n	cured pork rib
Rotkohl	**roht**-koal	red cabbage
Rüben	**rhoob**'n	turnip
Rührei	**rhoo**-er-eye	scrambled eggs
Saft	**zuft**	juice
Salat	zal-aat	salad

Salz	zults	salt
Salzkartoffeln	zults-kar-toff'l	boiled potatoes
Sauerkirschen	zow-er-keersh'n	cherries
Sauerkraut	zow-er-krowt	sauerkraut
Sekt	zekt	sparkling wine
Senf	zenf	mustard
scharf	sharf	spicy
Schaschlik	shash-lik	kebab
Schlagsahne	shlahgg-zarn-uh	whipped cream
Schnittlauch	shnit-lowhkh	chives
Schnitzel	shnitz'l	veal or pork cutlet
Schweinefleisch	shvine-flysh	pork
Spargel	shparg'l	asparagus
Spiegelei	shpeeg'l-eye	fried egg
Spinat	shpin-art	spinach
Tee	tay	tea
Tomate	tom-art-uh	tomato
Wassermelone	vuss-er-me-lohn-uh	watermelon
Wein	vine	wine
Weintrauben	vine-trowb'n	grapes
Wiener Würstchen	veen-er voorst-sh'n	frankfurter
Zander	tsan-der	pike-perch
Zitrone	tsi-trohn-uh	lemon
Zucker	tsook-er	sugar
Zwieback	tsvee-bak	rusk
Zwiebel	tsveeb'l	onion

Numbers

0	null	nool
1	eins	eye'ns
2	zwei	tsvy
3	drei	dry
4	vier	feer
5	fünf	foonf
6	sechs	zex
7	sieben	zeeb'n
8	acht	uhkht
9	neun	noyn
10	zehn	tsayn
11	elf	elf
12	zwölf	tserlf
13	dreizehn	dry-tsayn
14	vierzehn	feer-tsayn
15	fünfzehn	foonf-tsayn
16	sechzehn	zex-tsayn

17	siebzehn	zeep-tsayn
18	achtzehn	uhkht-tsayn
19	neunzehn	noyn-tsayn
20	zwanzig	tsvunn-tsig
21	einundzwanzig	ine-oont-tsvunn-tsig
30	dreissig	dry-sig
40	vierzig	feer-sig
50	fünfzig	foonf-tsig
60	sechzig	zex-tsig
70	siebzig	zeep-tsig
80	achtzig	uhkht-tsig
90	neunzig	noyn-tsig
100	hundert	hoond't
1000	tausend	towz'nt
1 000 000	eine Million	ine-uh mill-yon

Time

one minute	eine Minute	ine-uh min-oot-uh
one hour	eine Stunde	ine-uh shtoond-uh
half an hour	eine halbe Stunde	ine-uh hullb-uh shtoond-uh
Monday	Montag	mohn-targ
Tuesday	Dienstag	deens-targ
Wednesday	Mittwoch	mitt-vokh
Thursday	Donnerstag	donn-ers-targ
Friday	Freitag	fry-targ
Saturday	Samstag/ Sonnabend	zums-targ zonn-ah-bent
Sunday	Sonntag	zon-targ
January	Januar	yan-ooar
February	Februar	fay-brooar
March	März	mairts
April	April	april
May	Mai	my
June	Juni	yoo-ni
July	Juli	yoo-lee
August	August	ow-goost
September	September	zep-tem-ber
October	Oktober	ok-toh-ber
November	November	no-vem-ber
December	Dezember	day-tsem-ber
spring	Frühling	froo-ling
summer	Sommer	zomm-er
autumn (fall)	Herbst	hairpst
winter	Winter	vint-er

Berlin U-Bahn and S-Bahn

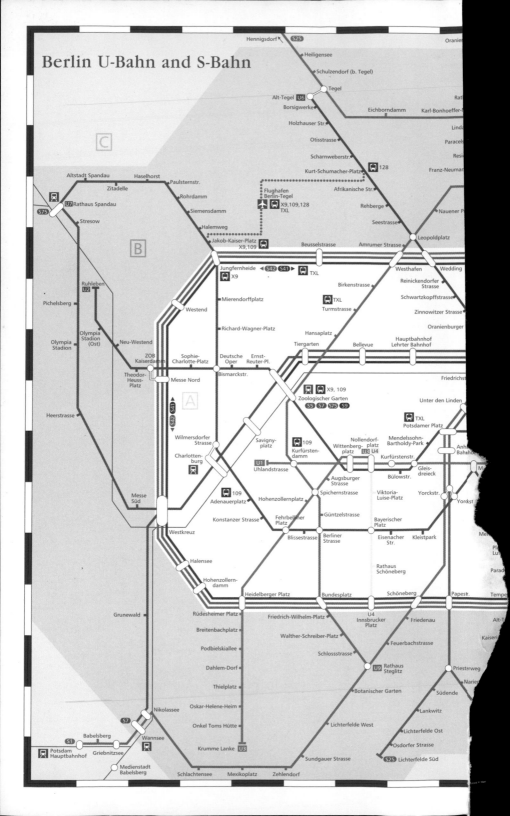